SIXTY YEARS
IN THE
20TH CENTURY

A Pilot's Memoir

To my Precious
Granddaughter
Kayla

D. ALLEN BUTCHER

With Love & Best Wishes

Papa

To those who are yet to be...

ACKNOWLEDGEMENTS

A writer does not create within himself alone. The encouragement and talents of others are necessary to bring those thoughts to fruition. With that in mind, I would like to express my appreciation to those who had a part in birthing this endeavor: to my faithful wife, Carolyn, for planting the seed and watering it, to Caleb Sizemore, Roy Francia, and the publishing team at Create Space, who did the really hard work and answered all my questions, and finally to my fellow writer, neighbor, and friend F. LaGard Smith, who was there at the right time.

GLOSSARY OF ABBREVIATIONS

AFB: Air force base

AFROTC: Air Force Reserve Officer Training Corps

ATC: Air Training Command

ATS: Air Transport Squadron

DF: Direction finding

DFW: Dallas-Fort Worth

FAA: Federal Aviation Administration

FAIC: Flight attendant in charge

FLL: Fort Lauderdale

IP: Instructor pilot

LAX: Los Angeles International Airport

MATS: Military Air Transport Service

ROTC: Reserve Officer Training Corps

SAC: Strategic Air Command

TMC: Transport Movement Control

TVA: Tennessee Valley Authority

UPT: Undergraduate pilot training

VOQ: Visiting officer quarters

VOR: Very high frequency Omni-directional Range

PROLOGUE

When the idea of beginning this work was sown in the seedbed of my mind, I began to think, after the passage of some time, that this seed would be like that sown among the thorns, as described in Holy Writ, and that the cares of this world and the lust for other things would enter in, so that I failed to bring the idea to fruition. Then one day, I happened across the words of Frederick Buechner, relieving me of my fears and doubts. In his work entitled *Listening to Your Life,* he stated the following:

Before anybody else has a chance to ask it, I will ask it myself: Who cares? What in the world could be less important than who I am and who my mother and father were, the mistakes I have made together with the occasional discoveries, the bad times and good times, the moments of grace…But I talk about my life anyway because if, on the one hand, hardly anything could be less important, on the other hand, hardly anything could be more important. My story is important not because it is mine, God knows, but because if I tell it anything like right, the chances are you will recognize that in many ways it is also yours. Maybe nothing is more important than that we keep track, you and I, of these stories of who we are…because it is precisely through these stories in all their particularity, as I have long believed and often said, that God makes Himself known to each of us most powerfully and personally. If this is true, it means that to lose track of our stories is to be profoundly impoverished not only humanly but spiritually.

As I begin my story, you will note that my grandfather was in the great Civil War. When he died in 1915, he left no written record of his life. How I miss that! How I would love to have just one hour with him, beyond the curtain of time, to understand who he was and to learn the details of the life he led. This was further motivation for me in that I did not want to fail my progeny in that regard.

I have made an observation about this current generation of young people that has also added motivation to write my story. It seems that with all their self-absorbed activities and electronic gadgetry and the proliferation of social media, there is no time or interest left for asking the questions that the fading generation is eager to answer. Out of respect for the privacy concerns of family members, I prefer to make this book primarily a chronicle of my own life as a pilot.

I will only add that this is not a "scholarly" work. There are no footnotes, and there is no bibliography. And if some meticulous historian should find any errors of time and place, I can only say that this is my life as I remember it through the cobwebs of my memory, and I must beg his indulgence and understanding. Here, then, is my story.

D. Allen Butcher
Murfreesboro, Tennessee
April 30, 2012

CHAPTER ONE

"BEGINNINGS"

I have always been proud that I was born on a Sunday, since it was the Lord's Day. It was the twenty-fourth day of September in the year 1939, a warm day, according to my mother, who gave birth that morning to a nine-and-three-quarter-pound boy at the home of my Grandmother Butcher in Clinton, Tennessee. Having children at home was common in that day. The doctor came by to finish the work of the midwife and pronounce me healthy, I suppose. This midwife was my aunt Mary Cooper, who loved to tell me how she greased me in lard and how they had fried chicken that day and didn't give me any.

Twenty-three days earlier, on September 1, 1939, the Germans had invaded Poland, marking the beginning of World War II. I guess you could say, then, that I was among the first of the war babies. But one thing was certain: This war would change the world in ways we couldn't imagine at the time.

My folks named me Doyle Allen Butcher. The name Doyle was given in memory of Doyle Martin, a "big brother" friend of my father, who was killed in an accident sometime before my birth. Allen was my maternal grandfather's name. Sometime in the early 1930s, while working as a lineman in Shreveport, Louisiana, he touched a hot wire and was electrocuted. His body was shipped back to his home town of Catletts-burg, Kentucky, where it was buried in the city cemetery; the location of the grave is unknown.

In any event, I began life representing the dead, and I hope, should they be watching from another dimension of time, that I have not brought too much reproach on their names. Like many, I never cared too much for my name. From the beginning, I was called Allen. Being the middle name, it presented problems in a world accustomed to the form of "first name-middle initial." At least I had the luxury of knowing that anyone who asked for Doyle was a total stranger.

My parents were poor, but most everyone else was in the same boat. The nation was coming out of the Great Depression, and work was scarce. Shortly after my birth, Grandmother Butcher bought a bigger house on Medaris Street in Clinton. This included a small two-room house next door, which was to be my first home.

At a very young age, my grandmother had married a Civil War vet-eran, William Butcher. He died in 1915, leaving her to raise three chil-dren by herself. Sometime later, she began to receive a small pension as a Civil War widow. Her favorite saying to me was, "It's not the making of money that counts. It's the saving of it." Her maiden name was Mary Jane Edwards, but everyone called her "Aunt Molly." She and my grand-father came up the Tennessee River on a steamboat from Sand Moun-tain, Alabama, sometime around 1900. They landed in Loudon, Tennes-see, and came overland to Clinton, where they set up housekeeping in a cabin with a dirt floor.

My grandmother was a strong woman who had a cow and a big gar-den. She cooked on a wood stove and did her laundry in a kettle in the back yard. Once, when I asked about all her canned goods in the base-ment, she replied that they were put back for "the cold, snowy days." She was a devout Baptist. I was impressed that she had used the Bible to teach herself to read and had read it completely through more than once. She had long hair that fell far down her back. I only got to see it once, as she always had it put up in a bun. She dipped snuff and loved to sit in her swing on the front porch. With that tobacco juice, she could "baptize" any fly within ten feet. She died in 1959, never having been remarried, and was buried in the Clinton Cemetery near her husband William.

My father was the only son and the baby of the family. He never knew his father, having been born shortly after his death. There was an old wives' tale that certain maladies among babies could be cured if an only son, who had never seen his father, would breathe into the child's mouth. My father said that he was called from play on many occasions to perform this service. Whether or not it produced additional income or benefit to the babies concerned, I do not know. My father's name was Jesse Lee Butcher. I always wondered how the "Lee" got in there, seeing that my grandfather fought on the Union side. My mother asked what the "L" stood for, shortly after they met. Fearful of being rejected, my father told her it stood for "Leroy." They must have enjoyed the joke. To commemorate it, they gave that name to my younger brother.

My mother's maiden name was Roxine Mae Hogue. I have never seen her first name cited anywhere, although my sister Vickie said she once saw it in an English novel. Somewhere along the line, the last name was changed from the English spelling of "Hogg." I assume that this was to avoid any association with the four-legged creature of the same name.

My mother had a stepfather named Claude Blackmon, who came on the scene shortly after my grandfather Hogue was killed. It was said among the family that he helped my grandmother go through my grandfather's insurance money in short order, through bad investments, although I'm certain that his being an alcoholic was a contributing factor. He was a construction electrician who followed work wherever he could find it. Consequently, he and my grandmother, Margie Hewlett Hogue Blackmon (We called her "Nana"), led a vagabond life, never staying anywhere more than a few months and taking along three children: my mother, a younger brother, Allen Jr., and a half sister, Suzie. My mother attended thirteen different schools before graduating from high school and never had a "home" until she married.

In both her body and spirit, Nana bore the strain of that vagabond life. She was a "loner," who had never had time enough in one place to establish friendships. She was a quiet person, perhaps given to depression. She loved to smoke and play solitaire, particularly a game called "Wandering Jew." Maybe it was apt, considering her lifestyle. She was a stickler for cleanliness, however. Once when she was visiting us, she observed my adolescent face complete with blackheads and pimples. I can still feel the scrubbing she gave me with that washcloth. One of my last memories of Nana was when she and Claude were pulling out of our driveway with everything they owned packed in an old Packard, heading for the next job. Perhaps there was something within me at that time that wanted to go with them. Nana died young, and alone, of a heart attack in East St. Louis, Missouri, when I was sixteen years old. I can remember helping Claude drive his new 1953 Buick out to get her few things in the apartment and then on to Catlettsburg, Kentucky, her only "home" town, where she was buried. With this family background, then, I began my life.

My first home was my mother's first home. My father found work with the Tennessee Valley Authority (TVA) as a common laborer, earning one dollar a day on the Norris Dam project, and he and my mother settled in as new parents. Changes, however, were in the wind.

As everyone does at some point in life, I try to recollect the first thing in my memory. It occurred in Memphis, Tennessee, when I must have been about two years old. We were staying with Claude and Nana. Claude had found my father a job as a lineman with the local utility. The fact that my father had never been a lineman didn't seem to matter. Their hiring him was either due to union politics or to a desperate need on the part of the utility. I don't know which, but I suspect the former. There is a picture somewhere of my father up on a power pole, so he looked the part, if nothing else. My Aunt Suzie was eight or nine years older than I was and was attending elementary school at the time. My first memory was the sight of her going out the front door of this big house one morning, on her way to school. Another first memory had to do with my step grandfather, Claude, who loved to tease. Apparently I had sensed some order to the world around me. He would disrupt that sense by turning over the dining room chairs, for no reason that I could see, and getting me upset. I guess things just had to be a certain way with me from the beginning.

Shortly after my father's lineman work, we were headed back to east Tennessee. Whether my father was homesick, tired of living with Claude, or understanding of the dangers of being an inexperienced lineman, I can only surmise. Perhaps it was all three. In any event, we moved back to Grandmother Butcher's place until my father landed a job as a guard on the Watts-Bar Dam project in Spring City, Tennessee. This was followed by another move to the South Holston Dam project near Bristol, Tennessee. It was an unsettling time for everyone, as the country prepared for war.

I always had a fascination for trains. During this time, I remember sitting on the front steps of my grandmother's house, looking down at the railroad tracks a few blocks away. Several locomotives were at work, constantly bringing coal down from the mines in nearby Jellico, Lafollette, and Lake City. I learned to recognize each locomotive by its distinctive features or sound, and I spent many hours absolutely absorbed. When the tracks below were deserted, I would play with my own "railroad." My tracks were the concentric circles on the "manhole" cover in the front yard, and my locomotives and cars were fashioned out of mud.

Our move to the South Holston Dam brought about a short period of stability in my young life. We lived very near the dam, in an old log house. My father always seemed to have a hunting dog around, and this location was no exception. Peggy, a birddog, gave birth to a litter of pups under the house. I can remember my father inching his way under the floor to retrieve them. Another memory was the discovery of a large nest of duck eggs in the bubbling spring that was our water supply. I was beginning to notice the world around me.

Early in 1943, when I was three and a half years old, misfortune began to fall my way. First off, I came down with a bad case of the measles. Then my mother tried to explain to me that she had to go to the hospital in Bristol to get another baby. Was *I* not enough? I remember my Grandmother Butcher coming up on the train from Clinton to help during this crisis. I must have picked up my first "bad word" during this period. (Can you blame me?) I can remember having to stick out my tongue while my grandmother sprinkled it with red pepper. I quickly learned how to differentiate between words.

On March 21, 1943, my mother gave birth to another boy, whom she and my father named William Leroy Butcher. Like me, he was called by his middle name from the beginning, although he reverted to "Bill" as an adult. Perhaps this was due to the association of the name "Leroy" with the Afro-American community. Or perhaps he simply grew tired of living out the joke about the "L" in my father's name. My brother and I had the typical sibling rivalry experiences growing up, but because of the age difference, we were never really close. In the 1970s, he took up motorcycling. One afternoon, he was traveling out the Alcoa Highway near Knoxville, Tennessee. A man, a painter by trade, pulled out in front of him. The motorcycle almost went through the car, killing both men instantly. Leroy's body was buried in the family plot in Claxton, Tennessee. I always wondered why it happened to him and not me, since I was exposed to much more danger over my lifetime. Only God knows. I miss him.

As World War II wore on, the call for manpower grew so rapidly that my father began to feel the heat of the draft, even though he was married, had two children, and was already working for the government in a security role. Soon we were back at my grandmother's house in Clinton. My father quickly joined the US Navy and was shipped out to San Diego, California, for basic training. His first assignment was to Pensacola Naval Air Station, Florida, as a gunnery instructor. During this time, I resumed my train-watching activities and perhaps began to wonder if these unsettling times would ever end.

A short time later, my father sent word that he had found a place for us near the naval base in Pensacola and called on us to join him. I can remember going with my mother and brother to the train depot in Clinton. Finally I was going to get to ride on one of the trains I had been watching, except that this time, it was pulling passenger coaches instead of coal cars. The first leg of our journey took us from Clinton to Birmingham, Alabama. I can remember looking out the window and catching sight of the steam locomotive as it negotiated the curves. On arrival in Birmingham, we were to transfer to another train bound for Pensacola. But apparently, there was a misconnection, as the authorities told us that we would have to spend the night and continue the next day. They directed us to the traveler's aid facility, where we were issued an army cot and were directed to a large empty warehouse across the street. I have a vivid memory of almost being hit by a streetcar as we attempted to dash across the street to locate our quarters for the night.

Our accommodations in Pensacola amounted to an old multistory house that had been converted into apartments. We were on the top floor, and I can remember that access to our apartment was via a long outside stairway. Mother tried to keep us quiet, but I can imagine that our landlady regretted renting that upstairs apartment to a couple with small children. I began to explore my new surroundings and discovered a large yard with tall trees draped with long strands of Spanish moss. There were luxuriant shrubs, among them a big wisteria bush in front of which I was coaxed to pose for a photograph. Mother spent a lot of time with us in the yard, hoping perhaps that we would burn off enough energy to take a nice long, quiet nap. I can remember that she put a little harness on my brother and, by means of a leash and a swivel hook, chained him to the clothesline to limit his sphere of operation.

One of our favorite things to do was to walk to the downtown area. I can remember walking on the sidewalk with my mother on one occasion. A store was playing the radio over a large loudspeaker out front. We stopped to listen to a news flash, informing us that President Roosevelt had just passed away. I didn't understand why everyone was sad and the mood so somber.

Another memory of downtown Pensacola was more joyous. I can remember sitting in the booth of a drugstore and having my very first banana split. I never dreamed that such delicacies existed. And so the days went. Somehow I knew, however, that there was more change to come.

In 1944, victory in Europe was achieved, and the war effort now turned to the pacific theater of operations. As 1945 dawned, the country could see that the end of war was near. At the Pensacola training center, the need for naval gunnery instructors was declining. Consequently, the navy reassigned my father to the Pawtuxet Naval Air Station in Maryland, to work in the commissary. Again we went back to stay with my grandmother in Clinton, while my father went ahead to find a place for us. After a few weeks, we got the call and headed for the train station one more time.

My "new world" was a trailer park located on a highway leading to the base near the little town of Leonardtown, Maryland. Our trailer was not large, but we managed. My mother had little to do while my father was working except to keep up with two active youngsters. She began to read to me, and we spent many hours together with books. Somehow my father came up with a car. On weekends, we would go into town for a movie or an ice cream cone. Once, in touring the nearby Chesapeake Bay, my father came upon a good buy in a sack of oysters. The fact that he had never shucked one before didn't seem to matter. I can still see him with a hammer in his hand, trying to get those oysters open. It became a family joke that lasted for many years. My folks had a tough time with privacy in the trailer. I can remember seeing my father with a bottle of beer and a cigarette and hearing the record player late at night. Their favorites were songs by Dinah Shore and a blues number entitled, "When the Lights Go down Low."

I got my first pet soon after we arrived—a dog named Smokey. We would explore the scrub timber behind the trailer together, that is, until I reported seeing a large multicolored snake on one of our forays. My mother quickly put a limit on how far we could roam. We had to leave Smokey behind when we left that place. After that, I was careful never to be overly attached to a pet.

When my father was at work, we would often catch the bus to the base. There was a base exchange and a movie theater that we would often frequent, plus a museum of sorts, which had various displays of naval operations. My favorite thing was the route the bus took around the base. It would go along the flight line, where I could see the airplanes and the large "blimps" that often flew over our trailer park. On one remote section of the ramp, the navy had parked several strange looking aircraft. They were dark green in color, with large red circles on the wings. I did not understand at the time that these were Japanese aircraft that the navy had captured and that they were here to undergo testing and evaluation.

While my visits to the base were sporadic, that was soon to change. Although I was not yet six years old, having been born in late September, my parents decided that it was time for me to begin my schooling. One day, a large orange bus stopped on the highway outside our trailer. I joined the other waiting children, with lunch box in hand, and boarded the bus that transported us to the on-base school. Somehow I sensed that I was entering a new phase of my life.

Because of the preparation my mother gave me, I took to school immediately. I could already read a little, and the lessons came easy. I also discovered my peer group as well as those in grades ahead of me. Once, during recess, an older boy persuaded me that kicking in the ground level window would be a good idea. I agreed, and the shattered glass was the launching of my ship of youthful disobedience. A teacher offered that perhaps I was only tying my shoe and had "slipped." This sounded good to me, so I readily agreed that that was the case. Therefore, you might say that I came into the world "speaking lies."

I do not remember my first teacher, but I still remember her methods of punishment. She took me out into the hall on more than one occasion, where I quickly learned her approach to discipline. The scenario would take one of two forms. The first was to scold me verbally and then give me a resounding whack on the head with a textbook. The second involved the same verbal scolding, followed by a command to hold my hands out. She would then brandish a ruler and deliver several sharp blows to my knuckles. This second method seemed to get more of my attention, and I always hated it when I saw that ruler in her hand. Perhaps that method of punishment was the reason I never became a piano player or a neurosurgeon.

I don't know why I was in trouble most of the time. Most likely, my lessons were boring and unchallenging to me. I am certain that the greatest news to my teacher was that I would be leaving before the end of the term. She must have seen some academic potential in me, however. She was going to recommend that I be "double promoted" to the third grade, had I returned the following term. However, because I was leaving and she didn't know where I would continue my schooling, she simply promoted me to the second grade.

In the spring of 1946, my father received his discharge from the navy. He had a late thirties Plymouth coupe that we loaded to the gills and headed the nose toward Tennessee. I can remember the car having a shelf between the back seat and the back window. That was my "seat" and "bed" for the trip back to Clinton and to the familiar environs of Grandmother Butcher's house. Somehow I was hoping that we would now lead a more settled life.

Since it was mid-spring when we returned to Clinton, school was still in session. Not wanting any questions about truancy, my parents put me back in school to finish the first-grade term. My teacher was a rotund lady whose name was Mossie King. Whether the name was for real, I never knew. She held each of us in turn on her ample lap as she taught us to read. I can remember watching her painted fingernails as she moved her index finger across the page, pausing until I responded with the correct word before going on. When a student completed each book successfully, she would give a reward of a few marbles, at least to the boys. I earned several, but lost them quickly to the "marble sharks" who ruled the playground. Although the teachers prohibited "playing for keeps," I was content to lose my cache of marbles, just to be invited to play.

Getting to and from school was the adventure of the day. Since we lived inside the city, there was no school bus. My parents decided that I would walk to school. Today's parents would shudder at the mile or so I had to walk. Sidewalks were available, but I shunned them in favor of the more direct route, down the railroad tracks to the station and then up the main street to the school. I got pretty good at walking the rails and even sampling part of my lunch on the way.

I had an older cousin, Jack Cooper, son of my Aunt Mary. Jack was in the sixth grade, and I always looked up to him and would go up to his house whenever I could. He was into building model airplanes, and he had an electric train, which I encouraged him to set up on each visit. The route to his house was up and over the hill behind my grandmother's house. On Sundays, after services at the Second Baptist Church and a sumptuous meal at my grandmother's table, I was allowed to head over to Jack's house to see what he was into. Although I am certain that he was never overwhelmed to see me, he never showed it. As I was saying, the route was up and over the hill, and took me by a strange church that held services long into the afternoon. There was always a lot of noise coming from inside, and I often heard screaming and shouting. I would always pass by on the other side of the street, just to be on the safe side. I asked my Aunt Mary about it, but she just said not to pay it any mind.

My grandmother was one of the honored widows at the Second Baptist Church, and it was her only social outlet, to my knowledge. Two events that she always looked forward to were the annual Christmas program and the annual all-day singing and dinner on the grounds.

At the Christmas service, there was a large decorated tree up front in the sanctuary. At the end of the service, "Santa Claus" would appear, after much excitement and anticipation on the part of us children, and would hand out "pokes" of candy treats. The big chocolate cream drops and jellied orange slices were always my favorites.

The singing (inside) and dinner (outside) were reserved, seemingly, for the hottest Sunday of the year. As a courtesy, the local funeral home provided hand fans, and the preacher kept the service short so the business of setting up the tables and food could commence. The quantity of food boggled my mind. It seemed that each contributor tried to outdo all the others, and I can remember my grandmother asking if I had gotten a piece of "her" cake.

Sometime during this period, I was introduced afresh to the moving picture. My mother had taken me to see "movies" on the naval bases, of course, but it was a different environment, and I was too young to understand what was going on. Now, however, I was permitted to go to the downtown theater on Saturday morning, either alone or in the company of Cousin Jack. Here began a ritual that stayed with me for several years. The theater would open around 10:00 a.m. I would then pay my admission of nine cents, buy a large bag of hot, sweet-smelling popcorn for five cents (when I had extra money), and find my favorite location in the semidarkness of the theater's folding seats. Soon the whirring of the projector could be heard, the curtains would part, and parading before me would be the greatest of things, to my young mind.

A color cartoon was always first, followed by previews of coming attractions. Then there would be the latest installment of the current "serial." It would pick up where the last installment had left off, showing the hero or heroine surviving some seemingly impossible situation from the past episode. My favorite was Tarzan, although Superman and Buck Rogers were close seconds. The feature or double feature, if we were lucky, would come next. These were usually of the western variety. The first of my cowboy heroes was "Sunset Carson," although he quickly gave way to the "Durango Kid," "Lash LaRue," and "Hopalong Cassidy." I liked Gene Autry and Roy Rogers too, but they spent way too much time singing and hanging around the women who, for some odd reason, were also cast in these films. The plot was always the melodrama, with evil seemingly having its way until the good guys with the white hats and white horses galloped their way to the "showdown" with the mustachioed bad guys, who always wore dark hats and rode black horses. This showdown was normally accompanied by loud cheering from the audience, as we knew justice was at hand. With evil finally subdued, the lights would come on, and, returning to reality, I would file out into the bright afternoon sun to find my way home, reflecting on the happenings of the past few hours.

TVA rehired my father after his stint in the navy. He was assigned to Fort Loudon Dam, located in Lenoir City, Tennessee, as a public safety officer. Once again I had to leave the confines of my grandmother's house and settle into a new location. Initially, we could not find housing near the dam. For a short time, we had to live in a small rental house in nearby Loudon. The six-mile drive involved crossing a toll bridge over the Tennessee River. I can remember stopping at the tollbooth, but do not remember if we had to pay, since my father was a TVA employee. Toll systems were not, and never will be, popular with the citizens of Tennessee.

Finally, a "project" house became available near the dam in Lenoir City. It was located on East Second Avenue. A short time later, we "upgraded" to another house up the street, which had more amenities. There were several of these houses, which had been built by the federal government to house people assigned to the dam. They all looked alike, for the most part, but some had been better kept than others. Here we had the best living conditions we had ever had, up to that point. For the first time, I was introduced to indoor plumbing, a telephone (I still remember the number: 459J), and the radio, of which I rapidly became a fan. This was to be my home for the next three years, encompassing years seven through nine, and elementary grades two through four. The times were exciting, as people were transitioning into peacetime. Wartime technology was bringing an ever-increasing number of new products onto the scene, and revolutionary change was in the air.

Family Photo 1946, author on right

CHAPTER TWO

"GROWING UP"

Something new, called a supermarket, was built near our neighborhood. It was not large, by modern standards, but was very different from the small mom-and-pop grocery stores to which we were accustomed. Mother would send me to pick up odd items as we needed them. I can remember bringing home a new product called "oleo" (margarine). It was white, but it came with a small package of coloring that, when mixed in, gave the margarine the appearance of butter. Although it became very popular, there was still something about it that never measured up to the real thing. My father must have felt the same way. Fresh butter and milk was always the household choice whenever we could get them.

My second-grade teacher at Nichols Elementary School was Mrs. Bradford. I must have picked up where I left off in my approach to education. She wrote on my report card that I was a good student but that I "disturbed quite a bit." She moved me on more than one occasion, apparently so that I would not be a bad influence on the better behaved students around me. Lunch and recess were naturally the big events of the day. Sometimes I would take my lunch, my favorite being a butter and sugar sandwich on white bread. However, I really liked the hot lunches served in the cafeteria, particularly the mashed potatoes smothered in peas. Recess was a chance to work off some of that unlimited energy, and

I gave it everything I had, alternating between the swings and the merry-go-round, which I could bring up to phenomenal speeds.

The greatest highlight began when the final bell rang and I was released from my academic prison to begin the adventurous walk home. As the crow flies (or as the sidewalks would take me), I lived about one mile from school. However, I had a more scenic route that added to that distance. I began by walking down a street that transitioned to a gravel road. This road led to a point where I could cross a large creek at the site of an old milldam and could then go by the ruins of an old factory and up an abandoned railroad spur. The rails passed a gulley that I would turn into and would then connect to the street where I lived. Many were the adventures I had along the way. I was careful never to mention the snakes, which liked to sun themselves on the rocks of the dam for fear that I might be forced to abandon my preferred route.

Play was the order of the afternoon until around five o'clock, when I would huddle by the radio to listen to *The Lone Ranger*, a program sponsored by the Merita Bread Company. This naturally became the bread of choice for my favorite sandwiches. (Even back then, marketers knew how to pitch to youngsters). With the radio, I had to add the action through my imagination, and I spent many hours visualizing the righteous masked man and his great horse, Silver, as they rode for truth and justice. Another favorite was *Let's Pretend*, which came on at 10:00 a.m. on Saturday, sponsored by Cream of Wheat Cereal. Again, this became the hot cereal of choice around the house. Meanwhile, I was ready to head for town after the radio program was over, so I would not be late for the movie theater and my Saturday routine.

My third-grade teacher was Mrs. Campbell. She must have challenged me, because I seemed to settle down a little. Perhaps it was because I was sick most of the time. My parents took me to a doctor, who advised that I should have my tonsils removed. I can remember the drive to Knoxville and how we entered the Medical Arts Building to have the procedure performed. The only good thing to come out of that was the ice cream needed to soothe the accompanying sore throat. The doctor also prescribed a "tonic." I never knew what was in it, but it apparently had a desirable effect. That was followed, however, by the news that I would need braces for my teeth, which required another trip to Knoxville and another specialist. I was becoming an expensive medical liability to my father, in a day when there was no such thing as medical insurance. I can remember that when it came time to remove the braces, my father performed the operation himself with a pair of pliers, rather than incur any additional expense.

Mumps and chicken pox followed soon thereafter, and then polio was a big scare in the area. A neighborhood girl contracted it and had to be placed in an "iron lung." I can remember the solicitation for "The March of Dimes" on the main street downtown, as research to find a cure continued.

When I wasn't sick, I loved to play cowboy, shoot marbles, or play "rolley-bat" with others in the neighborhood. The latter activity involved one person who would bat a baseball or softball and then lay the bat on the ground. The person fielding the ball would then roll it on the ground in an attempt to hit the bat, thereby winning the right to be the batter. In the evening, we would play "whoop-e-hide" (hide-and-seek) or "red rover," or we would have foot races on the lawns as all the parents watched from their screen porches. On other nights, we would crowd around the radio to listen to programs like *The Hit Parade*, *Jack Benny*, or the scary *Inner Sanctum* which began with the sound of an eerily creaking door.

It was about this time that I learned to swim. My father was a qualified Red Cross instructor, and I remember his taking me to the swimming area near the dam, where he taught me to "dog paddle." I loved the water and went swimming whenever I had the opportunity. He also introduced me to fishing, boating, and hunting. He loved all of this himself, and I was getting big enough to tag along. Once, he let me shoot his shotgun. Although the recoil knocked me down, I was proud that I had accomplished a "manly" thing. Another time, he decided to try golf. Since you had to have a caddy at the local course, he took me along to carry the clubs and keep an eye on the ball. My reward was the opportunity to hit a couple of balls off the last tee, although I later held out for a "caddy fee," which was usually fifty cents. My father liked to wager a little bet with his playing partners. Once he was playing with the owner of the movie theater in town. I was thrilled when he won a free admission and gave it to me. I remember redeeming it very proudly at the next Saturday matinee. Unfortunately, my father's enthusiasm for golf dropped suddenly after he hit a woman in the head with his golf ball. I can still remember the sight of blood and the woman being carried off the course. He never played much golf after that.

My fourth-grade teacher was Mrs. Robinson. She was the youngest, prettiest teacher I had ever had, and I must have had a "crush" on her. Her husband's name was "Lum," and he was part of a family who owned a furniture business in town. Through them, my father became a big fan of the Lenoir City High School football team, and we began attending all the games together. Since my teacher was in the group, I felt really special to be a part of this arrangement.

For Christmas that year, I asked for and received a Daisy BB gun, complete with the "Red Ryder" carving on the stock. I grew very accurate with it after I learned its idiosyncrasies. Birds were the target of choice, and I became the scourge of the neighborhood, even to the point of having my own burying ground for my victims. One day, while investigating a new house under construction, I decided that newly installed windows would also make a nice target, so I broke a few just to mark my territory. Naturally the builder traced this destructive deed back to my house, since I was the only kid in the neighborhood with a new BB gun. I handed over my gun and watched helplessly as my father broke it over his knee. It would be over forty years before I would receive another one. God had exacted revenge for the senseless destruction of his feathered creation.

Another time, while walking with my father, I picked up a sizable rock and, for some unknown reason, threw it accurately at a neighbor's mailbox, producing a large dent. After sending me to cut my own "switch," my father proceeded to whip me ferociously. In the melee, he hit me over the eye, opening a large cut that required a trip to the doctor and several stitches to close. I was trouble coming and going and, unfortunately for me, there were no child cruelty laws in those days to fall back on.

On still another occasion, after I had discovered matches, we paid a visit to Grandmother Butcher's house. I ventured outside and, again for some unknown reason, decided to set her backyard on fire. Seeing all the smoke, everyone rushed outside to fight the fire before it could spread to the neighborhood. After a few anxious moments, the blaze was brought under control. My father announced my coming punishment to the family, and I bravely stated that I certainly deserved it. But he never whipped me for that episode. I believe now that he probably thought I was temporarily insane. If behavioral scientists can ever figure out what causes young people to do such things, they will have discovered one of the great mysteries of the universe.

As I look back on these three years, I realize that they comprised the happiest days of my childhood. The days were long and seemingly unending. They were filled with so many things: Sunday trips to Grandmother Butcher's house, riding with my father in his TVA patrol car as he made his security rounds at the dam, riding the Ferris wheel when the carnival came to town, and so many more good things that have been lost from my memory.

The greatest single thing that happened to me during this period, however, was that God began to deal with my heart. (Wasn't it about time?) He apparently saw that I had "run out my string" of misbehavior and decided to have mercy on my parents and teachers. My mother was always quick to find us a "church home" wherever we went, and Lenoir City was no exception. With the exception of my father, we quickly became part of the congregation of the First Baptist Church, where my mother became a Sunday school teacher. This was fitting in that she was in the process of working on a college degree to become a teacher and was already teaching at a one-room school at nearby Martel, Tennessee. One Sunday, when the pastor gave the "invitation," I felt an urge to go forward and "join the church." I was baptized soon thereafter. I had taken a spiritual step, but was not equipped to understand the full meaning of what I had done.

In the spring of 1949, my father grew dissatisfied with his job. Possibly it was due to either politics or personalities. Years later, mother stated that he had gone as far as he could with TVA. In his spare time, he began attending Knoxville Business College. I remember the lessons he brought home and the evenings he would be away. These were the days of the "GI Bill," and most veterans applied for their share of the free educational opportunities provided by the federal government.

In conjunction with his decision to look elsewhere for employment, my father was also ready to fulfill his dream of having land that he could develop and live on according to the "old ways" he remembered from his youth. One weekend, my parents saw an ad in the paper listing a ten-acre tract for sale north of Knoxville. This tract included a livable old log house, a tenant house, and several outbuildings. The price was seven thousand dollars, an astronomical figure for a man who was about to become unemployed and whose only income was an educational benefit from the government. But somehow he convinced the bank of his future ability to pay the debt. The deal was signed, and we set about the task of moving again. With this move, I was to give up much of what I had enjoyed in my life, but I was excited about the prospects of a new place and unknown adventures that might lie ahead.

Another event that occurred about this same time was also the result of an ad placed in the newspaper. The State of Tennessee had just formed the new State Game and Fish Commission under Governor Frank Clement. The ad was a call for conservation officers who would serve each county in Tennessee. My father answered the ad, sent in an application, and promptly forgot about it. My parents were shocked when someone from the commission finally tracked my father down. Apparently he had given his Lenoir City address, and the letter indicating his selection for the job had not been forwarded. He was told that his class had already started, but that if he still wanted the job, he could catch up by reporting right away. The school was held at Standing Stone State Park near Cookeville, Tennessee, and my father hurried there to pursue what was to become his livelihood for the next few years.

Upon arrival at our new home, I found a jumble of buildings in the midst of overgrown vegetation. The last tenant of the property had attempted to raise goats, perhaps in an attempt to arrest the undergrowth. He also apparently liked to smoke his pipe in the process. I remember that one of my first jobs was to pick up the hundreds of "Prince Albert" tobacco cans that littered the area.

The house itself, long gone now, warrants some description. It was the classic two-story log house with hand-hewn logs and concrete chinking. You could see the ax marks where the builders had dressed the logs, plus a few small holes, reputed to be bullet holes from a Civil War skirmish, although this was never verified. The main room was relatively large, with a fireplace and a planked floor. A narrow, winding stairwell near the fireplace led to an upper floor of the same size, where my brother and I slept. The pitch of the roof was the ceiling, and there was no insulation, no heating, and no cooling. We had one naked light bulb hanging down from the ceiling, which provided lighting. It was unmercifully hot in the summer, and the snow would blow in through the cracks in the winter. Wasps loved to build nests in the recesses of the ceiling, and it was always necessary to do a "wasp check" of the bedding before retiring for the night. Bedding was comprised of old quilts and blankets, although I added a sleeping bag when it was really cold. This was to be a real "pioneer" experience.

The front of the house had a large covered porch with steps leading down into a yard that dropped steeply to a portion of the Old Maynardville Pike. The bank was lined with large Mimosa trees. I can remember playing a tag game wherein we ascribed magical powers to the beautiful pink blossoms. The rule was that if you put a blossom to another player's nose, he was obligated to "fall down unconscious" for a full minute. I can still remember the sweet smell of those blossoms in the midsummer air.

An addition had been made to the rear of the house. This included space for a kitchen and dining room on one side, a "sunroom" on the opposite side, and my parents' "bedroom/parlor" in the middle. Here there was an oil-burning stove that was fed by a copper line leading from a fifty-five gallon drum outside the house. This was my favorite room in the winter because it was the warmest. Since we now had no indoor plumbing, this was the location selected for placement of the galvanized washtub, which was brought in from the back porch on Saturday night for our weekly bath. My brother and I would use the same water, since there was only one filling. The rest of the time, our "bathing" would be at the kitchen sink, using a dishpan, soap, and washrag.

Since there were no indoor toilet fixtures, we had to make our way to the "outhouse," approximately thirty yards away. Careful planning was necessary to arrive at the precise moment of need. The weather, time of day, and competition from other family members had to be taken into consideration. On arrival, the usual "wasp check" was performed and, with the Sears Catalog on hand for reading material, the matter was concluded. While chamber pots or "slop jars," as they were commonly called, were kept in the house, their use was for the direst of emergencies, and they were largely frowned upon by all. From time to time, when the hole below the outhouse reached its capacity, we were forced to move the outhouse to a new location. First the new spot was selected. Then a man in the neighborhood, who had the reputation of digging "the prettiest hole," completed the excavation. The outhouse was then dragged on its skids by horses, tractor, or truck and placed over the new hole. The dirt from the newly excavated hole was then used to fill in the old location. Initially, this added a new planning factor in making a trip to the outhouse; you had to remember where it was.

My new world consisted of many features that I began to explore. On one side of the house, a hill led down to a creek that bordered the property. As a boy, I found this creek a natural draw to my exploratory mind, and I spent many hours there. I remember fishing for minnows, with hooks fashioned out of safety pins, damming the creek to make a swimming hole, and collecting "crawdads" in a bucket. The hill itself was also perfect for winter sledding.

On the other side of the house was a grove of pecan trees. Since one of the trees presented a suitable limb for a swing, my father obtained some guy wire cable and bolts, and we were soon enjoying the swing and pushing it to its limits. Later, my father tried a stand of bees in this same area, but he had to destroy them because of disease. He then built a kennel to house beagle hounds that he entered in field trial competition.

The rest of the property on that side was composed of open fields, which ran to the property line bordering the community of "Black Oak." These fields were, at various times, used as hay fields or as pasture for horses and cattle, or they were planted in various crops, including corn, tomatoes, and strawberries.

The rear of the house extended past the outbuildings to another bank that overlooked the new Maynardville Highway, which formed the boundary of the property to the west. Here sat a small tenant house inhabited by the Johnson family. My father had an agreement with Mr. Johnson that his rent would be free if he was willing to earn that rent by working on the property. When Mr. Johnson underestimated my father's call for work, he became difficult to find at home. Once, my father sent me to get his assistance for a chore. I knocked on the door, and Mrs. Johnson opened it to announce that her husband had gone to town to "sign up" for unemployment benefits. I must have considered the open door as an invitation to enter, so as she was telling me this, I barged on into the house, to find Mr. Johnson hiding behind the door. While this was an eye-opener to me about human nature, it proved a disadvantage to the Johnson family. My father soon gave them an eviction notice and tore the house down.

The location of the tenant house was important in other ways. This was the perfect vantage point for viewing the outside world as it passed by. My brother and I would sit here for long periods of time, watching the traffic pass and playing a game we called "Cars," for lack of a more imaginative name. One of us would begin the game by announcing the make and year of each automobile that passed. That person would continue until challenged for wrongly recognizing a passing vehicle, at which time he had to relinquish his role to the other. Being older, I had a clear advantage in this game, which often ended in a dispute as to the exact identification of a particular car.

The most important aspect of this location, however, was that it offered the best location for viewing the large screen of the Skyway Drive-in theater, located directly across the highway. The fact that there was no accompanying audio made no difference. The action was all-important, and we could always use our imagination to fill in the missing sound. At dusk, several kids in the neighborhood would gather blankets and assemble on the bank to wait for dark and the beginning of the show. When older, we would "slip in" the Skyway by going under or around the corrugated metal fence and finding an obscure post with a speaker. However, we always had to be on the lookout for the theater manager and be ready to rapidly vacate the premises if he came around. In our teenage years, with money particularly hard to come by, we would alternately resort to hiding in someone's trunk to gain admission. Once safely inside, the driver would open the trunk, and the stowaways would join the rest of the group.

One last feature in this area was a large billboard, owned by a sign company who leased the location from my father. The display was changed from time to time by means of a ladder and catwalk. Naturally, this became inviting to all boys in the neighborhood, and we climbed it regularly when we ran out of other things to do.

Finally the family had put down roots, and we now enjoyed a period of stability. This was the parcel of land on which I was to live for the next eleven years.

* * *

In the fall of 1949, I entered the fifth grade at Halls Elementary School, located at the intersection of Emory Road and Maynardville Pike, commonly called Halls Crossroads. This building had previously served as the high school, and it included a "cracker-box" gymnasium that was heated by a wood burning stove. A wing had been added to the original building. It included an auditorium on the upper level and additional classrooms, plus a cafeteria, on the lower level. Outside was a large, well-used recess area, which consisted of several softball diamonds. At the crossroads nearby was a building called the Lone Star, which served as a store, a gas station, a café, and a meeting place for the local Masonic Lodge. Two churches, Presbyterian and Baptist, were located across the main highway, with the new high school situated just beyond on the crest of a rise.

The school bus, which stopped in front of the house, was our means of transportation to school. This bus ran very early and required us to sit around at school before classes began. A bus that ran later, through the Black Oak community, arrived as classes were set to begin, and I could wait for it with my friends. Accordingly, I immediately made this the bus of choice.

My teacher was Mrs. Kelly, a large, rotund lady who was very popular with the students and with parents as well. She arranged the classroom seating by alphabetical order, as did most of the teachers I was to have over the next few years. It was for this reason that I was to view the back of Norma Sue Brock's head for a long time to come. This was not all bad, because she was an excellent student from whom I was able to "borrow" information from time to time.

Mrs. Kelly believed that children misbehaved because they craved attention. When anyone, boy or girl, would disrupt, she would call them to her desk and sweep them up into her bounteous lap. She would then rock them in her arms like a baby, cooing and using "baby talk" to give them all the attention she could muster. The fear of such embarrassment was so great among us that we were the best behaved classroom in the school. Books to the head and rulers to the knuckles could be endured, but to be treated like a baby was unacceptable to any ten-year-old. One other thing I remember about Mrs. Kelly was a statement she made in class one day, which was indicative of the times. We were discussing hourly wages, when she emphatically stated that "*nobody* was worth a dollar an hour." My lessons came so easily that Mrs. Kelly granted me extra privileges. I learned to thread and operate the sixteen-millimeter movie projector in the auditorium, and I was in demand by all the teachers when a film was scheduled for their classes.

I really perked up when the high school announced that it was to have its first band and that elementary students were to be included. I loved music, and the thought of actually playing a musical instrument was very appealing. The new bandmaster, a Mr. Blackwelder, held a joint meeting for parents and students who were interested in being part of the band. After looking at the size of my lips, he immediately tagged me as a potential trumpet player. The big problem was that each student had to purchase his or her own instrument, and I was uncertain how that could come about. One morning shortly thereafter, my father called me into his bedroom area and told me to look on the other side of the bed. There, to my surprise and delight, was a case containing a new Harry Peddler B-flat trumpet.

With "band" added to my curriculum, I would report to the auditorium for practice each day, much to the chagrin of those who had to remain in the classroom. Naturally I had band homework, which my father quickly relegated to the friendly confines of the barn, well out of hearing range. The school principal must have had similar leanings, as band practice was moved to the basement of the Beaver Dam Baptist Church not long afterward.

The band came together quickly and was formed into a marching band as well as a concert band. I earned a high school letter that first year, as a fifth-grader, and went on to play "first chair" in the trumpet section over the course of my secondary education. The band marched in the downtown Knoxville parades and traveled to many band "festivals" at colleges and universities in the area. Mr. Blackwelder was a dedicated man of few words and even fewer compliments. A highlight for me came one evening after the halftime show at a high school football game. It was Veterans Day, and I had been tabbed to play "Taps" after a "moment of silence" in memory of those who had "given all" in the nation's wars. Leaving the field, Mr. Blackwelder approached me, seemingly with a tear in his eye, saying that my playing of "Taps" was the best that he had ever heard. Later, when sports began to take up more of my time, I gave up the marching band, took up the baritone as an instrument, and continued to play in the concert band. I enjoyed the band very much and always wished, in later years, that I had continued to play the trumpet.

Our first winter in the log house was full of new experiences. Grandmother Butcher came to stay for "hog killin'," for several days during the first cold snap in November. This process began early on the first morning when my father would take out his single-shot .22-caliber rifle and dispatch the hog with a carefully placed bullet behind the ear. With neighborhood help and the additional help of a hoist comprised of pulleys and ropes, he would suspend the hog by the hind legs from a tree limb. After he had slit the throat, he allowed the carcass to "bleed" and then removed the entrails, followed by the tedious task of scalding and scraping off the hair. Grandmother usually tended a fired cast-iron kettle, to ensure an ample supply of hot, boiling water to expedite this process. One part of the entrails was the bladder. After drying it out, you could blow it up to the size of a football and play with it. Hence, the term "pigskin" came to be part of the vocabulary associated with the sport of football from its early days.

After the carcass cooled for several hours, the work of cutting up the meat began. The fat was placed in the kettle for rendering and was then poured into metal buckets to be used in cooking. What remained in the kettle after rendering was called "cracklins," or what we would call "pork skins" today. My father was particularly fond of "cracklin" cornbread, and my grandmother always made certain that a freshly baked "pone" was part of the evening meal. My favorite part of the hog was the tenderloin. This was usually served at breakfast on the second day, complete with fried eggs, biscuits, and "red eye" gravy, which was made by pouring hot coffee into the drippings left behind in the skillet after frying the slices of tenderloin.

Over the next few days, all the meat was "worked up" into its various forms: the hams and shoulders salted with sugar cure and hung to age, the belly salted away to be used for seasoning and the remainder ground into sausage using special "spices," which my grandmother saved from her garden for the occasion. So that nothing was wasted, grandmother took everything left over, including ears, snout, and feet, and ground them up and pressed them into a loaf. She would then slice the loaf and put it into pickling brine. The result was what we called "souse meat." The older folks liked it, but I was content to hold out for the tenderloin.

At school, a favorite trick we played on the teacher during hog killing time was to present her with a "present" wrapped in a large box. When she opened the box, there was a smaller wrapped box inside. This went on through several gift boxes, until she came to the last one. To the squeals of delight from the children, the teacher would open that box to discover and display the pig's tail, which was her "gift." It was hard to pull this on the veteran teachers, but newcomers were fair game.

In November of 1950, a massive snowfall paralyzed the area for several days. Since we depended on an electric pump for our water, we had to melt snow for drinking and for what little bathing we could do. With no fan blower on the oil stove, we had no heat except for the fireplace, which was kept roaring most of the time. Since the stove was also electric, mother was forced to use the fireplace for cooking as well. After the fire was allowed to die down, she would place on the coals a covered "Dutch oven," which contained our one-dish meal for the day. Without radio (transistor radios had not yet been invented) or television (we had none until 1955), we were perfectly snowbound and isolated from the rest of the world. The odds of a modern-day family having a similar experience seem very remote, and yet I think they would be the lesser for it, having missed one of the better "pioneer" experiences.

My sixth-grade teacher was Mrs. Smelser. She was a nice lady and a good teacher, who had to deal with the maturing bodies of her students. From time to time, one of the girls in the class would begin to cry and have to leave the room, with Mrs. Smelser right behind. After a few minutes, they would return with everything seemingly back to normal. In her kind way, Mrs. Smelser would explain, without going into any detail, that a transition to "womanhood" had occurred and that we would resume our lesson from the point of interruption. While all the boys were familiar with "the birds and bees" by this time, it made little impact on us except for the break from the lesson.

One thing did occur, however, that changed my attitude about life from that point on. While I had had my moments of vandalism and misbehavior outside of school, when I was at school itself, I had always been an obedient student, never questioning authority or instruction by those placed over me. One day, a boy in the class "stubbed up" and refused to follow Mrs. Smelser's instructions in some matter. In some odd way, I admired his behavior, and I suddenly realized that authority could be challenged. I filed this away and began to practice the behavior myself as time went on. The seed of teenage rebellion had been planted.

Back at home, I began to explore more of the neighborhood around me. Although I never had a new bicycle, my father found an old one for me, and my world greatly expanded. The bicycle was a "Ranger" with a "New Departure" rear axle. I learned to take it apart and put it back together over time, and became, out of necessity, something of an accomplished bicycle mechanic.

Across the road from the log house was an expanse of fields and gullies known as the Murphy farm, which became a subdivision in later years. This was one big playground for the boys in the neighborhood, and we spent many hours there playing football and cowboy, building "clubhouses" in the pine thickets, picking blackberries in season, and doing anything else our imaginations could come up with. Later, when my father got into horses, I would come home from school, saddle up, and ride these fields until suppertime.

In the Black Oak community, there was a place simply called the "ball field," where we would choose sides to play softball or baseball, depending on what playable ball was available. Wherever I was, I was careful to listen for the sound of the horn on the family car. This was the signal to halt my activities and head for home; it was nearing suppertime.

There was also a steep, hardwood-covered ridge, located behind the Black Oak Baptist Church, where we would swing on grapevines, carve our initials on trees, and race our homebuilt wagons down the hill. These were fashioned out of scrap lumber, with wheels and axles cannibalized from metal wagons bound for the junk heap. We also scratched out a small racing oval where we used discarded tires as our racing machines. Running and rolling them around the track, we raced to determine the winner.

This interest in racing came about when the Broadway Speedway was built just north of us, beyond the gap on the Maynardville Highway. It began as a quarter-mile track, but it was later expanded to a half-mile banked oval. The racing heroes of the day assembled here on Saturday nights, beginning with the "Midget" cars powered by their Offenhauser engines, which were small copies of the Indianapolis racing machines and which were normally raced by the same drivers who drove those. The Offenhauser engines screamed so loudly that they could be heard two valleys over in each direction, every night during the season. These cars later gave way to "jalopy" and late-model stock cars, while a drag strip was added in order to accommodate the growing interest in pitting one car and driver against another.

Since tickets for the races were expensive, I had to find alternate means of getting into the stands. The perimeter was well patrolled, so going over or under the fence was not an option. Interlopers were quickly apprehended and escorted to the nearest exit. By chance, I attracted the benevolent attention of the man taking up tickets at the gate, who had the double duty of handing out programs to the paying customers. He gave me the duty of handing out the programs and then, as the incoming crowd began to thin, he would nod to me and look away as I headed to the stands to take in the action. Later, I sold hotdogs and soft drinks in the crowd. That way, I was able to see the races and add some pocket change in the process.

That year, I ascended to my first position of authority, as a safety patrol boy. I had a white military-style belt that came diagonally across my chest and joined to the portion around my waist. While this position was minimal in responsibility, it did have one benefit that was to produce a lasting influence on my life. Each year, all safety patrol boys were admitted free of charge to a University of Tennessee (UT) football game, usually a "breather" on their schedule. I attended the game and was totally enthralled with the stadium (it held forty-eight thousand fans at the time), the crowd, and the action. This was the national championship team, coached by General Bob Neyland, in a game that matched Tennessee against the University of Chattanooga. Tennessee had an all-American tailback that year whose name was Hank Lauricella. On the first play from scrimmage, he ran off tackle for eighty yards and a touchdown, but it was called back for an illegal block. After the penalty, Tennessee ran the very same play and Lauricella took it all the way again for a touchdown. This was an example of the action that day, and I was "hooked" as a UT fan. Later, I sold soft drinks in the stands and was present at nearly all of the games during my academic days in high school and college. When I became an air force pilot, I would fly into McGhee-Tyson Airbase on a weekend "training mission" to take in the action. Eventually I had season tickets and rarely missed a game. It became almost a "religion" with me, and it was only after a spiritual change later on in life that I was delivered from that aspect of it.

Another thing that had an impact on my life during this period was a Gospel ministry that was welcomed into the schools at that time. About once each calendar quarter, an older couple would come to the school and tell Bible stories on classroom time. The main part of the program, however, was the reward system for memorizing Bible verses. For so many verses memorized, you could receive a wall motto, a Bible, and the ultimate reward—a free week in the summer at Camp Ta-Pa-Win-Go, located near Elizabethton in upper east Tennessee. This program seemed a good thing to me, so I plunged into it with great enthusiasm. I completed all of the requirements and attended the camp for two summers. The camp program consisted of concentrated Bible study interspersed with typical camp activities such as softball and swimming. Cabins were provided for both boys and girls, and the food was not only good, but there was plenty of it.

During the last year of camp, two important events took place. The first occurred during a private interview with one of the counselors. He asked me, "Are you saved?" and I said that I was. He then asked me, "How do you know?" Seemingly without thinking, and a little bit uncomfortable about being interrogated, I said, "Because I believe in the Lord Jesus Christ." He smiled, and we both knew that I had given the correct answer. It was my first spiritual revelation. The other event took place around a huge bonfire on the last evening of camp. Campers who wanted to "dedicate their life to God" were invited to select a piece of wood and throw it into the fire. I can still remember the eerie glow of the fire as most of us filed by and threw our wood onto the pyre. Although I thought for many years that I might have been "just following the crowd," time has brought that early commitment to a degree of manifestation.

My mother had always wanted her children to be in "Sunday School and Church." I believe that in all her traveling about, she had discovered an element of stability about attending church that transcended the uncertainties of life. She enjoyed singing in the choir and was always called on to teach a Sunday school class wherever she went. After beginning his new job, my father was usually away on Sundays with our only car, which presented a problem in getting to church. Mother decided that the Second Baptist Church in Fountain City, about four miles away, was the church we would attend. An elderly man in the neighborhood, who was a member there, volunteered to pick us up each Sunday. The night before, I would polish my only pair of shoes, bathe, study my Sunday school lesson, and lay out my one outfit of "Sunday" clothes. The next morning we would all pile into this gentleman's car for the trip to the church and back to the house afterward. This continued for some time, until the man decided to leave this church and join the Beaver Dam Baptist Church at Halls Crossroads. Not to be outdone and lose our way to church, mother decided to move us also. I always wondered if the man's decision to move was based on spiritual need or on the secret desire to be rid of his noisy passengers each week.

My seventh-grade teacher's name was Mrs. McPhetridge. She was an older lady who had a nervous "tic" that caused her head to jerk slightly from time to time. After awhile, this became "normal" to her students. She was an excellent teacher whose pet project was the appearance of her room. In that particular year, she decided to put curtains at the windows of her classroom. At that time, livestock feed was sold in patterned, colored sacks. Someone brought a sack in that she approved of, and it became the material of choice for the project. Since most students had livestock of some kind at home, we launched a search to come up with enough of these feed sacks to do the job. After several weeks of manipulating our parents into purchasing these particular sacks, the final ones were obtained, much to the delight of the entire class.

In the meantime, we launched a cash project to obtain money for the curtain rods and pulls. All students used either "Blue Horse" or "Top-Flite" brand notebook paper. These companies had a "cash-back" program based on the number of wrappers sent in for redemption. By adding our wrappers to everyone that we could beg, borrow, or steal from the other classes, we finally came up with enough for the required funds. When our beautiful feed-sack curtains went up at last, we were the proudest class in the school.

On the home front, my mother decided to join the workforce. Money was tight, and most of it went into developing our property. (Perhaps that is the reason I never wanted to own any land). Accordingly, my mother went to work in the cosmetic department of Miller's Department Store in downtown Knoxville. Later, when Rich's came to town with a larger, newer store, she transferred there in the same capacity.

While I was somewhat resentful toward my mother for her decision to abandon our home, it did open a whole new world for me in the city. Each Saturday, she and I would catch the bus to the downtown area. She would go on to her job, while I was free to roam and explore. After checking out the market square with all its sights and smells, I would usually go to the Orange Julius for a ten-cent hotdog and a five-cent Julius. This concoction was made with orange juice, malt, and ice that were whipped into frothy foam. Next I would head for the department store to check in with mother, and then I would ride the escalators several times and afterward make tracks to the Riviera Theater across the street for the latest movie. This was often the usual western or, now that the Korean conflict had started, a war film. Afterward, I would wait for mother to get off from work, and then I would join her and ride the bus back home. In this manner, I was able to recapture an element of my former lifestyle in Lenoir City, while at the same time escaping the responsibilities of the farm.

Those responsibilities increased as I got older. On more than one occasion, I was kept out of school to help put in fencing or to dig fence posts. At various times, my father had pigs, chickens, guineas, dairy cows, beef cows, plow horses, saddle horses, and dogs of various breeds. He enjoyed all these animals and would often just stand and watch them. He loved hunting dogs most of all. Once he borrowed the use of a champion bird dog from a friend in Union County, where he was assigned as Tennessee wildlife conservation officer. He chained this dog in our barn and left him there for the night. The next morning, as we entered the barn, we noticed that the chain was extending out an open window that was several feet above ground level on the backside of the barn. His worst fears were realized when we went around the building. There, with his hind feet only inches from the ground, hung the champion bird dog that had run out of chain. He was dead and destined never to point another bird. I never knew how my father explained this tragedy to the owner, but he never borrowed another dog.

My father got interested in beagle hounds for rabbit hunting and then for entering them in "field trials." There he won several trophies and ribbons, including a "Field Champion" designation for one female dog in the thirteen-inch class. Her name was "Bond's Becky." After winning the three field trials necessary to receive the Field Champion designation, she was so loved by my father that he had "Becky" painted on the front of a truck that we shared together. I had trouble explaining this to a couple of girlfriends who would not believe that it was a dog's name.

Later, my father and I judged a few field trials together. The trial would begin by drawing the dogs' names out of a hat and dividing them into "braces" of two dogs each. The owners, handlers, and judges would then form a line and sweep across the field until one of us jumped a rabbit. This sighting was confirmed by a loud "tally ho" from the person. The first brace of dogs was then unleashed at the point of sighting and was allowed to run this rabbit until one dog's performance was clearly superior to the others. At this point, the judges would say "pick 'em up." This continued with each brace in succession, until all braces had been run. The judges would then call the winners from these braces back for what was called the "second series," where the process was repeated again. These series continued until the judges determined the clear winner. While ribbons were awarded to the top finishers, the real value in winning was the increase in stud or breeding fees that accrued to the owners, particularly after one produced a field champion. As a judge, all this was physically challenging in that we had to follow the dogs wherever they went. By the end of the day, I was as ready as the "briar hogs," or rabbits, to take a long break from the action. In addition, there was an element of politics involved in these trials. Although never proven, it was suspected that some judges favored certain professional handlers who traveled the field trial circuit, along with their dogs, so my career as a judge was short-lived.

I preferred the actual hunting phase of owning beagle hounds. Each Thanksgiving, the official rabbit season would begin, and my father began a tradition that would last for several years. We would rise early on Thanksgiving morning, dress as warmly as possible, load the dogs, and drive to the Bridges farm located off the Norris Freeway near Andersonville. Here we would unload the dogs and begin our sweep across the fields. We had a rule that we would not shoot at the rabbit "on the jump," but would let the dogs do the work of running it and turning it back to our position. Unless the rabbit had a favorite hole to run to, it would invariably circle around to the area where we had jumped it. The skill in this type of hunt was in trying to determine what path the rabbit would take on its return and in positioning oneself for a shot. Fortunately, for me at least, if not for the rabbit, I was often in the correct spot.

The Bridges were big gardeners and, as such, had no great love for the rabbits that seemed to thrive on their produce. Consequently, I was always welcomed when I showed up with the dogs, and I did so many times, even extending this activity into my college days. The Bridges loved rabbit on the dinner table, so it was a win-win situation for everybody.

One particular Thanksgiving Day really stands out in my memory. We began our hunt as usual when, at about mid-morning, a light snow began to fall. It was a beautiful sight, and it added to the pleasure of the hunt for both hunter and dog. The joy of this magical wonderland was tempered somewhat by the fact that the snow began to fall more heavily, and we had some difficulty getting home.

Waiting at home was a huge Thanksgiving dinner that Mother had prepared for us. Nothing will whet one's appetite like tramping through the woods and fields on a crisp November morning. Overeating was anticipated and expected, and I did all I could to carry on the tradition, which usually called for a "long winter's nap" thereafter, coupled with attending the traditional football games later on in the day. While rabbit hunting was the staple hunting activity, I also enjoyed limited amounts of squirrel, dove, and quail hunting as well.

As I grew older, my father took me along on some of his workdays as a conservation officer. He loved to comb the back roads of Union County, interrupted by stops at the local country stores that served as the focal points of activity for these remote areas. On entering, one could expect to see several men in overalls, surrounding a wood stove and playing checkers with bottle caps while enjoying a "center-cut" baloney sandwich, a "Moon pie," and an RC Cola. This was followed by tobacco of some form, usually of the chewing variety. Here I was introduced to many of the "characters" that my father had come to know. These were mountain people who, for the most part, were honest, hardworking, and keenly aware of their constitutional rights. The fact that they made moonshine, shot deer out of season, and fished without a license was, in their minds, part of those rights. However, my father gained their confidence, probably because he kept secret the location of their "moonshine" stills and refused to shoot their deer trailing dogs as the last game warden had. Moreover, by working with the upcoming generation through an educational program in the schools, my father was able to effect some change of attitude toward game and fish management.

When my father was not roaming the backwoods, he would go out on Norris Lake to check fishermen for licenses and creel contents. He would launch his fourteen-foot aluminum boat at one of the docks and spend most of the day checking, but would always reserve some time to fish. He knew most of the good spots, and we usually caught a nice stringer of crappie to take home or drop off to a needy family along the way.

At one time, the state appointed my father as a personal fishing guide to General Mark Clark, who was serving as commandant of The Citadel in Charleston, South Carolina, after his illustrious service in World War II under General Dwight Eisenhower. Clark was the guest of another friend of my father, Colonel Claude Reeder, owner of the Chevrolet Company in Knoxville. When the fishing action dropped off, the conversation turned to moonshine whiskey. Soon the two were parked in the front yard of a county resident who was known to produce the best "shine" in the county. Assured that the General was "okay," the farmer went out back and returned with a half-gallon Mason jar filled with his homemade product. The general never said too much about the fishing afterward, but he was always interested in the possibility of obtaining a resupply of that "mountain dew." I enjoyed my time on Norris Lake and went back to most of the old haunts for many years thereafter.

CHAPTER THREE

"HAPPY DAYS"

My eighth-grade teacher was Mrs. Loy. She was a good teacher whose main goal was to prepare her students for high school. Accordingly, we spent a great deal of time with things like algebra and communication skills. I enjoyed her class, but I was most excited about being in the high school building itself, having transferred from the elementary school across the highway, with all its "younger students." Surprisingly, one girl in my class got married that year, so I knew that things were changing all around.

At age fourteen, my own body was beginning to undergo some physical changes, complete with pimples, aching joints, etc. My other grandmother, Nana, moved into the area for a short time with her husband Claude. On her visits, she did not neglect to scrub my face with the usual soap and hot water. I was a willing subject, being desperate to endure whatever was required to feel better about myself and to avoid embarrassment.

My rebellion and challenge to authority continued to increase, particularly at home. My father had always given me sound whippings as punishment for my misdeeds, but that was not sitting well with me at this point. One day I found a piece of my football equipment missing and learned that a neighborhood boy had appropriated it for himself. I confronted him, reclaimed the item, and gave him a fist to the mouth as a reminder not to do that again. Unfortunately, I broke off a piece of his front tooth in the process, which upset his parents, who then came to my father for restitution. While no monetary solution was offered, my father did promise that I would be given a good dose of my usual punishment. This seemed unfair to me, and since I believed I was getting too big to be whipped, I decided to run away from home. I thought of Boys Town in Nebraska and of Colonel Claude Reeder's winter home in Fort Meyers, Florida, but I decided to head for my grandmother's house first, in order to sort things out. Nana and Claude had rented a house west of Knoxville near Dixie Lee Junction. I was pretty good at hitchhiking, in a day when people would actually stop and pick you up, so I set out after school that day and within a short time, arrived at Nana's door. After we talked for awhile, she placed a telephone call to my father, who said to come on back home, and we would work out an alternate means of punishment. She fed me a good supper and put me on a bus back to Knoxville and home. I had some privileges taken away for a time, but I was never whipped again, although I had some very narrow escapes.

At school, I tried out for the eighth-grade basketball team and made the cut. I was neither the greatest shot nor the quickest player on the team, but I could out jump everybody, which apparently caught the attention of the coach. I hung around the gym quite a bit, and in so doing, inherited the job of keeping the time clock and the official scorebook for the varsity teams. This granted me free admittance to the home games and the privilege of riding the team bus to the away games.

The varsity teams were made up of both girls and boys. The girls' game in that day was a slow-paced half-court game. The offense of one team was paired with the defense of the other team at one end of the court, while the opposite took place at the other end. Neither group could cross the centerline, so there was very little running involved. The girls' game always preceded the boys' game, and it was a nice transition to the full-court game the boys' team played. These were the days of small "cracker-box" gyms with limited seating, often heated by freestanding stoves. I remember many great plays and players as the action on the court unfolded amid the permeating smell of freshly popped popcorn. All this motivated me for a later time when I would be able to play varsity basketball.

In addition to playing in the band, I developed an interest in singing. As my voice began to deepen, I moved to the lower registry and started to sing the bass part. I had learned to read music, so the transition from band instrument to choral music was relatively easy. I used every opportunity to sing at school and began to do choir work at church. Three other fellows and I developed an interest in "Southern Gospel" music, and we formed our own quartet called "The Happy Rhythm Boys." We would attend every gospel concert that came to town, and we tried to emulate, in our singing, the great quartets of the day, such as the Statesmen and the Blackwood Brothers. We sang at school and in a few churches before divergent interests caused us to disband. However, one member of our quartet went on to a career in gospel music as a piano player with the Prophets Quartet. Singing became a joy to me, and I have enjoyed it immensely in various ways down through the years.

"Putting up hay" was another one of my summer jobs. I remember that after eighth-grade graduation, most of my classmates went to the local state park for a swimming celebration, while I reported to the hay fields. My father had some of his own land in hay, but he had a friend, a veterinarian and dairy farmer, who did most of the hay baling in the community. I went to work for him that summer and began to realize what real work was all about. While the farmer and his foreman would operate the tractors, rakes, balers, and trucks, another boy and I would walk along behind, lifting the heavy bales. First, we would hoist the bales onto the truck to be stacked, and then to the barn to be lifted and stacked again in the loft. I begin to "itch," just thinking about it. It was hard, hot work that seemed to be never ending. Occasionally we would have an easier "rainy-day" job of cleaning out the dairy barn.

What made this job particularly bad was that the farmer was slow in paying our wages. Once, out of frustration, I worked up the courage to confront him in front of my father for the money I was owed. He paid up, mumbling something about it "slipping his mind." I worked in hay for two summers but set my sights on better work for the future. One thing I did learn was that I never wanted to be a farmer or to run a dairy operation.

* * *

At last I was fifteen years old and a freshman in high school. Fifteen is probably the worst age for a human being, particularly for a boy. You are too old to go by a girl's house on a bicycle and too young to drive by in a car. There was some light at the end of the adolescent tunnel, however, in the form of the "learner's permit," which was granted to those who had reached the magical age of fifteen. An adult driver (usually a parent) was required to be in the car while the "learner" was driving. While it was embarrassing for you to be seen driving with your parents, at least you were driving, and that was what counted most. At the time, my father had purchased a new 1954 Chevrolet with a new fangled option called a "PowerGlide" automatic transmission. After my having driven a few trucks with "straight-shift" transmissions in the hay fields, this creature was a cinch to operate. You just put the gear lever in "Drive," mashed on the accelerator, and it "went." Naturally I took every opportunity to drive, and I even sneaked the car out once to go for a short "solo." My mother was nervous about my driving on the main roads, so on Sundays, we would leave home earlier than usual and drive a long, circuitous, back-road route to church. It seemed that I would be fifteen forever.

At school, I was so eager to be a part of everything that I was willing to try anything. I was too fragile for the football team, so in an effort to be near the action, I volunteered to be part of the cheerleading team. An older teacher, who had grown up in the days of mixed teams, decided to revive that tradition at a time where the trend was to all-girl squads. Naturally the other male teammate and I suffered the slings and arrows of outrageous derision from all the other boys, including the players. But what the heck, I got in free at all the games, had the best seat on the sidelines, and got to hang out with the prettiest girls in school. It was a fair trade.

The year 1955 brought new changes to my life. There was a new spirit in the air, one that catered to the rebellious spirit in every young person of that era. Someone said that its author was the devil and that its name was "rock 'n' roll." The sounds of the Hit Parade were quickly drowned out by the electric, African beat of a new music form that combined rhythm and blues with other forms, to generate a sound that spoke to the unrepentant souls of young people. The beat was everything, while the words were superfluous and often nonsensical. This was "our" music, and we embraced it vigorously, much to the chagrin of our elders. This music recognized no skin color, as both black and white artists made their contributions to this rapidly growing genre. If Elvis Presley was the "King," then Chuck Berry was the "Prime Minister."

My mother bought a revolutionary record player for the house. It played small records that had a single song on each side and a big hole in their middles. This "45 rpm" player became the basic tool for playing the latest "hits." Mother's contributions of outdated "big band" tunes just never sounded right and were soon relegated to the bottom shelf. Area radio stations noticed the new sound and quickly ditched their old formats to embrace that of the youth culture. Television was just coming onto the scene, and a program entitled *American Bandstand* became the visual connection to all the latest songs, dances, and entertainers. A new era was dawning. The world was changing, and I was changing with it. Rock 'n' roll was merely the fanfare.

* * *

While I thought it would never arrive, it finally did: my sixteenth birthday, on September 24, 1955. Becoming sixteen meant one thing, a car, and more importantly, it meant solo, unsupervised use of that car. Many years later, in a letter to a granddaughter who was also sixteen and longing for her own car, I explained how I got my first one. Rather than repeat the details of that momentous event, here's the letter I wrote to her.

To: Sarah Cannon
Fr: Papa
Re: How I got my first car
Dear Granddaughter:

Believe it or not, I was in your very position at one time. I wanted a car in the worst way, not so much for transportation, I suppose, but for the freedom that it offered. I was too old to ride my bicycle by a girl's house and too young to drive a car. It was a very difficult time in my life, and I was embarrassed that I was not older and more independent than I was. I had it a little easier than you did, perhaps. I was a boy who grew up poor but did not know it. I did not have any friends whose parents were better off financially than mine were. All of us were in the same boat. My parents would let me drive when I got my learner's permit, but of course they had to be with me, and we went where they were going, not when and where I wanted to go. Therefore, this was not really the freedom I was after. The possibility of my own car seemed like a distant dream.

My father must have sensed my frustrations, so he came up with an offer for me to consider. If I would work during the summer (putting up hay, paper route, etc.), save my money, do well in my schoolwork, be pleasant (no complaining about not having a car), and help around the house, he would match what I had saved, and I would have a car for my senior year in high school. At the end of that year, I had managed to save two hundred dollars (remember, this was in the 1950s). My father was in the car business at the time, which was another advantage. He matched my two hundred dollars and bought a 1940 Ford for four hundred dollars. It had to be titled in his name because I was not of legal age. He told me not to try to "straighten out any curves" with it, and if he ever heard of my driving recklessly, the car would be sold. How I wish I had that car back today! It would be worth a lot of money. Anyway, I had to continue to work to pay for my own gasoline, plus I had to run family errands when asked, but I had "my" car. I do not think it ever had over two dollars of gas put in it at a time, and I was willing to take anyone anywhere who could come up with fifty cents for gas. One thing I did not know was that my father's auto insurance went up substantially and was canceled after I wrecked the car. One night, I was trying to pass a line of traffic. A car turned left in front of me, and I plowed into it. Nobody was hurt, but my car was badly damaged. I was devastated! Luckily, one of my friends had a father who ran a car repair garage. I had to scour the junkyards for parts, but I got that old Ford back running in a few months with a lot of hard work and a good bit of money, all of which I had to earn.

Since those years long ago, I have had many cars, the last two being among the world's finest automobiles, but I never forgot the lessons I learned on that old '40 Ford. First, owning a car is a responsibility of the first order. Someone has to take that responsibility, and it has to be the person who drives it. The initial cost is a consideration, but the title, license plates, insurance, repair costs, gasoline, tires, etc., can end up costing that much and more over the life of the car itself. You cannot expect your parents to meet all these costs. Secondly, driving a car is the most dangerous activity you will ever be involved with. Statistics prove it! It will take you to the graveyard or disfigure you for life in a second.

Therefore, showing off behind the wheel, or riding with someone who decides to show off, is unacceptable. Ask to be let out at the next corner and walk home. Once, when I was about your age, I was supposed to go to the mountains with some of my friends after church. I ran late in meeting them, so they left without me. Four were in the car. On the return trip, the car left the road at high speed and struck a telephone pole head on. The driver was killed, and the other three, if they are alive today, are brain damaged and crippled. I believe that God was looking out for me that day, but he expects me to remember and to be safe behind the wheel.

Now, what all this is coming to is this: Mimi and I want to give you some hope in having your own car by making you an offer similar to what my father offered me. If you are willing to work at a full time job these next two summers, plus what you can pick up on a part-time basis during the school year, and save your money, we will match what you save and come up with a car for your senior year. It would be up to you to continue to work to help meet the expenses of ownership, but not at the expense of your schoolwork. You would have to be a good student, be on good behavior at home, and keep a good attitude. By holding up your part of the bargain, it will be a win-win situation for everyone.

What do you say? Talk it over with Mom & Dad and let us hear what you have decided to do. We love you, Sarah.

Papa

While this letter reflects the wisdom that comes with age and experience, it is certainly not a reflection of my attitude and mindset at the time. Once when my mother asked to be transported somewhere at my inconvenience, I told her to "get there the best way she could." For the next week or so, I was the one looking for transportation, as my father took away my keys as punishment for my "lip." Another event comes to mind when I think of keys. My Ford had a locking gas cap, the key to which I kept on a separate key chain. My mother took the car to town one day and ran out of gas right in the middle of the busiest street. After snarling traffic and being pushed clear, she discovered that she could not remove the gas cap. The key was in my pocket, and I was ten miles away at school. After hearing the tone of her voice during the telephone call that followed, I set record time in hitchhiking to downtown Knoxville, in hopes of avoiding another "grounding." Sharing one's car with the family was not the total independence I had hoped for.

Turning sixteen and having my driver's license opened many avenues in my life. One of my greatest desires was to see more of the world around me. A friend of my Aunt Suzie had a grocery store and an old tractor trailer that he used for hauling produce. One day, during the Christmas holidays that year, I learned that he was going to New Orleans to get a load of bananas and that he needed company. I got word to him that I wanted to go, and against my father's wishes, rode with the man toward the sunset, in an old Mack tractor trailer. Comfort was not a major feature of this ride, as we bounced along the highways, feeling every crack in the road and trying to find some degree of comfort in the worn out seats. The man apparently did not trust me to drive this beast, so somewhere in Alabama, I finally grew tired enough to drop off to sleep. Unbeknown to me, we entered Mississippi in the wee hours of the morning. This state had an "open range" policy that allowed livestock to roam wherever they desired. My slumber was suddenly and violently interrupted as the tractor trailer brakes were applied to the maximum. I picked myself up out of the floorboard, peered outside, and discovered that we had come to a screeching halt in the middle of a herd of cattle. From that point on, we were at maximum alert all the way into Louisiana.

After arriving in New Orleans, we found our way to a large warehouse adjacent to the Mississippi River. In the river was the largest ship I had ever seen. We backed our rig up to the loading dock, along with hundreds of others, and awaited our load. Soon conveyor belts began to send large stalks of bananas out of the ship's hold. Black men began unloading the stalks, one stalk per man, hoisting the bananas on their backs and carrying them to the designated trailer. As the work progressed, I could sense a certain rhythm in their labor. Soon they began to sing individually or chant together in some indiscernible language, as they moved in single file from ship to trailer and back again. A few paused, on occasion, to take a long swig from a bottle of wine wrapped in a brown paper bag. After a long interval of time, it was apparent that no bananas were being directed to our trailer. The reason, it seemed, was that the appropriate boss man for our dock had not been "properly compensated." My friend then folded up a twenty-dollar bill and placed it in his shirt pocket, where it was visible to anyone standing close by. After passing on the required bribe, we finally began to receive our load. Nearly all these bananas were green, but on occasion, a stalk would come by with one or two "vine ripened" specimens. These were highly prized for their flavor, and I was fortunate enough to acquire one for a taste test that did not disappoint. This was the good part. The bad part was being on the alert for the large black tarantula spiders that used the stalks as nesting places.

Finally we were loaded and ready for another nonstop run to East Tennessee. As we pulled out late in the day, bananas were still coming off the ship, and I wondered if we had even made a dent in the total cargo load. The return trip was uneventful except for a broken fuel line, which involved a lengthy delay while my friend tried to manage a repair. After a temporary "Band-Aid" fix, we were on our way again, and we arrived safely home with our banana load intact. I had to take some light punishment from my father for going against his wishes, but I had seen some of the country outside of the local area, and it only whetted my appetite to see more.

In 1955, Chevrolet introduced a radically different line of automobiles and power plants, including a "hot" V-8 engine. These cars, particularly the hardtop sport coupes, became the rage among new car buyers, and demand was high. This afforded a great opportunity for a sixteen-year-old whose father happened to be a Chevrolet salesman. Firstly, I was able to drive his "demonstrator" models, thereby invoking a great deal of envy when I made the rounds of the local Blue Circle drive-in restaurant. Secondly, and most importantly, I was selected by the dealership owner to retrieve cars from other dealers throughout the South.

The scenario went like this. A customer would place an order for a particular model that was not in the Reeder Chevrolet inventory. The dealership would then search to see if that model was available from another dealer in the southern territory. If so, they made an inventory trade, although in some cases it was a straight purchase. In that situation, transportation to that dealer had to be arranged, usually by public conveyance. Throughout 1955, 1956, and 1957, I traveled by car, bus, train, and airplane to Chevrolet dealers all over the region, bringing new cars back to Knoxville, for nothing more than the privilege of driving them and the experience of traveling.

A side benefit was that I was usually called out of school to make a trip. I can remember sitting in class, "praying" that my father would place a call to the school, and on occasion, it worked. I would race downtown in my old Ford, receive enough money for gas and food, and be off to exotic places like Somerset, Kentucky, or Chamblee, Georgia. Sometimes I would take an equally excited school chum along with me to help with the driving. Most of the cars had radios, but the antennas had not yet been installed. Not to be deterred, we would rig up a coat hanger, attach it to the antenna terminal, and cruise along listening to whatever rock 'n' roll station we could find on the dial. Where else would a young man want to be? I had to remember to disconnect the speedometers on all cars so that they could be delivered "as new" to the customers. I always felt a little pang of guilt about this practice, and I wondered if the buyer ever knew that teenage drivers had put his car through its paces for two hundred miles before he took delivery.

But not everything connected with the newly engineered automobiles was beneficial. As speed and power increased, so too did injury and death. An adjunct of teenage rebellion was "drag racing," and while it was legitimized later on with specially built tracks, it had its beginning on any straight stretch of highway. The only safety consideration was to conduct the racing late at night, when traffic was light or nonexistent. First, a car owner would issue a challenge to another, after which all interested parties would ride to the selected site to witness the duel. The two cars would then line up abreast, with a designated "flagman" standing out front between the two cars. With engines revved to the maximum, the two drivers would wait for the "flag" (usually a white handkerchief) to drop. At the first downward movement of the flag, the drivers would release their clutches and go screaming off into the night, in a cloud of burning rubber and smoke. The goal was a line painted across the highway one quarter of a mile ahead. A "judge" would be posted at the finish line to determine the winner.

While these were usually single events to determine "bragging rights," sometimes there were multiple races to determine the "king" of the community. Having the fastest car was a badge of honor, and he who held it was given a large measure of respect, at least until he lost it to a faster car. I knew early on that I was not to be "king." My old "'40 Ford" could not compete with the new machines, so I was content to be a spectator to these happenings or to ride "shotgun" (in the front seat beside the driver) with one of the participants.

I will never forget the tragic event that spelled the beginning of the end for "country" drag racing in the Halls community as well as in the surrounding area. In the fall of 1956, the professed "king" in the community was a young man in his twenties, who worked at a filling station on a straight section of Maynardville Pike. He had a Lincoln that had been modified especially for drag racing. No one had come close to beating him for some time. When the '56 Chevrolets came out, my father sold one of the "hottest" models to the older brother of one of my classmates. One night the challenge came. After closing the service station, the "king" pulled his car out onto the highway in front and waited while the brand new Chevy pulled up alongside. The flag was dropped, and the race was on. They raced down the highway side by side, past the quarter mile mark, with neither giving in to the other. As they rounded a slight curve at an estimated speed of one hundred miles per hour, the Chevy met another car and, with no place to go, hit it head on. Both drivers died instantly, with the driver of the Chevy being decapitated in the process. People came from all over to view the wreckage, and it was agreed that no such impact had ever been witnessed before. Such was part of my introduction to automobiles and the world of transportation.

In the spring of 1956, as I was finishing my junior year of high school, I began to look around for a summer job. I had carried a paper route, worked in a grocery market, put up hay, and done odd jobs in the neighborhood, but I was looking for something more permanent and rewarding. As it happened, my father had a friend who was the superintendent of Big Ridge State Park, located north of Knoxville on Norris Lake. It was a popular getaway location for people in the area, and I had already been there on several occasions to swim, fish, or picnic. Since I was a strong swimmer and possessed my Red Cross lifesaving credentials from the Knoxville YMCA, I decided to meet with Mr. Jim Robb, the park superintendent, and to submit my application to the State of Tennessee for a job as a lifeguard. The swimming area was open on weekends in May, and I was available to work, so Mr. Robb hired me for the entire season, which extended through Labor Day. He also passed on a little philosophy about life, which I never forgot and which I adopted as part of my own. He said that the quality of life was made up of "experiences," and from that point on, I was determined to experience as much of it as possible.

This began three summers as a lifeguard at Big Ridge State Park. The summers of 1956, 1957, and 1958 were filled with many hours on the lifeguard stand, punctuated with much of what the youth of that era did in their free time. Perhaps freedom was the watchword. The "guards," as they were called, lived in "the guard shack" on a hill above the swimming area. Consequently, I was away from home for the entire summer and had my '40 Ford on hand for transportation. I did have one day off each week, which normally brought me home to do laundry and to get my "flattop" haircut from my favorite barber in Fountain City. Sometimes, however, I would skip a week, much to the displeasure of my parents, and just go fishing, visiting, or whatever occurred to me to do at the moment. My pay was $120 per month. This paid my "bill" at the dining hall for a month's worth of eating plus transportation expenses. After subtracting for a few incidentals and putting a small amount into savings, I was able to survive very well on the remainder.

Depending on the crowd, workdays entailed a rotation of thirty-minute "shifts" on the guard stands, punctuated by bathhouse duty, followed by periods of free time. There was a pavilion above the pool area, with a grill that served burgers and such. Here, too, was the main attraction for all the young people: the jukebox. During those three summers, that jukebox constantly played every rock 'n' roll hit, and it could be heard throughout the swimming area. I spent a good portion of my free time up there, watching the dancing and trying to get up the nerve to try it myself. Finally, one rainy day, when the crowd was light, a "local" girl, one who was there every day, took me in hand and taught me a few steps. I grew more confident after that, but made certain that there was a sizable crowd on the floor before I ventured forth. Girls were part of the scene, and the boys in the area knew it. Big Ridge was the place to be, and the crowds, at times, were almost overwhelming. Maintaining order in the crowded swimming area was a real task, and on several occasions the rangers had to be called in to break up altercations.

Lifesaving events were relatively rare, but there were always a few each summer. One event I distinctly remember occurred during one of my shifts. A group of girls entered the deepest part of the swimming area and began making their way to an outlying wooden raft. In all the splashing and confusion, one of them slipped beneath the water, unnoticed by me or her friends. When the rest of the swimmers reached the raft and missed her, they began screaming and pointing to the spot where they thought she had gone down. I immediately blew the three long blasts on my whistle that signified an emergency. Another lifeguard and I swam to the spot and began to surface dive into the dark depths of the lake. By spotting the paleness of her skin in the shadows, we were able to locate her and bring her to the surface. Passing her lifeless body up to the other guards on shore, I watched as they frantically began to administer artificial respiration. After a few moments of fear and tension, she suddenly began to cough and vomit. Finally she began to breathe and cry, much to everyone's relief. She was then whisked away to a hospital for further treatment. Afterward, I learned that she had contracted pneumonia from the experience and had almost died. Although she never came back to thank us (none ever did, probably due to embarrassment), the superintendent praised us highly for our rapid response and coordinated teamwork in making the save. I was always proud of the fact that during those three summers, with the thousands of swimmers in attendance, there was no drowning on our watch.

Growing up is a time of experimenting and of testing limits, and my youth was no exception. My father had bought me a beer once, when I turned sixteen, but now I had the opportunity to experiment further in that area. The guards came up with a number of big inner tubes that we rented out to the swimmers, and the proceeds of the rentals became our "beer money." After the swimming area was secured for the night, we would, on occasion, pile into one car and drive to the nearest package beer store. Since a couple of the guards were in college and could pass for twenty-one, we always made certain that one of them was included in the group. After we secured our supply, usually a quart bottle for each participant, we headed for some isolated spot on the lake, spread out blankets under the stars, tuned the car radio to our favorite rock 'n' roll station, and drank our brewed libations. All this went well for a time, until one night it was my turn to drive back to the guard shack. I woke up in my bunk the next morning and could not remember how I got there. I knew then that I was experimenting in a dangerous area, and I endeavored thereafter to place some limits on this activity.

I cannot let this subject pass without mentioning the local "moonshine," which was not a favorite beverage among the guards but which did make its appearance from time to time. One night, some of the "peach" variety found its way into the guard shack. After a few sips all around, bedlam must have broken out, as the rangers, headed by Mr. Robb, suddenly appeared on the scene to establish order and to get us into our bunks. I was embarrassed by all this and had a hard time looking Mr. Robb in the eye thereafter. I don't believe this was one of the high quality life "experiences" he intended. Such was my introduction to the "demon" of alcohol.

The opposite sex was a subject that was heavy on the minds of the guards, as we must have been on theirs. The reader has to remember that these were the innocent "Happy Days" of the 1950s, so there was a great deal more "talk" than there was "action" when it came to relationships between the two. Girls came in several categories: the "locals," the high school girls-club groups with names like "Top Hats "and "Penguins," who came to spend a week each summer, others who came on vacation with their parents to occupy the cabins, and roving groups of girls who had Big Ridge on their list of places to be on an irregular basis. Each guard had his favorites, some with one from each of the four groups. On occasion, this presented a "delicate" situation when two or more of the favorites showed up on the same day. Desperate measures were called for in these circumstances. To save himself from the wrath of a maiden scorned, the philandering guard would banish himself to bathhouse duty for the entire day, thereby neglecting all in order to avoid the ire of any. Over the course of those three summers, most of the guards I worked with met their future wives in that swimming area, and I was no exception.

When I returned in the fall of 1956 to complete my senior year of high school, my fellow students failed to recognize me. I had grown several inches, had put on weight, and was as dark as an Indian. All my subjects went well, and I took part in just about every extracurricular activity offered. I tried football again, but I had no great love for the contact. Basketball was my game, and I became somewhat proficient at the "forward" position. My strongest point was rebounding the ball after a shot, since I was able to out jump most players I competed against. I remember one game that involved our team, the Halls High "Red Devils," and the Lanier High "Poets." It was an "away" game that involved a trip to our opponents' gym in Vonore, Tennessee, about fifty miles distant. I had come home after school that afternoon and dined on a big T-bone steak. Whether that was a factor or not, I don't know. All I do know is that everything I shot at the basket that night went in. When the final score was tallied, I had scored twenty-eight points and had led the team to victory.

Another highlight occurred a few weeks later, when our team from a little country high school beat the much bigger Central High School in Fountain City, for the first time in history. Shortly after this high point, I began to have back trouble, most likely from my rapid growth. I continued to play but was in pain most of the time. The team ended with a good record, but due to lack of depth, average coaching, and injuries, we never went very far in the postseason tournaments. I always enjoyed basketball, and I went on to participate in it for many years thereafter.

In the spring of 1957, I came to the end of my high school days. The school "annual" of that year ascribed the following four years of activities to me:

ALLEN BUTCHER, son of Mr. and Mrs. J. L. Butcher, Route 13, Fountain City, Tennessee.

Honor student 1, 2, 3, 4; Beta Club 2, 3, 4, Secretary 3, President 4, Glee Club 2, 3, 4, President 3, 4; Biology Award 2, Chemistry Award 3, Science Club 1, 2, 3, Reporter 2, Vice-president 3; Delegate to Boy's County 2; Band 1, 2, 3; Student Council 3, 4, President 4; Distributive Education 3; Football 3; Basketball 4; Class Social Chairman 3; Cheerleader 1, Most Versatile Boy 4; Who's Who in American High Schools 4; Delegate to Volunteer Boy's State 3; H Club 4; Monitor 4.

It is just as well that the class picture accompanying this list of activities is forever lost to posterity. I had always worn the popular "flattop" style haircut, but I had decided that as a sophisticated senior, I should adopt a more mature image by letting my hair grow out and combing it. The result was that I looked like a "bellhop" at a fancy hotel. How the decisions of youth can forever haunt the maker.

There was one last summer in the sun at Big Ridge State Park before I entered the University of Tennessee for the fall quarter. I had no inkling of the work, study, and pressure to come. For now, I was carefree and reveling in the fact that I was a high school graduate. I knew, however, that another wind of change was in the air.

CHAPTER FOUR

"COLLEGE DAYS"

As I approached my freshman year at the University of Tennessee, I had no idea what I wanted to do with my life or what direction I should take. My mother wanted me to be a doctor. So for want of a better idea of my own, I registered and enrolled in Premed. The University of Tennessee was, at the time, a "land grant" college with a mandatory requirement that all male students participate in two years of military training through the Reserve Officers Training Corps (ROTC) programs. I had been alerted to this requirement ahead of time, and I was warned that if I did not want to "go army" and carry a rifle, I should list Air Force ROTC as my preference. I did that, but I also improved my chances by indicating interest in an air force career on the questionnaire handed out at registration. Soon enough, my desire was fulfilled, and I was enrolled as a freshman cadet in AFROTC, Detachment 800, the University of Tennessee.

My freshman advisor was a nice lady who taught in the Natural Sciences Department and who promptly loaded me down with twenty-one hours of academics. Thus I launched off into the world of "academia," characterized by eccentric professors and their lectures and the pressure of preparation for "pop quizzes," exams, term papers, and incessant study. I found out quickly that my performance and preparation in high school was sadly inadequate at this level of learning. My first big shock was a D- on my first "theme" in English 101. While this was a low point for me, I reached a high point later in the year. The English Department selected one of my themes for inclusion in the *Theme Vault*. This was a university publication designed to give incoming freshmen various examples of well-written classroom assignments. Could it be that I was to be a writer?

AFROTC involved classroom work as well as a weekly drill on Hudson Field, a large area near the athletic center where the football team held practice. I was issued a blue uniform, complete with shirt, tie, and insignia, plus a pair of black shoes, which I was to polish to a high sheen. For headgear, I was issued a blue "wheel hat" that had a visor (also to be kept polished) and the air force eagle insignia on the front. Since the air force was considered an "all-weather" arm, we were also issued a raincoat and a hat cover.

The cadet corps, which numbered about one thousand strong, was designated as a "wing." The wing was subdivided into "groups," the groups into "squadrons," and the squadrons finally into "flights" of about thirty men each. Upon receiving my flight assignment, I reported that first week to learn the basic rudiments of drill. Perhaps because I displayed some small measure of military bearing (having marched in the high school band), or because I was tall (the flight was "dressed" from shortest to tallest), I was designated as an "element leader" by my flight commander. There were four element leaders in each flight, each responsible for six or seven other cadets in his "file" and each the reference point for alignment. While the other cadets corrupted our title to "elephant breeder," I did not let that rob me of the joy and prestige of my first command. The organization, discipline, and the cut-and-dried relationship of the command structure were not lost on me. I enjoyed this environment, and I quickly added the military as a potential career path.

I survived my freshman year as a college student, and I spent one last summer as a lifeguard at Big Ridge State Park before beginning my sophomore season. Things did not get any easier academically, and I struggled to keep up with the workload. I had to drop one difficult course, inorganic chemistry, because there were not enough hours in the day to meet the study requirements. This was a difficult year in that I had not yet found my "niche" or a career path that I seriously wanted to pursue. But that was to change as the year wore on.

The Air Science Department came up with the idea of having a cadet glee club. As mentioned previously, I had always enjoyed singing, so I thought, "Why not give it a try?" While the glee club idea never got off the ground, it did demonstrate my volunteer spirit, and it allowed me to meet the senior cadets who were to hold the high-ranking positions the following year. First, however, I had to volunteer for Advanced AFROTC, which would commit me to two more years of college training and a potential air force career. As Julius Caesar once said, before he crossed the Rubicon River of his life, "The die is cast," and so was it cast in my life. I set my goal to become a military man.

As my sophomore year came to a close, I began to look around for another summer job. Capitalizing on my experience as a lifeguard, I applied for and was hired as manager of the pool at Beaver Brook Country Club in north Knox County. While the lifeguard time was similar, I had to spend additional time with chemicals. This was in order to maintain the proper pH of the water, which was subject to inspection at any time by the county health department. I also had a learning experience in human relations. The same club members were there almost every day, and their attitudes and values were different from those of the crowd at Big Ridge State Park. Mix in some alcohol and a few "brat" children, and it was not the most ideal workplace. Fortunately, I had the backing of the club manager, so I was able to exert some control over the pool environment. I also had other advantages, such as picking up extra money by teaching swimming lessons and being able to play golf on Mondays when the course was closed. This was my summer job for two years, which took me up to graduation.

The beginning of my junior year at the University of Tennessee was the start of my career path. I was selected for Advanced AFROTC, and because of the impression I had left in the glee club project, I was appointed to the cadet wing staff, with the rank of cadet sergeant. My duties were largely administrative, ensuring that proper orders were cut for drill and parade activities; in addition, I was a "gofer" for the wing commander and his staff. This proved, later on, to be invaluable experience for me. At the time, I did not realize that a cadet chosen for the position I was given was being looked at closely for future advancement to the highest level of command. The only thing on my mind at the time, however, was that I had finally found my "niche."

I also found a home in the academic world. I had a number of Latin and Greek courses in the Classics Department, and I felt comfortable there. Since becoming a doctor was not to be my calling, I was forced to choose a major. As it turned out, I had more hours in the Classics Department than any other at the time. Accordingly, my degree was destined to be a Bachelor of Arts with a Latin major and minors in English and chemistry. Later, this major had many command and administrative military personnel scratching their heads, trying to figure out how this guy ended up in the military. While many of my fellow officers had engineering degrees, I was always happy that I had a liberal arts education, and I never felt that it hindered my career efforts in any way whatsoever.

So here I was, looking at a possible air force career and suddenly conscious of the fact that I had never been up in an airplane. Like many aviators of days gone by, I began to hang out around the airport. As it turned out, my father's job as a conservation officer with the State Game and Fish Commission gave me the wedge I needed to hitch a ride. The state had a single engine Cessna, as I recall, that was based at the Island Home Airport near downtown Knoxville. The conservation officer who was assigned to fly this aircraft on surveillance missions over the area lakes knew my father. One day I confronted him as he was performing his inspection of the airplane before taking off on a routine flight. He must have sensed what was on my mind. Without my having to ask, and with very few words spoken, he said, "Hop in the back and stay low." I was too excited to think about the risk he was taking as he taxied out for takeoff. Soon he added full power, and we went bumping down the sod field, finally lifting off into smooth air, climbing to the east over Douglas Lake. What exhilaration! What a view! We seemed to be hanging in the air with no sense of movement, although I could see the ground moving slowly by beneath me. In my ignorance of what was involved in this scenario, it seemed to me that there was nothing to this flying business.

As my junior year continued, the Air Science Department began to take the advanced cadets on field trips to air force bases around the area. The instructors who were rated pilots had a requirement to log flying time each month. Accordingly, they would travel to Maxwell Air Force Base (AFB) in Montgomery, Alabama, check out a C-47, fly back to McGhee-Tyson AFB in Knoxville, pick up the cadets, and proceed to another base in the south (usually the one with the best Base Exchange for shopping or the best officers club for drinking or chasing after women). Sometimes we would stay overnight in open bay barracks, if the base could accommodate us. In this manner, I began to see how the air force operated and how a base was run, as we were exposed to orientation training in each locale. The highlight, however, was during the return trip. In cruise, if the weather was good, each cadet took his turn in the copilot's seat, wrestling the wheel of that beloved old C-47 "Gooney Bird" and doing his best to keep it on heading and altitude.

One thing I vividly recall from those trips was how the interior of the aircraft would fill with cigarette smoke as soon as we were airborne and the "No Smoking" light was turned off. Somehow, smoking (and drinking) was synonymous with the image of being an air force officer and particularly with that of a pilot. As one fellow cadet exclaimed, "With the price of cigarettes and whiskey, you can't afford not to smoke and drink." This was a true statement in the sense that cigarettes sold for as little as nine cents a pack, and liquor for seventy cents a bottle, at some base exchanges. As to tobacco, I had begun experimentation with it as a youngster, trying to learn to "roll my own," using a pouch of Bull Durham tobacco and a sleeve of OCB brand papers and slipping around the barn or gymnasium to light up. In college, however, it was the goal of the tobacco industry to get you "hooked" on their product. Students were hired to stand outside the student center and hand out sample packs containing four or five cigarettes each. The research results linking smoking with cancer were still under debate, so many students, myself included, took the bait. Tobacco became a major part of my life and would remain so for many years; this included not only cigarettes but pipes, cigars, and snuff as well. At the time, however, I was most concerned with fitting the image of the mature officer-pilot candidate.

In the spring of 1960, assignments for the summer training unit (STU)came down. Summer training was six weeks of "boot camp," designed to test the mettle of AFROTC cadets prior to placement for their senior year. Those who survived the course would be given a class ranking that would determine their rank and position in the cadet wing for the coming fall quarter. The training was scheduled at various air force bases around the country, so there was an air of excitement and anticipation as we eagerly awaited our assignments. Finally the list was posted. My orders, along with others from the cadet corps, were to proceed to Eglin Air Force Base in Fort Walton Beach, Florida, for the second six weeks of the summer.

After a final abbreviated lifeguard summer job at Beaver Brook Country Club, the time came for departure. Bobby J. Payne, a fellow cadet whose career would parallel my own, had a relatively new Ford Falcon, into which several of us piled one evening for the trip south. After driving all night from Knoxville, we pulled into Eglin's main gate and received instructions to proceed to an area called Postal Point. We didn't know what lay ahead of us as we passed the rows of "open bay" World War II barracks, the training fields, and the parking lot that lay just ahead. As we entered the lot, a training officer yelled at Bobby J. and said, "Park that car over there, Mister, and don't even think about it for the next six weeks." With barely time to grab our gear, we were marched off to stand in line for our barracks assignments while being verbally harassed by the training officers. The UT cadets, as well as those from other universities, were immediately separated from each other and assigned to barracks, so that no one knew any of the others around them. Cadets in my barracks were largely from the south, both black and white, with a few "Yankees" from the eastern states of New Jersey and New York.

After drawing our bedding and exchanging introductions, we were told to stand by for inspection. We stood at attention at the foot of our iron cots, as the training officers entered to give us their expectations of what our barracks was to be in terms of order and cleanliness. Any discrepancies would result in "demerits," which would be erased by walking "tours" on the drill field during designated times, usually during the few free minutes we had each day. After this briefing, we "double-timed" (ran) to the mess hall for our first meal. Since the facility was relatively small for our number, we had to eat in shifts. Those waiting were to stand and advance in line at attention while training officers verbally harassed each cadet in turn with questions, the answers to which the cadets were expected to know. "Who is the chairman of the joint chiefs of staff, Mister? Who is the secretary of the air force?" If you knew the answers, the harassment would then fall on some misalignment of your uniform or on the shine of your shoes. Other than the specific answers to the questions, which were always prefaced and ended with the word "sir," the only answers that were acceptable were "Yes, Sir," "No, Sir," and "I'll find out, Sir."

Once inside the building, you filled your tray in front of a big sign that read, "Take all you want, but eat all you take," after which you sat at the next vacant table. All meals were "square meals," wherein you sat at attention, eyes straight ahead, the fork or spoon lifting a bite of food straight up off the tray until it was level with your mouth. At that point, you guided the food straight into your mouth, withdrew the fork or spoon, and returned it to your tray in the same square motion. Deviation from this procedure or putting too much food into your mouth at one time called down more verbal abuse on your head. After the meal was finished, we formed up and marched back to our barracks to get ready for the next activity or inspection. And so it continued until "lights out" and "Taps" sounded at 10:00 p.m. Then, totally exhausted, we fell on our cots into instant, welcome, and dreamless sleep.

To say that it was hot during this training would be an understatement. The humidity always matched the temperature, which was always in the nineties. To put on a fresh uniform was to be wringing wet within a few minutes. But somehow we became acclimated, as the days continued with classroom work, physical training, and athletic competition. After the third week, we received a "free" weekend. Everyone headed for town where, instead of partying, most opted for an air-conditioned motel room, a soft mattress, and uninterrupted sleep.

First Jet Ride, Eglin AFB, Fl 1960, Author on left

By the fourth week, we had all learned the routine, and things began to ease up a bit. One highlight was the exchange program with the US Navy in Pensacola. They sent their cadets-in-training to tour the large Climatic Hangar at Eglin, while we bussed to Pensacola Naval Air Station to board the USS Antietam, a World War II aircraft carrier used for naval air training. On boarding the ship, each cadet saluted the colors on the fantail and requested permission to come aboard. With a crew of over six hundred sailors, we were soon steaming out of the harbor and into the Gulf of Mexico.

Air operations soon began, as the ship started to recover and launch aircraft in turn. The naval cadets arrived first in their propeller driven T-28s, followed by the marines in their A-4 jets. At noon, we descended into the bowels of the ship for lunch in the officers' mess. I noticed that the tables had a retaining strip all around the edges and wondered what purpose it served. I soon found out! An announcement to "Prepare for a turn to starboard" crackled over a loudspeaker, followed by an abrupt tilting of the mess room to an angle sufficient to send all the china and silverware rushing madly toward the table edge. The navy stewards laughed at us "landlubbers," vacillating between saving our food and supporting ourselves.

The T-28s returned for the afternoon training session, and after a short period, operations were halted to conduct a ceremony observing the ten thousandth landing on the Antietam. The cadet who made the landing was produced along with a giant cake, which was cut on the hangar deck. During the short ceremony and celebration, one of my fellow cadets asked the naval cadet, "You mean to tell me that you have made ten thousand landings on this ship?" All the navy personnel burst out laughing, while the air force was looking for a place to hide.

Years later, I was fortunate to return to Pensacola for a "public relations" cruise aboard the carrier USS Enterprise, to observe similar air operations. I always enjoyed my experiences on navy bases and wished, at times, that I had become a naval aviator. Many years later, however, an ex-navy flyer confided to me, "We took off one morning for our first carrier landing. As I watched the land disappear off the trailing edge of the wing, I knew right then I should have joined the air force."

After this welcome interlude, we were transported back to Eglin and the realities of summer camp. Things began to build to a crescendo as we approached the apex of our training, which consumed the final week. This was the survival phase, which included learning escape and evasion techniques, living off the land, and navigating to selected points for final pickup. The pet name for this exercise was "Swamp Stomp," which was not far off in its descriptive term. For the entire time, we were out in the watery recesses of the Florida panhandle, camping, marching, and staying generally tired and hungry most of the time.

Two highlights come to mind as I reflect on that experience. The first was my introduction to so-called "ethnic food." I had never eaten rattlesnake, alligator, or grubs before, but was served a "lunch" of these delicacies by the army rangers who conducted this phase of our schooling. They assured us that these foods would keep us alive to fly another day, and that when hungry enough, we would eat *anything*. We made halfhearted attempts to sample the fare, but we had not been away from the mess hall long enough to appreciate what was laid before us. "Tastes like chicken," someone said, but in our minds we were thinking about the real thing.

The second highlight occurred during an afternoon when we were practicing "stream crossing techniques." We were marched to the banks of a rather small but swiftly flowing river, where each flight took its position. The key to success of this operation was for one cadet to swim across the stream while holding on to the end of a rope and then to secure it to a tree on the opposite shore. Proud of my former prowess as a lifeguard,

I volunteered for the mission. (This was before I learned never to volunteer for anything.) Stripping down to my underwear, I grabbed the rope and bravely plunged into the raging stream. All went well for the first few seconds, but then, as the force of the current caught me, I felt my jockey shorts being swept off around my ankles as I kicked to prevent being swept downstream. Howls of laughter greeted my emergence on the other side, as I went about the business of selecting a tree and securing the rope in nothing but my "birthday suit." The first cadet who came across via the rope brought my gear, including a steel helmet, which we were required to wear at all times. At the same time, it began to rain as I attended to my secondary duty of assisting each cadet, in turn, to transition from the rope to the bank. So here I was, standing in the river in a pouring rain, wearing nothing but a steel helmet and vacillating between pride and embarrassment.

Such happenings, however, are not without their reward. My training officer had witnessed this event and made a note of it. When I went in for my personal interview at the end of the course, I found that he had written an account of this event into my training report and had rewarded me with a place in the "upper third" of my class. How far up in this "upper third," I did not know at the time. A few days after my return to Knoxville, however, a call came from the University Commandant of Cadets. I had placed first in my class and was designated as the cadet wing commander for the fall quarter, with the rank of cadet colonel.

The reception of the phone call naming me as the cadet wing commander was followed immediately with a sense of panic. While I was unofficially tabbed as the number one cadet in my class, the honor was somewhat lost in the enormity of the task that lay ahead. I had learned, however, that the way to success was to surround myself with the best people and to let them perform their assigned duties with minimum interference. Assembling a wing staff became the first order of business, and being an independent rather than a fraternity man, I was able to make my choices based on ability and performance rather than on politics based on associations or friendships. The wing staff was composed of the deputy commander, the operations and training officer, and the administrative officer. In addition, I had to name three group commanders, six squadron commanders, and twelve flight commanders. Somehow all the positions were filled, without complaint as far as my ears were concerned, and we began to organize for the upcoming quarter and the first day of drill for the new cadet corps.

All these newly appointed cadet commanders eagerly anticipated one other selection process: the selection of the female "sponsors" who would march with their respective units. These were sorority girls who vied to bring credit to their organization by being selected. After the necessary number was elected, assignment to a particular unit was based on seniority. Being the most senior, I had the first choice among these beauties, but having become a married cadet that year, I deferred my choice and agreed to take whoever was last to be chosen. This seemed to please my fellow bachelor cadets, who enthusiastically entered into the assignment process. Not surprisingly, and perhaps unbeknown to them at the time, a few cadets selected candidates who were to become their own future wives.

Finally it came down to the last girl, who was to be my sponsor and who was to march at my right hand, leading the entire corps of cadets. The oddity of the situation was that I was six feet, four inches tall, and she was perhaps five feet tall if she wore high heel shoes. We must have looked comical together as we marched along, she trying to keep up with my long, slow stride, and me trying to take quicker "baby steps" to stay in step with her. It all came together, however, as the organization and filling of vacancies was completed and the fall quarter of my senior year began.

That quarter was such a blur of activity: a full schedule of classes, Thursday drills on Hudson field, and marching the corps, in both good and bad weather, all around the streets adjoining the campus. This was to prepare us for the two major events of the season, marching in the Veterans Day parade in downtown Knoxville and the presentation of the corps at halftime of the Homecoming football game. All these came off without any major blunders by me or by any of my commanders and staff.

What sent throes of anxiety through my system, however, was the cadet wing briefing I had to deliver to the air force commander of the entire AFROTC program at the end of the quarter. This was a real air force general, who flew in once each year to inspect the detachment operation and to review the cadet corps. Part of that review was receiving a briefing by the cadet wing commander. After marching the corps of cadets past the reviewing stand on the drill field, the cadet staff assembled in nervous anticipation in an Air Science briefing room. Soon the general arrived, accompanied by the entire Air Science faculty. I called the room to attention as they entered and took seats facing the podium. Having relied heavily on the briefing given by the cadet wing commander of the previous year, I rose to greet our visitor, and I gave a short, concise briefing on the status and progress of the Air Force ROTC program at the University of Tennessee, losing some of my nervousness as I went along.

The major concern, however, was providing the necessary answers to any unanticipated questions the general might have at the completion of the briefing. He listened placidly until my presentation was complete, and then, after saying something like, "Very well done, Colonel," he asked his one and only question: "Colonel, what is the number of cadets that make up your wing?" This was a simple question, but obviously one for which I was not prepared. I was ad libbing something about the enrollment changing from term to term, when I spied one of the administrative enlisted men in the rear, waving eight fingers in the air. I then transitioned from the ad lib by saying that the cadet wing for this quarter was made up of approximately eight hundred cadets. This seemed to satisfy the general, who stood up, bringing us all to attention as he left the room. As we all breathed a sigh of relief, I resolved to be intimately familiar with the assets I had at my disposal in future situations.

Two other events that concerned me took place during that senior year at the University of Tennessee. The first was my entry into the flight instruction program (FIP), and the other was the annual University Awards Day.

The AFROTC flight instruction program was designed for senior cadets who were designated potentially as "Category One" and who were bound for the fifty-three week Undergraduate Pilot Training (UPT) program after being commissioned as air force officers upon graduation. The program involved thirty hours of flight instruction, in either a Cessna 140 or a Piper Super Cub, leading to solo flying and a private pilot license. All of us were very excited to finally get our hands on our own aircraft, regardless of what it was. When the schedule was posted, I was assigned to the Piper Super Cub. As airplanes go, the Cessna was the prettier of the two, but we who drew the "homely" Super Cub took satisfaction in the fact that it had a "stick" for control versus a "wheel" in the Cessna. This would give us an advantage, we thought, in the UPT program, where all the jet trainers were flown by a "stick."

After extensive air force physicals, psychological testing, and "ground school" on a variety of subjects related to flying, the big day finally arrived. I drove out to a little sod field near Knoxville, called Cox's Sky Ranch, where I met my instructor. After all the preliminaries, paperwork, and briefing, which lasted much too long in my opinion, we headed out the door and approached the aircraft. This Piper Super Cub was red in color, and it was powered by a single 115 hp Lycoming engine and fitted with a tandem wheeled or "rough field" landing gear. After an extensive "walk-around inspection," the instructor directed me into the front cockpit, where we began the "checklist" in preparation for the flight. Little did I realize that all of these preflight procedures would be repeated thousands of times, in various forms and on many different aircraft, throughout my flying career. Finally we were ready to start the engine. After yelling out the mandatory warning "Clear!" the instructor pushed the starter button, and the propeller began to rotate. After a few turns, the instructor advanced the fuel lever, and the engine sprang to life, belching a puff of smoke into the morning air.

First Flight Piper PA18 Super Cub,
Cox's Sky Ranch, Knoxville, TN 1960

Taxiing this little Super Cub was a feat in itself. Due to the conventional landing gear arrangement incorporating a tail wheel, visibility was restricted directly ahead. As a result, the pilot had to perform a series of thirty-degree turns to either side of his intended taxi direction in order to clear the area ahead. The instructor let me have a try at it, and after some over-controlling of the rudder pedals (which included excursions into little-used areas of the airfield), I was able to get her headed toward the departure end of the runway. After performing our "run-up" check of the magnetos and completing all the checklists, we were finally ready for my first takeoff. With the engine roaring at maximum throttle, the instructor released the brakes, and the little Super Cub bolted forward, bouncing down the sod field. The instructor pushed forward slightly on the stick, raising the tail, then pulled back harder, lifting us free of the earth and into the air. There was that exhilarated feeling again! Although I was to perform that same maneuver thousands of times over the next forty years, in a variety of aircraft, it never failed to produce that same feeling.

We climbed to altitude, again performing clearing turns, as we left the traffic pattern. Since we were very near the McGhee-Tyson Airport and were operating under visual flight rules, we had to keep our heads "on a swivel" to keep clear of other aircraft that might be in the area. I don't remember too much about that first flight except that we flew over the City of Knoxville and on to a practice area, where the instructor began to give me visual references for level flight and to introduce me to basic flight maneuvers.

Very quickly, it seemed, it was time to return for landing. As we approached the Sky Ranch, I spotted it in the distance and wondered how we were going to get our craft out of the sky and on to that little patch of earth below. The instructor entered the traffic pattern and set up a long "downwind leg," parallel and opposite to the direction of landing. He then turned ninety degrees to the runway on a "base leg," and made another ninety-degree turn to line up on our "final approach." All this time, we were slowing and configuring the airplane for landing. Now we started our descent, so as to arrive at the "threshold" of the runway at the proper altitude for landing. When we reached that point, the instructor eased back on the throttle and began to slowly pull back on the stick, holding the airplane just off the ground as the airspeed began to drop. Finally, just as the airplane was about to run out of airspeed and was about to stall, we touched down on all three landing gear at the same time—a perfect three-point landing. Once again I experienced that rush of exhilarating adrenaline, as we rolled out and taxied to the parking area. Although I had no inkling of how much I had to learn about flying at that point, my main thought was, "When can I go and do this again?"

The winter and spring quarters of my senior year at the University of Tennessee were somewhat less stressful. Having served as the cadet wing commander for the fall quarter, I was relegated to a special staff position, thereby giving other cadets an opportunity to serve in the command slot. My new position was not without responsibility, however, as I was assigned the laborious task of rewriting all of the cadet wing regulations. At last I was to become an author and leave some short-term legacy of my passing this way, although in this instance, I had to be guided by military form and format.

Finally the time for graduation crept upon me, and so much happened in such a short time. First, after passing all my flight checks, written tests, and solo cross-country work in the Super Cub, I received my private pilot's license. Having done so, I was now given the permanent designation of "Category One," which meant that I was now eligible for the air force pilot training program. Based on my academic record, I was designated as an "Outstanding Military Graduate." This meant that I was eligible for a commission as an officer in the "regular" air force rather than in the air force reserve, and could look forward to a full thirty-year career. The possibilities were endless, including advancement to the rank of general.

The second event, University Honors Day, occurred a few days before graduation. The military portion of these proceedings was held on the Hudson Field parade ground, where both air force and army ROTC contingents were formed. Photographers and reporters from the local newspapers were on hand to record the event. In addition to the honors mentioned above, I received the Academic Achievement Award for the senior class from the Professor of Air Science during these ceremonies.

I was glad to receive my diploma at the end of the graduation exercises, but I was most excited about the ceremony that was to take place immediately following. I was so excited, in fact, that as I departed the podium, I failed to move the tassel on my mortarboard cap from the right side to the left, indicating my graduated status. Immediately following the graduation exercises, all senior cadets assembled in the administrative office of the Air Science Department. There we took the commissioning oath and were sworn in as second lieutenants in the United States Air Force, my date of rank being June 4, 1961. The enlisted men of the detachment all crowded in after the ceremony in order to be the first to salute the newly commissioned officers. It was, and perhaps still is, the custom for those so commissioned to produce a dollar bill for the enlisted man who renders the first salute. Not to be negligent of tradition, we paid our dues, in turn, after rendering a snappy return salute. It was hard to imagine, but I was now a college graduate, an officer in the United States Air Force, and a holder of a pilot's license. Where would I go from here?

CHAPTER FIVE

"WINNING MY WINGS"
PART ONE

Where I was going from here was, in a word, nowhere, at least for awhile. There was a backlog for pilot training, and I was not scheduled to go on active duty until October. What was I to do for the four intervening months? With my first child having arrived on the scene, I now had another mouth to feed, and I needed a job badly.

My father also had a friend who was in charge of transportation for East Tennessee Packing Company, located in Knoxville. One day shortly after graduation, I visited the plant and asked him for a job. He looked at me, and spying a tractor trailer rig waiting to be positioned at the loading dock, said, "Back that trailer up to the dock, and you are hired." I jumped up into the cab, got it started somehow, and managed to slowly back the trailer until it was fairly lined up with the loading dock. How, I never knew. I could tell he was not very impressed, but he said, "Report to the personnel office and then be here at five in the morning." I was hired as a "driver's helper," which meant that the other fellow did most of the driving, and I did most of the work.

This work consisted of carrying heavy sides of beef into the walk-in coolers of butcher shops and restaurants throughout east Tennessee, southwest Virginia, and western North Carolina. This was my first introduction to transportation, and looking back, I can see that many of the principles employed would be the same on down through my flying career.

First I had to buy some uniform items. These consisted of a pair of dark-green work pants, a shirt and hat of the same color, and a pair of nonslip work shoes. Next I had to report at a given time, sign in, and proceed to my assigned truck, where I did a safety check, refueled the tanks, and checked the load. After my "driver" companion (captain?) for the trip appeared on the scene with the load manifests, we were off to the first stop. Further, I had to keep a time log, both for pay purposes and for showing ICC officials, if they stopped me, that I had not exceeded the limit for hours on duty. In addition, I was enrolled in the Teamsters Union, but would have to work out a ninety-day probationary period before I could become a full-fledged union driver. What this meant was that I had to work for the low pay offered by the company until I came under the aegis of the union, at which point my pay and benefits would markedly increase. However, it was a job. And if I could not be a jet pilot for awhile, I could at least be involved with transportation and see some of the countryside.

In this job, I also got an introduction to the human relations aspect of working with other people. Most of the company drivers were what one might refer to as "good old boys," with not much formal education, but good at heart, for the most part. They were the kind who loved mom, the flag, country cooking, and country music, and who believed that professional wrestling was "real." They were also pro-union. Some of the older and more senior drivers suffered with bad backs from years of sitting at the wheel and carrying beef on their shoulders. I always liked to team with the older drivers. I usually had to work harder, but I learned more and enjoyed hearing the tales of past events on the road. They also always had the best "runs" to the most scenic places. Each driver had his own special place to eat, to tarry for conversation, or to pull off for a nap in the cab before returning to the terminal. They all knew by first name everyone along their route. Each stop involved as much "catching up on happenings" as it did resupplying the meat coolers. Lunch was my favorite time, and I had many a hearty country meal in those small-town mom-and-pop restaurants. The work was hard, but I was a growing young man, full of vim and vigor.

Two stories come to mind when I think of those days, and I learned a lesson out of both. The first involved my going out solo on a "city run" in a small truck designed for light loads. These deliveries were to stores in the Knoxville area, and they belonged to a group of drivers who, for whatever reason, wanted to stay close to home. One day I was called in to cover a particular driver's route, and I left the terminal at his usual hour. Not tarrying along the way for extended conversation, lunch, or a nap, I finished the route and was back at the terminal around two o'clock in the afternoon, eager to find something else to do. I did not realize that the regular driver normally returned to the terminal after five o'clock. The next day, a kindly old driver pulled me aside and suggested that the next time I was called on to take another driver's route, I should check to see about what time he normally returned to the terminal, and should not get back before then. Labor lesson: Don't do in five hours what can be done in eight, if the regular man takes eight to do it, or initiative does not always have its reward and can result in possible bodily injury if taken too far.

The second event involved a trip that was composed primarily of delivering boxed meats to several small stores in neighboring North Carolina. The truck was loaded according to the stops, so all one had to do was to open the back door and "Presto!" there would be the boxes for that stop. The driver, wanting to practice good human relations, asked if I would like to start out in the driver's seat. Naturally I jumped at the chance, because I normally only got to drive at the end of the day when we were headed back to the terminal. Climbing up into the cab, the driver asked me if I had ever driven one of these before. "One of these" was a big International truck with a two-speed transmission that had to be carefully "clutched" when shifting through the gears. Not wishing to lose my opportunity, I forsook the truth and mumbled something like, "No problem," as I settled into the driver's seat.

We pulled out of the terminal, and all went well, until we came to the first traffic light, which was located on a steep hill. Releasing the brake, I "dropped the clutch," and the truck began to shake violently. I recovered from this action in some way and continued on to the first stop. When we opened the back doors, I could not believe the mess. Boxes that had been loaded in the front were now in the back. Those that were loaded on top were now on the bottom. That driver began to "cuss" and did not stop until we sorted through the last of the load at the end of the run. For some reason, I was never paired with that driver again. Lesson learned: Never venture forth without due experience, or don't do anything to make another man's work more difficult.

* * *

Finally the air force orders I had been looking for came through, and I was rescued from my life as a trucker. However, I left the packing company on good terms, with the invitation to return if and when my military days were over. I must say in retrospect that I enjoyed the job, particularly getting to see the countryside and meeting the people in those little out-of-the-way stores and restaurants throughout the region.

My active duty orders finally came through, with instructions to report to the 3615th Pilot Training Squadron at Craig Air Force Base, Selma, Alabama, in October of 1961. I was assigned to Class 63-C, which was comprised primarily of other AFROTC graduates from universities around the country. In addition, there were a few higher-ranking officers in the class, who had been accepted for training from other active duty posts, plus one or two candidates from the Air National Guard. We would also share this training experience with several Allied students from the Republic of West Germany.

To help protect West Germany from Communist East Germany, the NATO countries had elected to train pilots for a West German Air Force. Before this decision, and since the end of World War II, West Germans had been prohibited from engaging in any aviation activity, except for the use of gliders as a sport. Consequently, the German students had hundreds of hours of glider time, but they had no experience with powered aircraft. These men were non-commissioned officers who, upon completion of this training, would go on to advanced schooling in the F-84 and would ultimately go back to their country to fly the F-104 "Star-fighter."

The US students had great fun with these fellows, and they added a welcome contrast during the rigors of training that lay ahead. They loved big American-built cars and could often be seen riding around together in some ancient four-door Cadillac. When weather prohibited flying, we would often watch old "Air Power" films, narrated by Walter Cronkite, in the squadron "ready room." Our favorite, when these Allied students were around, was the "Victory over Europe" series, which featured the exploits of the US Army Air Corps pilots over Germany in World War II. When gun cameras would show an American pilot shooting down a German Me-109 or blowing up a German train, we would all cheer, much to the chagrin of the Allied students. They, in turn, would return the favor when an American B-17 fell out of the sky at the hands of the Germans. Perhaps all this seems sadistic and sophomoric, but it actually helped break the tension between the two groups. Never again, we hoped, would Americans and Germans try to kill each other in the skies.

The Air Force UPT program consisted of fifty-three weeks of training, leading to the award of wings for the uniform and to a designation as an air force pilot. The first week was devoted to "orientation." This involved meeting our training officer and receiving briefings on every subject appropriate both to life on an air force base and to the training we were to receive. The wives were also a part of this program, the idea being that things would go smoother at home if the wives understood what was expected of their husbands. The first twenty-six weeks were to be composed of "primary" flight training in the Cessna T-37, followed by another twenty-six weeks of "basic" flight training in the Lockheed T-33.

T-37 Primary Jet Trainer, Craig Air Force base, AL, 1961

Availability of housing on the base was very limited and was reserved for the bachelor officers only. Consequently, the married students had to seek suitable housing for themselves in the nearby town of Selma, Alabama, hopefully at a cost equal to or less than the "housing allowance" that the air force now added to our pay. Searching about town, I came upon a somewhat weathered "mansion" on one of the main streets; the mansion had a "carriage house" located to the side and rear. A portion of that had been converted into an apartment that was available for rent. I knocked on the door of the big house and was met by an elderly southern lady whose name was Belzora Kemp. This lady was right out of *Gone with the Wind*, oozing grace and charm with her southern accent. She always referred to black people as "nigras" and never appeared in public without being immaculately dressed. Her carriage house was available, the rent was acceptable, and the deal was made.

The transition from college to pilot training was equal to the one from high school to college, but I did not realize it at the time. I had experienced the pressure of test-taking and of meeting academic deadlines, but never the level of pressure I was to encounter during my ensuing training. The continual pressure to achieve an ever-increasing level of performance and proficiency in a specialized area was something new to me. What made the pressure doubly heavy was that my future and my very life depended on it.

* * *

Before beginning my recollection of this training, I would like to point out that the air force view was that you were an officer first and a pilot second. Good "sticks" (pilots) are a dime a dozen, I was told, "but a good officer is worth his salt." Consequently, our class was assigned a training officer who was sort of a "mother hen" or a "big brother," to help us adjust to being an officer while undergoing the strenuous training at hand. Since I held this same position later on in my air force career, I will save that experience for treatment later on. I do want to point out the social expectation brought to bear on us as new officer-pilot trainees. Not only were flying and academic performances to be measured, but the manner in which a "student" (and his wife) fit into the social structure of the air force "family" was to be evaluated also. While other factors such as leadership and a sense of responsibility were a part of a student's overall evaluation, the social aspect was heavily weighted.

Nearly all of this social activity centered on the officers club, and you were automatically expected to become a dues-paying member. While most "O clubs" had a nice dining room, the main attraction and gathering place was the bar. Many years later, during my airline career, a Northwest Airlines captain lost his license for a time, after he consumed sixteen gin and tonics the night before a flight and reported for the flight the next morning smelling of alcohol. While the flight he flew that morning was perfect in every respect, the report of his "excess" could not be tolerated. In order to shed some light on why this unfortunate individual ended up in this situation, and to make a counterpoint, I wrote a paper, which was published in the October 1991 issue of *Airline Pilot*. The article read as follows:

Commentary

By Capt. D. Allen Butcher (Delta)

Why they drink

"The Most Expensive Set of Drinks you'll Ever Buy," (June), asserted that "pilots who drink and fly airplanes are subject to full-scale criminal prosecution." I have yet to see an article that addresses the true reasons for the association of alcohol with the flying profession—namely, *tradition* as perpetuated by the military services.

I'll never forget that October day in 1961, when I was first introduced to "The Bar" at Craig Air Force base, Alabama, during the indoctrination of my undergraduate pilot training class. Up to that point, my drinking experience consisted of a few six packs of beer at the University of Tennessee and a few sips of Union County moonshine, which I will heartily endorse as an alternative fuel when our kerosene begins to run low. But on this day at the Officers' Club, a whole way of life was introduced to 60 nervous second lieutenants.

"The Bar," as we were briefed by our training officer, would be the social focal point of the squadron. Our presence and participation was expected, and our absence from any squadron function would be duly noted. Even the Air Force *Officers' Guide* included a section on the importance of responsible drinking in upholding the customs and traditions of the Corps.

We all quickly learned that "The Bar" was a place to unwind from the rigors of training, to settle personal differences, to increase our chances for "most favored status" by our commander as a "complete" officer, resulting in better efficiency reports and positions of increased responsibility. It was a place to parade our wing commander on our shoulders after he received a No.1 rating by the Air Training Command (ATC) Stan/Eval team. Then, after we dunked him in the pool, he bought "The Bar" for all the Corps.

So what if a few staggered and fell along the way. A buddy would pick us up. This was our reward, and it was all in the name of custom, tradition, and esprit de corps, founded by all those who had gone before us, all the way back to World War I.

So what if there were a few moments of pain as we headed for the cockpit the next day. We were *real* pilots now. As one of my instructors said, "A *real* pilot with a hangover needs only a cup of coffee, a cigarette, and a puke to be ready to aviate under any circumstances."

The epitome of this drinking tradition was a ceremony called "Dining In." This involved one hour of cocktails, copious amounts of wine with dinner, more copious amounts of wine with dessert leading up to after-dinner drinks with the traditional cigar. Concentrating on the speech of the visiting general was sometimes difficult as fork-launched peas flew about the room and *real* pilots threw up on their mess dress uniforms.

After earning my wings and reporting to my first assignment, I discovered that "The Bar" and its customs and traditions were perpetuated at the "O club" of every military installation I ever flew into. One featured 10-cent martinis, and paying more than 50 cents for a drink anywhere was unusual. Most bases had a package store with prices as low as 70 cents for a fifth of brand name liquor. As my roommate in Vietnam said, "At these prices, how can you afford not to be an alcoholic?"

Today, many of my fellow officers from that group of 60 second lieutenants from long ago occupy the left seat of this nation's airline fleet. Most have put alcohol in its proper perspective relative to their positions of responsibility and the demands of society for an alcohol-free cockpit crew. A few have needed the assistance of ALPA's HIMS program to counter the traditions of "The Bar" relative to flying. One or two probably have had their careers ended prematurely with "medical retirement." Fortunately, none to my knowledge has been faced with "criminal prosecution."

Let us always remember that when a pilot/alcohol problem rears its head within our ranks, long ago some of us had very good training in making alcohol a part of our lives.

* * *

The squadron "ready room" was a busy place that first day. While thirty or so excited officer students tried to find their assigned tables, the commander was on the raised platform at one end of the room, preparing for his initial briefing. Instructors sat at their tables preparing grade books for the three or four students assigned to them during the course of training. There was a large chalkboard at the other end of the room that listed each instructor's name and the schedule for each of his students. An enlisted man was in charge of posting the training and keeping each student's time card up to date.

A coffee bar was located outside the ready room in a lobby area. Each student had his own individual cup hanging on a peg. As alcohol was associated with pilots who were off duty, so caffeine found its place among the favored beverages for on duty consumption. The students rotated coffee bar duty to keep the place clean and orderly. Nearly everyone smoked, so the room was filled with a myriad of smells including smoke, stale coffee, and sweat-soaked flight suits.

Finally I met my flight instructor and the other students at my table. After a period of getting to know one another, the squadron and flight commanders called us to attention for their greetings and briefings. This began the seemingly endless days of briefings relative to our preflight training. These briefings covered a broad range of subjects, with emphasis on safety, along with a myriad of procedures that were to be followed on the flight line. Afterward we marched to an adjacent building to be fitted with parachutes, oxygen masks, and helmets with pull-down sun visors. We were responsible for this personal equipment with regard to its cleaning and suitability for flight. Here the equipment was stored on individual racks bearing each student's name, and it could only be removed prior to a training mission.

Following these fittings, we reported for ejection seat training, which involved being propelled out of a simulated cockpit with a twenty-millimeter shell. When fired, the force drove the ejection seat several feet into the air on a rail. Emphasis was placed on assuming the correct posture and following the appropriate emergency procedures. While this was great fun in the simulator, I was hoping that I would never have to perform this maneuver in reality. Being long-legged, I always imagined that I would break both kneecaps when propelled out of the tight confines of these jet-trainer cockpits.

Next we received a refresher course in parachute deployment, learning to fall properly and to get out of the harness before the wind could drag us along the ground. Another piece of equipment was added to our flight suits at this point: an "optic orange" knife with an open, hooked blade attached to a length of cord. This knife was stored in a pocket within easy reach on our left thighs, in the event that we needed it to cut the parachute cords.

The next session involved a visit to the "LINK" building where several Link trainers, simulating the actual T-37 cockpits, were located. These were electronic marvels manned by enlisted-men instructors. Their job was to introduce us to procedures related to aerobatics and instrument flying before we performed them in the actual aircraft. This began a long association with flight simulators, which every pilot I ever knew hated with a passion. Using simulators was not actual flying, and your performance in these contraptions could be used against you. The only "U" (Unsatisfactory) grade I ever received throughout the entire course was for a Link session for which I was ill-prepared, both in knowledge and attitude. Later on in my airline career, Delta Airline's pilots hated simulators so much that if a man's job was affected by his failure to perform in a simulator, he had the option of taking the flight check over again in the actual aircraft. This was written into the contract between the company and the Air Line Pilots Association (ALPA).

Our next stop was the altitude chamber, or "physiology training," as it was titled. Here we donned our helmets and oxygen masks and entered a simulated airplane fuselage that could duplicate the atmospheric changes to which we would be subjected in flight. Seated in facing rows, we watched the altimeter as we "climbed" to altitude in the eerily lit chamber. After reaching a given altitude, the instructor gave a signal that immediately produced a rapid decompression in the chamber. Suddenly we were enveloped in fog as the pressure was rapidly reduced to that of the preset altitude. All was well, however, as we were on supplemental oxygen.

Now came the point of the lesson. How could we recognize the symptoms of oxygen deficiency, or "hypoxia," if it occurred in flight? To find out, we were divided into two groups. Those in one group would remove their oxygen masks and begin writing on a pad of paper. People in the other group would observe this activity and would reapply the oxygen mask when performance of the task at hand began to deteriorate and continue to a point short of unconsciousness.

When my turn came, I took my mask off and began to write on the pad while taking deep breaths. Suddenly I was aware that the mask was being placed back on my face. I saw the reason after my head cleared. After a line or two of normal writing, my penmanship began to resemble chicken scratches, and I had come close to "blacking out." The lesson that oxygen deprivation could lead to rapid onset of physical debilitation and unconsciousness was not lost on me. I was always careful to check my oxygen equipment before, and periodically during, every flight.

Finally, after all this preflight training, it was time to get on with the program. One day I walked into the ready room, looked at the chalk-board, and saw the designation "C-1" beside my name. The "C" stood for "contact," that portion of training to be performed under visual flight rules and in good weather conditions. The "1" indicated that this was the first mission in that category. Other mission designations, such as "I" for instruments, "F" for formation, and "N" for navigation would come later in the program.

C-1 was known traditionally as the "dollar ride," when the student pilot gave his instructor a dollar after completing the flight. (This tradition must have been started by the same fellow who came up with the first salute idea). This rite of passage had been upgraded, however, in that now, a bottle of the instructor's favorite whiskey was given instead of a dollar. This introductory flight was basically a "free" flight, since the instructor did most of the flying and the student was, more or less, along for the ride in order to observe, handle the controls, and get used to the operational environment.

After a short briefing, the instructor and I proceeded to the personal equipment room. There we safety checked our parachutes, helmets, and oxygen masks, and walked outside to catch the flight line "trolley" that would transport us to the rows of aircraft on the ramp. This conveyance was a roofed, open-air trailer with benches all around, and it was pulled by a small "tug" tractor. Students and instructors crowded the benches as we made our way down the line. As we passed each row of aircraft, those who were assigned aircraft in that row would disembark until the trolley was empty.

Finally we came to a row of aircraft that had the tail number of the one we were to fly that day. Shouldering our parachutes, we walked in step between the rows. Even with earplugs and earmuffs, the noise was piercing. The T-37 jet trainer was known affectionately as the "Dog Whistle." From its J-69 engines, it emitted what was known as a "pure tone," which could, and did, damage the hearing of those who had to work around it without ear protection. The story was told that you could walk up behind any of the T-37 mechanics in the engine shop and speak their names in a normal tone, and they would just keep on working, oblivious to the normal sounds around them.

Throwing my parachute up into the left seat and hanging my helmet on the canopy rail, I donned my issue gloves and accompanied my instructor as he began to demonstrate the preflight inspection routine. I held a checklist booklet in my left hand for continual reference. Just as I had experienced in the Super Cub, many of the items were the same. We began with a check of the aircraft logbook, noting the status of the airplane and that all discrepancies had either been signed off by maintenance or had been deemed not serious enough to affect flying the aircraft. We also checked that the airplane was properly fueled and serviced. Moving around the airplane in a clockwise fashion, we checked every item as we came to it: tires, gear doors, pitot tubes, windshield, static ports, fuel caps, and flight controls. After the instructor was satisfied, he motioned for me to put on my chute and get into the left seat of the cockpit, while he went around to the right seat.

Once I got into the seat, getting everything hooked up was an exercise in itself. If you were lucky, an airman crew chief would be on hand to help separate and fasten all the parachute and shoulder straps while you were hooking up the oxygen hose and microphone cord. Removing and stowing my plugs and muffs, I quickly donned my helmet and made the final adjustments to my oxygen mask, sun visor, and interphone volume. Packed into this tiny cockpit, I now felt almost a part of the airplane itself. After an interphone check, with my instructor's voice crackling in my ears, we completed the "before starting engines" checklist. With the ground crew standing by with a large red fire extinguisher, the instructor raised his arm and made a circular motion with his index finger. This was the signal that we were ready to start engines. The ground crewman gave a "thumbs up," and we began the start sequence.

Starting a jet engine is a multistep process. Power, either electrical or pneumatic, is supplied to a starter motor, which in turn starts the compressor/turbine assembly rotating and begins pulling air into the engine. At a given rotation speed, and after the incoming air is compressed, fuel is introduced into the burner cans and ignited by ignition plugs. This action causes the turbine/compressor assembly to rotate even faster as the exhaust gases exit the rear, allowing the starter motor to disengage. The engine can now run on its own, not only providing the thrust necessary to fly the airplane but also powering all of the accessories attached to the engine. These would include generators, fuel pumps, etc. I never forgot how one of my instructors explained the operation of a jet engine in very simple terms: "Suck, squeeze, and blow. That's all you need to know."

With both engines running at idle and the "after starting engines" checklists were complete, the instructor raised both arms, and with thumbs extended outward, gave the signal to pull the "chocks" out from under the wheels. When this was accomplished, the ground crewman rendered a salute, which was returned by my instructor. He then directed us to move forward, turn down the lane formed by the rows of aircraft, and taxi toward the runway. I was to repeat this sequence thousands of times in a similar form over the years, but I was not thinking about that at the time. My heart was racing. We were taxiing and were actually going to go out and fly this jet.

Taxiing along the ramp or "tarmac" as it was sometimes called, we completed the taxi check. This involved setting wing flaps and checking flight controls and the proper movement of flight instruments. Suddenly we were at the takeoff end of the runway, in line with other T-37s awaiting takeoff. The instructor called "Canopy Clear," and actuating an electrical switch, lowered the Plexiglas canopy to the closed position, its surface now only an inch or so above our helmets. Ramming the yellow locking handle forward, he checked to see that the red "Canopy Not Locked" light was extinguished. The temperature of the cockpit began to rise rapidly, and sweat began to trickle down my neck. I could hear my oxygen regulator cycle with each breath as we awaited our turn for takeoff.

Air traffic was controlled from a mobile tower housed in a yellow-glassed trailer alongside the takeoff end of the runway. It was manned by an experienced instructor, who handled the radio, and by one or more others (students at times), who acted as spotters. Their job was to visually check each airplane for proper configuration, whether taking off or landing.

Finally a voice from the mobile unit crackled in my headphones, "Cleared onto the runway six at a time." This meant that six airplanes at a time were cleared to line up on the runway heading and to take off in turn. Counting the airplanes ahead, I realized that we would be in the next group. Completing the "before takeoff checklist," the instructor increased power and took the runway, responding with his call sign and the words, "Canopy down and locked, light out." Our squadron call sign was "Red Stick," an English interpretation of the French "Baton Rouge." The selection of this call sign was rumored to be the work of a Louisiana State University alumnus from Baton Rouge, Louisiana, although I never got the truth of the story.

Lining up, the instructor set the brakes. After the airplane ahead of us lifted off the runway, it was our turn. Advancing the throttles to takeoff setting, he made one final check of the engine instruments and released the brakes. The airplane leaped forward, and using the nose wheel steering to maintain directional control, we began the takeoff roll. At fifty knots (nautical miles per hour) of airspeed, the rudder became effective for directional control, allowing the release of the nose wheel steering button on the stick. At around one hundred knots, the instructor pulled back slightly on the stick, lifting the nose wheel off the ground. Continuing to accelerate, the T-37 lifted off the ground and into the sky, breaking the "surly bonds of earth," as one poet has aptly described it.

Things began to move so quickly after that. The gear was raised, flaps were raised, checklists were accomplished, clearing turns were made, and throttles were adjusted for climb as we bored through the sky at an ever-increasing speed. It was exhilarating enough, but would I ever be able to master this? I could hardly keep up. As one instructor put it to his student, "Lieutenant, you were so far behind the aircraft, you wouldn't have gotten hurt if it had crashed." This was no Super Cub, and I quickly realized that I would have to "stay ahead of the aircraft" in my thinking, if I was to become a pilot.

Proceeding to the local training area, we broke through a thin layer of clouds. The instructor lowered the nose and allowed the T-37 to accelerate to its maximum speed of two hundred and fifty knots. This was, and always continued to be, one of the most thrilling experiences of flying: racing along the top of a cloud deck at maximum speed. It seemed that we were going a zillion miles per hour.

"Enough of that," the instructor pilot (IP) said, as he jerked back on the stick and climbed the T-37 to our working altitude. There he demonstrated turns, stalls, and other basic flight maneuvers. Finally the big moment came. I had been following him on my control stick with light hand pressure, when suddenly he shook the stick slightly and said, "You have the aircraft." I grabbed it with a death grip and tried to maintain level flight. "Relax, relax!" the IP shouted. "You can't fly this bird if you're all tensed up." I tried to relax and did some better as I went along, but I was still rough and abrupt on the controls, failing to "trim" out the control pressures as they increased and decreased. The keys to solving this would come later. For now, I was content to know that I was actually flying a jet and keeping it right side up.

Soon it was time to return to base. We descended through the arrival corridor and maneuvered toward the traffic pattern entry point, constantly "clearing the area" for other traffic. By this time, I was soaked in sweat and feeling a little woozy. The traffic entry was a geographical point usually defined by a small town, a junction of highways, bends in a river, etc. After clearing for other traffic, we approached the entry point at fifteen hundred feet above the terrain and at ninety degrees (or perpendicular) to the direction of the landing runway. After flying this heading or "base leg" for a short period of time, and with the runway in sight, we shortened the turn to the "initial" leg by making a forty-five-degree "dogleg" turn toward the runway. This turn helped make alignment with the runway much easier than trying to make one big sweeping ninety-degree change of direction.

All changes of direction were made by rapidly snapping the aircraft into a steep bank and pulling two g's (twice the force of gravity) to maintain altitude. "Yank and bank" was the aviation term applied to this maneuver, which was referred to as a "two-g turn." If you were not flying the airplane, you had to anticipate these turns in the traffic pattern and during certain acrobatic maneuvers, and remember to tense your muscles, particularly the stomach muscles. Otherwise your blood would rapidly vacate your brain, producing a "blackout." Even with muscle tension, maximum g-forces would sometimes produce what was called "gun barrel" vision, narrowing your peripheral vision so all you could see was a small area looking straight ahead.

Two stories come to mind when I think about pulling g's without a warning. One day we were returning from a training mission. The IP was flying, and I was in a post-lesson relaxed state. Suddenly the IP laid his head back and racked the T-37 into a tight two-g turn. After nearly blacking out, I asked him what had happened. He said, "Oh, I like to drain my sinuses after going to altitude, and I've found that this is the best way to do it."

Another time, with another IP, the same thing happened when I was relaxed and inattentive. Again I almost lost consciousness, after which I asked the proverbial, "What happened?" He said, "Didn't you see that other jet? We almost hit him!" After that, I made a point of being aware and part of the "crew," and not just a passenger along for the ride.

But getting back to the traffic pattern, once aligned with the runway on the "initial" approach leg, the IP alerted the mobile controllers to his position by transmitting his call sign and adding the word, "Initial." Normally the controller would respond with an acknowledgement and instructions as to the next required radio call, for example, "Roger, Red Stick 56, call the "break," or, "Check final with the gear." The "break," or "pitch out," as the maneuver was called, was a steep banked turn to a "downwind leg," 180 degrees opposite the initial leg heading. This was accomplished by snapping the aircraft smartly and rapidly into the prescribed bank, rapidly retarding the throttles, and extending the speed brake (a small panel on the underside of the aircraft designed to produce drag). By holding everything steady throughout the turn and rolling out of the turn parallel with the runway headed in the opposite direction, one would be in position and at the correct airspeed to configure the aircraft for landing. Later, in formation training, I would come to understand the efficiency of this "overhead" pattern. Four aircraft in close "echelon" formation would come down the initial leg; the leader would pitch out, followed by the other three at three-second intervals. This would place them in perfect position relative to each other on the downwind leg, and would allow a quick recovery of all aircraft.

The downwind leg, as previously mentioned, was designed to accomplish two things. It was meant to slow the aircraft and to configure it for landing. With the throttles at "idle" and the speed brake extended, the airspeed would drop rapidly, allowing the extension of the landing gear and flaps (extendable panels on the trailing edge of the wing). The decision now was when to start the turn to "Final" and to line up with the runway for landing. Aviation is based many times on references to other objects outside the aircraft. Since this was my first landing, the IP pointed out that it was normally "the approach end of the runway disappearing off the trailing edge of the wing." In other words, when you could no longer see the end of the landing runway out of the corner of your eye, it was time to start the turn.

Now began the most difficult part of getting an airplane back on the ground safely—lining up with the runway and descending to a predetermined touchdown zone on that piece of terra firma. My old instructor put it this way: "Imagine that you are falling off a table and making a turn in the opposite direction all at the same time." This description seemed to work for me, as I never forgot it throughout my flying career. The final approach, then, began with a turn *and* a descent, plus judgment through experience, to bring the aircraft to a predetermined altitude and distance from the end of the landing runway. Not to forget communications with our controllers on the ground, the instructor keyed the mike and said, "Red Stick 56, gear check."

After the spotter in the mobile cab "glassed" the aircraft with his binoculars, to confirm that the gear was indeed extended, the controller responded, "Roger, Red Stick 56; cleared to land." I must admit that there are many words I love to hear in this life, words of affection, praise, and so on, but to a pilot, the words "cleared to land" are music to his ears. They mean that in spite of everything that has gone before, he has put himself in a position to end this flight safely and perhaps live to fly another day. Now, if we can just get this beast on the ground and get it stopped.

The descending path to the runway was again based on outside references, the approach end of the runway and its position on the windshield, among others. If you appeared to be going high, you reduced power and dropped the nose. If going low, you added power and raised the nose to return to the ideal picture reference. The idea was to have a "stabilized approach." Otherwise you might hear those dreaded words from the controller, "On final, go around!"

The sequence just described was to be repeated several times over the next few weeks, as I moved closer to that first goal of being able to fly solo. The days were filled with academics, physical training, link training, open ranks inspections of uniforms and flying gear, study of airplane and flight manuals, and unending briefings. Flights concentrated on stall recovery, spin prevention, slow flight maneuvers (simulated landing approaches at altitude), and "go-arounds," with maximum time in the traffic pattern for touch-and-go landings.

One day, I was working on touch-and-go landings in the traffic pattern with my IP. I was not having a particularly good day. Sensing my frustration after a rather poor turn to the final approach, he said, "I have the aircraft." Relinquishing control, I heard him key the mike and ask for a midfield turnoff after landing. My thoughts were that the training mission was over, that the IP had seen enough, and that I was destined for a "Fair" in my grade book. After landing and exiting the runway at the midfield turnoff, he suddenly brought the T-37 to a stop, set the parking brake, and opened the canopy. As he began to unbuckle his straps, he keyed the interphone and said, "You're scaring me! I'm getting out of this thing before you kill us both! You're on your own! Go fly this jet by yourself! I'll be watching from the safety of the mobile control unit." I was stunned! He vacated the cockpit, gave me a grin and a half salute, and headed toward the mobile cab. I looked at the vacant seat, heard the screaming of the two J-69 engines behind my seat, looked back at the instrument panel, and had the sudden realization that I was all alone.

In each person's lifetime, there is a handful of experiences that one would call "defining moments." Those moments could range from the birth of a child to landing that much sought-after job. What I experienced that day was one of those moments. I nervously started the aircraft rolling forward and began taxiing back around to the takeoff end of the runway. Somehow I completed all the checklists, got the canopy "down and locked," and found my way back to the takeoff position. Everything that I had learned, everything that I had worked for, had brought me to this point.

"Red Stick 56, Canopy down and locked, light out," I transmitted.

The reply from mobile control was, "Cleared onto the runway, Red Stick 56, you're cleared for takeoff when ready."

I taxied into position, held the brakes, and ran the engines up to takeoff power. I looked down that runway, as I would so many times in the future, and released the brakes. Without the added weight of the IP, the T-37 leaped forward down the centerline of the runway. Hopefully I would remember my procedures. At fifty knots of airspeed, I remembered to release the nose wheel steering button and began to maintain directional control with the rudder pedals, as the airflow made them effective. At the prescribed airspeed, I eased back on the stick, lifting the nose wheel off the ground. Holding this attitude, the main wheels lifted off the ground, and I was airborne! Raising the gear handle, I felt the familiar retraction sequence as the wheels were sucked up into the gear wells. I proceeded with the flap retraction schedule and accelerated to traffic pattern airspeed. I leveled at traffic pattern altitude and made my first turn, heading for the landing pattern entry point.

While I was tempted to celebrate my first jet takeoff in some way, the sobering thought occurred to me that while I had gotten myself into the air, I now had to get myself and the aircraft back onto the ground. Not only that, but my IP would be watching closely to grade my performance. I cleared the area around the entry point and entered the traffic pattern. Everything went smoothly as I lined up on "initial," pitched out onto the downwind, and turned final with a gear check call to mobile control.

"Red Stick 56, you're cleared for touch and go," came the reply.

I proceeded down the final approach, brought the T-37 over the end of the runway, settled into the flare, and made a perfect touchdown right in front of mobile control. Adding power, I lifted off for the second of three landings I was to make that day. It was at this point that the exhilaration of the moment became too much for me. I raised my fist and yelled out a "Yahoo!" that drowned out the scream of the engines. I had done it! I had "soloed" my first jet! Where some had failed, I had shown that I could hack the course. I had passed the first test in becoming an air force pilot. It was a confidence builder of major proportions.

I parked the aircraft and boarded the trolley back to the squadron building. A West German student had also soloed that day, and the news about being the first in our class to accomplish this goal had reached the ready room ahead of us. Approaching the entrance, I noticed a gathering of my classmates along the walkway. They suddenly rushed me, picked me up bodily, and carried me to an aboveground pool in front of the squadron building. There I was given the traditional "dunking," another rite of passage for all aspiring pilots who record their first jet solo. Back in the ready room, after a change of flight suit, I was presented with a "First Solo" certificate and an unusual complimentary performance debriefing by my IP. It was a heady day. This flight training was going to be a "piece of cake," I thought.

The days ahead were filled with more traffic pattern work along with an introduction to aerobatics. While I had indeed taken the T-37 for a solo flight, I had not developed any precision or judgment to go along with the manual skills of manipulating the controls. Much to the frustration of my instructor, I would fail to level at prescribed altitudes or to roll out on assigned headings, and I was generally "behind the aircraft" most of the time. In aerobatics, I was not aggressive enough, and I lacked precision in executing the aileron roll, barrel roll, loop, chandelle, lazy eight, cloverleaf, and immelman. While it might be of interest to the reader for me to go into detail about each of these maneuvers, I will simply say that they all required the utmost in planning, precision, and judgment in order to be accomplished successfully.

One maneuver I did master rather quickly (out of fear, for the most part), was recovery from a spin. Nicknamed the "death spiral" by World War I pilots, the spin basically involved an aircraft out of control, out of flying speed, and corkscrewing in a downward plunge to the earth below. Many World War I pilots died at the end of this condition, until one day, an unknown pilot wishing to go out in a blaze of glory rapidly "popped" the control stick forward as he was attempting to stop the rotation with opposite rudder. Suddenly the aircraft came out of the spin, and he lived to fly and fight another day. After he shared his experience with his fellow aviators, they quickly adopted his recovery procedure, and it remains the spin recovery standard for most aircraft today. While spins were uncomfortable at best, learning to recover from one was a confidence builder.

After a few more training missions, I was put up for my first check ride. I was still having difficulty putting everything together. That fact, coupled with nervousness and uncertainty about what to expect, did not lead to a happy result. I received a "Fair" grade and felt fortunate to get that, considering my performance. Perhaps the check pilot saw some promise, but I was embarrassed, and I began to doubt that I was cut out to be a pilot.

And then it happened! One afternoon, shortly thereafter, I was involved in a PT class involving gymnastics. I was working out on a set of overhead rings and decided to do a "skin the cat" maneuver, which was basically a back flip. I turned loose of the rings too early at the end of the maneuver and landed heavily and unevenly on my feet. My right ankle buckled and cracked like a rifle shot. It was then that I experienced the greatest pain in my life thus far. I was rolling around on the mat, crying and screaming with pain while holding my leg. The base ambulance showed up soon after. I was given a shot of morphine and loaded on a stretcher. Since there were no facilities at Craig AFB to treat my injury, I was immediately transported to Maxwell AFB in nearby Montgomery, where the flight surgeons made their diagnosis. I had a shattered ankle and would require immediate surgery. The surgical procedure involved the insertion of a "pin" or nail to hold the broken bones together until they could heal. I was told that the pin could be removed later if it caused any problem. It never did, and it still holds my ankle together to this day.

My recuperative period began in the orthopedic ward of the Maxwell AFB hospital. An interesting fact about military hospitals is that you shed your rank when you enter as a patient. There is no separation between officers and enlisted men, nor are there special privileges granted to any. Consequently, I was placed in a large wardroom with several other servicemen from all areas of the military, men who were suffering similar injuries. We got to know one another rather well, and we quickly settled into a daily routine of eating, bathing, physical therapy, and general camaraderie. My classmates sent their well wishes, and a few made the drive to visit on the weekend, in the midst of their busy study schedule. One even sneaked in with a bottle of Jack Daniels whiskey, which I kept hidden away until my departure. Since my injury had occurred in the few weeks leading up to the Christmas holidays, my immediate goal was to progress to the point where the flight surgeons would release me in time to avoid a "hospital Christmas." Finally my pain and swelling began to subside, and I was able to stand up on my good leg, holding on to the side of the bed. The first time I tried this, I nearly fainted dead away, as my heart had not been in the habit of pumping blood to a vertical brain for several days. When I showed that I could hobble around on a set of crutches without pain, the good news finally came down. I was granted convalescent leave at home for the duration of 1962, with orders to report back after the New Year for reevaluation.

CHAPTER SIX

"WINNING MY WINGS" PART TWO

With the advent of 1963 and my return to Craig AFB, Alabama, my main concern was whether I could remain with my classmates in UPT Class 63-C. With my injury, I had fallen so far behind the rest of the class that there was no time for me to catch up. Finally the word came down. I would "wash back" to Class 63-D, which had started training six weeks after my original class had begun. Not only did I have to come back from injury, but now I would have to adjust to a whole new set of classmates, a new squadron, and more importantly, a new instructor.

I found that most of my new classmates were too busy worrying about their own progress to pay much attention to a new addition, so I quietly took my place and got back down to business. Strangely, I found that the time interval between my injury and my return to training had had a beneficial effect. By having time to reflect on my mistakes and get in extra study time, I was able to see things more clearly. Consequently, my performance began to improve.

I was a little nervous, however, when my new instructor and I taxied out for the first training mission after my injury. While my ankle had nearly healed, I still walked with a slight limp, and I was fearful that I might not be able to rotate my foot properly to hold the brakes during engine run-up prior to takeoff. All went well, however, and I was in the air again. It was a feeling that I had missed more than I realized. I was allowed to go solo again shortly thereafter, and fell into the old routine of flying, academics, and physical training.

The missions began to change now, as the "contact" phase of the training syllabus was nearing completion. The emphasis now turned to instrument flying, the instructor acting as an observer with the student "under the hood." The "hood" was simply an oversized visor that the student fitted over his helmet in such a way that, during flight, he could only see the instrument panel. This was a precursor to much of the type of flying I was to do later on in my career.

The first rather exciting, maneuver I learned to perform was the instrument takeoff. Here the IP would position the jet on the centerline of the runway and give the student control of the aircraft. The student, who was now "under the hood," would then set his heading index needle to the runway heading, release brakes, and take off with reference to instruments only. This made for some exciting takeoffs, with IPs yelling out corrective commands and having to retake control of the jet, at times, in order to stay on the concrete. Luckily I got the picture early on. The key was to make very small changes in rudder pressure as the airspeed increased. After that, the instrument takeoff was a routine maneuver.

The basic instrument phase continued with Link training and missions concentrating on mastering turns, climbs and descents, airspeed changes, etc. All of these took place under the hood, simulating weather conditions. After passing the basic instrument check ride, I progressed to the next phase, where all of these maneuvers were brought together for one purpose, to get the aircraft airborne and back on the ground safely during any weather condition. This meant learning to fly published approaches to selected runways at a particular airbase or airport. These approaches were standardized in graphic form and were available for nearly all airports around the world. When you see a pilot carrying his "flight kit," it primarily contains the approach charts for the area into which he is flying. This new phase of learning also meant learning about onboard radio navigational aids as well as about ground-based equipment designed to work in conjunction with those aids.

My introduction to approaches was one called a "direction finding (DF) steer." Basically, the pilot contacted the appropriate tower, requested a "practice" DF steer, and followed the heading instructions given by the controller in order to bring him to the airport for a visual approach and landing. This involved keying your mike for the controller. He, in turn, would observe the direction-finding needle as it pointed to the source of the radio signal, and he would give the pilot a heading to fly. This would be repeated at intervals until the pilot called the "field in sight." In reality, this approach method was taught and used primarily by student pilots who got lost in the local area. Accordingly, it was used in emergency situations rather frequently during early solo missions. Such use usually resulted in much grief and embarrassment for the student pilot involved. The story goes that one day an excited call came in to Craig tower for a "practice" DF steer. Since the controllers were busy at that particular time, the reply to the call was that Craig Tower was only available for "emergency DF steers." After a short pause, the still more excited voice came back with, "Okay, give me one of those."

Two events come to mind as I remember this in-training time period. The first involved a foreign student, Afghan as I recall who was on one of his first solo flights. A foreign student alone in a jet airplane created an unpredictable situation, at best, due to the language barrier and to the different cultural ways of looking at things. Consequently, the student's IP was always on hand in the mobile control unit to help, should a problem arise. On takeoff, one particular day, the foreign student radioed excitedly that his canopy was not down and locked.

The IP radioed back with the instructions, "Put the switch down. Put it down!"

The student, interpreting the "it" to be the airplane, made a near perfect belly landing in a cotton field just off the airfield. Fortunately, he was not hurt. The jet was retrieved from the field, loaded onto a flat bed trailer, and returned to the base. After minor sheet metal repair and a thorough inspection, the aircraft was returned to service. I never learned whether the cotton farmer was reimbursed for damage to his field.

The second event was much more serious and nearly tragic. This incident involved a solo student practicing aerobatics and a "dual" ship, with an IP and a student "under the hood" on an instrument training flight. While performing an aerobatic maneuver, the student pilot apparently strayed into a departure corridor for outgoing instrument flights, and he pulled up into the dual ship, breaking both ships apart. All three pilots ejected safely. The dual ship pilots had normal parachute deployment and landed on the ground safely. The solo student got his parachute shroud lines tangled in the ejection seat, however, and was plunging toward the earth in what is known as a fatal "streamer." With quick thinking, he was able to climb up the shroud lines, disentangle them from the seat, and effect a normal chute deployment. There were many tense moments in the squadron ready room until we learned that all pilots were safe and uninjured. The loss of two aircraft produced several squadron "changes of command," changes in the local training airspace and unending "see and be seen" safety briefings.

As students completed final check rides in the contact and instrument phases of training, we were introduced to the last two phases of the primary flight training program: navigation and formation flying.

Excitement began to build as the thought of actually "going somewhere" in an airplane began to build in our minds, as did the idea of flying "with" each other instead of constantly trying to avoid one another.

Academics prepared us for the navigational phase with emphasis on map reading, plotting courses, and computing time, distance, airspeeds, etc., on a handheld slide rule computer. This little device was called the E-6B computer, and it was standard equipment for all pilots until replaced by electronics in the modern era. I was introduced to another subject, at this point, which would be the greatest obstacle I would ever face in my flying career: weather. It was to be my constant antagonist until the day I retired, and I learned a healthy respect for it, sometimes the hard way.

On the flight line, we began to spend more time at the flight planning tables in the base operations building. Here we had access to maps, weather information, and everything necessary for the preflight planning of a cross-country mission. Many imaginary flights were planned and plotted with the anticipation that one day; we would do it "for real." That day came when I entered the squadron ready room one morning and noticed an "N-1" beside my name on the mission board. I was actually going to "go some place" in a jet airplane. At base operations, I laid out the route given to me on a sectional chart. As the name implies, these are small-scale maps of certain sections of the United States that include most topographical and man-made features. These early training routes were usually "round-robin" or circuitous routes, which began and ended at the home field. Checkpoints might include a bend in a river, a railroad crossing, a water tower, or a drive-in movie theater. Naturally these routes were flown at low altitudes, to allow identification of the checkpoints.

After the IP checked my flight plan, map, and fuel calculations, we received a weather briefing and headed out to the aircraft. After the preflight inspection, I got situated in my seat, strapped a mini-clipboard containing the checkpoints to my right leg, and laid my map (folded to the route of flight) on the left console. Takeoff was normal, and we were cleared out of the area to our first checkpoint. Luckily, I remembered to check the takeoff time, as it was critical to determining the estimated time over the first checkpoint. I suddenly discovered that navigation was going to increase my workload tremendously. I now had to fly the airplane (maintaining proper altitude, heading, and speed), locate features on the ground and try to match them to those on the map, make entries on my clipboard, and make radio position reports to the local flight service station.

This last task was new and intimidating to me, as it was and is to all new pilots. The position report had to be given in a prescribed format, and might go something like this: "Montgomery Flight Service, Red Stick 56 over Plantersville at 1432 Zulu, altitude 5 thousand, 5 hundred, estimating Demopolis at 1451 Zulu, Centerville next; over." It was easy to goof up, say the wrong thing, or simply draw a mental blank when you pushed the mike button, and I'm certain that the flight service station operators had many a laugh and/or moment of frustration in trying to interpret and log the flight progress of these new jet jockeys.

With superior airmanship, I managed to find all the checkpoints, and soon my surroundings began to look familiar. We checked back into the local area with Craig Tower, entered the traffic pattern, and made a normal landing. Taxiing back in to the ramp, I experienced a great feeling of accomplishment; I had "planned the flight and flown the plan!" Going places was "fun" in spite of the work involved. Little did I know how much "fun" I was to have in the years ahead.

* * *

In the midst of primary training, a world event occurred that produced a sobering effect on the training squadron as well as on the entire base and community. This event was later given the title of the "Cuban Missile Crisis." The Soviet Union had established a military presence just ninety miles off the coast of Florida on the island nation of Cuba, which had embraced communism under the revolutionary dictator Fidel Castro. In the summer of 1962, Nikita Khrushchev, leader of the Soviets, decided to establish missile bases in Cuba from which to attack the United States if the "Cold War" degenerated into a hot one. In October, large Soviet ships were loaded with all the missile hardware and sailed toward Cuba. US president John F. Kennedy, not willing to tolerate such a threat to national security, placed all United States forces on alert and threatened all-out nuclear war if the ships failed to turn back. B-52 bombers from the US Strategic Air Command were kept constantly in the air, ready to strike at the heart of Russia should the Soviets carry out their plan. Security was tightened at Craig AFB, and fear spread rapidly as the ships continued toward their target. What if we came under nuclear attack? What about our futures, if war should suddenly break out? Tension was at a breaking point. And then the news came down. The ships had turned back. There would be no nuclear war, at least for the time being. Everyone relaxed and got back to the work of training and becoming pilots, but with the knowledge that the world was becoming an increasingly dangerous place. What part would each of us play in facing that danger?

As navigation and instrument training progressed, I learned to navigate on instruments using the Very High Frequency Omni-Directional Range (VOR) radio stations located throughout the country. Courses from one station to another were called "victor airways," and I had cockpit instruments that enabled me to orient myself relative to a particular station and to fly a published course to another. I could also use these VOR stations to fly published instrument approaches to airports during marginal weather conditions. In addition, we were introduced to the "radar environment." Here, a ground-based controller could pick up my jet on his radarscope, and he could either help me navigate safely along my route of flight or guide me down to a safe landing when the weather turned "sour." Everything was coming together now as our proficiency increased, but there was still one bloc of training remaining, one we knew would be demanding and yet would be the ultimate thrill: formation flying.

The idea of flying in proximity to another (or several) aircraft probably began with the dawn of aviation. The tactics of war evolved this idea to a science. Now, instead of a number of lone aircraft individually engaging the enemy, aircraft would be massed in formations designed to concentrate attacks on ground targets as well as to provide protection for one another in the air. Now, instead of several aircraft attempting to navigate to the target, only one, designated the leader, would have that responsibility, while the other aircraft would simply follow his plane, maintaining a prescribed, relative position in-flight. After World War II and the advent of the jet airplane, the large, loose formations previously flown gave way to "close formation," with a tremendous increase in concentration and skill on the part of the pilots. Now the pilots were expected to fly "wing tip to wing tip," at near-sonic speeds and in every kind of weather.

This tactic had its use in the public relations and recruiting missions of the armed services as well as having wartime applications. While the US Navy had its Blue Angels, the US Air Force had its Thunderbirds. These were special units composed of the best young pilots flying the latest jet fighters in the inventory. They developed routines to display formation skills and painted the aircraft in special colors. Then the air force scheduled air shows around the nation to "wow" the spectators (some future military pilots) with these high performance demonstrations. I was fortunate, during both the military and civilian portions of my flying career, to witness these air shows and, on one occasion, to be a part of one.

One day, I came into the squadron ready room and found an "F-1" posted beside my name on the mission board. The ensuing briefing was more extensive and detailed than usual, with two IPs, two student pilots, and two aircraft involved. To begin with, we would not take off in formation, but would use a timed interval between takeoffs. One of the leader's first jobs was to take off and begin a shallow turn out of traffic. The "wing man," or number two, would then take off and effect a "rejoin" with the leader. This was no easy maneuver, requiring the utmost in judgment and skill while trying to close the gap and arrive in the "slot" position next to the lead ship. There were plenty of tense moments early on in our training. "Overshoots" were common, as we tried to get the picture.

Formation flying was one of the most demanding, yet one of the most exhilarating of all in-flight maneuvers. As leader, you were responsible for the safety and navigation of the formation. As wingman, you were expected to maintain your position relative to the leader and to stick to him like glue. This "slot" position was determined by maintaining a visual reference relative to the lead aircraft. It might be something like "line up the outer flap hinge with the lead pilot's head" or "put the leader's wingtip on the nose of his ship." Whatever the reference, a good wingman was bent on maintaining position. One IP said, "If you are a wingman and the formation crashes, make certain that when they dig out the wreckage, your aircraft was still in the slot." Since formation was usually flown under "radio silence," the pilots used head and hand signals exclusively for communication. Knowledge of these hand signals was imperative for successful formation flying. The sight of aircraft flying in a close, precision formation was always a beautiful sight to me, and I was fortunate to fly formation in several military and civilian aircraft myself. The air shows of the Blue Angels and the Thunderbirds were a recruiter's dream, as every aspiring aviator had the dream of handling the latest "hot" jet.

Finally there came a day when all the check rides had been completed, all the training missions flown, all the academic subjects passed, and all the physical training completed. Those of us who were left had met the challenge. We had completed the six months of primary undergraduate pilot training. We were not yet full-fledged air force pilots, and we knew that much lay ahead in the remaining six months of basic flight training, but we began to develop just a bit of swagger in our step, to tilt our caps a certain way, and to display a little of the "cool" that characterized our instructors.

Basic training? The T-33? Bring it on! We can hack it!

* * *

One thing you get accustomed to in the military is change. Nothing remains the same for long. And so it was with primary flight training. You file away the experiences of one training period and try to find something to connect it to in the next. Basic flight training began with transfer to another squadron, a whole new set of instructors, new academic subjects to master, and in this instance, a new aircraft.

The Lockheed T-33 was a training derivative of the F-80 "Shooting Star" fighter widely used in the Korean conflict. It was the first and slowest of first-generation jet fighters, and it quickly gave way to the high performance F-86 in the Korean theater. However, as a trainer, it made the perfect teaching aid for many classes of future aviators, until replaced by the T-38 in the 1960s. Known affectionately as "the T-Bird," it was a favorite of all who flew it. It was simple to fly and maintain, it had great range, and it was the pick of the command staff to maintain their flying currency. Throughout the air force, nearly every wing commander had his own personal T-Bird. It was the "shiniest" airplane on the base, and it usually sat in front of base operations, ready to go at the whim of the commander.

The T-Bird was powered by a single axial-flow jet engine. That's not important to know, except for the fact that it was very sensitive to "over temping" if you dumped too much fuel into the burners with rapid throttle movement. After the appropriate amount of screaming by the instructor, the student quickly learned to move the throttles very smoothly and slowly, with one eye fixed on the exhaust gas temperature gauge.

Emergency procedure was simplified in the T-33. The procedure was basically a two-step process. If the lone engine failed for any reason, the pilot activated a "gang start" switch that supplied extra "fuel and fire" to the burner cans, to get the engine running again. If the first procedure failed, you went to step two: EJECT!

What I most remember about the T-33 was that it was the only aircraft I ever flew that had a "yaw string." Sitting in the front cockpit, the pilot peered out over the nose at a piece of twine, which, if the aircraft was being flown in a coordinated fashion, would align itself perfectly with the centerline of the fuselage. Otherwise, it would flare off to one side or the other, giving the IP another reason to chide the student for misapplication of the rudder. One last thing, for which I was thankful, was that we would not do spins in the T-33.

At first, moving to a new aircraft was difficult, but I quickly learned to "brain dump" everything I knew about the old, and I attempted to fill the void with everything I could learn about the new. There were different "numbers" to learn, such as speeds, limitations, weights, etc., and different procedures, for example, emergency, normal, etc. This change was to be true of every transition I would make in my flying career, and it was accelerated by the use of "cockpit time," additional Link training, rote memory, and dealing with those new numbers while flying the actual aircraft.

As to the schedule of training, it was almost identical to the primary phase, that is, learn to take off and land, gain precision in aerobatics, show that you were safe enough to go solo, then move on to instruments, navigation, and formation. This training was backed up with additional academic subjects such as weather, principles of flight, and the learning of Morse code, as well as with increased physical training. All of this was still challenging, hard work, even though it was somewhat more relaxed and increasingly familiar.

One thing that helped me relax was the Korean veteran IP to whom I was assigned. Being an older captain who had experienced the "real air force" firsthand, he was a laid-back, mild-mannered relief from the lieutenant IP types who had never been out of the air training command. Flying under his tutelage was a pleasure, and I began to look forward to our training missions together. From him I learned that becoming part of the aircraft itself was essential to being a good pilot. The transition phase came easy for me, and I soloed in minimum time.

The T-33 had a couple of radios that the T-37 did not have. The first was a low frequency radio, a throwback to an earlier time in aviation when it served as the primary radio for instrument approaches. Called an automatic direction finding radio (ADF), the pilot would tune in the appropriate frequency of the ground station, orient himself to the station using the needle on his instrument panel, and then fly a published approach to the airport served by that station. While low frequency stations were still being used to identify navigation points, the practice of using them for instrument approaches was rapidly being replaced by more reliable systems. While all of this is "nice to know" information, the big thing about this radio was that it had an AM broadcast band. As a result, we student pilots spent many solo "training" hours piercing the sky with aerobatics while listening to the popular hit music of the day. Interestingly, Japanese pilots had used this same radio system, using a local Honolulu radio station, to guide them to Pearl Harbor on December 7, 1941.

The other radio was an IFF (Identification, Friend or Foe) radio, commonly called a transponder or a "parrot." This radio was used to dial in a code, or "squawk," which allowed radar controllers to pick your aircraft out from all those other "blips" on his scope. Failing to set in the appropriate code or forgetting to turn the transponder on after takeoff was certain to incur a sometimes nasty comment from the controller, along with certain sarcastic wrath from your IP, if he was so disposed.

As we progressed in our flying skills, competition began to creep in between student and IP. One of the first areas was in parking the jet after a mission. To park the T-Bird absolutely perfectly, you had to bring the nose wheel to rest in the center of an eighteen-inch circle painted on the ramp. The other pilot usually treated the one who had a "perfect park" to a free cup of coffee. Unbeknown to any student who got too good at perfect parking was the collusion between the crew chief and some instructors. The crew chief, at a signal from the IP in the back cockpit, would give "slightly erroneous" hand signals to ensure a "less than perfect park" if the student was parking, or extra-precision signals for the IP, if he was at the controls. We quickly learned not to bet with certain IPs when this deception came to light. Interestingly enough, these parking games continued throughout my career. On aircraft with several crew members, we would each make a mark on the nose wheel, after anteing up the appropriate bet money. The crew member whose mark was nearest the pavement when the aircraft came to its final stop at destination was the winner. This game was also played with the blades of a propeller. Such are the actions of airmen in their quest to add interest to the field of aviation.

The training pace began to pick up quickly, as the class moved into advanced instrument work and formation flying. "Washouts" were less frequent now, as the class settled in with those who could "hack the program." I felt sorry for those few who came so far and failed to get "the big picture" about some phase of training, and who would then have to find another niche for themselves in the air force. Some went on to navigator training. Others filled the "current needs" of the air force in various specialties. I thought of all those hours of study, the physical training, and the early morning get-ups with "open ranks" inspections waiting on the flight line, all for naught now. But perhaps it was for the best. The "weak" pilots, and I flew with several of those throughout my career, would always be a danger to themselves and a burden to those with whom they flew.

Instrument flying in the T-33 was a good bit different from that in the T-37. Here the student sat in the rear cockpit. A hood was pulled forward and secured to the top of the rear instrument panel, totally closing off all outside references. The IP sat in the front cockpit, acting as an "observer," and landed the airplane after the instrument mission was completed. After a few missions to work on "basic" instruments, we advanced rapidly into instrument approach work at surrounding air force bases. Much of my training was at nearby Maxwell AFB near Montgomery, Alabama. I can remember many hours "sweating it out" in the rear cockpit as I tried to maneuver through ILS (instrument landing system), VOR, and ADF approaches to their little-used runways. I was always relieved to hear the IP say, "That's enough for today. I've got the stick. Let's head for home." I could then pull the hood back and relax, remaining vigilant for other air traffic while the IP flew us back to home base. Instructors normally landed from the rear cockpit, so this was training of sorts for them to remain proficient from either seat.

Again formation flying was my favorite phase of training. In the T-33, we would fly four-ship formation instead of the two-ship missions we had flown in the T-37. The big difference, however, and one that was not lost on instructor or student, was that the student pilot would fly solo. It was said that the most dangerous time for an IP was to be in the lead ship with three solo students flying wingman. Beginning with the "rejoin" after takeoff, this was a "fear factor" mission for the IP, and the radio transmissions proved it.

One day, three other instructors slipped into the students' cockpits to play a joke on one of the other instructors who had become a "screamer" on the radio during these formation flights. The radio frequency was set up to be heard in the squadron ready room, and a tape recorder was brought in to record the instructor's voice. This tape was to become a legend throughout the air training command, and it was played endlessly for the humor and the lesson as well. Of course, these "students" could do nothing right, even flying "inverted" on the wing and designing every move to frustrate and scare the wits out of this IP. He yelled and screamed so much, finally ordering the flight back to base, declaring the mission over, and promising dire consequences for the "students." He realized the subterfuge when he got back on the ground, but it was too late. I understand that he became the mildest IP on the base after the tape was played back in his presence.

One technique used to reduce a student's tendency to make "stupid" mistakes by failing to follow procedures or use good judgment was the "boner fund." A "boner" was worth one dollar, and it was assessed to the student pilot in various denominations, depending on the severity of the offense. Hurting the "pocketbook" was bad enough, but posting your "boners" on a chart for all to see was even worse. The only good thing was that the proceeds of the boner fund were to be used for a graduation party at the end of training. I was feeling pretty cocky about not having posted any boners, as I surveyed the boner board and my fellow students' contributions from time to time. But this was to change.

One day, we briefed a four-ship formation mission. I was to fly solo on the wing of my instructor, who just happened to be the squadron commander. We had to meet a preplanned takeoff time, so I proceeded to the aircraft, hurried through my exterior preflight inspection, and jumped into the cockpit to complete my interior check. I was all set (I thought), when the call came for taxi-out and takeoff. All proceeded normally as I joined on the lead ship for climb to our maneuvering altitude. Suddenly the instructor's voice crackled over the radio, "Red 2! [That was me.] Break out of formation and look at your left wing!" I slid out as instructed and looked out on my left wing. A vaporized stream of JP-4 jet fuel was coming out around the fuel cap. The T-33 was siphoning fuel at a rapid rate, and the tank could quickly have emptied, had the stream not been noticed. Fear gripped me when I realized that in my haste to complete the preflight, I had not checked the security of the fuel caps. The voice continued over the radio, "Return to base immediately, Red 2! Advise mobile control of the situation, and get that bird on the ground as soon as possible!"

I did as instructed and landed without further mishap, but I dreaded what lay ahead when the rest of the flight returned for debriefing. As my commander pointed out in that debriefing, I had failed to complete the mission. Had it been an operational mission, I would have jeopardized its success and possibly the lives of my fellow officer-pilots. To reinforce his point, he said, "Take ten boners." Needless to say, my ship had the tightest fuel caps on the base from that point on.

There is a sequel to this story, however, which I will move ahead to relate. I was the first in my class to complete all major check rides prior to graduation. After completing the last check, I passed by my squadron commander in the ready room. He asked me if I thought I "had it made" now. "No, Sir," I replied, "I've still got a lot to learn." He must have liked my response. The next day, when I reported to the flight line, I found a note from him on my table. It read, "Lieutenant Butcher, congratulations on being the first in your class to complete all major check rides. When you receive your wings, you can look any other pilot in the eye. Erase ten boners." I still have that note somewhere in my records. It meant a lot to me at the time, and I never forgot it.

The training days now seemed to accelerate toward the main goal of receiving the silver wings of a rated air force pilot. But there was one last highlight to look forward to: the overnight cross-country flights that would complete navigation, the last phase of basic training. As luck would have it, I fell in with two instructors and another student from the New York area, and our cross-country training mission began to take shape. Our plan was to fly as a two-ship formation, exchanging lead position from time to time, with Stewart Air Force Base in upstate New York as our first destination. There we would check into the visiting officer quarters (VOQ), rent a car, and drive into New York City to spend the rest of the day and evening. This all came off without a hitch, and we drove down the Hudson River on the Palisades Parkway, crossed the George Washington Bridge into Manhattan, and found a place to park for what I thought was the exorbitant price of five dollars. The other student had family in the area, so he headed for the subway system, while the rest of us set out to explore the city. I had never seen such tall buildings or experienced such urban energy as I did that day. This was a far cry from the backwoods of Alabama. The people looked and acted differently, and I was taken aback when I saw a black man and a white woman walking hand-in-hand down the street.

Walking the streets was an experience in itself. At the time, I did not realize how many times I would walk those same streets later on in my airline career. We split up for awhile, but we agreed that all would meet later on in the evening for dinner. My IP, who was wise in the ways of New York, made a reservation for us at Mama Leone's, an old family-run Italian restaurant in the theater district. We met as planned and stuffed ourselves with the specialties of the house. Too soon, our time was up. We dug the car out of the garage and retraced the drive to Stewart. Luckily, I did not have to drive. The last thing I remember was falling asleep in the back seat with the lights of the city disappearing behind us.

Morning came way too early the next day, but we were up and out to base ops for flight planning the next leg. We split from the other two aviators and decided on Charleston AFB, South Carolina, as our second destination. Working out of the New York area with its "less than courteous" air traffic controllers was a lesson in itself, but it was Sunday, the traffic was light, and we were soon headed south along with memories of my first visit to the "Big Apple." While New York had been cool and delightful, with fall foliage in full color, we were soon back in the heat and humidity of the south as we landed at Charleston, with its Spanish moss and live oaks lining the base perimeter. We parked the jet, headed for the VOQ, and went on to the officers' club. Here I discovered the main reason for the popularity of Charleston AFB as an overnight destination: shrimp! Not just any shrimp, but all-you-could-eat pails of big, succulent, peel-and-eat shrimp, dipped in the best cocktail sauce I had ever eaten. Stuffing myself again with this local delicacy, I began to see that flying was very closely associated with eating, and from that moment on, I began to combine the two. The reader will notice this connection as the events of my life move forward. Turning in early to rest up from our New York experience, I drifted off to sleep very quickly, to visions of Italian-stuffed shrimp.

My class having completed all phases of the undergraduate pilot training program, it was now time for us to receive our hard-earned wings and to choose assignments based on our class finish. I ended up number eight out of forty some-odd, but was not certain as to what would be left when the choices got down to me.

Naturally there was a great deal of excitement running through the entire class as we contemplated our future. What assignment slots would come down? Which one should I choose? The big fear was that what had happened to a previous graduating class, composed primarily of air force academy graduates, could happen to us. The Strategic Air Command (SAC) assignments had been going to those students finishing at the bottom of the class. This was somewhat understandable, as most who went to SAC got very little flying time in the B-52 bombers, instead sitting hours of alert, and in some cases, ending up as missile commanders in remote "silos" somewhere in Montana. This pattern of selection so incensed the SAC commander that orders came down assigning the entire class to B-52s with no other options available.

Our fears were put to rest, however, when the assignments were posted and a wide range of aircraft and commands was included. But "what to pick" was still the question. The number one guy in the class took a plush assignment to a four-engine jet, the C-135 (B-707). With this gone, there were a few fighter assignments to F-100s and F-102s, a few slots for return to ATC as instructors in the T-37, a few multi-engine assignments to C-130s, followed by the dreaded assignments to SAC, and the evil of all evils: a helicopter assignment. We knew that would go to the last guy in the class, because our squadron commander had once given ten "boners" to a student for going over to an adjacent hangar just to look at a helicopter.

After seeking the counsel of several instructors, each of whom had a different slant on things, I finally came up with a decision. Although my instructor wanted me to stay in the ATC as an IP and so recommended me, I went with more veteran advice to go out into the "real air force" and fly something in which I could quickly build flying time. Accordingly, I reviewed the list and centered in on a C-130E assignment to the military air transport service (MATS), 86th Air Transport Squadron, with stationing at Travis AFB, California. If this assignment was available when it got down to me, I would take it. And, as fate would have it, it came to be. The guys above me all took other assignments, some to fighters, some to ATC, leaving me with my first choice. While my instructor was disappointed that I didn't take an available F-102 assignment to the Air Defense Command, I was determined in my choice. And as we all expected, the helicopter assignment did go to the last man in the class, and I hope that he prospered wherever he ended up.

With assignments decided, it was now time to prepare for the ceremony of receiving our wings. The commanding general flew in to deliver the congratulatory address, as family and friends gathered outdoors on a bright, sunny day in December 1962 to witness the event. It was an air force custom (superstition?) at the time, and still might be, not to wear the initial set of wings awarded to you. Rather, you were to break this set of wings in two, thus ensuring that you would never break a real set of wings throughout your flying career. Accordingly, we each purchased another set to be pinned on our uniforms, following the tradition. While I place my trust in powers above, the fact that I am writing these memoirs gives testimony to some validity of that tradition, although it did not protect all.

Now that I was a "rated" officer, I was also eligible to hold a civilian commercial pilot's license with instrument rating, based on my training. The only thing lacking was the passage of a Federal Aviation Administration (FAA) written exam, which an officer on base was happy to administer for a small fee. While some of my fellow graduates passed on the opportunity, most signed up to take the exam, if for no other reason than to have the commercial "ticket" in their wallets. At the time, I did not know how important it was to have those "tickets," as they were required later on for seeking an airline career.

After clearing the base, it was time to say good-byes to those with whom I had endured the most demanding fifty-three weeks of my life. Many of those I would meet again in other circumstances. Some would not survive the experiences that lay ahead. Others I would never see again. And yet, on that day, we were convinced that there was nothing we could not conquer. We were the best this country had to offer, because we were told so, and we had come to believe it ourselves.

CHAPTER SEVEN

"THE BIG AIR FORCE"

I took some of my military leave back in Knoxville, where I began to contemplate the trip to Travis AFB, California. I decided to leave the family in Knoxville until I completed training on the C-130 and got settled into my new assignment. I had a 1961 Chevrolet four-door sedan that I knew would make the trip, but I thought it a good idea to have someone travel with me. Accordingly, I advertised my departure date in the newspaper, inviting someone to go along to share the driving and the expenses. Almost immediately, I received a call from a marine who was also in Knoxville on leave and who needed a ride as far as Gila Bend, Arizona. He also had family there and wanted to visit, prior to getting back to El Toro Naval Station in Southern California. I had my Aunt Suzie living in El Cajon, near San Diego, at the time, so it worked out that I would drop the marine off, visit with her, and work my way north to Travis, which is located in the Bay area just north of San Francisco. I was about to discover just how big the United States of America really was.

The first night, we made it as far as Texarkana, Texas. Getting an early start the next day, we spent the next eighteen hours driving across Texas, arriving in El Paso around midnight. We caught up on our sleep at a wayside motel, and then we pressed on to Gila Bend, arriving around lunchtime. My travel partner had been telling me about his family and how good Mexican food was. He called ahead, and we met at a local restaurant for my introduction to some of the best food I had ever eaten. From that point on, Mexican was my favorite for many years to come, and I always went out of my way to find the perfect Mexican restaurant—always searching, but never quite reaching the level of what I had that day in Gila Bend, Arizona.

I bid the marine and his family good-bye and set out for the California line, arriving at my Aunt Suzie's in the early evening. She was a registered nurse married to Tom Stanton, a sailor stationed at San Diego Training Center for recruits. Ironically, my father had received his basic training in World War II at this same facility. The next day, Tom gave me a tour of the facility, and I watched some of the recruits undergo some of their physical training on the parade ground. It was a little cramped in Tom and Suzie's trailer home, and I sensed that they did not have much money to entertain guests, so I bid them farewell and struck out for my final leg to Travis AFB. I found US 101, as I recall, and headed north, up the central part of the state, passing cities with names like Modesto and Merced. I turned west, crossed the Sacramento River at a place called Rio Vista, and pulled in the front gate of Travis as the sun was setting.

Checking into the bachelor officer quarters, I reflected on the past several days and on the number of miles it had taken to get to where I was. It was then that I thought of those poetic lines that would remain with me until the end of my career: "I have promises to keep, and miles to go before I sleep." How many more miles would I travel in my lifetime? If I had known the answer at that time, I would have been staggered.

Up early the next morning, I was eager to find the 86th Air Transport Squadron (ATS) Headquarters and to get a look at the C-130s I would be flying. I thought it strange that there were no 130s parked on the ramp; nor was there a sign advertising my squadron on any flight line building. I parked the car and asked several people if they knew where the 86th ATS was located. They told me that the 86th was a newly formed squadron, and they gave me directions to the temporary administrative offices that had been set up in a nearby building. I continued walking, and I soon located the designated building. It was a two-story wooden structure, and on the handrail of the stairs was an arrow pointing upward with the words "86th ATS Upstairs." I paused at the top, adjusted my uniform, and rehearsed my "reporting for duty" routine, which involved knocking on the door of the commander's office, stepping smartly inside at his command to come in, standing at attention in front of his desk, giving him a smart salute, and saying "Lieutenant Butcher reporting for duty, SIR!"

I entered the building, only to be shocked and dismayed. There was nothing at all on the second floor except for a desk, a chair, and an enlisted man shuffling papers as I entered. He asked if I was lost, and I mumbled something about reporting for duty to the 86th ATS. He said that I was in the right place, that the 86th was just being organized, and that it would be some time before it was operational. "Where are the aircraft?" I asked. "Oh, we don't have any yet," he said. "Those will be picked up at the Lockheed-Georgia factory later on. In the meantime, you will be attached to the base operations squadron to maintain your flying currency." "What aircraft do they fly?" I queried. "T-33s and a T-29, I believe," he said. "Check back in a couple of weeks, and I should have further orders for you."

My disappointment could not have been greater. Here I was with no squadron to speak of and no aircraft relative to my assignment, left to hang around base operations hoping for a chance to fly my old trainer in order to maintain flying proficiency. This assignment was not, to my way of thinking, working out well at all. What I did not realize at the time was that to be part of a new outfit was a unique experience, about which not many other young aviators could boast.

During the next few days, I checked in at base operations to see if anything was going on. Finally a flight to Hill AFB in Utah was posted, and there was room for me to go along in the back seat of the T-33. At last, I would get into the air again. I met the crusty old major who was flying the airplane, and I sensed that he was not really all that happy about having to nursemaid a wet-behind-the-ears second lieutenant. He did a quick flight plan, an even quicker walk-around inspection, and basically told me to get in the back seat and keep my mouth shut. I was very happy to comply, knowing that I was going to get back in the air.

This was a courier mission wherein we delivered the "mail" to another airlift wing and picked up what they had for our wing on the return. The flight over the Sierra Nevada to Utah was quick and scenic, and I never touched the controls. Ground time was minimal. After refueling and grabbing a snack at the flight line snack bar, we launched off again for Travis. The major relented somewhat and allowed me to fly the jet en route. However, apparently sensing my rustiness on the controls and my unfamiliarity with local procedures, he resumed the controls and made the landing; so ended my very first mission as an air force pilot.

A few days later, a trip to the Air Force Base in Wichita, Kansas, was posted. The aircraft was a T-29, the military version of the Convair 440, which was used primarily for navigator training and administrative purposes. I asked for and received authorization to go along and to log some copilot time, to get my time in for the month. At least four hours of flight time was required each month in order to be eligible for flight pay, and I was still short after the T-33 flight to Hill AFB, Utah. We took off from Travis in the afternoon and landed after dark in Wichita. I rode in the observer's seat most of the way there and back, except for a couple of opportunities to hand-fly the airplane in cruise. We received certificates of non availability for overnight accommodations and obtained government transportation to a Wichita hotel. I can still remember the wakeup call I received the next morning. The operator said something like, "Good Morning! It is ten degrees in Wichita. Have a nice day!"

Returning to Travis the next day, I checked in at my squadron office. My days of assignment to base operations were over. I had received further orders at last. I would travel to Stead AFB, Nevada, for two weeks of combat survival training, and I would then proceed to Sewart AFB, Tennessee, for C-130 school. It was a good start to 1963; time to pack my bags.

* * *

The Sierra Nevada Mountains are beautiful in wintertime. That drive, in February of 1963, from Travis to Stead AFB, Nevada, crossed the upper San Joaquin valley through Sacramento and began a gradual climb to the Donner Pass at the California-Nevada line. Snow was piled high on either side of the highway at the top, a grim reminder of the ill-fated Donner wagon train that was once stranded near the pass for an entire winter. Back then, the few survivors had to resort to cannibalism to survive.

Survival was the purpose of my trip: to complete combat survival school before continuing on to Sewart for my C-130 flight training. Soon I would be out there, somewhere in these mountains, with the same goal as the Donner survivors. From the pass, the road winds down the eastern slope, past Lake Tahoe to the town of Reno, a short drive from Stead. In those days, Reno was a "cow town," a Las Vegas "wannabe." Gambling casinos made up most of the town, and the best-known fact about the town was that people could get a "quickie" divorce here without the hassle of lawyers and waiting periods. As such, it became a "Mecca" for the rich and famous wishing to disentangle themselves from unsatisfactory unions as well for as those who just wanted to party, gamble (legally), and enjoy big-name entertainment.

The Truckee River runs through the town, and upon my arrival that day, it was in full-flood stage due to snowmelt and rain. Stead AFB personnel had been pressed into service to help sandbag the riverbanks in town. Arriving on base, I checked into the VOQ, met some of my fellow classmates, and spent the rest of the afternoon exploring the area. The next day, we picked up our training schedules and reported for our initial briefing. This school was considered an "advanced flight training course," we were told. Anyone failing to complete the course would automatically lose their wings and would be reassigned to another branch of the air force. This got everyone's rapt attention. The course was comprised of three phases: classroom, compound (simulated prisoner of war), and the "trek," which consisted of navigating on foot through the mountains, utilizing escape and evasion techniques, and surviving with minimum food and equipment, all while being pursued by "enemy" forces.

After this series of briefings, the base commander greeted us and gave us some precautions about patronizing the casinos of Reno. He ended by saying that we should go on downtown that night and "make our contribution to the local chamber of commerce" in the casinos, to get it out of our systems. I did go, but having been forewarned not to gamble what I could not afford to lose, I only watched. Silver dollars were the tokens of choice, and I can still remember stacks of them on the blackjack and crap tables. Coming back to base, a few classmates bragged about winning a few dollars, but most had little to say for their gambling experience in the brightly lit casinos of Reno, Nevada.

The classroom phase of training consisted of lessons on the use of survival equipment as well as the "dos and don'ts" in survival situations and physical training in the martial arts. We were required to run everywhere we went on base, in preparation for the physical test ahead. Due to the high altitude at which we would be training, great emphasis was placed on avoiding dehydration.

With the classroom phase completed, we assembled one evening, got a short briefing, and loaded ourselves onto a bus. We were allowed nothing other than the clothes we were wearing. Being a smoker at the time, I attempted to bypass this restriction by sewing a few cigarettes and a pack of matches into the lining of my flight jacket. After unloading in darkness, we were directed to make our way across an adjacent field to a "pickup point." As we began this scenario, the sky suddenly lit up with flares, explosions, and machine gun fire. We hit the ground and continued toward the goal, crawling on our bellies. There were barbed wire and "bomb craters" to negotiate along the way, while live ammunition was being fired just above our heads. Reaching the end of the field, already exhausted by this experience, we were "captured" by "enemy forces" dressed in the uniforms and wearing the red insignia of a Communist country.

We were herded into a makeshift hut and told to strip to our underwear while our clothing was searched for any items we might have forgotten to leave behind. I learned later that in warm weather, you were ordered to strip naked and were then doused with a blast of water from a fire hose. A "guard" found the cigarettes I had hidden, and he was agitated that he could not get to them in the sewed lining. But because there were several of us to search, he threw them back at me in mock disgust. Because of this, I was one of the first chosen to go into solitary confinement.

This was a small box, like a tiny outhouse, in which there was no room to stand or sit. The only way to obtain any comfort was to lean against the wall of the box in such a way as to support the weight of your body. Tired, thirsty, hungry, and claustrophobic, I drifted off into a dreamlike state of sleep, only to be awakened at intervals by the "guards" yelling and beating on the box with a stick. There were other boxes nearby, and as time went on, I could hear a fellow "prisoner" crying and finally screaming to be taken out of the box. This was done, and all returned to quiet. Understandably, I never saw that fellow officer again.

After several hours in the box, unable to sleep, my mind turned to the cigarettes sewed into my jacket. With a nicotine craving, I tore at the thread until *I* gained access to my contraband treasure. I had lit up and was enjoying my nicotine treat, when the guards, apparently alerted by the smoke boiling out of my box, were suddenly on the scene. After they yelled and beat on the box more vigorously than before, the door suddenly opened, and I was dragged out. The performance of push-ups by the" prisoner" was punishment in this training scenario. There was no physical contact allowed between "guard" and "prisoner," so I was ordered to the ground and given the push-up equivalent of a rifle butt to the head for my offense. I was afraid that they were going to put me back into the box, but apparently I had "done my time." I was subsequently marched to a POW "bunker," where I joined several of my classmates who were already there.

It was here that I began to lose contact with the passage of time. The body desperately wanted to sleep, but was kept from its goal by the incessant blare of loudspeakers calling the names of "prisoners" to report for interrogation. At regular intervals, all prisoners were called out of the bunkers and forced to fall prostrate on the ground while listening to verbal propaganda abuse. Finally, they called my name and I was marched to a tent to meet my interrogator. The interior was dimly lit, and I could barely make out a figure seated in front of me. A light was placed so as to produce a bright glare in my eyes. We had been instructed that, according to the provisions of the Geneva Convention, POWs were required to give only their rank, date of birth, and serial number. Our Communist enemies of the day, however, were ignoring this provision and treating captives as "war criminals." Therefore the scenario had to be taken a step farther. I was to fabricate a story about my mission and its objectives and try to mislead my captors as much as possible.

The interrogator began calmly, but he became vocal and frustrated when he could not extract any valid information. He then began a line of interrogation designed to induce "despair." He named members of my family, saying that I would never see them again and that they could be harmed at will; he said that I would grow weak, sicken, and die in this place, and all for what—failing to help provide proof that the United States was a criminal nation. In my exhausted state, the line between reality and the training scenario began to blur. Was I really experiencing this, or was it just a bad dream? I could almost believe that this was for real. I was almost on the verge of crying, when the interrogator abruptly ended the session, ordered me to the ground for push-up "punishment," and had me marched back to my bunker, where the program to prevent sleep continued.

One interesting phase of this training, of which I was not a part, was the designation of a covert "escape committee." I learned later that they were successful in getting a few classmates out of the compound. While they were required to turn themselves back in, it was purported that one man returned to the barracks for a hot shower and a meal at the officers' club before doing so. Escape had its own reward, at least in one man's opinion.

At last the compound phase was over. We had been "liberated" by friendly forces. The last test, however, was the toughest. There were no buses standing by to transport us back to the barracks. We had to walk. I can still remember being barely able to put one foot in front of the other as I negotiated the hill leading to the base, all while in a dreamlike stupor. I had never been so tired in my life, nor have I ever been since. Somehow I reached my room, and having gone beyond hunger and a desire for cleanliness, I collapsed onto my bed and slept for a solid twelve hours.

When I awoke, it was evening, and I was still groggy. My thoughts turned to food, so I showered, dressed, and went to the "O club," where

I ordered the largest steak on the menu. Something had happened, however, during my period of captivity and the deprivation of food. My stomach must have shrunk, for I could only eat a few bites before feeling extremely full. This was one occasion when my "eyes were (truly) bigger than my stomach." I returned to the barracks, where I immediately fell back into blessed sleep. The next day was Sunday, as I recall, a rest and preparation time for the last phase of training—the "trek."

* * *

This phase of combat survival school began easily enough. We were bused to a "static camp," where we were introduced to a range of demonstrations including camouflage techniques, survival foods, navigation, map reading, etc. The next morning, we were divided into elements of a dozen men or so and were given maps, our destination objectives, and last minute survival gear, including minimum food rations. After choosing a leader, we set off through the high Sierras toward our first bivouac point. It was follow-the-leader through the woods, always maintaining distance between you and the man in front but never losing sight of him. I was "tail end Charlie," so my only duty was to keep the man ahead of me in sight.

While the various elements were proceeding in the same general direction, it was not intended that they intermingle at any point along the route. Somehow, most likely by miscalculation on the part of one of the leaders, another element crossed our path. I noticed that the man in front of me changed direction slightly. When I came up to him at the next rest break, I found out that in the confusion, he had followed the other element instead of our own. Now, not knowing where the rest of our element was, we had no choice but to join the one he had followed, with hopes that we could rejoin our unit later on.

Part of the evaluation process for this phase involved carrying a "punch card." Any time you made a mistake or were "captured," you

were given so many punches. (Had "boners" given way to "punches?")
If you amassed too many, you had to repeat the course. The two of us
wondered aloud how many punches we would receive for this blunder,
not to mention the blunder of our own leader in "losing" two of his men.
Things were not going well thus far.

We were received amiably by the other element, however, and continued on to our first encampment. Each man carried one-half of a tent
shelter on his pack, so we paired up for sleeping. Food rations were in
short supply, but we pooled what we had and made a community stew
over the campfire. It was here that I began to see what hunger could do to
a man. One was caught stealing an extra share from the pot and suffered
the embarrassment of being called to task by the others. Would I have
done the same, had I the opportunity? This was a time of experiencing
a conflict between personal desire and the overall welfare of the group.
What other lessons lay ahead?

Things did not get any better. The next morning, in a predawn "raid,"
we were "attacked" by an enemy force that overran the encampment.
Those who reacted quickly enough escaped into the dark, chilly morning
with nothing but their underwear. Exhausted and half asleep, I snuggled
down in my sleeping bag and tried to remain motionless as the "invaders"
poked around inside the tent shelters. Previous students had obviously
overused this ploy, and it wasn't long before a hand grabbed my shoulder
and someone demanded I produce my card to receive a punch for being
"captured." There was nothing to do now but get dressed, stoke up the
fire, and wait for the escapees to return, at which time we recounted our
own "raid" experiences to each other.

At the next checkpoint, my buddy and I reunited with our original
element. It was good to see more familiar faces. The leader was relieved
to see us all safe and sound, and we tried to answer the question, "What
happened to you guys?" This checkpoint was the "jumping off" location

for the final phase of training. We were divided into pairs and given our destination objectives. The plan was to spend the next two days navigating over mountainous terrain to a "safe point" and a final pickup. We checked our gear, counted our few food rations, and set out at the designated time. Our packs became increasingly heavy with each hill. I can remember us resting at the bottom of one extremely steep hill and eating a Lifesaver or a portion of fruitcake as we waited for the sugar to enter our bloodstream, and then shouldering our packs and using that newfound energy to conquer the hill. Hopefully, we had more Lifesavers than there were hills. We chose a campsite off any obvious trail that evening, with the hope that we would not be subject to another raid. Apparently we chose correctly, and we enjoyed a night of welcome, uninterrupted sleep.

With sunrise on the last day of training, I was feeling pretty good in that I had received only one punch on my training card. It took five punches, as I recall, before an officer had to repeat the course. Our final leg that day took us on a direct route by an abandoned sheep farm. Instead of taking a more indirect route to our destination, we decided to gamble and go for the shortest route home. We were marching along in single file through a grove of fir trees adjacent to the sheep farm, when a figure stepped out from the grove behind us. The command to halt startled us, and we were too exhausted to do anything else but comply. Too late! I had been captured *again*! We produced our training cards, and each of us received two punches for taking an obvious route when we should have detoured around the farm.

I was up to three punches, and the day was not over yet. We were released to continue on our journey. This time, however, we were all eyes and ears, and navigated well off the beaten track. If we were to be captured again, the "enemy" would have to work at it. At last we neared our objective. We could hear laughter and talking as we came up to the pickup point. We quickly joined the group that had made it in ahead of us, compared punch cards, and joined in the exhilaration that we had survived and made it in spite of the mistakes that we counted as part of learning the art of "escape and evasion." With the bus ride back to the base behind us, we turned in our gear, hit the showers for our first real bath in several days, and made it to the "O club" for "celebratory libations" and some real food. Combat survival was now behind me. What other adventures lay ahead? Had I known, the knowledge would have overwhelmed me.

* * *

With combat survival school completed, I was now ready to get on to the next challenge, getting checked out in my assigned aircraft at Sewart AFB in Smyrna, Tennessee. Three other fellow officers were headed in the same direction, so we piled into my '61 Chevy, left the fair city of Reno in the afternoon, and headed for Tennessee. We intended to drive straight through, driving in relays. But after we started seeing imaginary "pink elephants" on the highway in the wee hours of the morning, we decided that the better part of valor would be to spring for a motel room and get some sleep before proceeding on our trip. We accomplished this stopover in Flagstaff, Arizona, and completed our journey the following day and night.

Arriving at Sewart, I got settled into "student" quarters, an old World War II barracks with an oil-fired furnace. It was a cold spring day, so I decided to turn up the heat and catch up on the sleep I had been deprived of for so long. It must have been midmorning when I dozed off, the old furnace humming along, making the room nice and toasty. I was to meet some fellow officer-students for dinner in the evening, and I remember them knocking on my door. I mumbled something to the effect that they should go on and I would join them later, after which I returned to the "sleep monster" that had me in its clutches. His grasp continued throughout the night and into the next morning. When I finally arose to turn down the heat, I realized that I had slept for twenty-four hours. I had not been aware of how exhausting the previous few weeks had been, but the body knew and responded accordingly. After a few groggy hours, I was energized and ready to tackle all challenges.

I would venture to say that there are, in the careers of most pilots, one or two aircraft that they learn more about than any of the others. The C-130E was one of those for me. I had acquired a copy of the airplane manual, or "Dash-One" as it was referred to, before I had left Travis, and I had already started reading and studying, to some degree. I still recall that the manual began something like, "The C-130E is a high-wing, all metal, land-based mono-plane...," and even after forty years, I can still remember engine settings, emergency procedures, and aircraft limitations. All this was drilled into my subconscious during the next two weeks of combat crew training school (CCTS).

C-130E Hercules, Travis AFB, CA 1963

There was no simulator training available at Sewart in those days, so upon completion of ground school, I went directly to the aircraft on the flight line for flying training. I reported to my instructor at the assigned aircraft on that first day of flight training, and I discovered that I was paired with an older fellow pilot. I noticed something odd about these training aircraft and discovered that they were "B" models, the difference being the absence of the "extended range fuel tanks" between the inboard and outboard engines. Obviously, there was no need for "extended range" in a training environment, so the C-130B was the "trainer" of choice.

We assembled in the cargo compartment and began discussing different things about the aircraft. I was eager to show that I had retained a good working knowledge of the aircraft systems, so when the discussion turned to the fire protection system, I piped up with the fact that the fire detection system on each engine was made up of fifty-three feet of "Inconel" (heat sensitive) tubing. My instructor gave me a strange look, made an obscene gesture with the middle finger of one hand, and said something like, "That fact will never save your (blank) in a critical situation. Forget it." This was the beginning of my understanding of the great gulf between the men who build airplanes and the men who fly them. You could know every engineering fact about an aircraft and still not know how to fly it and survive. It was a lesson I never forgot, and yet there were many people I was to interact with throughout my flying career who erroneously believed that the more "facts" you knew about an aircraft, the better a pilot you were. While in their minds, this knowledge was a measurement of "skill," in mine it only served to produce confidence in the "nuts and bolts "of the particular machine I was engaged to fly.

With the discussion at an end, we proceeded to the cockpit where the IP and my fellow pilot, being senior to me, occupied the pilot and copilot seats. I strapped into an observers seat and watched as they read and accomplished the checklists. Heavy emphasis was placed on "crew coordination." Now, instead of everything being accomplished by one individual, the aircraft would be flown as a team; one man flew and all other crew members (copilot, flight mechanic, navigator, and loadmaster) provided input to ensure accomplishment of the mission. At the time, I didn't know the inherent difficulties that would result later on in utilizing "human resources" to "aviate and navigate."

The four big Allison turboprops soon came to life, making that distinctive sound that would identify the plane to anyone who ever flew it, and we were soon at the takeoff end of the assigned runway. The IP brought the four big turboprop engines up to full power, and we almost leaped into the air after a short takeoff roll. This machine might have looked ungainly, almost ugly, but it was a performer and was the best for what it was designed to do. I used to razz some of the "fighter types" by pointing out the fact that the C-130 could take off and be at one thousand feet of altitude before their "ground loving" fighters could get airborne. Add jet-assist-takeoff bottles (JATO) to the racks on either side of the fuselage, and you could make that three thousand feet. Facts are hard for some people to swallow, particularly those people with enlarged egos.

After the IP put my fellow pilot through the paces of the usual air work, we switched seats, and I finally got the chance to put my hands on the controls of the aircraft I was to fly over the next three years. I was surprised to discover how easy and precise the movements of the controls were. With hydraulically boosted flight controls, you could almost fly the airplane with one finger. Power and maneuverability—this was going to be one great plane to fly.

Checking out on the C-130 was a real joy, and I took to it with great zeal. Since there was to be a simulator in place back at Travis, there was very little instrument training involved. We just took off, flew around, and spent most of the time in the traffic pattern. Finally the day came for our final check. Since he outranked me, my fellow pilot got into the seat first. He didn't do too well, showing a nervous and hesitant technique on the controls and having trouble with his landings. We switched seats, and I accomplished the same maneuvers and landings, ending the mission with the best "grease job" (meaning "smooth") touchdown I had ever made. At the debriefing, our instructor went over the good and not so good on each of our check ride items. I was shocked when he looked at us both and said, "Lieutenant Butcher, you did a good job, but Captain_____, you need your butt kicked." While we both passed, and I was exhilarated by his praise, I felt sorry for my fellow airman and hoped that I had not made him look bad with my performance. Ironically, this same officer later applied for, and was granted, a release from flying status on the basis of "FOF." That is, fear of flying.

As I was completing training, orders came down that added a special punctuation mark, of sorts. Instead of returning to Travis via the normal means of military or commercial air, we would proceed to the Lockheed factory in Marietta, Georgia, pick up a brand new C-130E, and ferry it back to Travis. Not only would I finally get to see one of my squadron's aircraft, but I would be part of its delivery.

On the appointed day, those of us who had completed training loaded on to one of Sewart's C-130s for the short flight to Dobbins AFB, collocated with the Lockheed factory in Marietta, Georgia. It was a warm spring day, and the humidity really hit us hard as we disembarked on the ramp. I had become accustomed to the drier conditions of California and Nevada; this was an instant reminder of my previous days in the Deep South. While the higher-ups completed all the necessary delivery paperwork, we underlings set about flight planning and hanging around base ops until we were given further word on our departure.

At last we were "good to go," and we boarded a shuttle to the Lockheed ramp. There it sat, the shiniest, most beautiful C-130E ever produced, at least in our minds. It was our ticket home, and except for a few test flights, we would be the first to fly it. The Lockheed technicians met us with a brand new logbook. I remember that in the "Status" block, there was a black initial. This designation was reserved for aircraft that had no known discrepancies. I had never seen that designation before and was never to see it again. We were to start out with a "perfect" aircraft. Seniority has its privilege, and although we were all drooling to take the controls, the "field-grade" officers (major through colonel) took their places in the pilots' seats while the rest of us looked for seats to strap into for takeoff.

With the four big Allison turboprops cranked up and emitting that familiar whine, we taxied out, took off into the afternoon Georgia sky, and turned westward. I didn't realize that the route we were to take would be repeated many times later on in my flying career: over the hills of Alabama to the Mississippi River at Memphis, across the plains of Kansas to the Rocky Mountains of Colorado, on through the Great Basin of Utah and Nevada, descending now over the Sierra Nevada and the San Joaquin Valley to home base. We each had our turn in the copilot's seat on the trip out, and all enjoyed the view from the big "greenhouse" cockpit we would become so familiar with in the months to come. Touching down on the runway at Travis, we all sensed the meaning of the moment, that although there was much training remaining to become "combat ready," the 86th Air Transport Squadron was now for real, and we had the airplane to prove it. The only thing to mar the trip was the entry placed in the new logbook, replacing the black initial with a red dash. The discrepancy read, "The American flag ("Old Glory") not painted on tail."

* * *

The next several weeks were a blur of transformation for the 86th Air Transport Squadron. Personnel and aircraft delivery increased dramatically, changing the squadron building into a beehive of activity. Simulator and actual flight training in the local area were paramount, as the mission of becoming combat ready was laid out before us. Aircraft were in the air daily, practicing instrument approaches and landings at little-used facilities in the area. Some of these were Beale AFB, McClellan AFB, and civilian fields like Portland, Oregon. Several pilots would board these "trainer" aircraft and switch seats to allow each one his turn to complete aircraft qualification. Naturally we took every opportunity to enjoy the scenic beauty of the area from Lake Berryessa and the distant Pacific Ocean in the south to Mount Shasta and the volcanic peaks of the Olympics to the north.

Every pilot is assigned an "additional duty" in a flying squadron. Mine was that of assistant training officer. I and the other training officers had our own little cubicle with a large Plexiglas status board mounted on one wall. Listed on this board were the names of every pilot in the squadron along with the status of every requirement they needed in order to be current and available for assignment to a mission. These included a current physical, an altitude chamber refresher, periodic check rides, and so on. We used grease pencils of various colors to denote status; black meant "current," green stood for "nearing non-currency," and red signified "not current." After you achieved currency in all items, the squadron commander was not happy with any "red" on your currency line. As crews were assembled to fly missions, no one could become part of the crew unless he was cleared by someone in the training section. When I wasn't flying, my job was to report to this office for duty each day.

The next phase of training involved transoceanic flying and learning overwater procedures. For this training, a series of "turnaround" missions was scheduled between Travis and Hickam AFB, Hawaii. These missions would not only serve for training and qualification, but we would be flying actual cargo for the first time. As always, seniority was the key in order to be assigned to the next mission. Since a few other second lieutenants and I were low men on the totem pole, we had to wait our turn, however impatiently.

I arrived at the squadron one morning to discover the name "Butcher" posted on the scheduling board. My time had finally come. We took off early one afternoon, climbed out over San Francisco Bay, and headed for the Faralon Islands Beacon, west of the Golden Gate Bridge. With the exception of a ship called *Ocean Station November*, positioned midway between the mainland and Hawaii, there was nothing but water between us and our destination. Beyond the range of radar and of our normal radio communications, we would have to depend on our navigators to fix our position using the stars and long-range radio air navigation (LORAN) stations. Communication would be by high frequency radio (HF), which was very unpredictable and, at times, depending on atmospheric conditions, virtually unusable.

After droning on for hours over nothing but the open sea, we picked up a VOR station on Molokai, intercepted the inbound course, and reported our position at the air defense identification zone (ADIZ). This is an area surrounding all of the United States. You must be positively identified to enter this zone. Otherwise, you have an automatic date with a flight of fighter jets that will look you over personally and send you a bill for the effort. Soon we were in VHF(very high frequency) radio and radar contact with Honolulu Center. The navigators folded their maps and charts and began to dream about what they would do on their fifteen-hour layover in Honolulu.

Hickam Field is collocated with Honolulu International Airport, and both civilians and the military utilize the same runways. We mixed in with the DC-8s and Boeing 707s from United and Pan Am in the traffic pattern while eyeing the beauty of the mountains and beaches below. Finally we settled on to the runway, approximately eight hours after our departure from Travis, and taxied seemingly forever to the cargo ramp at Hickam. The loadmaster, who had little to do other than sleep on the flight, now sprang to his duty of offloading the cargo, while the rest of us headed to the VOQ.

After stashing our crew bags, we reassembled at the "O club" for "mission debriefing." This was the traditional after-mission indulgence in alcohol-based liquid refreshment, regardless of one's state of fatigue. It was here that I was introduced to a local Hawaiian drink called a Mai Tai. The veteran pilot I was crewed with set me up on this one. The drink itself is composed of fruit juices topped off with large amounts of regular rum and 151-proof rum. It is served in a hollowed out pineapple shell with a straw. As one sips the drink through the straw, the tongue becomes slowly desensitized to the alcohol, disguising its effect. I liked the taste of the first one, so I ordered another one, not picking up on the grins on the faces of my fellow crew members. It was near the end of the second Mai Tai that something seemed to hit me in the back of the head. Somehow I made it to my room and into bed, where I slept until time for pickup and our return trip to Travis. Thereafter, I vowed to forever limit myself to one Mai Tai, or less.

The short missions to Hawaii continued for several weeks until all squadron crew members were "overwater" qualified. After this, the squadron began flying stateside cargo missions and gearing up for global operations. We came to understand that although we were a MATS unit, we were flying an aircraft with "tactical" capabilities. In other words, we could do so many other things with the C-130E than simply droning along over the ocean, carrying a few pallets of cargo. We could drop troops and equipment; we could land and take off on short, hastily prepared runways, etc. The uses were unlimited, and the future was to prove the C-130 to be one of the most versatile aircraft ever produced. What this meant was that we would now serve two masters and perform two main tasks. One would involve carrying mainline cargo for MATS. The other would involve being attached to tactical air command (TAC) for "special missions."

TAC was already flying the C-130B in close support of the army's 101st Airborne Division at Fort Campbell, Kentucky, and the 82nd

Airborne at Fort Bragg, North Carolina. Accordingly, our next training step was to become "combat qualified." One day in October of 1963, I walked into the squadron building to learn that I, along with several others, had orders to go on temporary duty (TDY) to Fort Campbell for "drop school." What hurt was that we had to exchange our beloved air force flight suits for army combat fatigues, or "Sweeney's Greenies," as they were affectionately called in honor of General Sweeney, the Commander of TAC. While we were somewhat repelled at the thought of looking like the army, the excitement of doing something entirely different eased our concern somewhat.

In preparation for this training, the emphasis shifted to flying formation in the local area. We would take off at one-minute intervals, rendezvous, join up in a close "V" formation, and practice our air work. The older pilots, who had flown only cargo throughout their careers, were a little nervous at the thought of all this aluminum being in such close proximity. We young guns, however, were enjoying every minute of it, reliving our recent UPT days in flight school. Consequently, we got most of the actual flying time under the watchful eye of the old aircraft commanders who, when we were flying wing, almost always thought we were "in too close" on the lead ship. The great thing was that the C-130 was an excellent formation aircraft. With its rapid throttle response and boosted controls, it was what we called "a piece of cake" to maneuver. It didn't get much better than this.

* * *

Fort Campbell, Kentucky, was a vast complex of airfields, drop zones, and old World War II barracks. We arrived one sunny October day to take up temporary residence and to begin our training. The first training mission involved a "dummy drop" of a simulated load onto a drop zone target. This was a total crew effort. The navigator determined the point of release, the pilot maintained correct heading and airspeed, the copilot activated the air delivery switch (ADS), and the loadmaster monitored the deployment of the drag chute and the egress of the load out the back of the aircraft. Naturally there was competition among the crews to see who would have the smallest margin of error, and my crew was elated when our load landed closest to the "bull's eye" on the circle target. After several of these day drops, we went to night drops, with only "smudge pots" outlining the drop zone. Accuracy was not as great, but we did get the "goods" into the circled area.

Now it was time to drop troops instead of cargo loads. I wish I could adequately describe the atmosphere inside an aircraft just before a group of sixty-four army airborne paratroopers leave the aircraft for their descent to the earth. In charge is the jumpmaster, who, after every trooper is hooked up and all safety checks are complete, becomes the motivator to ensure that no one hesitates at the door when the "jump light" goes from red to green. Stamping their feet and yelling at the top of their voices, the paratroopers stampede out the jump doors as though they can't wait to get out of this confining aircraft and into the freedom of space.

The loadmasters on our crews were enlisted men who wore parachutes and who were stationed in the rear in order to secure the cabin and doors after a jump. It seems that one of them was giving the army boys some "lip" on one of these missions. So to teach this "flyboy" some respect, the last paratrooper out the door grabbed him and took him along as he left the airplane. Witnesses on the ground said that there were sixty-four small white chutes that opened, followed by a large, bright orange air force survival chute. Everyone landed safely, and while the commanding general was greatly miffed at this incident, the offending loadmaster was last seen at the service club being treated to free drinks and initiation as an honorary member of the 101st Airborne. While this increased the camaraderie between the army and air force somewhat, our other loadmasters were careful to keep a tight lip and to secure themselves to some part of the airframe during subsequent jumps.

Another event that comes to mind occurred on our first troop drop. Experienced jumpers were to be dropped at 125 knots of airspeed, while first-timers were to jump at 110 knots, to lessen the opening shock. My aircraft commander innocently asked the assembled paratroopers which category they were. "Oh, we are beginners for sure, Captain," they all responded. After the nice, easy jump, we learned that this group was one of the most experienced in the 101st. Lessons learned: Never believe a paratrooper, and don't stand too near the door over the drop zone.

Our last mission was a clandestine night drop designed to infiltrate an individual behind enemy lines. Flashlights on the ground were our only reference points, and we had to fly without lights, gliding in as silently as we could over the drop area. The C-130 was a favorite of all paratroopers. With its rounded fuselage and air deflector doors in front of the jump doors, all a person had to do was stand in the door and release his grip, and he would be basically sucked out of the aircraft. This worked well for mass troop drops, but these special-mission types had a more preferred method. The loadmaster would drop the aft ramp, and on illumination of the green light, the trooper would simply walk out the back, plunging into the darkness of space. I watched one of these, and when the man was gone, I wondered what motivated a man to jump out of a perfectly good airplane at night, not knowing for certain that his equipment would work properly, not knowing where he would come down, and not knowing whether he would survive or what would be waiting for him if he did survive. Of such stuff are heroes made.

With our training complete, we departed for home base, not realizing how much of what we learned would be put to use in days to come. For now, however, we were all content to separate ourselves from the army, put our flight suits back on, and get back to the business of transoceanic flying.

CHAPTER EIGHT

"FLYING THE LINE"

With tactical training behind us, the 86th ATS began expanding its operation in the Pacific. Having attained a C-1 rating, we were now "combat ready" to take on any mission the nation's military might throw our way. We were now flying cargo missions to Japan, Korea, India, Thailand, and the Philippines, with stopovers in Guam, Okinawa, Wake Island, Midway Island, and Hawaii. Unfortunately, the first mission that went beyond Hawaii did not go well. Since the C-130E was new to many of the stations, proper servicing procedures, parts, and repair facilities had not yet been taught or put into place. The crew of our first aircraft to land on Wake Island learned this the hard way.

When the engines are shut down on the C-130, the level of hydraulic fluid that moves the propeller blades has to be checked almost immediately. Otherwise it will drain out of the reservoir and will indicate a "Low Oil" condition. This was the case with this aircraft. After a few hours on the ramp, the ground crew checked the four prop reservoirs, found them low, and serviced them up to the "Full" mark. Fifteen hours later, the crew started all four engines and immediately blew out all four prop seals, due to the excessive fluid pressure. It took eighteen days for four propellers to get there from the factory in Marietta, Georgia. In addition, a crew of mechanics had to be airlifted from Japan to "swing" the new propellers into place after removing the old. All the while, the crew, which was composed of the commander and other senior officers, had to stay with the aircraft. What do you do on a small pacific atoll for eighteen days? "Relax" was the most common answer, but I am certain that they were all glad to see the island disappear behind them when they departed. Without question, C-130 "prop servicing" became a top priority item for all ground personnel throughout the Pacific as well as for the crews who flew her.

My first mission after returning from Fort Campbell was a routine stateside cargo run. November 11, 1963, found me at Corpus Christi Naval Air Station, our last stop before returning home. At around noon, we took off, heading north by northwest over the Dallas-Fort Worth "metroplex," for the first leg of our flight. Suddenly air route traffic control came on the radio, advising that there was an "emergency" in that area and directing us to take up a new route due west over El Paso for our initial leg. We assumed that there must have been an aircraft accident in the area, as we proceeded on our new routing. After a routine flight, we landed at Travis and taxied to our ramp. When the front door opened, a crew chief ran up the stairs and delivered some shocking news. President Kennedy had been shot and killed in Dallas. We looked at each other in disbelief, now realizing what the "emergency" was all about. We all participated in the nation's mourning over the next several days, as it unfolded over television, and a spirit of gloom settled over the entire squadron with the loss of our commander-in-chief.

* * *

With the advent of 1964, we were back to the business of moving cargo. I had several trips into all the countries mentioned previously, plus a new one named South Vietnam. MATS crews were always bringing back "souvenirs" of their travels, and you could always tell a MATS man's home by its furnishings.

I will bypass the pineapples of Hawaii and go straight to what was called "the land of the big BX" (Base Exchange), Japan. To fly into Tachikawa AB, Japan, was to fly into a shopper's dream, among other things. Some headed to the "hotsy" baths located just off base, while others, who had Japanese wives, headed to the local grocery stores for foodstuffs not available back home. But everybody ended up eventually at the large Base Exchange, where everything imaginable was available at unbelievably low prices, including cameras, tape recorders, crystal, jewelry, watches, furniture, Japanese art, and so on and on. The most popular item, however, was a large green ceramic charcoal cooking pot called a "hibachi," which could be bought for something like five American dollars. It was not unusual to see several of these loaded as "ballast" during the last minutes prior to departure. I never bought one, but I understood that they did cook a good steak and that they are still available today at exorbitant prices. As to sightseeing in Japan, I'm afraid I failed to ever get off the base. With all that was available "on base," why would anyone have ever wanted to?

* * *

This brings to my memory one particular mission involving getting back home with the "goods." One year, near Christmas, we were headed home to Travis with the aircraft looking more like Santa's sleigh than a cargo ship. We lost an engine and had to divert into Hickam AFB, Hawaii. Since we had to stay with the aircraft, we knew that there was little chance of being home for Christmas, considering the time needed to effect an engine change. We were all "down in the dumps," when a surprising call came from the command post duty officer, putting us on "Alert." A C-130E flown by our US Navy "sister squadron" at Moffett Naval Air Station, California, was inbound to Hickam. MATS Manual 55-1 had a provision that if a crew had a broken airplane, they would supplant any crew transiting that station, take the "good" airplane, and leave that crew to await repair of the other one. The navy aircraft commander, when advised of this move, flew into a rage, threatening the duty officer with every known source of influence, but to no avail. We quickly shifted all our Christmas gifts to the good ship and made haste our departure. We had to feel sorry for the other crew, however, knowing that they wanted to get home for Christmas as badly as we did. The feeling was tempered somewhat in knowing that they would have done the same to us.

* * *

The next great shopping destination was Bangkok, Thailand. After arriving at Don Muang Airport, we would be whisked downtown by taxi to a US-leased hotel for our layover. The ride itself was a thrill a minute, as we navigated streets choked with every kind of air-polluting vehicle. Charged up by the ride, we would usually change clothes and hit the streets, making our way to the one or two gift shops that all crew members frequented. Salesmanship was not lost on the Thai shopkeepers. As soon as we came through the door, the "mama-san" who ran the shop turned on all the display case lighting and produced bottles of a local beer for our consumption. This beer came in large bottles labeled "Singh Hai." After drinking a bottle, "singing high" was exactly what the indulgent felt like doing and, if he had the funds, purchasing one of everything in the store. Special buys were carved teakwood elephants, sets of locally made bronze tableware with teak or rosewood handles, star sapphire rings, and bolts of beautiful Thai silk. Bargaining and haggling over price was normal and expected. And if this was your first time in Thailand, mama-san was prone to give you an extra special discount price.

With the shopping done, it was off to see the sights. These included the Floating Market, where everything from fish to flowers was sold from small, shallow-draft sampans, the Reclining Buddha, the Emerald Buddha, the Golden Buddha, the temple "wats," and the Snake Farm. At night, the attractions were Thai boxing matches and classical dancing.

After a meal of Asian lobster, it was back to the hotel for a much-needed sleep.

I will mention my one mission to India here, because it was the only time I flew west of Thailand. We took off out of Bangkok on a routine cargo run. We could not fly over Burma, due to some diplomatic agreement, so we had to fly a southerly deviation over the Indian Ocean and turn back northwest to reach New Delhi, our destination. This was a turnaround mission, so we did not leave the airport or the vicinity of the aircraft. While it was being offloaded, I noticed a group of people clamoring for the clear plastic sheeting used to cover the pallets of cargo. I asked one of the ground people what this was all about. He said that the sheeting was highly prized and was used primarily for window material by the natives, glass being far too expensive.

A few minutes later, an old truck pulled up near the edge of the ramp. It was completely loaded with shiny brass trays. Each tray had a beautiful design, hammered out by hand, with a piecrust edge all around and a set of teak wood legs that allowed it to be used as a coffee table. The going price was forty American dollars. The problem was that I did not have the money. My aircraft commander bought one and, sensing my interest in one particular tray, asked if I was going to get it. I explained my plight, to which he replied that I might never have such an opportunity again, and he offered me a loan of the purchase price. This was unusual because the unwritten rule among officers was, "Neither a lender nor a borrower be." But he was right. I never got back to India again. Because of his sensitivity and generosity, that tray hangs in my home today, a treasured souvenir of India. I have never seen another like it, although I did see one similar, but of lesser quality, some years later at a gift shop in Chinatown in San Francisco; the price? Six hundred dollars.

Kadena AFB, Okinawa, was another destination I always enjoyed. The main souvenir of Okinawa was an oriental room-divider screen made of rosewood. Although I never bought one myself, almost every MATS family home had one.

This large island was a verdant green subtropical location with pleasant temperatures year round. It was often referred to as "the best kept secret" in the air force. It had the finest officers' club and a golf course with spectacular views of mountain and seacoast. During World War II, the Japanese had built a rest and recreation (R&R) site called Okuma, on the northern tip of the island. A few of us rented a car one day and drove up to check it out. The drive took us through the farming area with its thatched roof houses surrounding rice paddies and vegetable gardens. While the road was not in the best of condition, we did make it to the end, where we were greeted by a beautiful beach area with recreational facilities, run by the US Army for personnel stationed on the island. We could only imagine the great loss of life that had occurred here during our World War II invasion. The native people, the Ruyukus, had been told that the American troops were monsters who would eat their children. Consequently, many committed suicide, hurling themselves off the surrounding cliffs onto the rocks of the seashore below.

Clark AFB, Philippines, was another common destination. It was a depot and repair facility for all air units operating in the South Pacific. Clark was a damp, hot, tropical location, with rain a daily occurrence. It was not a favorite of the aircrews. Unrest had begun in the islands, and security was a concern. Communist guerillas roamed the mountains nearby, and we were nearly always restricted to the base. The officers' club was nice, however, and that was usually where everyone congregated. The mandatory souvenir from the Philippines was a large fork and spoon set carved out of Koa wood, or anything else carved from Koa wood. It could be said that "Koa was common" in the homes of MATS crew members.

Agana Naval Air Station, Guam, was an interesting stopover. In 1964, on this island, there were still Japanese who had not yet surrendered after

World War II. They took no aggressive action against their "enemy," but they were content to hide in caves in the more remote areas of the island. To surrender would have meant bringing shame to their families back in Japan. It was not until some years later that the last one came out of hiding. The air station itself was not large, and the buildings were still of the old World War II-era corrugated metal construction. There were beautiful beaches nearby that contained a vast array of seashells, many of them large and very rare. They could be purchased at the Navy Exchange and were the Guam souvenir of choice.

Other routine refueling stops on our Pacific routes were Wake and Midway Islands. In World War II, the US Navy had blockaded Wake Island after its capture by the Japanese. With the defenders starving, supply ships had to run the gauntlet of US submarines and surface warships in nearby waters. One such ship, a *Something-Maru*, after being torpedoed, ran itself up on the island reef in a desperate attempt to get its goods to the defenders. In the 1960s, the rusted hulk of the ship was still there at the approach end of the runway, and we would use the radar return from it to practice what was called an airborne radar (ARA) approach. There were a great number of other World War II relics still on this and on other islands at that time. But later, the United States gave Japanese companies the right to salvage all this spent steel. The rumor was that it was all taken back to Japan, melted down, and turned into Hondas for the American market. Midway Island also had a great deal of World War II history associated with it, the Battle of Midway being a turning point in the war. This island was a quick refueling stop on our way home, and I spent little time there. The big attraction here was the local "gooney bird," a gull-like bird that made its home on the island. These birds were not known for their beauty or grace in landing, and there was always a laugh to be had, watching their clumsy antics. Taking one as a souvenir was never considered an option.

Three local irregular missions I was assigned to out of Japan were to Kimpo AB, Korea, near Seoul, and to Marcus Island and Iwo Jima on mail runs. The run to Kimpo was a routine cargo flight, but the other two were memorable for different reasons.

Marcus Island is a blip on the earth's surface, lying midway between Wake Island and Japan. It is an ancient volcano slowly sinking into the Pacific Ocean. With the exception of a few small buildings housing the radio equipment and the men who operated it, the runway made up the remainder of the atoll. We were assigned a "mail run" out of Tachikawa AB to deliver both the mail and other needed supplies of food and parts. Our arrival was greeted with great enthusiasm, not only for what we were bringing in, but also due to the fact that a few of those stationed there were scheduled to go "on leave" back to Japan.

One look around this deserted isle was enough to explain their enthusiasm. The only recreational item was a large concrete swimming tank that several of us tried out while the aircraft was being unloaded. Finally all the happy faces leaving the island boarded, and we began to start the engines, only to shear a generator shaft on one of them. This was a "no-go" item, and we had visions of hours—possibly days—before maintenance could be airlifted in for the repair. Luckily, one of our crew was an old "maintenance type" who knew how to "pad" or disconnect the shaft of the generator in order to eliminate the potential fire hazard. Working with some of the island personnel, he crawled out on the wing, opened the cowling, and set about the work of disconnecting the generator shaft. Once this was accomplished, they buttoned everything back up, and we started the engine to see if the work would hold up. Sure enough, it did, and we took off to the cheers of those in the back, as we saw the atoll disappear off the trailing edge of the wing, all the time pondering what it would have been like to be marooned on Marcus Island. Officially, however, this repair never took place, and the write-up entered into the log was that we had "lost a generator in-flight." Sometimes you have to do what you have to do.

The other mail run, to Iwo Jima, was routine from a maintenance standpoint. We landed on the island after carefully reviewing our procedures in the event of a go-around. The runway ended at the foot of Mount Surabachi, and extreme maneuvering was necessary in order to avoid contact with the mountain, in the case of a missed approach. An air force captain who was the island commander greeted us, and in appreciation of our services to him, offered us a tour of the island. We hopped in his jeep and began the climb up the still-smoking volcanic Mount Surabachi.

We could look back down on the World War II invasion beaches where so many American marines had given their lives to take this piece of rock and its airfield, so close to Japan. We could look up and see the numerous honeycombed cave entrances where the Japanese had hidden during the fierce naval bombardment that had preceded the invasion, and whose caves served as the tombs for those who refused to surrender. Finally we reached the top, where we arrived at the location of that famous American flag raising that was repeated so many times in picture and sculpture. It was a poignant moment as we paused to consider the sacrifice of so many, both American and Japanese, for so small a piece of real estate. Our captain guide related that the island was considered sacred by the Japanese, and that veterans' groups from both sides continued to meet together each year to commemorate their comrades lost in this tragic battle. As we departed, we circled the island one last time, observing that "Old Glory" was still waving proudly from atop the mountain.

* * *

In addition to the unscheduled missions assigned during routine cargo operations, the 86th was also tabbed for "special missions" originating from our home base at Travis. These were of a sensitive and highly classified nature, but with the passage of time, can be rightly recounted in these memoirs. Two such missions of which I was a part come to mind.

The first of these began with a flight to an obscure airfield in Canada. We left Travis completely empty of cargo, "buzzed" the airstrip upon arrival in order to frighten away any local caribou, and landed and taxied up to a complex of buildings enclosed by a tall security fence.

After we sat for a few minutes with engines idling, a figure wearing a white lab coat appeared and opened a large gate, giving us directions into the enclosure. We taxied in, parked, and shut down our engines. After a short wait, several other similarly attired men appeared, carrying a small metal tank similar to a propane tank. We were instructed to drop the ramp and open the cargo door. The men came onboard and, while the loadmaster was busy securing this tank in the middle of the cargo area with nets and heavy tie-down chains, began to hang small strips of tape from the ceiling of the aircraft. When this was completed, we were summoned together for a short briefing about our cargo. Although the substance in the tank was never mentioned by name, we quickly became aware of the fact that we were carrying a most deadly experimental chemical nerve agent.

At the conclusion of the briefing, we were issued vials attached to hypodermic needles containing a liquid called Atropine. Our instructions were that if any of the tape strips began to change color, indicating a leakage of the gas, we were to plunge the needles into our thighs and inject the Atropine as quickly as possible. Nothing further was said. The men departed the airplane, we started engines, they opened the gate, and we took off on our next leg to McCord Air Force Base, Washington, to refuel and obtain further orders. Be assured that all eyes were glued to the tape strips dangling throughout the cabin.

Upon our arrival at McCord, nobody wanted anything to do with us. We were directed to the most remote part of the base and were told not to leave the aircraft. A fuel truck appeared and quickly filled our tanks, and an air force blue pickup truck delivered our flight plan and orders along with supplies for the galley. Our orders were to proceed to Barbour's Point Naval Air Station on the Island of Oahu, Hawaii. There we were to transfer our "cargo" to the Department of the Navy, for further disposition. We were given priority for departure, and we were soon airborne, feeling somewhat rejected, but glad to be on our way to the next step in ridding ourselves of our dangerous cargo.

We arrived at Barbour's Point and were again directed to the most remote part of the airfield. Soon a team of "technicians" arrived, unloaded the tank, removed the tape strips, and collected our syringes. "Scuttlebutt" from the loadmaster was that the nerve agent was destined for Eniwetok, a remote Pacific island, for testing on sheep at one of the atolls nearby. Having completed our part of the mission, we were ordered to make the short hop over Pearl Harbor to Hickam Field and a much-needed fifteen-hour crew rest, after which we would fly a "normal" cargo mission back to Travis. We felt as though we had been released from jail. Never was I so glad to get rid of something as I was that tank. In violation of my previous vow, I believe we all had at least two "Mai Tais" at the "O club" that night, in celebration of the event.

The second of these special missions was also classified as "Top Secret," but was of a different nature. The classification was due to the sensitive nature of the mission itself—the recovery of human remains. The idea was that the nation should not arouse the emotions of living relatives who had lost loved ones in World War II. It seems that natives in Indonesia had discovered the wreckage of a B-24 bomber on top of a remote, jungle-infested mountain. Bones and dog tags indicated that the crew had perished in the crash. Missionaries got wind of the find and notified our embassy in Jakarta. Our job was to airlift an army grave identification team to the island of Biak, near New Guinea. There the team would be airlifted by light aircraft into an airstrip closest to the crash site, after which they would have a three-day journey, hacking their way through the jungle, to reach their destination. One factor that complicated this mission was the relationship between the United States and Indonesia, which was led by the Communist-leaning dictator, Sukharno. Apparently, however, diplomatic maneuvering had succeeded in allowing the mission to take place.

After picking up the army team at Tachikawa AB, Japan, we proceeded to Clark AB in the Philippines for refueling and to receive weather and intelligence briefings. No American aircraft had been to Biak in some time, and we did not know what to expect upon arrival. We approached the airfield, built by the Japanese in World War II, and landed uneventfully. Taxiing in, we were astonished to see another C-130E sitting on the ramp near the small operations hut. As we got closer, we could see that it had the markings of the Royal Australian Air Force, that country being on better terms than ours with their Communist neighbor. We were also amazed at the acres of fifty-five gallon oil drums and abandoned World War II military equipment still littering the Island.

We were greeted very formally by a government official and transported to a small "hotel" nearby. This structure was constructed of lumber and bamboo, with small cubicles serving as rooms, and with a small lobby where a ceiling fan rotated overhead. On the wall behind the desk hung a picture of the dictator himself, wearing a red "fez." This was like a scene from the movie *Casablanca*. We were given room keys, and we spent the few hours we had trying to rest and fend off the mosquitoes. The army team was gone when we went back to the airfield the next morning. I had talked with one of the army officers, urging him to keep a diary, hoping to hear from him or at least to read about his upcoming adventure and what he found on the mountain. But I never did find out the results of the mission and whether or not the families of those who were lost found peace at last. We departed, saluting the Australian crew as they taxied out with us for takeoff, and headed back to Clark and more friendly territory.

* * *

In the summer of 1964, the word came down that the 86th ATS had been selected to support "Operation Deepfreeze" to our research base at McMurdo Sound, Antarctica. This series of missions was designed to provide personnel and logistics to that facility from Christchurch, New Zealand. The US Navy, utilizing ski-equipped C-130A aircraft, had previously flown these missions. But with the research widening, greater cargo and range capability became necessary, resulting in assignment of our C-130E squadron to continue the mission. It was found that seawater, when frozen to extreme temperatures, had the same "braking coefficient" (or capability) as dry concrete. Consequently, a four-thousand-foot "runway" was cleared across frozen McMurdo Sound for recovery and launch of our aircraft.

This mission was the talk of the squadron, and everyone was eager to know who would be selected to go. Selection meant that you were among the best at what you did, and I was honored to be among those chosen. Naturally this mission triggered the need for additional training, since we would be operating in new territory and under adverse and unpredictable conditions. While the navigators began working with polar navigation and the flight mechanics with cold weather procedures, it was off to arctic survival school at Eielson AFB, Alaska, for the pilot crew members.

Prior to reporting for the school, we drew our survival equipment at Travis Base Supply. This equipment consisted of heavy insulated flying gear and white air-chambered flight boots, referred to as "Mickey Mouse" boots. We took off for Eielson and landed in minus twenty-degree weather. This was not going to be a fun adventure, it seemed. It was so cold that the tower closed the field for several minutes after a takeoff, due to the ice fog created by the exhaust of the departing aircraft. We were picked up and ferried to the VOQ through streets with high windrows of snow on either side. I noticed that the parking spaces were equipped with electrical plugs. These, I learned, were to accommodate the plug-in of the engine block heaters on each vehicle, in order to keep the oil from congealing in the crankcase. The rigors of operating in such an environment were becoming rapidly apparent.

After two days of classroom presentation on what was known about polar survival, we were split into small groups and transported to a remote area for a planned two-night stay. This area was actually sub polar, in that there were trees instead of open, frozen tundra. We had been issued additional gear, including double goose-down sleeping bags, a parachute, and a "crash ax," along with a basic survival kit containing a few rations, signaling mirrors, matches, etc. The idea was to simulate a forced landing and survival until we could be rescued. An instructor was assigned to each group as an advisor.

After being dropped off at our "crash site," our first order of business was to construct a shelter to escape the effect of wind chill. Taking turns with the crash ax, we each felled a small fir tree, cutting it three feet or so above ground level and leaving it partially attached to the trunk. I then trimmed out the lower branches of mine, spread the parachute material over the remainder, and packed snow over the whole thing to form sort of a "snow cave," with the opening at the tree trunk. The next step was to outline a sleeping area inside and to make a bed of pine boughs to provide some insulation from the frozen ground. On this I placed my sleeping bag, after which I fashioned a fire pit at the entrance and began to gather tinder and firewood. While it was very cold, all this activity caused us to work up a sweat. We were cautioned to remove our outer clothing if this occurred, to avoid rapid heat loss from the body. With our individual work completed, we turned to the tasks of gathering firewood for a signal fire, digging a latrine, and setting snares for any snowshoe rabbit that might be in the area.

Daylight ended quickly, and after cooking and eating our rations, we retreated into our snow shelters to endure the night. All of this does not sound too bad, except for the fact that the temperature was in the minus twenty-degree range and falling. The cold was numbing, and it obsessed the mind. We were told not to sleep in our clothes, as they would prevent the heat of our bodies from properly insulating our sleeping bags. Let me say that stripping to bare skin in that temperature and getting into a cold sleeping bag is not a task for the fainthearted. After a few minutes, however, I moved from freezing to just plain cold, as I began to toss and turn on my bed of boughs. Somehow I managed a few hours of restless sleep, only to awaken to the fact that I now had to get out of the sleeping bag and put my clothes back on. I started a little fire at the entrance first, while remaining in the sleeping bag, and fixed some hot tea and ate my breakfast rations. I dragged all my clothes inside the bag to get them as warm as possible, and then made a dash for it, outside the bag. I am certain that I have never put on as many clothes as quickly as I did that morning.

The instructor told us that a helicopter would circle the area that morning. Whichever group had the best signaling presentation would receive an airdrop of "special rations." Although already tired, hungry, and cold, our group rose to the challenge. We gathered everything we could find that would burn or produce smoke. The key, according to our instructor, was to light the fire at the first sound of the approaching chopper. Needless to say, we became "all ears," and soon we heard that faint sound. As soon as the helicopter arrived in the area, our fire was going strong, sending out large billows of smoke into the icy air. We all stood in formation, flashing our signal mirrors in the direction of the helicopter as it circled the area. It passed over us twice and headed away, leaving us in a momentary state of disappointment. Had some other group outdone us? Suddenly the chopper wheeled around, headed back our way, and dropped out a small package overhead, attached to a chute. We had won! We slapped each other on the backs and stomped up and down in jubilation, as we divided the spoil of candy and snacks.

The daylight passed quickly, and the wind began to pick up as the temperature fell. The grim reality of passing another night in these conditions began to seize my mind. Suddenly the order came down, "Balance of training cancelled. Bring everyone in." With the temperature in the minus twenties and the wind at thirty knots, the powers that be apparently felt that the resultant "wind chill factor" was too risky to subject us to another cold-suffering night. The celebration of this decision far outdid the extra food drop demonstration, as we packed up our gear and boarded transport back to the base. The celebration continued well into the night after long, hot showers followed by much liquid refreshment and consumption of Alaskan king crab at the "O club."

Back at Travis, training continued as we began to send flights "down under" for route training. I was lucky enough to be assigned to one of these that also included a stopover in Australia. Leaving familiar Hickam Field on Oahu, we headed due south, crossed the equator, and landed in the Fiji Islands for fuel. From there we pressed on to Australia and landed at Avalon Airfield near Melbourne. Taxiing in, we saw rows of B-57 Canberra jets parked on the ramp, and we were surprised by a P-51 Mustang taxiing by, canopy open, its pilot wearing the old World War II leather helmet with earphones. Was this part of an active unit or merely a local aero club interested in preserving history? We never found out, as our thoughts turned to spending some time in downtown Melbourne.

Someone had pulled the right strings for us, and we were whisked away to downtown Melbourne and to the Southern Cross Hotel for the night. To go "down under" in the 1960s was to return to the America of the 1930s and '40s. Everywhere you saw American-made cars from those decades as well as a well-dressed and well-mannered people. We had been told to take our "Class A" uniforms (coat and tie) and to wear them when off duty, remembering that we were to be goodwill ambassadors of a sort. We were received as such, being granted every courtesy and respect by all we came into contact with. I came to realize that these people looked on the United States and its armed forces with great appreciation for saving them from the Japanese in World War II. It was a standard rule among them, for example, that no American in uniform pay for a "pint" in the local pub, a rule that was welcomed and exercised freely by us all.

One thing we initially failed to understand about the pubs was that they were only open for one hour a day for the "public." This hour was from 5:00 p.m. to 6:00 p.m., and it was difficult to find a place to stand in any of these establishments, because they were jammed with patrons rapidly going about the business of downing their daily "bitters." Victorian law, as we came to understand it, established this restriction in order to get the working man home to his family in some semblance of sobriety, to carry out his duties there. As always with the ingenuity of man, there was a "loophole" to this law. If one was a resident of a hotel, or possessed a room key indicating that he was a patron of that hotel, the pub could stay open for him. Consequently, most pubs were part of a hotel, and after closing briefly to the public, would reopen to "hotel patrons" who would lay their keys on the tables to prove their place of temporary domicile. Even hotel patrons had a limit, though, being required to discontinue their consumption by 10:00 p.m., an hour at which all good men should be headed for a restful night.

It was midwinter in Melbourne on this July night, and I remember the wind howling at the windows as I drifted off amid the luxurious bedding of the Southern Cross, only to be awakened too quickly for our return to Avalon Field. It was rainy and cool, and after an English breakfast, our well-dressed driver, who was wearing all black, directed us to our vehicle. It was a late-model black Jaguar, of which he was very proud. We chose seats, and I rode up front. I can still remember the driver pulling on his black driving gloves as I admired the walnut dashboard. We had a pleasant drive through the city and countryside, this time in daylight, having come into town in near darkness the day before. I admired the city parks and the neatness of the countryside, and thought what a good place this might be to live, or at least to visit at length. Too soon, our time of indulgence and "hero" treatment was over, and we returned to the reality of our mission and the next leg to the South Island of New Zealand.

The flight to New Zealand was relatively short, and we were scheduled to spend minimum time on the ground for refueling before heading home, with additional fuel stops in Pago Pago, American Samoa, and Hawaii. Christchurch is the largest city and the capital of the South Island, Auckland being the same for the North Island. Christchurch was to be our base of operations for support of Operation Deepfreeze 1964. We departed, anxious to get back home, but looking forward to the mission that awaited us upon our return in November.

The mission of Operation Deepfreeze, as mentioned previously, was to support our research mission on the continent of Antarctica. This mountainous, frozen landmass had already been declared a nonpolitical zone, open to all nations for scientific research. Consequently, the continent had been marked off in zones and assigned to various countries for their individual research efforts. For the United States, this zone included our base camp at McMurdo Sound and at Byrd Station, further down at the South Pole.

When the final orders came down to the 86th, we learned that we would fly thirty turnaround missions from Christchurch, New Zealand, to McMurdo Sound, as well as making a few airdrops to Byrd Station, originating from McMurdo. There was no landing capability at Byrd. We would take three aircraft. One would fly the mission for the day, one would sit alert for rescue, and one would be held back as a spare, with each aircraft rotating through the three positions. Aircrews would do the same, flying a mission, having a day off, and then sitting on alert prior to flying another mission.

The mission launched in November of 1964, and with so many crews aboard, all three aircraft "fireballed" Hickam and the Fijis, flying straight through to Christchurch. We circled the city, to announce our arrival to the Kiwis, and landed. There was some fanfare as we taxied to the ramp and were greeted by the local dignitaries and military commanders. We had been told that the hunting was very good in New Zealand, and I had borrowed a .30-30 rifle from a neighbor to take along, in the event I had an opportunity to participate in a hunt. Others had done the same, but we were surprised when we were asked to surrender all arms for storage in a government facility. They could be checked out only for a specific hunt or upon departure from the country. So we got a quick lesson in New Zealand gun control, with hunting guns under government control and a complete ban on handguns. Not surprisingly, the murder rate in New Zealand was one of the lowest in the world, and none of those murders was from guns.

After getting settled in the old World War II barracks adjacent to the airfield, we found our way to the navy club nearby, where all the off duty action took place. One of the bachelor types leased an old '37 Chevrolet four-door Sedan from a local car dealer, to use as a "crew car." I was fortunate enough to ride along for a couple of local tours, but this vehicle rapidly turned into a "date car." It was not unusual to be sitting at the bar, have the telephone ring, and have the bartender announce in a loud, English-accented voice, "Miss Jones requests the presence of all 'eligibles' at her home this evening, for food and refreshments, her address being… "After which there would be a mad scramble to find a seat in the Chevy and to head out to the location given. The US Air Force had its mission in New Zealand, and the young women of New Zealand had theirs. Several of them would succeed and would eventually become US Air Force wives.

The first mission to launch was reserved for the senior officers, both pilots and navigators, and was done one afternoon with some fanfare. But we were surprised the following morning to discover that same aircraft parked on the ramp. The newspapers and local radio told the whole embarrassing story.

The mission had proceeded on course as long as the aircraft was in contact with land-based VHF navigational radios. Once beyond their range, navigation shifted to what was called "grid navigation," backed up by celestial "star shots" in order to confirm position. As the mission progressed, the navigators began to have trouble making celestial positioning line up with the assumed grid position. This continued for some time before it was finally revealed to the aircraft commander that the navigators did not know where they were. The pilots radioed out an SOS, and luckily, the operator of an antiquated low frequency navigational radio site answered the call. This facility was normally shut down at sunset, but because of the SOS, the operator would turn it back on. Lost at night over the open sea, with fuel running low, the pilots saw the skinny backup direction finding needle swing toward the station. They quickly turned to that bearing and, after a period of "sweating it out," finally came back into VHF range and landed back at Christchurch with minimum fuel remaining. What had happened?

Investigation placed the blame on navigator training and on the failure of the navigators to advise the aircraft commander as soon as they noted a discrepancy. It seems that in the use of grid navigation, a "latitude correction" was necessary in order to properly align the desired course. This correction was made with a latitude correction knob on a scale marked "North Latitude" on one side and "South Latitude" on the other. Since all training for Operation Deepfreeze had taken place in the northern hemisphere, the navigators had automatically set the latitude correction knob to that side of the scale. When plotted out on a map, this setting doubled the navigation error, sending the aircraft almost due east toward Chile rather than south to the pole. Without that faint old radio beacon, the aircraft, crew, and all personnel aboard could very easily have been lost at sea, leaving the rest of us with no idea of where to look for them.

As with all operational blunders of this type, some "heads had to roll." Headquarters back at Travis directed that all navigators onboard be reduced to "Unqualified" status and sent home. The aircraft commander was allowed to stay, but he was reprimanded for his failure to monitor aircraft progress and to turn back sooner. Needless to say, every aircraft that departed for the South Pole thereafter had the northern portion of the latitude correction scale completely taped over. After some limited ribbing by the locals, we launched subsequent missions successfully, without fanfare or drama.

Finally it was my turn to man a mission. The first portion of the flight was similar to all other overwater legs I had flown, but after we passed the equal time point (ETP), which was reckoned as the "point of no return," the scenery began to change. Large icebergs began to appear, at first fairly scattered about but growing more numerous as we flew further south. It was an eerie feeling as we surveyed the scene below, knowing that we were committed to land at McMurdo, regardless of what the weather might be, and that if we were forced down prior to destination, our chance of survival and rescue was nil.

As we droned on over this icy landscape, my thoughts turned to the training we had undergone back at Travis for the worst-case weather scenario we might face on landing at McMurdo. We had taken turns making totally blind landings, following the verbal instructions of radar controllers on the ground. The ground controlled approach (GCA) controller would guide the aircraft to a point approximately fifty feet over the end of the runway, at which point he would advise the pilot to "take over visually (if able) and complete your landing." Assuming "zero-zero" conditions, the pilot, flying and wearing a hood, would reduce the rate of descent to 200 to 300 feet per minute, bring the throttles to idle, and wait for the aircraft to hit the ground. Needless to say, there were no smooth touchdowns, or "grease jobs." Remember, too, that this training took place in relatively nice weather, with an "observer" pilot ready to take over if something went awry. There would not be that safety factor when we tackled the real thing. One thing that did give us some confidence was that the navy had handpicked the best GCA controllers in the service to man the radar site at McMurdo.

As we neared our destination, floating icebergs gave way to a solid shelf of ice and tall mountains in the distance. All looked good, weather-wise, as we were vectored to the frozen sea-ice runway, the surface of which was eighteen feet thick. The snow had been bulldozed to either side and piled at each end, creating the visual effect that we were landing into a sunken hole. Landing was uneventful, as we touched down on the frozen surface and braked to a stop, remembering to bring the props out of reverse sooner than normal, lest we produce a "whiteout" by blowing the loose snow forward and blinding ourselves.

We taxied into a ramp area of sorts, near a collection of World War II Quonset huts that housed an operations area, sleeping quarters, and a mess hall. Donning all of our cold weather gear, we stepped out into the cold, crisp air and made our way to the huts, as support personnel moved in to offload our cargo and direct the scientific teams to their appropri-ate area. Interestingly, I had the opportunity to talk with a member of one team and was able to learn something of their research projects in Antarctica. One project involved equipping seals with tracking devices, trying to determine how far they ranged out under the ice in search of food and how they were able to navigate back to the small blowhole where they had entered the water. Another project involved the taking of deep core samples of snow, in an effort to learn more about the atmos-phere in ancient times. Some of the snow that was sampled had fallen, we were told, before Christ walked the earth. These people made a dedi-cated group in that they were willing to spend a year of their lives in the most remote area of the world in order to carry out their research. We all wished them well.

Since it was daylight for all twenty-four hours of the day, we had to look at our watches to realize that we were hungry and in need of a nap after our long flight. Surprisingly, the food served in the mess "hut" was of the highest quality and variety. The scientific teams at least had this to look forward to during their long stay on the ice. After taking our fill, we found our way to a sleeping hut. Someone, in an apparent attempt at humor, had placed a sign over the entrance that read "Stalag 17," a reference to the infamous Nazi prison camp of World War II. Finding a bunk, we drifted off for few hours while the unloading, loading, and servicing of the aircraft was completed.

But all too soon, the word came down to report back to the aircraft for departure. The scene there was reminiscent of the scene I remembered on Marcus Island. People from the scientific teams were already there, excited and eager to return to civilization. The C-130 was all buttoned up, steam rising into the frigid, minus forty-degree air from the electrical power carts, cabin heaters, and engine heaters designed to prevent its oil from congealing. With passenger briefings and preflight procedures completed, the engines came to life, and we taxied out onto the frozen ice of McMurdo Sound. One thing I particularly remember about this takeoff was the action of the flight mechanic (FM). It was his job to monitor the throttles on takeoff, from his seat to the rear of the center console between the two pilots. This monitoring was to prevent any "over torque" of the engines prior to reaching takeoff speed. Normally, if any trend toward an "over torque" was noted, the flight mechanic would verbally announce it, and the pilot would stop advancing the throttles. What none of us realized, however, was that in this extremely cold, dense air, very little forward movement of the throttles would be necessary to bring the engines up to full power. Consequently, the pilot flying (not me) shoved the throttles forward rather rapidly, as was customary. This was followed by a loud scream from the FM, as he literally dived over the center console to help stop any further throttle movement. Luckily, the "over torque" was momentary and not of sufficient duration to do engine damage. We were learning to operate in this environment. Experience is the best teacher; this time we were lucky, and we never forgot.

Soon the last mission was flown, and it was time to deploy back to Travis. I had grown to like this beautiful, green land of New Zealand, with its homogeneous peoples. There were no racial issues here, and there was no crime to speak of. The people loved America and Americans, and there was no language barrier. The countryside was beautiful with its sheep farms and neat cottages, the city of Christchurch was modern and well planned with its parks and greenbelts, the mountains and the sea were nearby with excellent hunting and fishing, the food was outstanding, and the pubs were always cheery. How could one not love this land and want to live out his or her life here? The thought even crossed my mind about eventually retiring "down under" one day, to the extent that I inquired about the cost of living. Later, as I embarked on a career in commercial aviation, I even sent inquiries to Australia's Qantas Airlines and Air New Zealand concerning possible employment. They were courteous, but answered that you had to be a citizen of either country, so I abandoned the idea. With all its problems, America was still my home and my destiny.

I never had the opportunity to go on a hunt, so the deer rifle was delivered to the aircraft as our crew was winding up preparations for our departure. We said our good-byes to the station personnel and launched off, with a bit of sadness, for the long trip home, with stops in Pago Pago, American Samoa, and Hawaii. We had completed the mission without a hitch, except for the embarrassment of the inaugural flight. After our return home, we were presented with the Antarctica Service ribbon for our efforts. This was a beautiful blue and white ribbon worn on our dress uniforms. Very few people possessed this ribbon, and I always felt very proud to wear it, particularly when some other officer asked me what it signified. Operation Deepfreeze was over, but one last, great adventure with the C-130E Hercules lay ahead.

Before moving on, however, I must interject this one story that came out of our time spent in New Zealand. Practical jokes were a mainstay in the officer ranks. Fortunately, I was more often the instigator than the target. In this instance, it seemed that one of my fellow lieutenants had become particularly enamored with a young lady in the community of Christchurch. We suspected that this relationship had gone beyond the bounds of international "friendship," and we proceeded to hatch our plot accordingly. Someone managed to obtain (or forge) some US Embassy stationery on which we typed a story, the gist of which was as follows:

The US Embassy, New Zealand, has been contacted by the parents of Miss_____, resident of Christchurch Township. It seems that Miss_____ has discovered that she is to be a mother and has named Lieutenant_____ as the father. The family wishes to know the intentions of said lieutenant and what the US government intends to do to ensure his meeting all responsibility in the matter.

This "document" was then emblazoned with stamps of acknowledgement showing that it had been sent "through channels," which included Commander Pacific Forces, Headquarters US Air Force (Western), Wing Commander (MATS-Travis), and Commander 86th Air Transport Squadron, with a request for an immediate reply.

In order to lend the maximum degree of "believability" to our evil plan, we had to involve someone within the squadron who had rank, responsibility, and access to such communications. Our operations officer, who led the Deepfreeze mission, was briefed on our plot and willingly entered in to our subterfuge.

On a day when our subject had reported for squadron duty, we were all busying ourselves in our cubicles when the call rang out for Lieutenant_____ to report to the operations officer immediately. We peeped down the hall as he entered the Ops office and closed the door. After a few minutes, he reappeared, his head down and his stare glassy. This uncommunicative daze continued for the rest of the day and into the next, as he contemplated the possible repercussions to his career and the implied obligations for his supposed indiscretion.

Finally, after enjoying the ruse to its full extent, we decided it was time to put an end to it, lest he do something foolish, that is, get us into trouble. So we banded together and approached him with the truth. The strange thing was that, for a time, he would not believe that it was a joke. Had our plot been that perfect? After a time, however, he accepted the truth, returned to his normal behavior, joined us for a "peace offering" libation at the "O Club," vowing to get revenge, even if it took him years to do so. Luckily I was reassigned before his vengeance was heaped upon me personally. Such were the happenings amongst junior officers of that day.

* * *

With the completion of Operation Deepfreeze, the squadron settled back into the routine of regularly scheduled transpacific cargo missions interspersed with occasional stateside special missions. Something new was brewing, however, as we began to receive increased training in dropping troops and air landing cargo in the desert area of southern California. Some of this training involved the marines at Camp Pendleton, California, which, at the time, was undergoing an investigation for unexplained deaths due to spinal meningitis. While we were a little leery of landing there and working closely with these forces, we did so, and without contracting this disease, which had already taken several lives among the marine recruits.

Finally, the reason for our stepped-up tactical training was made known. We would take part in a joint airborne training mission with the armed forces of Iran, in what was called "Operation Delawar." While C-130B units from TAC would drop all the troops, we would join with our MATS C-130E sister squadron at Charleston, AFB, South Carolina, to airdrop all the equipment. Headquarters for this mission was established at Incirlik AB, Turkey. This was to be a large global mission designed as a "show of force" to the Soviet Union, demonstrating our rapid response capability in the event of an "international emergency." American and Iranian forces would combine to meet the simulated attack of an "enemy" invading force. The Shah of Iran was our friend, and it was the aim of this country to show that we would not let our friends down in the event of an attack. Protecting United States interests was the order of the day.

Crews were selected for the mission, and I was paired with my old crew from the Fort Campbell training days. We immediately called ourselves the "Number One" crew and set about building some "esprit de corps" around that concept, as we began to prepare for the mission. To get our eight aircraft to Turkey and back would involve "staging" our crews at Charleston AFB, South Carolina, and at Torrejon AB, Spain, with some flexibility at Lages AB, in the Azores, for the strong crosswinds that often closed down air operations.

The crews began to depart at intervals for the first leg to Charleston. Arriving there, we went into crew rest, awaiting the arrival of the next aircraft, which would be our "ticket" to Spain and a similar crew rest. From there, we would pick up the next arriving aircraft and complete our odyssey to Turkey. The time at Charleston was partially spent in seeing old friends from pilot training who had taken C-130 assignments. The "O club" was the marshalling point, and I rekindled my taste for the local boiled shrimp that was predominant on the menu. More of the mission was becoming clearer. There would be thirty-two C-130s taking part in this exercise, sixteen from TAC dropping troops and sixteen of ours, from MATS, dropping cargo. We would come over the designated drop zone in sixteen-ship formation and would disgorge our cargo, to be followed by the sixteen TAC aircraft dropping Iranian and American paratroops. It was going to be a big show.

From Charleston, our first leg was to the Azores Islands. As previously mentioned, this airdrome was long known for vicious winds that often prohibited the landing of any aircraft. This time we were lucky in that the winds, though unusually high and gusty, did not exceed our maximum allowable crosswind component. After a bumpy touchdown, we taxied to the ramp for more fuel and for a short crew rest, before pressing on to Turkey. The Azores Islands are a Portuguese possession, and they are particularly noted for prized handmade linens and the production of wine. One of these wines, called "Mateus Rose," had become a favorite of the crews for off-duty consumption. So we all pitched in a few dollars and hoisted a couple of cases aboard, for our stay in Turkey.

Later that evening, we departed for the long night flight across southern Europe and the Mediterranean Sea. Working with the various air traffic controllers and their unusual English accents was a challenge. Just getting the French controllers to answer was difficult in itself. There was not much sightseeing to be had, and after taking turns in the crew bunk for a nap, we descended and landed at Incirlik AB, Turkey. We lined our ship up with those that had arrived earlier and deplaned to consider the scene. Men and equipment were everywhere, and the open areas had been converted into a "tent city." We located the appropriate tent, where we were reunited with the other crews and were assigned our "quarters." This consisted of a cot located in a large tent that was fitted with roll-down flaps to keep out the blowing sand. But it was so hot that little concern was given to the sand. Consequently, the flaps were kept rolled up to let in the breeze. The only thing left was to await the start of the operation and to use what little spare time there was to check out the local town of Incirlik.

To say that the town was poor would be an understatement. The streets were dusty and constantly stirred up by the passage of two-wheeled carts, pulled by donkeys and guided by turbaned and robe-clad drivers. The cafes and shops were all open-aired; their wares piled and hung in every way imaginable. We entered a small café and ordered a cup of coffee. What was produced was a small cup of muddy liquid with a small spoon and a bowl of what looked like sugar. After one sip of this strong brew, which included the coffee grounds themselves, I realized the need for the sugar and poured in a good amount to dull the bitterness. Our reactions must have been a source of amusement to the proprietor as we tried to down this concoction in very small sips. Somehow we got it down. No refills were requested or needed as we left the premises and headed for the serious business of shopping.

The most popular items for purchase were oriental rugs, camel saddles fashioned into footstools, and beautifully carved white "meerschaum" pipes. Prices were cheap, and after some expected haggling, the visitors from America gave the local economy a sizable boost. I knew little about rugs at the time, and was not into pipe smoking, but the craftsmanship of the camel saddle footstools captured my fancy. I picked out one with a beautiful stuffed green cushion and, carrying my prize, made it back to base, where I stored it under my cot.

The next day, things began to stir, and we were called to the mission briefing, dressed in our "Sweeny Greenies" combat fatigues and baseball caps with rank insignia attached. The plan was to take off, assemble in formation, and proceed to the drop zone near the town of Vahdati. The winds were up, and the resultant dust storms limited the visibility. The pressure would be on to identify and hit the drop zone. In addition, we would be tracked continuously by Soviet radar in neighboring Turkish Armenia. The last thing we wanted was to create an international incident by straying off course and getting shot down by Soviet fighters.

Launch time came, and our rendezvous in the air came off without a hitch. In our formation, we were near the rear, one hundred feet above and one thousand feet behind the aircraft in front. The visibility was terrible, as advertised, but we concentrated on the job of maintaining position on the lead aircraft that had the responsibility of navigating to the drop zone. Finally we arrived at the initial point (IP), to begin our run to the drop point. The navigator was poised to activate the ADS system that would drop the drag chute into the slipstream behind the aircraft, pulling the pallets of cargo out of the aircraft. The signal came over the radio to "drop now," and our navigator hit the ADS switch. We could see cargo spilling out of the aircraft all around us, until our loadmaster came on the intercom with an excited voice. Our drag chute had fallen on the open ramp and had failed to deploy. By this time, the formation was pulling off the drop zone in a steep, climbing turn, and we were fearful of this "hot load" exiting the aircraft in the wrong spot or causing a control problem with the aircraft. Luckily, neither event took place.

After leveling out of our turn, we advised the lead aircraft of our situation. We were told to break out of formation and to "air-land" our load at a desert airstrip near the drop zone. Since we had a "hot load" (one that could exit the aircraft at any time), we had to leave the cargo door and ramp open. Accordingly, we made a shallow descent, being as smooth on the controls as possible, and proceeded to land as instructed. The terrain was the most desolate I had ever seen, with cracks in the dry desert soil and swirling winds of dust. Who would want this place, anyway? Maybe it was the oil below the surface that made this terrain worth fighting for. In any event, we were glad to get unloaded and to depart as soon as possible for the more pleasant environs of our tent city back at Incirlik.

Another crew in our formation had a similar experience with a hung load, but they were able to get the drag chute deployed and to dispense their cargo, although beyond the designated drop zone. Someone started the story that the Shah was really "ticked off" because an American C-130 crew had dropped a 155 mm howitzer right into his villa, scaring all the residents of his harem. Everyone picked up the story and began to foretell harsh measures that would surely result when this errant crew was identified and brought forward for punishment. Nothing transpired, of course, and the word came down that the big operation was a success.

Glad to leave the sand, dust, and dirt of Turkey and Iran, we departed for home, the first stop being Spain. Caught up in the staging of crews, we were given a twenty-four hour layover at Torrejon AB. Accordingly, nothing would do but that we visit Madrid. Someone hired a car, and we were soon off for the long drive to the city. The driver knew the city but not much about safe driving, as we hurtled through the narrow streets of Madrid on a wild ride to one of the city's famous restaurants. After dinner, we were driven to a nightclub frequented by American servicemen. It was 10:00 p.m., and I thought the place would really be "jumping." But to our surprise, there was hardly anyone there. We were escorted to a balcony area overlooking the main floor, where we cooled our heels and nursed a few glasses of liquid refreshment. At about midnight, people began to filter in, and the action began to pick up. An orchestra began to fill the hall with music reminiscent of the "bull ring," and energetic costumed dancers began the famous Spanish dance. On the floor below were several small tables with some very strange seating. At each table was a lone woman dressed in Spanish finery, awaiting the arrival of a "consort" to wine and dine her and, apparently, to work out plans for the remainder of the evening (morning?). None of us left the balcony, being mesmerized by the scene below and by the hypnotic cadence of the music. But even with the energy displayed below, our eyes soon became heavy, and we departed back to the base, having been educated in late night Spanish customs. The dinner hour was 10:00 p.m., and no night-life began prior to midnight.

The next day, we checked out the Base Exchange, where many Spanish-made goods were on display. I admired the many hand-tooled leather offerings but found nothing to tempt me into a purchase. We departed that afternoon, headed for Kindley AFB, Bermuda, for fuel, and finally into Charleston AFB for crew rest. We had to undergo inspection by

US Customs and had been told that they were a tough bunch, particularly the representatives of the Department of Agriculture. I was told that I would probably have to slit the cushion on my "camel saddle" and remove the stuffing, to avoid importation of any unwelcome vermin. Such was not the case, however, and we breezed through the inspection, making certain that we had listed everything we had brought with us. The inspector even let us pass through our remaining case of Mateus Rose as "table wine" and thereby avoid paying any duty. After another crew rest, it was on to Travis AFB and home. It had been a long journey. Operation Delawar was complete, and it was our hope that we had performed well, at least well enough to give the Russian something to consider should his designs on the area become more sinister.

* * *

After a few days off, I reported for duty at the squadron training office. I had no idea that this day would start my life off in a whole new direction. It was a typical workday around the squadron. There was "scuttlebutt" going around that the 86th ATS was in line to convert to the new C-141 "Starlifters" when they came into the inventory. These were four-engine jet transports with all the latest technology. We junior officers were all first lieutenants now. We were looking forward to checking out as aircraft commanders and possibly flying the latest transports the air force had to offer. The future looked bright and unlimited, from our perspective.

Suddenly the operations officer appeared in the doorway and asked to see me in his office. I quickly followed him down the hall, where he asked me to take a seat across from his desk. What was this all about? I did not think I was in any trouble that I knew of. He began by saying that some assignments had come down that had to be filled from the ranks of our squadron. These assignments were to fly C-123 aircraft in support of our mission in South Vietnam. He asked if I wanted to volunteer.

Stunned by the moment, and considering my rosy future with the 86th, I asked, "What if I don't volunteer?" He smiled slightly and replied that I would go anyway as a nonvolunteer. Realizing that for a career officer to have "nonvolunteer" posted to his personnel records for combat duty was the death knell for advancement, I quickly replied, "I'll volunteer."

I walked out of his office in a daze. My days with the 86th Air Transport Squadron were basically over. Everything now would be directed toward preparation for my new assignment. But I always kept track of the 86th thereafter, even when it converted to the C-141s that I had longed to fly. I enjoyed my time in the C-130E, though, and the experiences I had had. I would see that aircraft again, but far away in the future and in another place.

CHAPTER NINE

"WARTIME"

As necessary training preceded every new assignment, I was anxious to know what that entailed. A few days later, my orders came down with the details. First I would proceed to Albrook AFB, Panama Canal Zone, for the "Tropic and Ethnic Familiarization" course, better known as "jungle survival" school. From there I would report to Eglin AFB, Florida, Auxiliary Field #9, better known as Hurlburt Field, for C-123 pilot training. Following that would be a short course in counterinsurgency at the Air War College, Maxwell AFB, Alabama, prior to returning to Travis and shipping out for Vietnam. Projected date for arriving in the war zone was set for June 1, 1965.

The first phase began at San Francisco International Airport, where several of my fellow officer-pilots and I boarded a Pan American Boeing 707 for the long flight to Panama City, Panama. The overnight portion took us to Guatemala, where we landed for fuel and had a chance to deplane to stretch our legs. I ordered a coffee in the terminal and was introduced to the bitterest, most potent brew I had ever tasted. It was small in quantity but powerful in its effect, much more so than what I had experienced in Turkey. I was "wired" for several hours after getting it down. I learned later that what I drank "straight," the natives normally modified with large quantities of cream and sugar. While reboarding, I couldn't help but notice several Mitchell B-25s parked on the far side of the ramp. This was part of the Cuban Fighters "Air Force," which was formed to help free Cuba from the control of Castro. Unfortunately, the effort came to naught at the "Bay of Pigs" fiasco, and these aircraft were left without a mission, to waste away in the tropical heat.

Upon arrival in Panama, we were bused to nearby Albrook AFB, the headquarters for our mission in Central America. After getting settled into the barracks, we assembled for the initial briefing. This school, like most others of its type, was also divided into phases, in this instance, the classroom, static camp, and field phases. In addition, we were advised not to venture off base, as the base was on a "code yellow" alert. It seemed that political unrest, common to the hot-blooded temperament of the locals, was rampant, and that American military personnel could be targeted. Fortunately, this restriction was lifted at the completion of training, and I was able to see the nearby Miraflores Locks of the Panama Canal in operation.

After a couple of days in the classroom, covering survival techniques in a tropical environment, we were bused to a nearby camp for a survival-foods lunch. I had seen this before at AFROTC summer camp. This spread included fish, turtle, alligator, and python, which I sampled, and grubs, ants, and other insects, which I did not. While it might have been necessary to partake of these latter food sources in an actual survival situation, I was willing to wait until that situation occurred before indulging.

Finally, after drawing our equipment, we were ready for the jungle. Boarding a helicopter, we were whisked away over the jungle canopy and set down in a clearing on a hilltop. From there we hiked a short distance to our static campsite near a river. There we set up camp by hanging our hammocks in the trees, building a fire pit, digging a latrine, etc. We had a sergeant instructor along who helped us identify various plants that could be used in a survival situation. Some examples included lemon grass, which made a very nice tea, and orchids, which made a colorful, tasty salad. Many years later on a trip to Hawaii, I shocked two of my granddaughters when I removed the orchid gracing our luau table and downed it before their eyes. We also learned to get water from bamboo. We had limited rations, so it was necessary to supplement them with what we could add from the environment. We had been given a survival weapon in the form of an over and under .410 gauge/.22-caliber shotgun/rifle. One of my fellow officer students managed to kill an armadillo, which we dressed and cooked in its own shell over the fire. We added a few fish and a couple of birds to the stew as well. We bathed in the river and went to sleep to the sounds of the jungle and the river. So far, this duty was not so tough after all, but I had a feeling that it was going to change very soon.

The next day, we were divided into pairs and briefed on the escape and evasion phase of our training. The "problem" simulated our having been forced down in enemy territory. We were to navigate downriver to various safe areas, interact with the "friendly" indigenous people we encountered, avoid capture by the "enemy," and arrive at the pickup point for "rescue." My partner was an F-100 fighter pilot who was also slated for Vietnam duty. We decided that we would not rush off with the rest of the group, who were "chomping at the bit" to get started downriver. Instead, we spent the afternoon building a raft to keep our packs dry as we navigated down the river to the Indian village, which was to be our first assembly point. We decided to spend another night near the base camp and begin our journey the following morning. As it turned out, our plan worked to perfection. Each student had been issued a soft, bright yellow "jungle hat" to wear during training. The Indian tribe who inhabited the area had been offered a bounty of one hundred dollars American for each of the hats they could snatch from their wearers. To them, the offer amounted to a fortune, and they were lying in wait that first afternoon for all those who charged downriver. The next day, after a pleasant float down this beautiful river, my partner and I waded out of the river into the Indian village—the only ones who had survived the first leg and kept their hats.

The remainder of that day was spent observing the simple life of the Indian family. We watched one woman grinding grain in one thatched hut, another was cooking, and still another was weaving palm into rugs. The head of the family, whom we had nicknamed "Antonio," demonstrated his prowess with the bow and arrow and invited us to try his prized dugout canoe. He also posed behind a tree, showing how he would snatch those yellow hats as they came by. We all had a good laugh at his antics, and after a meal of "jungle stew" and a rest, we prepared for the next phase of our escape and evasion problem.

As night fell, we headed out by land trail to our next rendezvous point. At some point, we encountered a "friendly" native who volunteered to guide us to our destination. After playing "follow-the-leader" over several miles of jungle trail, we came to another village in the wee hours of the morning. We were tired, hungry and in need of sleep. The natives in this village, whether by nature or design, were not as friendly as those of Antonio's people. They did, however, offer us a welcome bowl of "mystery stew," which we all downed with gusto. Our guide then urged us up and out on the trail, purporting to lead us to our final destination—the designated safe area where we were to be picked up. Unfortunately, this "friendly" turned out not to be so, and led us into an "enemy" camp, where we were captured and confined. I was expecting a repeat of my experiences in the combat survival school at Stead AFB, Nevada, with solitary confinement, interrogation, etc. But after some discussion between our senior officers and school officials, an "academic situation" was declared, everyone took off their masks, and the problem was declared "over." No one wanted to argue the point, and we were soon on our way back to the barracks for a much-anticipated sleep.

After a debriefing the next morning, we reported to the waterfront, where we boarded a motor launch to receive "parachuting over water" training. Each of us, donning a parachute harness, was required to jump off the rail of the boat as it glided along. The boat would then drag us for a short distance, with simulated shroud lines, to simulate an actual water landing. The trick then was to find and release the chute from the harness, inflate the one-man dinghy attached to the harness, and paddle over to a twenty-man life raft. Once every man had his turn, we received instruction on the use of life raft equipment and on how to survive while awaiting pickup. That phase began shortly thereafter, as a rescue helicopter appeared on the scene. Each man, in turn, was required to grab the dangling harness, place it under his arms, grasp and lock his elbows, and be winched up into the chopper above. While each of us dreaded the idea of having to perform any of these maneuvers "for real," this was good training that might allow us to live to fly another day. We had a brief graduation ceremony in the afternoon, and then we headed out to see the locks of the Panama Canal before returning to the barracks to pack for departure. The first step on the road to Vietnam was complete.

* * *

The second step began with my checkout on the Fairchild C-123 at Eglin AFB, Florida. This was familiar territory to me from my days of summer camp back in the AFROTC program at UT. This time, the actual training took place at what was officially called Eglin Auxiliary Field #9, but was more familiarly known simply as Hurlburt Field, located a few miles from the main base. Its main claim to fame was its use by General James Doolittle during World War II. Here, the crews who were to bomb Tokyo early in the war trained for their short takeoffs from the carrier Hornet in Mitchell B-25s. The length of the carrier deck was marked off on the runway, and crews were trained to get airborne in that distance. For the reader who is not familiar with that particular mission, I would refer them to a book on the subject as to its outcome and effects. In 1965, the base itself had been upgraded with new housing, a golf course, and numerous other recreational facilities. It was totally dedicated to training aircrews for Southeast Asia in the C-123 and the A-25, an updated version of General Doolittle's old B-25.

Once settled into modern, apartment-style housing, I reported to the flight line for my first day of training. This was to be a different type of school. There was little "ground school" and no simulator. This was to be a "hands-on" school, with maximum time spent in the cockpit. I met my instructor, who had been transferred from Pope AFB, North Carolina, where the C-123 was still being flown in support of the 82nd Airborne at nearby Fort Bragg. I said something about the "Dash-One" airplane manual and its contents, and he replied, "This is TAC; we use it for a seat cushion." He would teach me all I needed to know. This was to be "non-standardized" flying at its best: Go get the work done, don't come back until you're through, and we don't really have time to see how you do it. What a departure from the rigid, standardized flight procedures of MATS.

As I approached the C-123 for the first time, I was struck by its similarity to the C-130. It was almost like a "baby" C-130 in shape, with its high wing, high tail, and cargo ramp and door. It had a roomy cockpit for two and a fold-down seat for the crew chief/loadmaster during actual mission flying. Two Pratt & Whitney R-2800 reciprocal engines provided power—the tough, proven veterans of World War II. Many still were the stories of how they could take a hit and still get you back home. I learned that the original design of the aircraft fuselage was for that of a powered glider. Our instructor pointed out the "towing ring" still in place behind the nose access panel, the steel tubing used to brace the fuselage for unpowered landings, and special "T-handles" in the cockpit that were used to jettison the entire engine nacelles from the airplane, if necessary. Fortunately, these were "wired off" and were not to be a feature utilized for our mission. He also pointed out the half-inch armor plating on the floor that would provide protection from small arms fire, something we were to be thankful for in future situations.

Training began with the normal takeoff, traffic pattern, and landing maneuvers. Having "grown up "on jets, I had to reacquaint myself with things like mixture levers, manifold pressure, and propeller RPM settings. One of the most challenging things, in the beginning, was starting the engines without "backfiring." This called for actuating the starter, looking at the rotating propeller, counting a preset number of "blades" of rotation, actuating the fuel primer button, getting the engine running on the primer, and finally, moving the fuel mixture lever forward to complete the sequence. After embarrassing myself a few times, as we all did, I finally got the hang of it. It was good that there was not a "boner" system in place, else we all would have been poorer as a result.

Soon we left the traffic pattern and took up our tactical training. The first phase was low-level navigation, which was the most exhilarating thing I had done with any airplane yet. The plan was to fly at maximum speed, fifty feet off the deck, and to complete a "round robin" route around the local area. It was similar to an automobile "road rally," in that one pilot would concentrate on holding heading, altitude, and airspeed. The other pilot used his map to locate ground checkpoints, keep track of time, and give out instructions to the pilot flying, in order to maintain the desired course. These routes were flown continuously, and a joke that went around was that if the cows you flew over "ran," you were off course. If they kept grazing, you were "right on."

The culmination of our training was to be night landings on an eighteen hundred-foot dirt strip called "Rock Hill," using only flashlights held by people on the ground to define the landing area. This was the most challenging and dangerous thing I had ever done with an airplane. After touching down and using maximum reverse to get stopped, the cockpit would fill up with dust, limiting visibility. With another aircraft landing right behind us, we had to clear the landing strip and avoid colliding with others who had landed ahead of us, taxiing back for takeoff. It was a tense situation, but one that would be seen again in actual combat support.

Graduation day finally came with the completion of all training and a brief check ride. On the last day, we were ushered into a room where an officer asked for volunteers for C-123 special missions. I had gotten wind of this from a previous graduate and "sat on my hands." These special missions included spraying jungle trails with Agent Orange defoliate to rob the Vietcong enemy of their jungle cover (codename: Ranch Hand) and clandestine missions into Laos and North Vietnam under cover of night and under direction of the Central Intelligence Agency (CIA). The latter missions used specially painted (black) aircraft with no markings, in order to minimize detection. It was not that I was fearful of any danger with these special missions, but I felt that being so "compartmentalized," I would miss being a part of the "big picture" in our combat support mission. Fortunately, an adequate number volunteered, and we were dismissed to clear the base and press on to the last phase of training: counterinsurgency school and an airpower demonstration.

The distance from Hurlburt Field to Maxwell AFB in Montgomery is only a day's drive, and I soon found myself back in school with many other officers headed to the war zone. The purpose of this one-week school was to demonstrate some of the air tactics being employed against the Vietcong in Vietnam, Laos, and Cambodia, and to give us an up-to-date picture of the current situation. That situation was to change dramatically, soon after the course began. In the midst of one presentation, a staff officer handed the instructor a note saying that American air forces had begun bombing facilities in Haiphong Harbor in North Vietnam, along with the "Ho Chi Minh Trail" in Laos and Cambodia, in an effort to cut the supply lines to the Vietcong insurgents. This was an escalation of hostilities of major proportion. We realized that we would be the vanguard of what was ultimately to be one of the greatest buildups of men and materials in the nation's history.

While this was somewhat unsettling news, we were heartened by the airpower demonstration that came at the end of the course. Vietnam was to be a great proving ground of air weaponry for future wars of insurgency. Nothing was ruled out. Old World War II C-47s were pulled out of mothballs and equipped with "Gatling gun" type cannon, firing six thousand rounds per minute that could turn a section of jungle into chopped salad in seconds. C-123s were modified to spray the defoliant Agent Orange on jungle trails, to deny the enemy cover. They were even used to deliver multiple barrels of napalm on selected targets, to incinerate the enemy. One account I heard was that when this tactic was employed, the heat from the ensuing fire was so intense that it created its own thunderstorm and extinguished the fire. The B-52s, designed to deliver atomic weapons on the Communist Bloc of nations, would now be employed to "carpet bomb" areas of suspected troop concentrations. This experimentation went on and on without end. My reaction to all this was that we might be involved in a limited war but we surely had the airpower to end it in short order.

We were all greatly impressed with the display of available air power, that last day of class. How could a few black pajama-clad insurgents utilizing small arms stand up to all this? We left with this thought: With the war escalating to a more "conventional" type of war, we would make short order of this insurgency and would maintain what we thought was freedom and democracy in South Vietnam. Perhaps there has been no greater underestimation of an enemy in our history.

Next stop: South Vietnam.

* * *

In the first week of June 1965, I boarded a Continental Boeing 707 at Travis AFB, California. My ultimate destination was Tan Son Nhut AB, Republic of South Vietnam. This was a military charter flight, filled with military and civilian personnel of every description. It was a night flight over a familiar ocean route to the first refueling stop in Kadena AB, Okinawa. It was a relatively comfortable flight, and everyone tried to sleep as best as they could. It was somewhere in mid-ocean that the realism of what I was about to do struck home. I would not be coming back home for an entire year (I thought), and during that year, I would be in a hostile environment. I accepted the situation as my lot, however, and determined to do my duty as I had been trained. After landing at Kadena, we were disappointed to learn that we would not be allowed to deplane, so we moved around the cabin, stretching our legs as much as possible under the circumstances. The turnaround by the ground crew was done quickly, and we were back in the air very soon for the short flight to our destination.

My first sight of Vietnam was when I stepped out of the 707's cabin door and was greeted with bright sunshine, oppressive heat, and humidity. After collecting baggage and processing in, I was assigned temporary quarters in an old downtown Saigon hotel until I could arrange a more permanent situation. There was no housing available on base. Those of us in the same boat exchanged some United States money for the local piasters (commonly referred to simply as "p") and hailed taxis at the main gate for the downtown area.

To paint a picture of Saigon in 1965 is to go back in French history to its colonization of this part of the world. Driven out of the northern part of the country in the mid 1950s by Communist insurgents, led by Ho Chi Minh, the French tried to protect their economic interests by negotiating a settlement after their disastrous defeat at Dien Bien Phu. Under the terms of the settlement, the Communists would control the north while the French would set up a free republic in the south. This shaky arrangement was not to endure for long. Soon the insurgents began to infiltrate the south, and the battle was on. The French had had enough. After their fashion, they pulled out, leaving the newly formed republic to fend for itself with no administrative expertise and little military capability. Enter the United States in an effort to shore up the south and to prevent another country falling victim to the "domino" theory of Communist domination.

What was left behind had a distinctive French influence. Swarms of petite Renault taxis in their blue and cream colors choked the streets and roads, along with man-powered tricycle "pedicabs," French motorbikes, and bicycles of every description. Add the myriad of civilian and military traffic, and you give a new meaning to the term "traffic jam." Traffic control was virtually nonexistent except at the French traffic circles, where the local white-clad policemen (called "white mice" by the locals) did their ballet routines in an effort to bring some order to the confusion of vehicles. Restaurants were decidedly French with their outdoor seating areas, now reduced in size and protected by sandbags to counter the rash of restaurant bombings by the insurgents. Important people and buildings were isolated behind broken glass-covered walls and barred gates, in the French style. The citizenry was alternately clad in western and native dress, the latter being the "ao zai" for the women, a thin, normally white pajama-type garment with flowing vertical panels in front and behind, accented by the "panty line" that was clearly visible to all. For the men, it was a plain set of pajamas, normally black, with the native straw hat as a common accessory.

As we neared our destination, it was increasingly apparent that the streets were nothing less than open sewers. I still have the image in my mind of the old man standing in the gutter, holding his ancient penis aloft and urinating for all to see. But as someone once said, "The whole world is a man's urinal!" The smells of the city would assault the senses of anyone not accustomed to being in a large city in that area of the world: engine exhaust, decaying garbage, woks cooking food on the sidewalks, all mingled with the faint smell of human waste. After awhile, the senses accept it and prayer is offered for the daily rain to wash everything clean once again.

I was assigned a small room on the upper floor of the old hotel. It was reasonably clean, though basic in its furnishings. The community bath was down the hall. After stowing my stuff, I hailed a taxi and went to the city center and the Rex Hotel officers' club, located on the roof. It provided a bar, a restaurant, a pool, and live entertainment in the evenings. This was the "gathering place" for all off-duty air force officers. Unfortunately, these and other like places in the city had become targets for the Vietcong. Several US personnel had already been killed in these locations by bomb blasts produced by so-called "plastic" explosives, which could be shaped into any form and could be hidden in things as simple as a bicycle. Being several floors up on the roof, however, gave us some form of security, along with the sandbagged entrance and armed guards. I spent most of the afternoon there before returning to the hotel, in an effort to get my body in sync with the new time zone. The thin mattress on a wooden platform did not deter my immediately becoming dead to the world. My first day in Vietnam was suddenly over. Only 364 days to go.

1st Air Commando Wing C-123, Tan Son Nhut AB,
Republic of South Vietnam, 1965. Author front row, far right

The next few days were very busy. I was assigned to the 310th Air Commando Squadron based there at Ton Son Nhut. After attending to the various in-processing tasks, we newcomers were assembled to meet our squadron commander, who gave us an update on the war zone situation. During his briefing, he kept referring to the Vietcong as the "North Koreans." This not only revealed something about his past military service but, along with other grammatical gaffes, showed that he was not the sharpest officer to come down the pike. This was confirmed in the months to come in that, to my knowledge, he never flew a combat support mission and was rarely seen around our operations hut. I came to understand that there were many "field-grade" officers (above the rank of captain) who were in the war zone solely to add combat command to their records in an effort to further their careers. Junior officers with no such aspirations would accomplish the real mission.

Getting around on base was an easy proposition. There was a steady, slow-moving stream of traffic from the flight line area all the way to the main gate. One just jumped on the first vehicle offering a place to stand or sit and hold on, and jumped off when the vehicle passed one's destination. There was a post office, mess hall, and most other support facilities right on base. So clearing in was a simple process.

All uniform items and accessories were issued on base, with the exception of one item. As "air commandos," we were authorized to wear a special wide-brimmed hat, with one side of the brim swept up and attached to the crown. The hat was commonly referred to as a "Go-To-Hell" hat. This was purchased from a local shopkeeper in the city, who seemed to enjoy the concept of the moniker. When I placed my order, he threw his head back and laughingly said, "Ah, go to hell." He must have made a small fortune. In any event, the hats were heavy, hot, and uncomfortable, and were only used for ceremonial purposes. The "Sweeny Green" baseball cap with rank sewn onto the front crown was the cap of choice, and the "Go-To-Hell" hats were relegated to being hardly more than souvenirs.

I remember one instance where I went to base supply in an effort to obtain a new pair of the latest canvas and leather "jungle boots" worn throughout the theater. I was told that they were all out and that there would be a lengthy wait to receive a pair. When I shared this with a fellow officer, he told me to go downtown to a certain area, and I could find anything I needed, including combat boots, on the black market. I did as he directed, and although I did not purchase a pair of boots, I did see that much of what was unloaded on the docks of Saigon City ended up on its streets.

As mentioned previously, the local currency was the piaster, with an official exchange rate somewhere around one hundred piasters to an American dollar. I say "official" because there was an "unofficial" rate offered by certain Indian shopkeepers around the city, usually between 110 and 120 piasters to the dollar, depending on the denomination of the bill. (They loved one-hundred-dollar bills.) Everyone quickly learned where these shops were and traded their dollars there. Later, the United States, in an effort to stem the flow of dollars to these sources, introduced what was known as MPCs—Military Payment Certificates—in lieu of the dollar. These could be exchanged only at the official rate. The dollar was outlawed. This set up a money exchange business in which, I am ashamed now to admit, I became a willing participant. With the privilege of flying into and out of the country and receiving uncensored mail from home, each man was able to keep a continuing supply of American money. This money was exchanged at the "unofficial" rate and then was used to buy MPCs at the "official" rate. These, then, could be exchanged back to dollars when leaving the country for short-term duty elsewhere, such as taking a C-123 to Clark Air Base, the Philippines, for repair, delivering mail and supplies to our bases in Thailand, etc. While the amount of gain achieved in all of this enterprise was negligible, it did give one the feeling that he was getting the most out of his dollar, even though it was strictly illegal. This was just one of many trading schemes that went on in the country, and there were many other stories about people trading cases of C-rations for jeeps, "bazookas," cases of grenades, rifles, etc.

As it turned out, my days in the hotel were few in number. A vacancy had come open in an apartment shared by three other pilot officers in my squadron, and they were looking for someone to share the expense. I immediately jumped at the chance, and it proved to be a good move. The apartment was on the second floor of a high-rise building not far from the city center and the Rex Hotel. Each of us had his own bedroom, fairly well furnished with an overhead fan, and we shared a living room, kitchen, and a sizeable bathroom.

Most importantly, we had two maids who were there six days a week to clean, do laundry, and have a meal ready at the appointed hour when we returned in the evening. To make it even better, one of the maids was trained in French cooking. Consequently, we were sometimes treated to a departure from our normal meat-and-potatoes regimen. To a country boy from Tennessee, crepes stuffed with crabmeat along with "flan" for dessert were truly exotic. We had access to a US military commissary for our groceries, and we rotated that rather unwelcome shopping duty among ourselves when it was time to bring in supplies. At other times, the maids would bring in local food in season. It was always comical to see one of the tiny Renault taxis, loaded to the gills with groceries, pulling up to our building to unload. Once a month, we would all assemble around the dining table to reconcile the expenses for the month and to pay the maids. All in all, it was a very satisfactory arrangement. I do not want to present this arrangement in greater terms than it really was. However, I do realize that, as a pilot and an officer, the living conditions of my Vietnam experience were much better than those of the typical GIs slogging around in the rice paddies and living in "hooches," as their tents were called.

Finally, after tending to all these affairs, it was time to get down to the business at hand. I could fly the C-123, but I still had so much to learn about flying it with someone shooting at me over now-unfamiliar terrain while I completed my assigned missions. My introduction began with a "theater checkout." I would be assigned to fly as copilot with the more senior, experienced officers, learning local procedures, locations, types of navigation aids, and preferred routes, and most importantly, landing and taking off from every location we were authorized to go into. The interesting part of this learning experience was the variety of mission types that we flew. They might constitute anything from a nighttime "flare" mission to a "mail run" completely around the entire country. Whatever was to come, boredom would not be a part of it.

My theater checkout began with an assignment as copilot on a night "flare mission," which became one of the most harrowing experiences of my flying career. We took off at dusk and navigated north to one of the so-called "strategic hamlets." This was a village, open in the daylight hours when it could be easily defended, but secured with a defensive perimeter at night to ward off attack. This was part of the military strategy to defend territory only in "strategic" locations around the country and to leave the rural areas to the enemy at night. As you might imagine, these hamlets were prime targets for attack. Our mission was to "loiter" over the hamlet and drop high-incandescent phosphorus flares via parachute. As they descended, these flares would light up the countryside to near-daylight conditions for about twenty minutes, making it easier to spot enemy activity. Word was that each of these flares was worth a small fortune. Such are the costs of war.

We arrived on station with a load of forty flares and began our slow circling of the hamlet, setting the mixture levers to the leanest setting in order to conserve fuel for the nightlong mission. We settled back in our seats, lit our cigarettes (pilots who didn't smoke back then were regarded suspiciously), and watched for "tracers" (visible enemy fire) directed our way. As the preceding flare would extinguish itself on the ground, the flight mechanic/loadmaster would kick out another flare to take its place.

After a couple of hours on station, we were startled by a scream over the interphone, from the flight mechanic in back, accompanied by a blinding bright glow in the cargo hold. A flare had gone off prematurely inside the aircraft, threatening to set off the other flares and turn us into a flaming meteor in the sky. Our only option was to bail out. I was tightening the straps on my parachute and getting ready to leave the cockpit when the cargo compartment went dark again. The flight mechanic had managed somehow to grab the burning flare and kick it out of the aircraft before it could do its damage. He suffered burns on his hands, but elected to stay at his post of duty for the remainder of the mission. Fortunately, all went smoothly thereafter, and we landed back at Ton Son Nhut as the sun was coming up. The flight mechanic was sent off for medical attention and was written up for a commendation and a Purple Heart. Shortly thereafter, the "strategic hamlet" concept was abandoned, and flare missions became rarer.

They were not so rare, however, that I would not fly another memorable one soon after. Down in the Mekong Delta, south of Saigon, the Vietcong were using sampans to move military supplies across the Mekong River at night. To counter this, the army had developed a clandestine aircraft called the "Mohawk," which was equipped with a device called a "side-looking" radar. This apparatus was capable of detecting movement down to something like two miles per hour. The attack plan, nicknamed "Snipe Hunt," was to use this aircraft to detect the boats moving on the river. We would then be called in to drop out a string of flares. Following this, A1E fighters and "Huey" helicopters would be called in under the flares in order to destroy the targets with rockets and twenty-millimeter gunfire. All this sounded good, but success depended on close, rapid coordination with several agencies. In addition, all aircraft would be flying without lights of any kind, to avoid detection and enemy ground fire.

This operation was an accident waiting to happen, and it almost happened to our crew. Having been called in on a section of the river, we had just completed our flare-dropping run. Suddenly an A1E fighter zoomed up right up in front of us, filling the windshield, so close that we could see the blue flame from his engine exhaust stacks. We took immediate abrupt action to avoid the impending midair collision and waited for our hearts to settle back into our chests. Fortunately, this was my last experience with flares. I always wondered how effective these missions were in denying supplies to the enemy. So one day I asked an army liaison officer that question. His answer was, "We don't really know about that. One thing we do know though. It really cut down on the night fishing along the Mekong."

I was soon checked out on most of the routes and airfields that made up the mission of the 310th Air Commando Squadron. We utilized tactical air navigation (TACAN) stations for navigation to most of the airfields, utilizing the bearing and distance information provided by these ground-based radios. After awhile, these bearings and distances were committed to memory, landmarks along the route became well-known, and little use was made of navigational radios.

Most of the missions were routine, involving shuttling rice, cargo, fuel bladders, and ammunition, with an occasional mail run around the circuit to Hue in the north and to Soc Trang in the south. One run that everyone fought for was the weekly run to Dalat to pick up fresh vegetables. This destination was located in the coastal highlands and was always a cool and comfortable place, compared to the heat and humidity of Saigon. It was little wonder that it was a favorite getaway destination for the South Vietnamese in better times. Another favorite destination was Vung Tau on the southeast coast. Here we could walk down to the beach and practice our marksmanship with the .357 revolvers that we carried and with the M-16 rifle that was aboard every aircraft and manned by the flight mechanic. Luckily, we never had to fire a shot in anger.

We began to get new people into the squadron as the veterans began rotating back stateside. Since I was becoming more qualified, I was paired with the newcomers on occasion. One day I was paired with a lieutenant colonel who had recently completed his theater checkout. He had come from the regimen of Strategic Air Command, with its emphasis on standardization and on carefully following procedures. We began shuttling supplies from one base to another down in the Mekong Delta area, using the canals for navigation and flying at a lower than normal altitude. After flying the same route for several shuttles, I discreetly suggested that we vary our route somewhat, to avoid establishing a pattern that the enemy might use against us. Seeing the same aircraft go by in the same location, time after time, was a sure way to draw enemy gunfire. My suggestion went unheeded, with a remark to the effect that, "There ain't anybody down there goin' to bother us." On the ensuing shuttle, we began to experience something like BBs striking the aircraft, and the controls began to shudder intermittently. We turned away from the canal we had been following and returned to base. Inspection revealed eighteen bullet holes in the wings and tail section. Luckily again, it was small caliber ammunition that had made the holes. Had it been anything bigger, we could have been shot down easily. As a result, varying one's routes during multi-shuttle missions and maintaining altitude above three thousand feet for as long as possible became hot topics in daily flight briefings from that day forward.

Another mission that stands out in my memory is one that took place in the central highlands at a place called Kontum. Here was one of the few concrete landing strips in the country, reportedly built by the Japanese in World War II. We were directed there one day to move some troops and vehicles to another location. We were relaxing in the operations hut while the flight mechanic, acting as loadmaster, conducted the loading of our aircraft. When we saw that the loading was nearing completion, we returned to the aircraft to check the paperwork and to figure out if we were within limits for our takeoff at that altitude and temperature. All seemed to be in order, so we started our engines and taxied out for takeoff.

We lined up on the runway, did our engine run-up, engaged the water injection system to give us maximum power, and released the brakes. We noticed that the takeoff roll was going slower than normal, but everything looked normal, so we pressed on. But it became increasingly apparent that we were rapidly approaching the end of the runway and had not yet reached flying speed. As the end of the concrete passed under the nose wheel, I jerked the control wheel back, and somehow the C-123 struggled into the air, shuddering on a stall, and fighting for every foot of altitude. There was a loud "thud" as we sucked the gear up, acquired minimum flying speed, and began a slow climb. Something was wrong, but what?

Landing at our destination, we rechecked our load. It was then that we discovered that we were seriously overweight. We had loaded a small "four-by" truck, loaded with mortar shells. The flight mechanic was used to dealing in "pounds" in determining weight, but this load was given to him in kilograms. Since there are 2.2 pounds to each kilogram, we had taken off with over twice the weight listed on the paperwork. In addition, we had taken out a barbed wire fence and two headstones in a cemetery adjoining the airfield. Had our water injection failed or had the Japanese poured a little less concrete, we would have plowed our own graves off the end of that runway.

July 4, 1965, was a routine day for my crew. We were shuttling rice from an airfield on the central coast, called Quin Nhon, to a place called Cheo Reo, up in the highlands. We were taking a break under the shade of the wing and wondering how we could celebrate our national holiday in such a wayward place. Suddenly, along the fenced perimeter of the field, we spotted an old "papa-san" pushing a wagon loaded with watermelons. What could be more appropriate on the fourth of July than watermelon?

We searched our pockets for a few piasters and rushed to the fence to make our purchase. The old man was happy to part with a portion of his load, and we were soon gorging ourselves on the best watermelon I ever tasted, under the shade of the wing. Happy Independence Day!

In the fall of 1965, the Vietnam conflict began to heat up and change the nature of the war. No longer was it a sunrise-to-sunset operation. Enemy troops and supplies were streaming down the so-called Ho Chi Minh Trail on the borders of Laos and Cambodia. More pitched battles were being fought in the open countryside. American forces responded by building a giant base at Cam Rahn Bay, stepping up the bombing of North Vietnam, and pouring over five hundred thousand military personnel into the country. Ton Son Nhut Airbase was inundated with aircraft and cargo. It was about this time that a call came down for duty officers to man a newly formed unit called Transport Movement Control (TMC). Some-how my name got into the mix, and I volunteered for the new assignment. I was transferred from the 310th ACS but remained "attached" to it for flying purposes. Later on, the 310th was relocated to Nha Trang AB along the central coast, and I was "attached" to a sister squadron, the 309th ACS.

The mission of TMC was to coordinate and control the loading, unloading, and ground movement of all transport aircraft arriving and departing Ton Son Nhut Airbase. To assist in this Herculean task, a two-story control "shack" was built, overlooking what was known as the "rebel" ramp area. On the top floor were situated various status boards to keep track of scheduled missions as well as communication radios to coordinate with aircraft and ground support agencies. Keeping the status boards manned was the job of two enlisted men, with the duty officer looking at "the big picture" and making decisions about how to keep everything from evolving into a big mess, which, with the number of aircraft and limited ramp space, it was prone to do. I was one of four duty officers, and a senior captain served as our immediate commander and filled in as the need arose.

The TMC shack was to be manned 24-7, which necessitated scheduling duty in shifts. After trying various combinations, we mutually settled on a schedule that entailed three "day" shifts (7:00 a.m.–3:00 p.m.), three "swing" shifts (3:00 p.m.–11:00 p.m.), and three "graveyard" shifts (11:00 p.m.–7:00 a.m.), followed by three days off. So I settled into this routine for the remainder of my tour of duty. While the duty was challenging in terms of planning, coordinating, and communicating, I missed the friendly confines of the C-123 cockpit, and I took every opportunity to return to the skies with my old unit.

TMC duty was not without excitement, however. As I approached the base one morning to begin a day shift, I saw plumes of black smoke rising into the sky. This phenomenon is normally associated with burning petroleum, so I was anxious to find out what was going on. As I passed the gate, someone yelled out that the base had been hit with mortar fire during the night. I hurried to the TMC shack and found the duty officer I was to relieve. He was somewhat dazed and shaken from the attack. When the first rounds had begun to explode on the flight line, he had grabbed all the secret documents and dived into the nearest bomb shelter. He was glad to be relieved, and I learned later that he was recommended for a Silver Star (a United States military decoration for gallantry in action). Everyone was viewing and taking pictures of the damage done in the attack. Several aircraft had been hit as well as fuel storage tanks, all burning out of control. The saddest sight, however, was neither of these, and it requires a little background.

The C-123 was an aircraft that had to be refueled "over the wing." That is, fuel hoses had to be lifted up onto the wing, and then the fuel caps removed, nozzles inserted, and tanks filled, at a very slow rate, from the tanker trucks we had to work with. Later, aviation technology developed "single point" refueling, where the fuel hose from the tanker could be hooked up to a panel on the aircraft, with valves to direct the fuel to various tanks. But that was not to be had, as yet, on the C-123. Accordingly, everyone had been excited about the arrival of a brand-new, shiny, bright yellow "jet pump" tanker truck that had just arrived the day before and was parked on the ramp. Here was the answer to our slow refueling and mission turnaround times. But as fate would have it, the very first mortar shell fired by the Vietcong went through the windshield of that truck, igniting the fuel tanks and leaving it a burning hulk. Aircraft were expendable, but a jet pumper was a "luxury" that we sorely missed in the weeks to come. Perhaps the enemy was smarter in their target selection than we thought.

Working in TMC had several side benefits. I was able to get out of the country from time to time, and I enjoyed "R&R" side trips to Hong Kong, Bangkok, and even Kadena AB, Okinawa, where the air-conditioned VOQs offered a temporary respite from the heat and humidity. I even donned my old MATS flight suit and hitched a ride back home to the United States for a few days, at a time when stateside return was prohibited east of Hawaii. Ferrying a C-123 to Clark Air Base in the Philippines for overhaul was another one-time opportunity to leave the combat zone, although security was tight there, and there was little to do except wait for a repaired ship to take back.

There were ribbons and medals to be awarded for Vietnam service, and I guess I received my share. In addition to the Vietnam Campaign Service ribbon, I was awarded the Air Medal, with silver and bronze "clusters" representing the combat support missions I had flown. The surprise medal was the Outstanding Achievement Award, which supports the idea of being in the right place at the right time. It came about in the following way. I was manning the TMC duty officer slot one afternoon, when a call came in, advising that one of our C-123s had crashed on takeoff from a remote landing strip down in the Mekong Delta. Complicating the rescue of the crew was the fact that the aircraft had ended up in a minefield off the end of the strip and was subject to enemy fire at any moment. Getting on the phone while maintaining contact with aircraft circling the crash site, I coordinated with helicopter and fighter units at nearby Bien Hoa Airbase for rescue and covering fire if needed. Response was rapid, and the whole episode was brought to a successful conclusion with no loss of life. I understood that after the minefield was cleared, the aircraft was "cannibalized" for parts and the tail blown off, in keeping with air force regulations.

CHAPTER TEN

"COMING HOME"

For me, the year 1966 began with the main thought that was the thought of every serviceman who served in the Vietnam conflict: what will my next assignment be, and how soon can I get there? I was due to finish my tour of duty in the war zone in May, and I really began to deal with the issue of where my military career would lead me next. The war was escalating rapidly, and things were not going well back home. Young men were escaping the draft by seeking asylum in Canada or by openly burning their draft cards in front of the TV news cameras. There were riots and demonstrations in the streets. It seemed that everyone was protesting for some cause. Drugs, free sex, and "acid rock" music were rapidly replacing the Happy Days of the 1950s.

To the serviceman, the events going on back home spelled out an oncoming lack of will to win this conflict. And that was reflected in the attitude of those very people who were sent to win it. The most noticeable emblem of this was the proliferation of so-called FIGMO charts, prominently displayed around squadron ready rooms, including the TMC shack. The word FIGMO is a military acronym that stands for "Forget it, I've got my orders," meaning, "What do I care about what goes on here; I've got my orders transferring me out of here." These charts showed a beautiful female genie, emanating from a lamp, with ninety-nine spaces making up her form. Each space represented a day remaining until transfer, and one space was to be colored in as each day passed. The one hundredth day was the tip of the genie's finger, which was strategically placed over the male apparatus of a sleeping airman. Hence the phrase, "Ninety-nine days and a wakeup," became the favorite saying of the day. While high-ranking officers frowned on these charts and even gave orders prohibiting their display, those doing the real work largely ignored these orders.

And so, my one-hundred-day period arrived, and my FIGMO chart was posted with the rest. My orders came through, sending me back to the air training command at Moody AFB in Valdosta, Georgia, as a T-37 instructor. I was tired of traveling the world, tired of war, tired of seeing body bags of United States dead loaded onto aircraft, and tired of seeing the weekly shuttle to the Philippines carrying those soldiers brought down by the venereal diseases of our ally. I was ready to settle into a nice "stay-at-home assignment," far from the sound of exploding bombs and the rush of battle. This assignment seemed to be just the ticket, so I asked for it and received it. Such is the finger of fate.

The remainder of my tour in the combat zone took on a measure of routine: three day shifts in TMC, three swing shifts in TMC, and three night shifts in TMC, followed by three days off, during one or more of which I flew the C-123 just to keep my flying skills up to snuff. The flying mission had changed drastically over the space of my tour of duty. We had gone from a daylight-to-dark operation, supplying Special Forces, to a twenty-four hour operation carrying fuel and ammunition to frontline combat units throughout the country. From the fifty thousand "in-country" military personnel upon my arrival, the number had grown to five hundred thousand. Instead of the "nice little war" described by a colonel seeking a general's star, we found ourselves in a hot war that nobody wanted, without the will to win it. The summation of all this was displayed on the back of a jacket I saw some years later. It read,

"PARTICIPANT: VIET-NAM WAR GAMES—1965–66, SECOND PLACE."

Finally the day came when my FIGMO chart was all colored in and taken down from the wall. I cleared the base, turned in my gear, briefed my replacement, and returned one last time to my apartment on Vo Than Street. I said good-byes to my roommates and to the maids who had cooked and cleaned for us so well, packed all of my personal things in a footlocker for shipment to my next duty station, and took one last cab ride to the airport along the route that I had come to know so well.

I boarded a military-chartered jet and watched the runway and terrain slowly disappear, as we launched eastward toward home. I had done my duty to my country and had survived, and was now ready to begin a new chapter in my life and in my military career. To the day, I had given a year of my life to a cause noble in its origin, perhaps, but a losing cause in its execution. I didn't know that at the time, but the succeeding years would bear it out. A fuel stop at Hickam and a second leg to the familiar ramp of Travis AFB brought me back to the United States of America, where a number of us, upon disembarking, knelt to kiss the concrete. There was no homecoming committee, and there were no "welcome back greetings" from anyone. Another couple of flights brought me back to the hills of Tennessee for a period of leave and an attempt to reconnect with the life I had left behind.

The country I returned to was even deeper into antiwar sentiment. There were no ticker tape parades staged for her returning veterans, and yet the struggle to stop "Communist aggression" in Vietnam continued. My new assignment was to help prepare young men to be a part of that struggle. And so I reported to the air training command at Moody AFB in Valdosta, Georgia, ready to become an instructor pilot in the undergraduate pilot training program. But first things first—I would have to complete the primary instructor training (PIT) school located at Randolph

AFB in San Antonio, Texas. This fulfilled the unwritten rule that no one in the USAF can avoid spending some time in his or her career in the great state of Texas.

I subsequently found myself on the road to San Antonio with a fellow officer in need of the same training. We checked into the visiting officers' quarters and reported to the classroom for our first day. The goal of this school was not so much centered on flying the T-37, which was already familiar to all of us, but on how to "talk" about flying the airplane. Developing "diarrhea of the mouth" was the way one fellow officer put it. Each mission involved a PIT instructor playing the role of "student," while we, the prospective instructors, would practice our methods of imparting knowledge and skill to meet ATC standards in the cockpit. After a final check ride in which I never stopped talking (teaching?), I was graduated to return to Moody and to my first set of students. But I cannot leave this part of my story without saying something special about the city of San Antonio. Its history and beauty along the River Walk were most enjoyable, and I was fortunate to get back there on several occasions in the years that followed.

Back at Moody, I reported to my squadron and was immediately assigned a table with four students. Much had changed since I had gone through the UPT program. It was now a "pipeline" program, with much larger classes and a shortened syllabus. Classes of forty were now classes of a hundred and twenty. Much of the formation and navigation training had been eliminated in order to expedite pilots through the program to serve the Vietnam War effort. In retrospect, I was thankful for the training I had gone through, and I felt sorry for the current student pilots who were, in my mind, shortchanged.

My most difficult adjustment, coming from the war zone, was the emphasis on administrative detail. I was now responsible for maintaining four "grade books" for my students. Every training mission had to be chronicled with grades in various pencil colors, comments, recommendations, etc. It seemed somewhat ridiculous to me, but for my higher-ups, one mark of a good instructor was the condition of his grade books. I had to force myself to adopt that concept. As to the actual work with the students, it was most enjoyable. Students came in all descriptions; some already gifted aviators, some never having flown much at all, some with a desire to excel, and others with the attitude of just getting by. My job was to discover what technique to employ with each one in order to accomplish the mission goal.

For some reason, I always favored students from the South. Perhaps this attitude was based on some common core of heritage or culture that helped me communicate with them more readily. In any event, I always looked at the universities that incoming students had graduated from and jockeyed to get southern men assigned to my table, no prejudice intended. (Remember, my grandfather fought on the Union side).

The next few months developed into a routine, as I helped move my first class through the program. Brief, fly, debrief, fill out the grade book; brief, fly, debrief, fill out the grade book, etc. My technique in teaching these prospective pilots was patterned after the better instructors of my own training experience. I immediately identified tension and stress as the greatest detriments to becoming a proficient aviator. So I guess my approach, if it could have a label, would be considered easygoing and relaxed, with an attitude of, "Let's enjoy what we are doing." This approach was not for every student, but I was fortunate not to have many that needed to be screamed at or slapped on their flying helmets in order to facilitate learning.

The most enjoyable time, of course, was turning each student loose for his initial solo. This event was to replay my own experience, except that I now had to replay it from the IP point of view. Thus I spent many anxious moments in the mobile control cab, watching my student circle the aerodrome and praying that he would remember to lower his gear, would not get lost, and would return to earth without killing himself. Luckily, my instruction was sufficient to ensure survival, and there was much celebration back in the squadron ready room, followed by the customary dunking and the gift of spirits (Jack Daniels Black Label of course) from the celebrant to the instructor.

While the student was learning, I discovered that it was a learning experience for me also, raising my own flying skills and giving me a confidence (cockiness?) that I had not known before. The film, *Top Gun*, produced many years later, captured this attribute perfectly. I was surprised to discover that my role as a model instructor went beyond the cockpit. One day a fellow IP mentioned something about seeing one of my students out on the flight line. I asked him how he knew it was my student. He replied that the student was carrying his parachute just the way I did (by one shoulder strap over the right shoulder). I then realized that I was being watched and emulated more than I thought.

All in all, the training went smoothly, but there were some mishaps and some fatalities, though not all at Moody or in my squadron. At a western training base, a T-37 hit a sandhill crane in flight. The remains of the bird came through the windshield, killing the student instantly. Encounters with birds would continue to become an accident factor in future years, as the impact speeds increased and birds found their way into the intakes of jet engines. In another instance, an IP decided to give his student an unauthorized low-level tour of the Grand Canyon. They probably never saw the cable that stretched across the canyon and ripped the aircraft apart, killing them both instantly.

The worst accident that I became involved with did occur at Moody. It was a Sunday afternoon, and aircraft were returning from weekend cross-country training. Part of that training included formation landings for the students nearing graduation from basic training in the T-38 aircraft. As one formation of two was landing, the wingman overlapped his leader's wing, encountered the wake vortex coming off that wing, and flipped over on his back. The jet impacted the runway upside down and slid down the runway, grinding the cockpit canopy away and coming to rest in a ball of flames. There were no survivors. My role in this was that I was appointed as the student pilot's personal affairs officer, a duty that I found to be the most difficult of anything I had ever done. It involved dealing with a young, grieving widow, going through the man's personal effects, paying his outstanding debts, and "clearing him off the base" one last time, for a final check that we all must face. I was never so relieved to be done with a duty as I was that one.

But there were some humorous happenings as well. One Sunday, I was serving as officer of the day. This duty involved representing the commander for any activity that might arise concerning the mission of the base. Mainly, that involved hanging around base operations, watching the recovery of our cross-country aircraft. Suddenly the tower operator called operations, saying that an object had been spotted on the runway by a landing aircraft. As officer of the day, the job of inspecting the runway fell to me. I jumped into a base vehicle, and after establishing radio contact with the tower, drove out onto the runway in an effort to locate the object. A few hundred feet down the runway, I spotted a large gopher turtle slowly making an illegal runway crossing without clearance. As I helped expedite his crossing (perhaps to some love feast awaiting his arrival), I radioed the tower that we had a turtle on the runway. "Roger that," the tower replied. Within a few seconds, the excited voice of the wing commander came on the radio asking for verification that we had a "total" (accident) on the runway. I can only imagine the relief in his mind as I corrected the miscommunication.

As one of the few Vietnam veterans on base, my tenure as a "line IP" was short-lived. After a few months, I was singled out and reassigned to the 3550th Student Training Squadron. I would now have the duty of being the training officer for alternating classes of students entering primary flight training. In addition, I was to be the "primary" source for an academic course in counterinsurgency. I would teach this course at Moody, as my contemporaries would teach it to all students at all bases throughout the air training command. Naturally this triggered a need for more training.

I soon found my way back on the road to San Antonio and to academic instructor school at Randolph AFB. Now I would learn to be a "platform" instructor. After this militarily slanted "speech" class, in which I learned everything from how to use gestures to how to operate an overhead projector, I was soon on my way back to Moody and to my new duties. A fellow officer was headed back the same way, and he invited me to stay overnight with him and his parents, who lived in Crowley, Louisiana. He had a new Porsche sports car, and soon got tired of running formation with my old clunker Chevrolet. He raced ahead and was well into his wait for me as I arrived later in the day. I relate this incident for two reasons: first, because on this overnight visit, I was introduced to the finest Cajun food and best-tasting coffee (Community Dark Roast) that I had ever experienced; secondly, because this bright young officer, with the entire world before him, possessed within his body a form of Hepatitis, contracted in Vietnam, that was slowly destroying his liver. His wasting away and subsequent death was always a source of sorrow for me.

The next few months involved adjusting to my new responsibilities. I now had a cubicle office in a World War II vintage building, along with three other training officers (another for the T-37 primary phase and two for the T-38 basic training phase), a commander, and a secretary to handle the myriad of paperwork. I was now responsible for the overall training, discipline, and evaluation of alternating classes of student officers entering the UPT program through their having completed primary flight training in the T-37. In addition, I was charged with writing a study guide and lesson plans for teaching the counterinsurgency course.

Add to this the public relations events in the local community and the on-base wives orientation program, and you can imagine how time challenging the job was.

The most difficult part of the job was getting to know each student under my supervision and preparing a training report for each one at the completion of the primary phase. While I tried to fly with as many of my students as possible, time would simply not allow it. I often had to depend on comments from their respective IP and academic instructors to augment what little I could gather for myself, in order to come up with something objective. After writing each individual report, I then had to have a personal, private interview with each officer to critique his progress. While these reports were not included in each officer's permanent record (they were destroyed upon graduation) they did serve to prepare him for the all-important, annual efficiency report that he would encounter out in the "real" air force.

There were several disciplinary incidents that come to mind, relative to these classes of officers that came through during the succeeding months. They are humorous to me now, but at the time they could have had serious consequences. The first of these involved a student who, after having had too much to drink at the "O club" and experiencing a severe case of homesickness, decided in the wee hours of the morning to depart for home. He fired up his new car and sped up the highway toward town. My fellow T-37 training officer lived off base near this highway, at a place where it took a sharp curve. He related to me that he was awakened by a long squeal of braking tires, followed by a loud metallic crunch and then dead silence. Fearing the worst, and not knowing the incident involved a student pilot, he called the police, dressed, and went to the scene of the accident.

He described the scene as one large cedar tree resting in the back seat of the car, with the driver outside on the ground, throwing up and apparently unhurt. Luckily the car had swapped ends just before it hit the tree. Otherwise the student would have been crushed in the front seat. At about 4:00 a.m., I received a call from the chief of police, saying that he had one of my boys in the "drunk tank," and asking, "What do you want me to do with him?" I told the chief to let him sleep it off and that I would be down later in the morning to take him into custody.

If he went in like a lion, he came out like a lamb with head hanging as he saw me waiting for him. My approach to this situation could be best described as anger tempered by shaming, compassion, and the instillation of fear, not forgetting that the student pilot was lucky to be alive. The first stop, after getting him a shower and a change of uniform, was to the flight surgeon for a physical exam, to ensure that none of the last night's proceedings had impacted the young man's ability to continue in the program. Afterward, he was confined to quarters, except for training, and was placed on Report for Officer Training, as documentation in the event of any additional violations on his part. Such were part of my "wet nurse" duties as a training officer.

The second incident that comes to mind involved a student pilot by the name of Lt. Dunn. At the time, there was a travel restriction limit consisting of a fifty-mile radius from the air base for all students. Lt. Dunn and a buddy decided to ignore the limit and enjoy a weekend of sun and fun at the beach in the Jacksonville area, some ninety miles away. They would have gotten away with it too, if they had not overlooked one small detail. They skipped out of town without paying their motel bill. A few days later, a memo came down to me from the base commander, saying that a motel proprietor had contacted him about the unpaid bill and that I should investigate and correct the officers involved. It did not help that Lt. Dunn's name had come up previously for some other minor infractions, so I was pretty "steamed" by the time he reported to my office.

After he entered my cubicle, I did something that I had never done before. I had him stand at attention (in a "brace," as it was called), and putting my nose only a few inches from his, proceeded to give him the worst "chewing" I had ever given anyone. I told him that if I so much as heard his name come up in any future situation, I would have him transferred off the base within twenty-four hours and headed to supply officers' school (nothing against supply officers. It was just the only non-flying specialty I could think of at the time). Restricted to base, placed on Report for Officer Training, and lighter in the wallet for his beachside lodging, Lt. Dunn left the building with his ears burning. My fellow training officers, who were eavesdropping from adjacent cubicles, said that what went on even scared them, and they gave me a good kidding. It was "One and done for Lieutenant Dunn," I retorted. Interestingly, every student of mine who ran afoul of the rules straightened up and graduated successfully, receiving their wings and going on, I would suppose, to become fine officers and pilots. And as I mentioned previously, all the reports of their misdeeds were destroyed upon graduation, never to follow them on to the "real" air force.

My other duties involved being the coordinator for the "Red Carpet" and "Wives Orientation" programs. "Red Carpet" was the name given to a program that was hosted and funded by the local community, welcoming each UPT student and family to the area. My responsibility was to help coordinate this event, to arrange transportation, and to attend with my classes as they were scheduled. The event was held at an old fish camp on one of the large ponds in the area, among the cypress trees laden with Spanish moss. The fare was Southern in all aspects, the appetizer being a large bowl of cucumbers, tomatoes, and onions floating in vinegar. The idea was to fish some of that out and to eat it on a soda cracker. Actually it was rather tasty, if unconventional, and prepared the diner for the fried chicken that lay ahead. There was an open bar too, if you drank Bourbon, and a good time of food and drink was had by all. After the dinner, the mayor of Valdosta would give a short welcoming address, followed by the police chief and other local dignitaries. The wing commander or his representative would then say a few words, thanking the townspeople, and reminding the students to be good citizens during their training stay. I thought that it was a very worthwhile program for cementing the relationship between the base and the town, and I thoroughly enjoyed each such event that I attended.

The Wives Orientation program had been retained and was similar in most respects. After the flight program had been under way for a few weeks, the students' wives were invited to assemble at the officers' club for a luncheon and to hear welcoming remarks from the wing commander and from the president of the Officers' Wives Club. These were followed by short talks from the flight surgeon and physiological training officers, explaining to the wives the stresses on their husbands. The usual "dos and don'ts" were given, relative to their roles as wives of aspiring aviators. That is, don't serve beans and cabbage before sending him to the base to fly, give him time to study at home, don't get into a big fight before a check ride, and so on.

Afterward, I would usher the wives to a waiting bus for a trip to the flight line. Here we would visit the actual training environment, where they could see their husbands in action. This included stops at the Link trainer, the altitude chamber, the squadron briefing room, and a static display of the aircraft their husbands would be flying in pursuit of their wings. While I thought the program very beneficial, I did have to take some ribbing about squiring all those women around the base, and their presence was somewhat disruptive to whatever training was taking place.

And so it went for the next several months, as each class made its way into and out of the UPT program, feeding the pilot pipeline to support the war effort in Vietnam as well as the "Cold War" preparedness against the Soviet Union. My schedule became so routine and repetitive that I would sometimes hear myself briefing a flight or teaching a class while thinking of something else.

The one thing that served to break this duty routine was the cross-country training flight. As I have stated, airplanes were designed to "go somewhere" and not to "fly around the flagpole," the term used to describe local training flights. Serving as IP for a student cross-country flight was okay, but that involved teaching, and eventually ended up with students traveling to the same air bases. The real sought-after cross-country flight was one where two IPs could take a jet and go somewhere on a mission totally (or at least partially) unrelated to student training. I was able to get in on a couple of these "boondoggles," as they were called.

The one I best remember was a trip west with another IP, in a supersonic T-38 that replaced the old T-33 in the basic course of training. The "mission" was to travel to all UPT bases, where we would meet and coordinate with our contemporaries who were teaching the counterinsurgency course. How we got that approved is still beyond my understanding. But off we went for several days in the "hottest" jet in the inventory at the time, hopping from base to base, going "supersonic" at times, enjoying the amenities of each base, and having a handsome time "coordinating" with our contemporaries. To top it off, we got to spend a couple of extra days at what was called the "garden spot" of all UPT bases: Williams AFB near Phoenix, Arizona. There, on our arrival, we blew an air conditioning turbine, which necessitated maintenance and flight-testing on the aircraft before it could be released back to us. In this situation, we were in no big hurry. Moody could operate without us for a little longer, we thought, although we did get a few comments (tinged with flashes of jealousy) from those in command upon our return. "Where in _____ have you guys been?" was not an uncommon question. Did they not know that coordination takes time?

Author as USAF Captain 1966

Sometime in 1968, I can't remember an exact date, I took notice of a phenomenon I had not observed previously: The really "sharp" officers were putting in their paperwork to get out of the air force. It was not for lack of valor, because many, like me, had already served in Vietnam. And those who had not were not of the caliber to shirk any duty called for as a commissioned officer and pilot. No, this was more to do with the air force as a career, one that was a "dead end" for men who wanted to fly. The typical scenario was that after flying the line for a few years, the air force took the officer-pilot out of the cockpit and put him behind a desk—a poor place from which to aviate. Then, unless you could play the politics game in the higher ranks, the best you could hope for was to rise to and retire as a "bird" Colonel, a rank signified by an eagle on the uniform, the rank just below "brigadier" general. In addition, as the needs of the air force changed, periodic reductions in force (RIFs) took place, denying full retirement to both reserve and regular commission holders, usually at a time when they should be in their highest earning years.

Granted, all of these conditions existed, but what was the alternative that was moving so many to apply for this transition to civilian life? That could be summed up in the calling of one US industry, the commercial airlines. They were all looking for pilots. World War II veterans in the industry were aging and retiring. The industry anticipated unprecedented growth as it entered the jet age. Plus, the "freeze" that had been placed on the release of any military pilots had dried up the pool of available candidates. Now, with the country's commitment to wage war in Vietnam beginning to wane, the freeze had been lifted. The race was now on to supply the nation's airlines with the pilots they needed in order to operate and expand their businesses.

I had always thought of myself as a "career" officer. So it took me some time to convince myself that this was the move for me. I held a regular commission, I had combat time, and all my efficiency ratings were good. The air force had been good to me, and I felt certain that I could finish a career with good result. Still, I had to look at the lure of the economics and the stability that an airline career could offer. Finally, after much research and soul-searching, I made a decision. I would resign my commission and pursue an airline career.

CHAPTER ELEVEN

"DELTA DAWN"

As my fellow officers began leaving the air force to pursue careers in commercial aviation, I inherited from them a plethora of information on how they went about the process of obtaining employment and securing a starting class date with a major airline. This information included employment applications, addresses, specific requirements, sample tests, and books to guide the prospect through the hiring pipeline. After devouring all of this information, I prepared and sent my applications and inquiries to all of the major air carriers as well as to the so-called "regional" carriers. I also journeyed to Atlanta, to the campus of Georgia Tech University, to take the "Stanine Exam." The results of this exam were required by some airlines and were an attempt to measure one's aptitude for becoming an airline pilot. While it did measure some things applicable to flying, such as reaction times and symbol recognition, I thought it somewhat comical that you had to know what wine to serve with certain foods and to know what "truffles" were. Were we to be purveyors of food and drink as well?

In the meantime, I began to "finagle" for a separation date from the air force. The freeze on "getting out" had been lifted, but I had incurred an additional time obligation by receiving additional training as an academic instructor. It looked like it would be late 1969 before I could be released. With all airlines hiring heavily in the spring and summer of 1969, I was afraid I would "miss the boat" in that hiring cycle. But what was I to do? It was here that a stroke of luck (one of many that were to follow) came my way. I had accrued sixty days of leave, and after finding an understanding fellow officer in Personnel, I convinced the air force to allow me to take this leave as "terminal leave," effectively backing up my separation date by two months. With that "indulgence" secured, I updated my airline employment applications and advertised myself as being available in September of 1969. I learned later that permission to take terminal leave was disapproved shortly after my departure and that my name was "mud" in the Moody AFB Personnel department for some time after.

While I was willing to consider employment from any air carrier at that time, I particularly wanted to go to work for Pan American Airways. I had seen their operation in the Pacific, operating out of most of the islands, and was most impressed with the uniforms and the gleaming Boeing 707s the pilots flew. It did not take long, however, to discover that such images did not necessarily equate with an airline that was a good one to work for. After I did some "talking around," it became obvious just how little I knew about commercial air aviation. Labor disputes, furloughs, unions—all of these were foreign terms to me at the time. It did not take long to discover that Delta Airlines was the one to go with, if it was possible, with American, Eastern, Continental, and Northwest as other considerations. Was my destiny tied to any of these? I had no idea.

When the job offers did not immediately begin to roll in, I became a little nervous and began to back up my airline applications with inquiries to other related industries. In fact, my first job interview was with the Singer Corporation, who built the "Link" trainers that I had learned to hate. But I was willing to set that aside if it meant gainful employment. I traveled to Orlando, Florida, for the interview, and while it went fairly well, the prospect of relocating to White Plains, New York, as a salesman was not immediately appealing. I would take my chances with "real" aviation. I also applied for some Air National Guard slots as a civilian instructor in various types of older propeller-driven aircraft. While I did get one response from a New York Air National Guard unit flying ancient C-119 "flying boxcars," it failed to offer much encouragement.

The first response to my inquiries came from Northwest Orient Airlines, with instructions to report to their headquarters in Minneapolis for an interview. They sent me a round-trip ticket, which began with the short hop on Southern Airways (a Martin 404) to Atlanta, connecting with Northwest (a Boeing 720) on to Minneapolis. It so happened that I had a student officer in one of my classes who was from Minneapolis. He learned of my trip and contacted his parents, who insisted that they would pick me up at the airport and provide me lodging the night prior to my interview. This all went like clockwork. I arrived on a beautiful sunny day and got a brief tour of the city, a home-cooked meal, and a comfortable bed for the night, before being delivered to the corporate headquarters of Northwest Orient Airlines.

After a short wait in the lobby, I was greeted by a personnel representative, who took me back to his office to review my application, to check my logbook, and to administer an additional exam. Afterward, I was ushered into the office of the chief of Flight Operations, who sat behind a large mahogany desk in very opulent surroundings. He was rather businesslike in telling me about the expansion plans of Northwest and how I would most likely be a captain within four years. His main question to me was why I didn't seek employment from some of the southern-based airlines, seeing that I was from Georgia. I replied that I felt that Northwest presented a great opportunity, and that I thought Minneapolis, what part I had seen of it, was a grand city. This seemed to satisfy him, as he abruptly ended the interview by standing, offering his handshake, and ushering me to the door with the statement that I would be hearing from them soon.

I hopped aboard the company shuttle to the terminal in a total state of exhilaration. I had the promise of a job with an expanding company in a beautiful city. What else could be better? When I arrived at the departure gate, the crew was just arriving. I introduced myself to the flight engineer, who invited me to go out on the ramp with him to preflight the Boeing 720 for the flight to Atlanta. Now I *was* in "hog heaven." This was the cherry on top of the whipped cream. I was so impressed with the front office and now, here I was, actually on the ramp, helping to preflight one of their sleek jets. But the flight engineer was a rather somber fellow, who broke my bubble somewhat. He said that not all was rosy with Northwest. It was a "union" airline, and there was constant friction between the various labor groups and management. He recommended that I not close off any other avenues with other carriers. I filed this away as I reviewed my experience on the flight back to Atlanta.

Arriving back in Atlanta, I had a rather lengthy layover before my flight to Valdosta. I wandered up around the ticket counters and struck up a conversation with a Delta agent. He urged me to walk over to the Delta general offices and initiate the pilot hiring process for employment, since Delta was in the process of a major expansion. I had nothing better to do, so I took his advice and made the short walk across the ramp to a low-slung brick building, where I was guided to the rather cramped and unglamorous office of the vice president of operations. I filled out the usual employment application, took a short "elimination exam," and was ushered into the inner office of the vice president himself. He was an older man with a disability, who had been a pilot at one time, but he now had the responsibility of screening potential pilot applicants. He had little to say as he thumbed through my logbook, advised me to keep my application updated, and dismissed me to return to the terminal. Compared to the Northwest experience, I was little impressed, as I weighed the options on the flight back to Valdosta.

In August of 1969, I received a letter from Northwest, hiring me into an October class and containing instructions to report to the Mayo Clinic for a physical evaluation. While it was satisfying to know that I had passed the hiring process for Northwest, I had seen by this point that Delta was the only way to go. Consequently, I began "bugging" Delta Personnel on a regular basis. Finally, the thing I had most hoped for came in the mail—a letter inviting me to join the Delta family, with class date beginning September 12, 1969. I quickly responded with an acceptance and invoked my plan to take terminal leave and make the class starting date. The key to this plan was having the squadron administrative sergeant "sign me out" on my separation date, almost a month later in October. A bottle of his favorite beverage was given as an incentive not to forget his responsibility to perform the task.

* * *

The class of sixty new-hires that came together at the CDC Training Building in Hapeville, Georgia on September 12, 1969, was composed almost entirely of military-trained veterans of the Vietnam conflict. The average age was thirty years. Because of our relatively advanced age, it was evident that we would never advance to the top of the pilots' seniority list. In fact, we were destined to fly copilot for many captains who were younger than we were. There were no "sour grapes," however. We were all just glad to be there and on the seniority list.

There was one last hurdle to the hiring process that each of us had to get by, which was the interview with the company psychiatrist. Rumor had it that he was the final authority on whether or not you joined the Delta family. He had a variety of chairs in front of his desk, and it was said that the one you chose had a great impact on his decision. So it was with some trepidation that I reported to his office, where I was ushered in and advised to have a seat. Sure enough, before his desk stood a rocker, an easy chair, and a straight chair. I took a seat in the straight chair, and after a few minutes, the psychiatrist came in to meet me. We shook hands and engaged in some "small talk" about my background as a UT graduate. (Andrew Holt, President Emeritus of UT, was on the Delta Board of Directors at the time.) The psychiatrist then stood up, thanked me for my Vietnam service, shook my hand once again, and ushered me out of the office. I felt strongly that I had secured his stamp of approval, but never knew if my chair selection was a factor. I did hear that one candidate had gotten into a verbal spat with the good doctor and was turned down for employment.

The first week of training was taken up primarily with getting all of our publications and study materials, being measured for uniforms, and ordering flight kits. The seniority list for the class was published, and I was listed as number one, based on my initial contact date with the company. But I was startled the next day, when it was announced that there was a change to the seniority list. It seemed that another member of the class thought that he had made initial contact with the company before I had. He contacted the Personnel office, the records were checked, and it was determined that he was correct. He was now number one, and I was number two. While it did not bother me at the time or have any material effect on my career, I had not yet come to realize how important one seniority number could be.

Other than class time, the biggest challenge was finding a place to live during training. Most of the class elected to go with "crash pad" apartments, with five or six guys sharing the space. I teamed together with another classmate, Elisha Patrick (Pat) Weaver, and found a two-bedroom apartment almost within walking distance of the training center. Pat and I had a unique arrangement. I would do the cooking while he studied, and he would do the cleaning up while I did the same. I remember hearing him in the kitchen late, still cleaning up after my culinary efforts. Pat did get me into trouble with his wife, Lou, when I met her some time afterward. He had told her that her cornbread was not up to what I had baked, and this did not sit well, although it was treated with great humor. Pat was a good friend, and we have maintained contact into our retirement years.

After an initial week of orientation, the aircraft and base assignments were posted, based on our choices, with seniority as the primary factor. The jobs for which we were hired were as flight engineers or "second officers" on either the Douglas DC-8 or the Convair 880, both four-engine turbojets. The Delta crew bases in those days were Atlanta, Dallas, New Orleans, Houston, and Chicago. I elected to stay in Atlanta to train on the DC-8 and was so assigned. The class was then divided, half to the DC-8 and half to the 880.

Flight Engineer Class, September 1969. Author front row, far left.

Our class of thirty or so now began the quest for the Turbojet Engineer License, the "ticket" we needed in order to perform the job for which we were hired. Preparation for the written exam and advancement to simulator and aircraft training would be all classroom work, while issuance of the license would come upon passing an FAA oral exam and a check ride on the DC-8. For the next six weeks, we plunged into the world of FAA Regulations, aircraft systems, weight and balance requirements, and so on, at the end of which we were administered the exam covering all this material. Although I don't remember my score, I did pass. More importantly, I took the advice of my instructor and reported to the local FAA office to take the air transport rating (ATR) written exam, which covered much of the same material and which would be required if and when I came up for promotion to captain. This was advice well taken. Although the test was difficult and covered some areas in which I had little background, I did score a seventy-nine. (Seventy was passing.) This test result was still valid twelve years later, at the time I reached my captaincy, and it kept me from having to take the exam at that time.

The next phase of training was the DC-8 simulator, where I was introduced to "normal" procedures, "abnormal" procedures, and "emergency" procedures in operating the flight engineer's panel. Most pilots say that over the course of a flying career, there is one aircraft that stands out as the one you knew best. For me it was the C-130E in my air force days, but here, it was the Douglas DC-8. She was the "queen of the fleet" at the time, beautifully engineered and beloved by all who flew her. I was fortunate to fly both the engineer's seat and the first officer (copilot) seat later on in my career. I believe that, as of this writing, I could still sit down and "work the panel "at the flight engineer position. First officer was a "dream" position in many ways, but you earned your pay when you had to handle her in a crosswind. The DC-8 had no hydraulic boost to move the controls, having only a system of wires tied to each control surface. I have seen the sweat pouring off the brow of many a first officer (myself included) as they wrestled the control wheel, trying to hold in a crosswind correction. But I digress.

After the pressure of training in the simulator environment, I was scheduled for my oral exam with an examiner from the Federal Aviation Administration (FAA). This was my first oral exam, and I was duly nervous. The two of us sat down with the DC-8 aircraft manual. He began to flip through the manual, asking me questions on various systems and operating procedures.

After a few minutes of this, he said, "Let's go get a cup of coffee." After a long break, we resumed the process for a few minutes, after which he slammed the aircraft manual shut and said, "See you on the airplane." I breathed a sigh of relief. It was over, just like that. What I did not realize was that Delta would never have put me up for the oral exam if I had not known the material "cold."

The next day, I reported to the "old hangar" area of the airport ramp, located behind the Delta general offices area. There sat a DC-8, designated for our use that day as a "trainer." Assembled there were flight instructors, flight engineer instructors, candidates for pilot and flight engineer positions, and the FAA examiner who would sign the "tickets" granting the ratings, if all went well. All flight training took place in the actual aircraft, in those days. Later on, with the further development of simulators, all training, including the FAA "rating ride," was done solely in simulators. I always thought it quite odd that a pilot could receive a rating authorizing him to fly an aircraft without ever having set foot aboard the actual aircraft. The company loved simulators because they did not have to pull an aircraft "off the line" to accommodate training. The pilots, on the other hand, hated simulators (how many times do I have to say this?), partly because it was never considered the "real" aircraft, but mostly because of the compound emergency situations to which you could be subjected without killing everyone aboard.

Because the pilot senior to me was also getting his flight check, he got in the seat first. As always, this was an advantage in that I could observe him while he performed the procedures that I was soon to accomplish myself. I don't remember which airport was selected for our "pattern" work that morning, but it was usually a nearby "unbusy" airport that could handle the multiple approaches and landings that had to be accomplished. It was usually Huntsville, Alabama, or Augusta, Georgia, or it could be one of several other possibilities, depending on the weather. In any event, the flight went well. Every candidate received his appropriate license and began his love affair with the DC-8. I finally was certified to do the job for which I was hired.

But wait! There was still more training to undergo. Although now certified, I had to accomplish several hours of on-the-job training, riding with a line-experienced flight engineer, before I could be turned loose on my own. I would occupy the flight engineer seat, with the regular engineer looking over my shoulder and offering tips to ease the transition from the training environment to actual line flying. It was here that I began to understand the sometimes vast difference between the two, the former being a hectic environment of aircraft "nuts and bolts," emergency and abnormal procedures, and nervous tension, and the other being a relaxed, professional atmosphere of doing a job. I was always amazed when some of my fellow pilots elected to trade the latter for the former and transfer to the training department. Those who elected to do so for extended periods, even for more pay and better working conditions, were never considered "real" pilots by those who flew the line. What pilot skills they possessed rapidly deteriorated in the training environment, and they were finally required to rotate back to the line to rehone those skills. It was the dread of every flight engineer and copilot to hear the words, "I'm your captain for this trip. I'm out of the training department." The smart ones would also add, "I'm a little rusty, so help me out."

One of the requirements of the on-the-job line training was to make certain that we flew every model of the DC-8 that Delta operated, which, at the time, amounted to three models. First was the DC-8-51, the original model purchased by Delta. Next was the DC-8-61, the "stretch" version with improved systems and passenger carrying capacity.

Lastly was the DC-8-33 owned by Pan American Airways and flown by the pilots of both airlines, in what was known as the Delta-Pan Am Interchange. A Delta crew would pick up the aircraft at Washington Dulles Airport and fly it domestically, while a Pan Am crew flew a Delta aircraft to London. Pan Am was the primary carrier on the routes to London and beyond, and it was hoped that by entering into this interchange agreement, Delta would be considered for an award to fly the route in the future. Pan Am, for its part, was anxious to add to its domestic routes.

Dubbed the "Chinese Bandit" because of the Pan Am paint scheme, this DC-8 model was a whole different animal, with an entirely different cockpit and system engineering. The level of Pan Am maintenance was also not up to Delta standards, so there were usually a great number of "maintenance carryovers," and the aircraft in general was in shoddy, although airworthy, condition. Although the DC-8-33 was covered in ground school "differences," it was always an unpleasant experience to find one of those sitting at your gate. But at last, every training requirement was met, and I became a full-fledged turbo-jet flight engineer, with the license to prove it. It was December 1969, and my career as an airline pilot was about to begin.

* * *

Upon being released to crew scheduling after completing my training, I was assigned a "reserve line" for the month as a DC-8 flight engineer. Reserve line holders were very junior pilots who did not have enough seniority to hold a "regular line" with a defined monthly schedule showing the exact flights the pilot would fly. A reserve line holder had defined off days only. The remainder of the time, he was "on call" to fly any trip that could not be covered by the regular line holders. Their inability to cover a trip could be due to sickness, training, vacation, etc. Being "on the hook" as a reserve line holder was not the best duty, due to the uncertainty of "when you would go". Also, most of the trips, or "rotations," were not the better ones on the schedule. It was the goal of every pilot to hold a regular line, or at least a portion of a regular line, for the coming month. Again, seniority was everything.

I did not have long to wait for a "call out" for my first trip, and I remember it distinctly. It called for me to "deadhead" (ride in the cabin as a passenger) to Detroit, link up with the captain and first officer in the crew lounge, and man the flight engineer position back to Atlanta. All went smoothly, and I was well received by the captain, Harold McEver (who was a relative of Gene McEver, an all-American football player at the University of Tennessee back in the 1930s). I was a little tense and nervous at first. Sitting in the flight engineer's seat, I was prepared for what I thought would be the inevitable emergency or abnormal event. Sensing my apprehension, the first officer (probably at the suggestion of the captain) turned around sometime during flight and said to me, "Relax, nothing is going to happen." Although I refused to believe that completely, he was right. Relaxed, though vigilant, became my approach, and as he said, nothing major ever "happened" on the engineer's panel in all the days of my manning that position.

That doesn't mean, however, that there was no excitement along the way. One morning, after a layover in Detroit, another DC-8 crew, along with ours, was transported to Detroit Wayne County Airport in order to fly two different trips. We were bound for Atlanta, while the other crew was headed to Miami. After breakfasting together at one of the most favorite employee cafeterias on the system (giant pancakes were the specialty), we two flight engineers headed out to the concourse to preflight our respective aircraft, which were parked at adjacent gates. All went routinely as we pushed back and taxied out together. We were the first to depart, and I had just sent our departure time to Delta's company radio, when the voice of my counterpart onboard the other DC-8 came over the air in my headset. "Atlanta Radio, this is Delta Flight_____. There is a man in the cockpit holding a gun to my head. He says he wants to go to Havana, Cuba, and we're going to take him." This was the closest I came to being hijacked during my career. The sad thing was that security measures were beginning to go into place, and things would never be the same again.

Another incident that comes to mind in reference to my duty as a DC-8 flight engineer occurred one morning in Atlanta. All preflight duties were completed, the passengers had been boarded, and we were just waiting on the final paperwork and dispatch by the gate agent. Suddenly the first-class flight attendant appeared on the flight deck and announced that she could not rouse one of her passengers, who had just been seated only a few minutes prior. This well-dressed elderly woman had simply taken her seat, turned her head to the window, and died. Medics were summoned, and after their unsuccessful efforts at resuscitation, she was pronounced dead in the Jetway (the covered passageway leading from the gate to the plane). One reason I so remember this incident is that the captain wanted the medic's report to indicate that the lady died in the Jetway and not on the airplane. Otherwise there might be some culpability on his or Delta's part, and besides, there was a lot of paperwork involved if a passenger died on your airplane. Having been assured that his wishes would be followed, the captain called for the door to be shut, and we departed, a little shaken by the episode, but philosophical that life and air transportation must go on.

A third incident that I distinctly remember involved an early morning preflight inspection of a DC-8, again in Atlanta. One of the required items to be checked was the "nacelle" or front opening of each engine, checking for nicks in the fan blades, obstructions, and so on. The engines on the left side (engines number one and two) were free and clear, but when I shined my flashlight into the number three nacelle on the right side, I was shocked. Blood, guts, feathers, and bones surrounded the entire intake. Apparently, whoever flew the aircraft inbound had encountered a flock of birds on final approach and had landed without realizing what had happened. Maintenance personnel, who normally did an abbreviated postflight inspection, had also missed the problem. After arriving on the scene, maintenance control grounded the aircraft, and Operations cancelled the flight. I learned later that the engine had to be changed. As mentioned previously, bird ingestion was becoming a serious concern in this era of jet aviation, and several accidents with great loss of life were attributed to this cause. Although I experienced a few "bird-strikes" in the years that followed, this incident was the closest I came to a serious, undesired meeting in the air with my feathered friends.

From November of 1969 through May of 1970, I was settling into my job as a DC-8 flight engineer. Delta was hiring heavily at the time, and the prospects of "moving up" to fly better trips were very good, as pilots who were junior to me were added to the seniority list. It was at that time that I received one of those "shocks" that often comes with an airline career. I walked into crew scheduling one day and wandered over to check the bulletin board. To my amazement, my name was listed among those who had been awarded a first officer bid on the DC-9! How could this be? I was just learning the job for which I was hired, only to be put back into the training environment to learn another. What had happened was that a DC-9 bid had been posted, and not enough pilots senior to me had filled out the positions.

When that happened, the provisions of the labor contract called for the bid to be filled by the most junior pilots in the base, one of whom was me. I had been "drafted" involuntarily for a position no one else wanted! To understand that, you would have to know how hard a DC-9 copilot had to work and how "miserable" the trips were out of the Atlanta base. As one fellow pilot put it, you were "busier than a one-armed paper hanger," flying trips that were primarily on the "backside of the clock," that is, between midnight and 6:00 a.m. And I was going to do this for $550 a month? In retrospect, it was good that I was able to occupy a "front seat" pilot position so early in my career, but it must be said that I earned every penny, and then some, of my "probationary" salary.

Before I relate my experience with the Douglas DC-9, let me say that as every pilot has a favorite aircraft that he flew, conversely, he has one that he detested. For me, the DC-9 was the latter. Perhaps this stemmed from the way I was introduced to it, or the trips I had to fly, or how hard I had to work, or the short time that I was on the aircraft. Most likely, it was a combination of all these.

My "upgrade" to first officer on the DC-9 followed the usual pattern: ground school and simulator training in Atlanta, flight training set up in Jackson, Mississippi, and the appropriate hours of on-the-job training on the line, with the regular first officer looking over my shoulder. Coming off the engineer's seat on the DC-8, this was a major transition. The training department had developed "flow patterns" to help with the multitasking that had to be accomplished in the DC-9 cockpit during line operation. This involved moving one's hand from panel to panel, activating or deactivating the appropriate switches, buttons, and other controls as they were called for, and backing it all up with the checklist after the fact. I had gotten pretty good with this technique and was intent on impressing the first officer on my first on-the-job training ride out of Atlanta. All went well, to my thinking, and after we landed at our first destination, he was quite complimentary.

"By the way," he asked, "what time did we leave the gate in Atlanta?" I had completely forgotten my additional duty to note "time out, time off, time on, and time in" for the flight and to transmit those times to the company. "Don't worry," he said with a smile, "I covered for you. You'll catch up with the airplane before long." There is nothing like embarrassment to keep you from making the same mistake twice. And so it was that I did "catch up with the airplane," and things became easier after that.

That was not the end of my embarrassments, however. Another occurred on one of my first flights after being released to the line. I usually signed in early, checked the gate of departure, and proceeded on out to do the preflight procedures, so as not to be rushed. I noted that the departure gate was gate 50. The old Atlanta terminal rotunda that served this gate had one Jetway that actually led to two gates, Gate 50A and Gate 50B. I glanced outside and saw a DC-9 sitting at Gate 50B, and I assumed this to be my aircraft. I preflighted that aircraft like no other, stationed myself in the cockpit, and had everything done. All the captain had to do was walk in and sit down, and we were ready to roll.

But I noticed after awhile that there was no activity on the airplane—no flight attendants boarding, no passengers, no agents, etc., and it was coming up to departure time shortly. I looked over at Gate 50A and noticed that another DC-9 was now positioned there. I suddenly experienced a deep sinking feeling. Had I preflighted the wrong aircraft? I rushed up the Jetway to the "Y" separating the two gates, and pushed past the boarding passengers. Stepping into the cockpit, I encountered a very irate captain who wanted to know, "Where the hell have you been?" It was five minutes before departure. While contacting crew scheduling to ascertain my whereabouts, he had had to do all the preflight procedures himself. I tried to explain myself, but he just said, "Sit down and help me get this flight off the gate. We'll talk about it later." I finally caught up with him, and the flight departed normally. Later, we both got a big laugh out of what had happened, but there was not much humor involved at the time. Needless to say, I became an expert at reporting to the correct gate and preflighting the correct aircraft.

One management philosophy that was instrumental to the success of Delta Airlines was known as the "hub and spoke" system. Smaller aircraft, like the DC-9, would make up the "spokes," shuttling passengers and cargo from smaller outlying stations into the "hubs" like Atlanta or Dallas. There, these same passengers and cargo would be transferred to larger aircraft, like the DC-8, and would be flown to the "hub" nearest their final destination. "Spoke" aircraft would then complete the process. While the larger aircraft might fly one-to-four "legs" a day, it was not unusual for the "spoke" aircraft to fly up to ten or twelve "legs" a day. This was a lot of "up and down" and a lot of work. As I began to gain experience in this new position, I learned quickly to "stay ahead of the aircraft" and of the captain, through anticipation and planning. The long, relaxing flights on the DC-8 were over, at least for the foreseeable future.

In addition, I began to learn about being a captain one day. It never ceased to amaze me how captains knew just what to do in certain situations. What I came to realize much later was that the captain had already seen that situation back somewhere in his career and was merely acting based on experience. One incident comes to mind that made a big impression on me, relative to a captain exercising his authority—one I never forgot, and was to use on more than one occasion. We were flying the DC-9 into Miami one afternoon, with thunderstorms all around. Air traffic control, whose personnel comprised a powerful union with a somewhat arrogant attitude in those days, had almost convinced the nation's pilot group that they had absolute power over what aircraft could do and could not do when under their control. This meant not deviating from a prescribed route, regardless of weather. That idea was gaining momentum until a controller denied the request of a Southern Airlines DC-9 to deviate around a thunderstorm near Atlanta one afternoon. Entering the storm, the crew lost control of the aircraft, "over-temped" the engines, causing them to seize, and attempted to land on a two-lane highway, with loss of the aircraft and of all souls onboard. The timeframe of the incident I am recalling was not long after that accident.

As we approached Miami, it was obvious that our flight path would take us directly into the center of a large thunderstorm cell just ahead. The captain told me to advise Miami Center that we would need to deviate around that cell, which I did. "Negative, negative Delta, you must remain on course," came the reply, in a not so friendly tone. When the captain heard this, he turned to me and calmly said, "Advise the controller that we are starting a right-hand turn to reverse course and will enter a holding pattern at this position." I relayed that message to the controller, who came back with "No, no, Delta, don't do that! Roll out on your present heading and continue west around the cell. Report when you are clear to resume course." That we did, and after navigating around the storm, we landed safely in Miami. I learned much about who was really in control that day.

Not long after this incident, the controller union went out on strike. President Reagan declared this strike illegal and fired all those who refused to report back to work. That firing rid the controller ranks of nearly all of those who were hard to work with. The new hires had a much more cooperative attitude and rarely denied a request to deviate around weather.

A close-to-home tragedy is the most memorable event of my days on the DC-9. It is very hard to imagine now, but at one time, there was absolutely no security at the nation's airports. Passengers simply checked outsize baggage and proceeded directly to the departure gate with whatever they wanted to carry on the aircraft. With the hijackings of the early 1970s, security measures began to be put into place, a little at a time, and were very inconsistent throughout the system. One of the first measures established was referred to as "at the gate" security. A security guard was posted at the point of boarding in order to screen carry-on baggage for illicit items that might be used in a hijacking attempt. One airport where this measure was in place at the time was the Baltimore-Washington International Airport.

One evening a Delta DC-9 was in the process of boarding a flight when a deranged man in the boarding line pulled out a gun, killed the security guard, and proceeded down the Jetway. Entering the cockpit, he shot and killed the copilot. He then pointed the gun at the captain and ordered him to take off, with the aim of flying the DC-9 into the White House. When the captain refused to comply, the gunman shot him through the body, ordered the boarding door closed, and took the aircraft and its passengers hostage.

Meanwhile, a SWAT team was called to the scene to confront the situation. One member of the team, stationed in the Jetway, took note of the small access window on the front boarding door. This window was used by the flight attendants to confirm the positioning of the Jetway upon arrival, before opening the door for deplaning. Stationing himself at the right angle, he was able to see inside the aircraft and locate the gunman, who was standing near the front door. With one well-placed shot from the SWAT team member through this tiny window, the gunman was killed, and the incident came to a conclusion.

This event, however, sent chills throughout the industry and the nation, leading to further steps toward the security systems in place today. But I remember this event in a more personal way. The murdered copilot, who never had a chance, could easily have been me, as this incident involved an Atlanta crew flying an Atlanta base trip. I had even flown with the captain, who was now in critical condition and fighting for his life, his career apparently over.

But what I most remember is the next night in Columbia, South Carolina, on the trip I was flying. We were due an aircraft change in Columbia on this particular rotation, and sitting at the gate was the very same DC-9 involved in the incident the day before. Entering the cockpit, I noted that new seat cushions had been installed. What I did not notice or recognize immediately were the bloodstains on the cockpit floor, bloodstains from the crew, which had not been caught during the cockpit cleanup. Flying that DC-9 on that night was a very eerie experience. Was the world going crazy? Would I be involved in a similar scenario in the future? Time would tell. But a pleasing footnote to this event occurred several years later. After multiple surgical procedures, months of rehabilitation therapy, and unending hassle with the FAA, the captain of that ill-fated flight returned to full flight status, with much applause from the pilot group.

One last memory of the DC-9 I call "the worst landing I ever made in a flying machine" event. Kansas City Downtown Airport was the scene of the "crime." This outdated airport was still in use in the early 1970s while Kansas City International was being constructed, well west of the city. The approach was very steep, to a runway sitting down in a "hole" alongside the river. In limited visibility conditions, the approach was known as the "Rudy Patrick approach," so named because the final approach course flew over a large hardware store, on the roof of which was emblazoned the name "Rudy Patrick Hardware." If you saw this, you knew you were on course.

It was my first time going into this airport at the controls, and I was a little tense. The weather was clear, with gusty winds, as I descended rapidly toward the end of the short runway, trying to stay "on speed" in order to get the DC-9 stopped in the shortest distance possible. As the end of the runway came up, I abruptly pulled the nose of the aircraft up and "wiped the power" off. Unfortunately, the DC-9 was still ten feet or so in the air at the time and ceased immediately to be a flying machine. Like an elevator dropping from the second story, the aircraft contacted the concrete with a bone jarring impact that must have severely tested the structural integrity of the ship's design.

The captain inquired, "What happened there?" He slowly taxied to the gate, agreeing to keep the cockpit door closed until all the passengers were deplaned, in order to spare my embarrassment. That did not work for the two stewardesses, however, as they gave me some grief for the rest of the trip. Lesson learned? "On speed," with a DC-9, was a bad landing waiting to happen. On that aircraft, and on every one I flew thereafter, I always added a few knots of airspeed, as one fellow pilot put it, "for mom and the kids."

I didn't know it, but my days on the DC-9 were about to end. Exigencies of the company, I was told. Checking the bulletin board for the "latest" one day, I learned that my DC-9 first officer position had been eliminated and that I was now reassigned to a first officer position on the Lockheed L-100, the civilian equivalent of my old air force friend, the four-engine turboprop C-130 Hercules. Delta had leased three of these aircraft to replace their old propeller-driven C-46s of World War II vintage. Pilots who had flown those "antiques" always remembered wearing their raincoats backwards to stay dry while aviating through rain showers. At that time, Delta was trying to get out of flying cargo, but still maintained a separate air-freight department to service a few special customers.

There were a lot of factors associated with flying freight at that time, and most of them were bad. Any semblance of a firm schedule was "out the window," as in, "This aircraft will be ready to leave when we get it loaded, so stop bugging us," from load planning and operations. It reminded me of my air force experience in MATS, wherein we changed that acronym from Military Air Transport Service to "Might Arrive Tomorrow Sometime." Mechanics hated the aircraft, as in, "We don't get much training on this bird, but we'll check with Lockheed to see what we need to do." Maintenance was all smiles when we brought one in with no "write-ups" in the ship's log.

Then there was the rule that freight moves only at night. Nearly all flying was on the "backside of the clock," that is, between midnight and

5:00 a.m. Cabin service was nonexistent, and so we had to pack a "lunch" or hitch a ride into the passenger terminal of our "turnaround" station, in hopes of finding an all-night snack bar. I will never forget the 2:00 a.m. trip into the terminal at Chicago O'Hare to get a "Thuringer" hot dog, one that would stay with you longer than you wanted. As to the actual flying, the aircraft was still noisy and limited to a speed of 250 knots, which was slow by jet traffic standards. This made us unpopular with air traffic control, who nearly always had to redirect other traffic around us. The altitudes we flew—usually twenty-two to twenty-eight thousand feet—were not high enough to avoid the weather. So we were in for a rough ride when weather was forecast along our route of flight. With very few exceptions, there were no layovers; most trips were turnarounds to freight terminals in Chicago and Newark, with stops in Memphis and Charlotte.

Cargo ranged from live animals to auto parts to any "outsize" cargo that would not fit into the belly of a passenger jet. Containerized cargo had not come onto the scene at this juncture. I remember one special trip to San Francisco to pick up a racehorse that had been shipped all the way from Australia. In Atlanta, he must have welcomed the sight of the horse trailer and the end of his long journey, as he was led off the aircraft on wobbly legs.

With all of the "bad" of flying freight, what, if any, was the "good" in my situation? For one thing, I was able to keep my "hand on the wheel" as a first officer, and secondly, as one captain put it, "Freight don't talk back."

Flight training on the L-100 was minimal, and the check ride was easy, since I had flown the aircraft before. These three aircraft were "B" models, without the extended range tanks under the wings. They were set up for maximum cargo loads, using aluminum pallets and a "rail system," whereby each pallet was lifted onto rollers, slid forward into place in the cargo compartment, and locked into the rail. This made for easier loading and unloading by eliminating the need for large, hard to work with tie-down straps.

Though we did wear our uniforms, flying the L-100 was very informal. Nonissue items were the norm, such as baseball caps to help cushion the heavy headsets we had to wear, heavy winter coats, and so on. At least we did not have to wear raincoats, as I mentioned earlier relative to flying the C-46. For entertainment, we were not immune to moving the dial of our low frequency radio to the AM broadcast band to search for a ballgame or a good music station. I remember one captain who had a favorite Chicago station that played the "hits" of the 1930s and that advertised a particular beer. We would cruise along listening to Gene Austin singing "My Blue Heaven" and other songs of that era, until the signal faded. Once I even brought my guitar along in order to work on my chords and to have a sing-along over the roar of the engines.

My most memorable event connected with the L-100 occurred on the night of December 11, 1970. We were inbound to Atlanta after a stop in Memphis, when the nose of the L-100 pitched up rapidly and violently. The captain yelled for me to join him on the control wheel, to help push forward on the control column. Seeing that we were losing the battle, I lodged my knee between the control column and the seat to help overcome the force. This stopped the pitch-up moment, and after we slowed the aircraft, we managed to reduce the force to a point where we regained control. What had happened was that the "trim tab," a small flap on the trailing edge of the elevator, which was used to zero out pressure on the control column, had run away full "nose up." This could easily have pitched the aircraft up into a stall, resulting in loss of control. Based on more favorable weather in Atlanta and on the fact that we could fly the aircraft at reduced speed, we elected to press on to Atlanta after we transmitted our intentions to Delta Flight Control and requested crash equipment to stand by on arrival. As it turned out, the landing was normal, and we breathed a sigh of relief as we rolled out on the runway with the fire trucks chasing us, their rotating red lights flashing. Loss of control is a pilot's greatest fear, and we had come close. A sore knee was a small price to pay for what could have been a major disaster and the end of my short airline career.

Once again, the changing needs of Delta came into play, and my position as a first officer on the L-100 was soon canceled. I would now revert to the position for which I was hired: flight engineer on the DC-8. This was accomplished with very little retraining, and I soon discovered that I had built up a little seniority in this position since my absence. Shortly thereafter, I was offered a return to a DC-9 first officer position. But I was tired of being "jerked around," so I turned it down, deciding to build my seniority and wait for a more opportune time to move up. I had completed my probationary year and was now a full-fledged member of the Airline Pilots Association union (ALPA), which represented Delta pilots. As such, my pay virtually doubled as I came under the union contract pay rates. Things were looking up. There was only one minus. As a flight engineer, I was not flying the aircraft.

CHAPTER TWELVE

"KEEPING A HAND ON THE WHEEL"

To remedy the fact that I no longer had my hand on the controls of an aircraft, I turned to the best option available to me, the Air National Guard (ANG). I initially inquired at Dobbins AFB in nearby Marietta, Georgia, but there were no vacancies in the units there. Although it required a commute, I then began to look at the unit based at McGhee-Tyson AB on the Knoxville Airport, flying KC-97 tankers. A few other Delta pilots were members of the unit, and the Delta chief pilot was granting jump seat privileges to commute back and forth on Delta flights to attend training. (The "jump seat" was an additional seat in the cockpit for observers, notably FAA inspectors.) Knoxville was also my hometown, and it gave me an opportunity to visit and stay with family. After interviewing with the squadron commander, I was welcomed into the unit and received assignment as a "first pilot" on the KC-97. I was now juggling three jobs: flying a full schedule each month as a DC-8 engineer, working part-time at a local Atlanta tire center, and commuting to Knoxville for participation in the Air National Guard.

How can I describe the KC-97? It had evolved from the civilian version known as the "Strato-Cruiser," which came into service at the end of World War II and was short-lived due to the advent of the turbo-prop and the jet age. The military saw a use for it, however, and acquired both cargo(C designation) and tanker (KC designation) versions. It had four large 4,360 horsepower engines, and on the tanker version, two J-47 jet engines slung under the wings for additional thrust. An interesting thing about these jet engines was that they were programmed to burn aviation fuel instead of jet fuel in order not to deplete the jet fuel supply for refueling. As a result, the turbine blades would become encrusted with lead deposits over time. To remove these deposits, the engines would be run up, and walnut hulls would be shoveled into the intakes. The friction of the hulls would remove the deposits without damaging the engine itself.

In pilot jargon, the KC-97 was referred to as a "flying gas station" and an "aluminum overcast." With reference to its engines, it was described as, "Four turning (the propellers) and two burning (the jet engines)." It was the only "six engine time" I was to ever record in my flight log. This aircraft, with its "greenhouse" nose, was big, heavy, underpowered, and a handful to fly, so much so that the flight engineer had a dual set of the reciprocating engine throttles at his station. During approach, he would adjust the throttles on the pilot's command, so that the pilot flying could concentrate on manipulating the control wheel and handling the jet throttles. The aircraft systems were complex, producing a nightmare of switches on panels throughout the cockpit. I managed to get some elementary knowledge of all that, but I was mostly interested in the actual flying, which, to some degree, was like an airline operation.

Crew coordination was paramount on this aircraft, and as first pilot, I was charged with reading the items on the checklist and ensuring that they were completed, from "before starting engines" to "engine shutdown" after the mission was complete. That, along with handling all outside communications and taking my turn at the controls, was "old hat" to me. Most of my flying was in the "local training" category, just working on takeoffs and landings and on flying instrument approaches. This was what I wanted most, to keep up my flying skills.

Later, I began to fly local missions, where we would arrive on a nearby "oil burner" track for refueling operations. These missions involved Air National Guard and Reserve fighter units who were receiving in-flight refueling training. The usual scenario was a two-ship formation of F-15s or the like, joining on our wing and then, in turn, dropping under our tail. At this point, the boom operator, who was lying on his belly looking out a rear window, would maneuver the "flying boom" onto the fuel receptacle of the fighter aircraft and would begin the transfer of fuel. After he got his "shot," he would pull off and fly formation with us, while his buddy repeated the process. Our job as pilots was to maintain a constant airspeed. There were some problems with the higher performance fighters in that our maximum speed in level flight was too slow for them to avoid going into a stall. Consequently, we had to maintain a slow descent and use our jet engines at maximum power to gain additional airspeed and effect a good operation. All went smoothly on these missions, and while we were probably viewed with some degree of humor by the fighter pilots, they all seemed glad to see us and to receive a full tank of jet fuel for continuing their missions.

The "primary" mission of this unit, however, was periodic deployment to Germany in support of our NATO fighter units based on the western side of the Iron Curtain. This was a political barrier erected in Germany by the Russians after World War II, separating East and West Germany. Tensions were still high in the area, and several people were shot trying to escape Communist East Germany, particularly along the Berlin Wall, which divided the city in half. This wall was torn down in the 1980s during the Reagan administration, and the two Germanys reunited.

Having done my duty to my country in Vietnam, I was not particularly interested in obtaining military leave from Delta to participate in a deployment. Fortunately, there were always enough volunteers to man the mission, and no pressure was applied to force me to go. I also had no desire to check out as aircraft commander, with its added requirements. I did qualify as a first pilot and was content with my level of participation. At times, though, I was dangerously close to going noncurrent, and I once received a call from the operations officer telling me to get up there "at all costs," to get my flying training periods in.

Two years later, I got wind that a RIF was planned for the unit, to include all of us commuting "part-timers." In addition, there were changes going on in the Delta chief pilot's office that precluded the use of the jump seat for attending military training. All of this, coupled with an expected Delta copilot bid looming on the horizon, let me see the "handwriting on the wall" for my continuation as a member of the Air National Guard. I figured that I would resign my commission before the reduction in force came, and so, months later, I did. If necessary, I would tough it out a little longer as a flight engineer, until I could get my hands on the controls once again.

* * *

While I had reverted to a second officer position in January 1971, I was still "dual-qualified" on the DC-9 and L-100 as a first officer, and I was subject to a call-out to fly a trip on those aircraft; couple that with trying to fly the KC-97 in the Air National Guard, and one can see that it was a very confusing time in my flying career. Sometimes I had to stop and remember what aircraft I was flying in order to avoid using the right procedure on the wrong airplane. I wasn't the only Delta pilot who encountered difficulty in this area.

One morning I was scheduled for a flight from Atlanta to Miami. Delta had just acquired the B-747, and she was now the "queen of the fleet." Only a few of the most senior captains were fortunate enough to check out and fly the airplane. Since the flying time scheduled for the 747 was somewhat limited, those captains were permitted to pick up trips on the DC-8 in order to fill up their time for the month. On this particular flight, that policy proved to be a major mistake.

Normally, when switching between aircraft types, the captain would let the first officer fly the first "leg" so he could look at one landing before having his turn. Not so with this particular captain. In his practice, the captain was the captain, and he *always* flew the first leg. All went fairly smoothly during takeoff, departure, and cruise, with the first officer having to nurse this rather "rusty" captain along with the checklists, procedures, etc. The weather in Miami was perfect, and we were cleared to land on runway "9 Right" at Miami International. We came over the runway threshold a little high and "hot" (too fast). The captain then "rounded out" (pulled the nose up) fifty feet above the runway and "wiped the power" (reduced the throttles to idle). The DC-8 "floated" (hung in the air) for a good distance down the runway until it ran out of airspeed, at which point it dropped suddenly, hitting the runway like several "tons of bricks." The captain then "stood on the brakes" (maximum braking), bringing the DC-8 to a shuddering stop on the runway, at which point all the main tires blew their "fuse plugs" and deflated due to the heat generated by the brakes.

So here we were, sitting in the middle of runway 09R at Miami International Airport, with blown tires and the possibility of a brake fire, listening to the tower advising the aircraft landing behind us to "go around" (abandon approach and landing). Meanwhile, fire and crash equipment was speeding to our location as the tower announced that runway 09R was "closed." Fortunately, there was no fire, and after a cooling period for the brakes, Delta maintenance was able to reinsert the fuse plugs, inflate the tires, and tow us to the gate. During all this, the captain seemed almost unconcerned and nonchalant about the whole affair, although I'm certain most of the passengers were terrified. (I know I was.) Hopefully the captain learned that landing a 747 with its cockpit fifty feet above the runway was no way to land a DC-8. I was glad it was the first officer's leg back to Atlanta. I don't think either of us could have stood a repeat of this embarrassing and dangerous scenario. Interestingly, Delta soon abandoned the "dual qualification" system, allowing each pilot to concentrate on flying only one aircraft until fully trained on the next one. Score one for safety as well as for economics. By July 1, 1971, I only had the DC-8 and the KC-97 to be concerned about.

For the next two years, I settled into a relatively normal routine, flying a full month as a flight engineer on the DC-8 and commuting to Knoxville to fly with the "Guard." I gave up my third job as a tire salesman, since I was now on "increment pay," having completed my probationary period and having begun to accrue seniority. There were two memorable events during this period.

One area of airline flying that departed from the routine of normal operations was flying "charters." This involved various groups and organizations who chartered an aircraft for a specific purpose, going to a specific destination for a specific time, with a return to their point of origin.

One charter that was employed by the casinos in Las Vegas was to fly a group of "high rollers" from the New York area out to the desert, so they could try their luck at the tables. Delta acquired a contract with one of the casinos to operate what became known as "Flamingo charters," shuttling gamblers out to the Flamingo Hotel on the strip in "Vegas." One night we were cruising along in flight under normal conditions, with the exception of one thing. We kept hearing an intermittent rattling noise behind the cockpit door leading back into the first-class cabin. After several of these occurrences, the captain directed me to go back and investigate this unusual noise. As I opened the cockpit door, I encountered a blanket lying on the cabin floor. Kneeling and standing beyond the blanket were several passengers who held money in their hands and who were most intent on what was happening on the blanket. One passenger was holding a large set of dice, getting ready to throw them up against the cockpit door and let them rebound onto the blanket. I realized that I had just interrupted a dice game among those who had decided not to wait until their arrival at the Flamingo to test their luck. I quickly apologized and shut the door, allowing the game to continue. After I related this to the captain and first officer, we all had a laugh and steeled ourselves to the clatter of the dice until it was time for descent. On charters, there were many such irregularities compared to normal flight operations.

Another memorable event occurred on a trip into New York. Layovers in New York were different from all the others in those days. They required packing a coat and tie for any layover involving the dinner hour, and the entire crew was expected to participate. Safety in numbers was the idea, and the whole crew usually stuck together on the streets of New York. On this trip, one of the "stews" (stewardesses, later to be given the title of "flight attendants") had a fiancé who worked at the United Nations (UN) as assistant secretary to our ambassador to the UN, then George H. Bush, who would later become president of the United States. Consequently, the crew was invited for a "behind the scenes" tour of the United Nations building. Meeting on the steps of the building overlooking the East River, we were ushered into Ambassador Bush's office, where we were given the royal treatment, followed by a tour of the chambers of the Security Council and the General Assembly. It was hard to believe that I sat in the same chair as Nikita Khrushchev, the Russian leader, who, only a few weeks earlier, had sat there, banging his shoe on the table and telling America, "We will bury you."

I had many New York City layovers during my airline career. Strangely, the city was a place you were always excited to get to, but were always glad to leave. One captain referred to it as the "land of tall buildings and dirty streets." It was also commonly said that "it was a great place to visit but, you wouldn't want to live there." Herding millions of people onto one small island called Manhattan was akin to crowding too many rats into a cage. Eventually they would kill and eat each other.

The traffic was murderous, crime was rampant, and the people ill-mannered, and yet, on a sunny spring day, there was no experience like being on the streets of New York. It seemed to be the center of everything: entertainment, food, fashion, and the arts. One could take in a theatre play on Broadway, attend a concert at Carnegie Hall, shop on Fifth Avenue or Canal Street, enjoy a jog through Central Park, or watch the skaters at Rockefeller Center or the precision of the "Rockettes" at the Radio City Music Hall Christmas Show, all this while enjoying the best food in the world from the "deli" situated on nearly every corner. To escape all this, one could even enjoy a moment of quiet reverence within the confines of Saint Patrick's Cathedral. Whether one was seeking out another museum, visiting Ellis Island, or climbing up into the "torch" of the Statue of Liberty, there was always something to do, someplace to go, and an efficient subway system to get you there. But alas, it was time to get back to the hotel for "pickup," an exciting ride with a city cab driver to one of the three airports serving the City (LaGuardia, Kennedy, or Newark), and for departure to a place more mundane and more in tune with reality. While I had layovers in cities that were more beautiful and just as enjoyable in many ways, I would have to conclude that there was no place like New York City in the entire world.

* * *

With the advent of 1973, my classification as a second officer and my duties as a flight engineer were coming to a close. Not thinking that I was senior enough to secure and hold a bid on it, I submitted a "wish list" bid for a first officer position on the Boeing 727. Delta had just acquired Northeast Airlines in a merger, and the B-727 was part of their inventory. During the prelude to the merger, the "powers that be" at Delta had let it be known that they did not favor the B-727. Consequently, the pilot group did not think that it would be around very long. And yet, here was a bid posting, and the aircraft was now flying on Delta routes. What happened was that these same "powers that be" discovered that the B-727 fit perfectly into Delta's route structure now that the airline industry had been "deregulated." Now, any airline could fly anytime, anywhere throughout the continental United States. The B-727 was to become the "workhorse" of the industry, and Delta became the leading purchaser and operator over the next several years.

Coming in from a DC-8 trip one day, I ran into one of my class-mates, who said, "You'd better check the bulletin board down in Opera-tions. Looks like you're going to be a '72' copilot." Sure enough, there was my name just above the last name on the list, awarding me an "advance entitlement" as a first officer on the B-727. It was shocking at first, that I could skip the DC-9 completely and go to the next level, ahead of so many who were senior to me. What I did not see at the time was that I was going to be junior on the B-727 for a very, very long time.

Since there were no training facilities set up for the 727 in Atlanta at that time, all ground training on the aircraft was scheduled to take place at the Boeing factory in Seattle, Washington. To be able to attend a "factory school" was a rare opportunity. Here, the instructors were the aeronautical engineers who had designed and built the aircraft. If a stu-dent had a question, he could get it "straight from the horse's mouth." I was also privileged to go down on the factory "line" to see the aircraft subassemblies come together to form the completed aircraft itself. To see the actual building of the airplane that you would later fly was something special. I had always identified an aircraft by its engines, but here they were more of an afterthought. The finishing hangar was full of completed aircraft just waiting for the Pratt & Whitney Jet Propulsion Team to attach the dynamics needed to launch these magnificent machines into the air. After their work was done, the factory test pilots took charge of the aircraft for taxi tests and for that initial takeoff into the environ-ment that the plane was designed for. After a series of "proving flights," it was ready for delivery to the customer. Every pilot envied the chief pilot group that was sent to take delivery and to ferry each new aircraft back to Atlanta.

The Boeing school itself was most interesting and enjoyable. As former "Douglas" aircraft operators, we did a quirky little thing each morning in an effort to "pull the instructor's chain." On our Styrofoam coffee cups we would write, "Douglas is Divine," and we would face the cups so the instructors could see them. Being the professionals that they were, they chose to ignore the cups. So in the last few days of training, we changed the slogan to read, "Boeing is Beautiful," a tribute both to the instructors as well as to the aircraft we were beginning to know. The class schedule kept us relatively busy, but we were able to enjoy the local seafood at dinner, and on the weekend, rent a car to explore the local area, nearby Mount Rainier in particular.

As our ground school was coming to an end, I was beginning to wonder about the next phase of training, the simulator. One morning during the last week, one of the administrators came into the classroom and announced that due to the limited space available for simulator training, only the captains would receive that training. Delta had decided that the first officers would get all further training "in the airplane." This announcement was met with mixed emotions; we were glad that we could avoid the rigors of simulator training, but were sad that we had to leave the Boeing factory and return to Atlanta. Delta had set up a flying "school" at the airport in Columbia, South Carolina, where we were to complete our checkout.

"We wuz robbed" would be the phrase that best described our flight training, in lieu of simulator training, on the B-727. With only one aircraft available, and with a host of copilots awaiting checkout, my days at the Columbia, South Carolina flying school were shortened to the minimum. Requirements were reduced to a "working knowledge" of the aircraft systems, and emphasis was placed on takeoffs and landings, with a few instrument approaches thrown in. After a couple of training sessions, I accomplished three successful landings and was signed off as "qualified" on the 727. I was told that anything I had missed I would learn "on the line"—so much for Delta's training of first officers.

Returning to Atlanta, I found myself the most junior copilot among those who had completed training, with the exception of one other pilot. He and I made up what was known as the "reserve contingent" for the few lines of time that were initially flown out of the Atlanta base. As you will remember, that meant that we were "on call" for anything that might require the need for a pilot to cover a trip. We were utilized to the maximum, and we often met each other "coming and going," realizing that there were no others besides us, as yet, to fill in when needed.

Since the aircraft was new to the base, flying was restricted to turnarounds. These were designed to have the aircraft back in Atlanta overnight for maintenance and for the training of mechanics for outlying stations. Therefore, there were no layovers for some time. New York City would have to wait.

The merger with Northeast had brought some of the oldest B-727s into the Delta inventory. In fact, Northeast Airlines was the original operator of the B-727 in the airline industry. These older airplanes came in two models, the old B-727-100 (the "short" model) and the newer B-727-200 (the "stretch" model). Both were powered by what was designated the "dash- nine" engine, one that was not the best in performance compared to the newer "dash- fifteen" engines coming on Delta's order from Boeing. Flying these old airplanes was like going back in time. The flight instruments were of another era and were scattered around the panel in no particular order. The short model had a slightly different control wheel that, I found out later, was used on World War II bombers. On the back of the wheel was stamped "Control Wheel-B-29."

The worst thing about these aircraft, however, was the color. Northeast had adopted the name "Yellowbird" as part of its advertising slogan, and had painted its aircraft accordingly. We took some "grief" throughout the system when we showed up in an old, dirty, canary yellow aircraft, with only a Delta "widget" decal on the passenger door. Luckily, these planes were quickly destined for the paint shop, and we were able to regain our pride in flying the "new kid on the block." Later, as the new B-727-232 models began to arrive, these aircraft were all pulled out of service, "painted out," and sold to other airlines, primarily in South America.

Now that the merger with Northeast was completed and the pilot seniority lists merged, I began to fly with several captains who had migrated down from the Northeast Airlines base in Boston. These guys knew the airplane in and out, and I was able to learn a lot about the airplane by flying with them. As we began to branch out with more trips and layovers, we began flying with former Northeast stewardesses as well as pilots. We all found great humor in each other's regional accents and habits. We enjoyed introducing them to such things as "grits," gravy, gumbo, catfish, and hushpuppies, while we were introduced to "lobsta," "chowda," maple syrup, and giant blueberry muffins. All in all, it was a successful merger, one that greatly expanded Delta's route system and the size of the company. Things were looking up for Delta Airlines in the 1970s.

In the midst of so much optimism, I was suddenly brought back down to earth by an event that was to change my flying career and my life, perhaps for all time. As a pilot with both Delta and the Air National Guard, I was subject to periodic physical exams. These were required on an annual basis as a flight engineer or copilot, but escalated to every six months as a captain. As I was in my early thirties, these exams had been just a part of the routine, without any discrepancies, and I had not given them much thought. One morning, while attending weekend training with the Guard at McGhee-Tyson, I was scheduled with the flight surgeon for my annual physical exam. As an enlisted medical corpsman was taking my blood pressure reading, he asked if I was "uptight" about anything. I replied that I couldn't think of anything. He said, "Your blood pressure reading is really high this morning." He had me lie down and rest for a few minutes, after which he took the reading again, this time apparently with a better result. What I did not know at the time was that this would become the routine for getting my blood pressure "within limits" for most future flight physicals, and I developed a real fear of having the blood pressure cuff wrapped around my arm. Later, I had to go on blood pressure medication and, on one occasion, had to take six weeks "sick leave" while my doctor "tweaked" the drugs and dosages to fit my situation. Luckily, my Air National Guard flight surgeon at McGhee-Tyson was also certified by the FAA to give airline flight physicals, and he "kept me flying" until the end of my career.

Somewhat troubled by this incident, I began to realize, on my return to Atlanta, that my flying career could be placed in jeopardy by a failure to meet physical standards. So I began to formulate a plan, in the event that that scenario should play itself out. Some of my classmates had elected to take out "loss of license" insurance, available from ALPA and other carriers, to offset the financial loss resulting from a failure to meet FAA physical standards. Others had skills in other career fields that they could fall back on in such situations. Since the insurance was relatively expensive, and I had no marketable skills other than my ability to fly airplanes, the answer for me became quite clear: I needed to go back to school. Before deciding what path to take in this area, I did what most pilots were doing at the first hint of a physical problem. I engaged a personal physician to treat my situation and to perform a "prephysical to the FAA physical" in order to catch anything ahead of time. I employed this strategy throughout my career and was able to retain my first-class physical certificate throughout, except for the six-week period mentioned previously.

With that accomplished, I turned to the next goal of obtaining additional education sufficient to see me through a job crisis. Since I was eligible for educational benefits under the "GI Bill" administered by the Veterans Administration, I could offset most of the expenses involved by signing up for them. At the same time, Georgia State University, with its campus in downtown Atlanta, had begun a two-year course of study leading to an Associate Degree in Aviation Administration. The curriculum was set up for the evening hours to allow those already working in the industry to attend classes. All this fit right into my plans, and after working out all the administrative details, I enrolled in the program.

While I had given up my flying with the ANG, I now had to juggle my flight schedule with Delta while attending classes at Georgia State. Since I was a reserve line holder, I had twelve off days or "X-days," as they were called, that I could count on for class attendance. The other eighteen days, I was subject to being called out on a trip. Enter the "beeper," a mobile device that would give me the freedom to go anywhere in the area while still being reachable by crew scheduling. This was before the advent of the "cell phone," and it afforded tremendous freedom from the task of sitting at home by the phone waiting for a call. If it looked like I was close to being called out, I would dress for school, pack my uniform and suitcase in the car, and drive to the downtown campus for class, wearing my beeper. By working with the crew schedulers, bidding the appropriate "X-days," and keeping my beeper handy, I missed very little class time over the next two years, and I graduated on time with an Associate Degree in Aviation Administration. Now I had a working knowledge of the intricacies of the airline industry, enough to allow me to transfer to another field within the industry, should I fail to meet physical standards as a pilot.

The first thing I did after receiving my diploma was to "Xerox" a copy and send it to Delta Personnel for inclusion in my personnel records. I did not expect a response, but was pleasantly surprised and pleased when I received a letter of congratulations from the Director of Personnel, a portion of the text of which follows:

October 20, 1976

Dear Allen,

Just a short note to offer you my heartiest congratulations on achieving your Aviation Administration degree at Georgia State. I know this represents a lot of hard, diligent work and you certainly are to be commended.

Next time you're over here at the G.O. (General Offices), please stop by my office and I'll buy you a cup of coffee.

Again, congratulations!

With this accomplishment now in my file, I felt confident that Delta would find another place for me, should I not be able to fly their airplanes. Luckily, I never had to go to the GO for that cup of coffee with the personnel director.

CHAPTER THIRTEEN

"FLYING COPILOT"

The copilot seat on the B-727 was to be my "home" for almost seven years. And as the fleet expanded with each new arrival from the Boeing factory, more and more 727 flight time was added in Atlanta and in other bases throughout the system. Those factors, along with the passage of time and an expanding economy, allowed me finally to attain some measure of seniority. As a result, I was able to begin holding a "regular" line of time, with a set schedule for the month. With my schooling behind me, I was able to concentrate, for the first time, on only one thing: flying my trips on the B-727. Being the number two man on a three-man aircraft was a relative luxury; the flight engineer did all the "dirty work," and the captain, at that time, had most of the responsibility. It was said that all the copilot had to do was show up with his flight kit and remember to say "clear right" and "I'll take the chicken" (in the rare case of a "steak or chicken option" for a meal offered by the cabin crew).

All in all, the "72" was easy to fly but hard to land smoothly. Because of the rearward placement of the main landing gear, it was easy to pull up on the control wheel prematurely and drive the main gear onto the concrete with a "teeth shattering" result. Once on a windy day in New England, we were engaged in a multiple-landing trip segment terminating in Portland, Maine. One of the passengers, who had endured several of these "positive touchdowns," stuck his head into the cockpit as he deplaned and asked, "Are you guys basketball players?"

We said, "No, why?"

He said "I thought you had to be, the way you've been dribbling the airplane all morning." Sometimes you just had those days.

The only other complaint pilots had with the "72" were the seats. These were rumored to be the same used for those World War II bombers mentioned earlier, and they were definitely not designed by orthopedic engineers. Most pilots who flew the airplane ended up, at some point, with back trouble, and I was no exception. Fortunately the newer aircraft had much improved seating, with lumbar adjustments for individual pilot differences.

The merger with Northeast, along with deregulation, had presented great opportunities for Delta to expand its route structure, particularly in the eastern portion of the country. This was where the bulk of B-727 flight time was utilized. San Francisco and the west coast would also have to wait for awhile. A favorite layover in the summer months was Bangor, Maine. The Holiday Inn, where we laid over, provided a van for the crew's use, and it was constantly in use with trips to Bar Harbor for sightseeing, seafood, and shopping. In winter, it was used either for transport to a local restaurant for a lobster dinner or transport to a nearby ski resort.

One incident that comes to mind, relative to flight operations in the state of Maine, took place just down the coast at Portland. A Delta crew had laid over the night before and had reported the next morning, only to find the airport shut down by heavy fog. Not to be intimidated by a little ground fog, the captain of this crew hatched a plan to lift the fog enough to attain takeoff "minimums" and to press on to whatever was calling him. With the tower's approval, he started all engines, groped his way out onto the runway, and began high-speed taxi runs up and down the runway, the idea being that heat from the engines would "burn off" the fog, causing it to lift. I remembered this technique being employed at a drive-in theater in my youth, so it did have some credibility. After a few of these taxi runs, though, unbeknown to him, the brakes became superheated, and a fire broke out in one of the wheel wells. Luckily, the fire was reported immediately by a panic-stricken passenger.

Stopping on the runway, the captain called the tower and declared an emergency. There was only one problem. They could not see the airplane, due to the fog, and they had no idea where it was on the runway. By the time fire and rescue could find the airplane and extinguish the flames, the fire had consumed a great deal of the gear and wing structure in that area. Fortunately, the passengers and crew were safely evacuated, and no one was killed or injured. The sad part about this affair was that the captain was dealing with "sea fog" and not the "ground fog" he was used to seeing in the south. No amount of heating could lift sea fog, as it was constantly rolling in off the ocean. His efforts had only resulted in multi-million dollar damage to the aircraft, serious danger to passengers and crew, and several months off for him, without pay.

But what was the company to do with the airplane? It could not be flown out or trucked out, so a decision was made to repair it on-site. The aircraft was maneuvered to a remote area of the ramp, and teams of workers from Boeing trucked in to begin restoration. For several months afterward, we would pass the site on taxi-out at Portland, watching the restoration activity under a giant canopy that had been erected over the airplane. Needless to say, that was the end of any future efforts to assist Mother Nature in clearing any kind of fog.

As mentioned previously, flying a charter operation was a great way to break the sometime monotony of everyday line flying. The one I best remember on the B-727 took place in May of 1974. Richard M. Nixon was president of the United States at that time, and he often sought refuge from the pressures of the office on Key Biscayne, near Miami, Florida, in the home of one of his longtime political supporters. Any time this occurred, the White House had to obtain and coordinate air transportation for the nation's press corps to follow along. Delta, through its Special Movements and Charters division, had acquired a number of these press corps charters, and it was to one of these that I was assigned to serve as first officer. The trip started with ferrying an empty aircraft to Andrews Air Force Base in Maryland, where we were assigned a special place on the ramp. After loading the airplane with all kinds of gourmet food, wine, and liquor, the press corps, many with their families in tow, boarded for the flight south. Meanwhile, President Nixon was being picked up on the White House lawn and ferried via helicopter to a waiting "Air Force One," a beautiful blue and silver Boeing 707 waiting on the ramp nearby. We took off first and proceeded to Homestead AFB, just south of Miami, with Air Force One following approximately ten minutes behind.

Upon landing at Homestead, the press corps quickly deplaned to set up a makeshift news conference setting on the ramp, prior to the president's arrival. In the meantime, press corps family members "looted" the aircraft of all the food, wine, and liquor they could carry with them as they deplaned. Had they been this way before? Luckily, the flight attendants were able to "squirrel away" a lobster and steak lunch for the crew. Soon, Air Force One landed and taxied to the ramp, and the president deplaned to meet the press briefly before being whisked away to his Floridian sanctuary. The press corps and their families then departed for a vacation stay to coincide with the president's visit. (Had I chosen the wrong career?) Back on board, the White House Transportation Coordinator presented the crew with ballpoint pens that had purportedly been used to sign various pieces of legislation into law, each pen bearing President Nixon's signature. Later, the crew received a letter of appreciation from the White House Chief of Transportation, relayed through the

Delta District Marketing Manager, a mister Hollingsworth, in Washington, DC. A portion of the text read as follows:

"I received a call today, May 21, 1974, from Mr. Ray Zook, Chief Transportation, White House, and was advised that our operation for May 20 was one of the best.

I wish to personally compliment the crew. They did an excellent job and certainly promoted Delta, and helped increase our standing with both White House personnel and the White House Press Corps in the true Delta professional manner."

This "commendation" was sent to each of the crew members with the following endorsement from the chief pilot:

"The continued success of Delta is certainly closely tied to the action you and the rest of your crew displayed on Flight 8702. I just want to add my thanks to those of Mr. Hollingsworth for a real professional flight, Allen.

It is certainly a tribute to all of you for going that extra step for all of us, and we do appreciate it."

It was always a good thing to get such letters into one's personnel file. The idea was widely circulated, however, that it took a "slew" of these "attaboys" to make up for one "Uh Oh."

And so my days as a B-727 first officer continued, interrupted only by events in my personal life that would change my flying career for all time.

* * *

Divorce is not an easy thing, but it happens among people, resulting in a redirection of one's pathway in life. For me, that "redirection" involved decisions that would place me in a different category relative to Delta Airlines, which would change my career path.

In early 1977, I made the decision to move back to Tennessee, rejoin the Air National Guard, and become a "commuter" to my job with Delta in Atlanta. I did not realize the added pressure that this move would bring to my job. A crew scheduler confided to me that Delta "did not like commuters." I assumed this dislike to center around the added circumstances of making it to "sign-in" on time and a tendency to employ "sick leave" when things went badly during the commute. One commuter pilot made the mistake of calling in "sick" at an outlying airport after he missed his flight to Atlanta. The scheduler turned around and placed a call to his home, only to be told by the pilot's wife that he had left for work and was at the airport. His punishment was thirty days off without pay. Abuse of sick leave was not an option with Delta Airlines.

In addition, Delta prohibited the use of the cockpit "jump seat" for use by commuters. Late in my career, this was changed in contract negotiations, thereby alleviating most of the "hassle" involved with getting to work. Obtaining the ten-year Delta "Annual Pass" helped alleviate the expense as well. In the interim, I had to bid trips very carefully and give myself plenty of lead time to get from Knoxville to Atlanta. Sometimes I commuted down the night before, for an early departure the next morning. In all cases, I left a four-hour window before sign-in, in case I had to drive the two hundred miles to the Atlanta Airport. I was also determined never to use sick leave except in a dire emergency, and I probably flew several times when I should have stayed home. As far as my career path was concerned, I could never afford to be "junior" or an "on-call reserve" pilot again. As a commuter, I would have to stay "senior" on equipment in order to hold a line of time conducive to getting to work.

This was a significant factor in retarding my upward mobility to better paying seat positions.

On the bright side, I was back home in Tennessee. After renting an apartment near the airport in Maryville and establishing my legal residence, I advised Delta Payroll, who released me from further payments of Georgia State income tax. This was a further assistance to my commuting costs, which involved extra hotel, meal, and transportation expenses.

My first stop was to my old Air National Guard outfit at McGhee-Tyson AB, to see if I could get back into the unit to help meet my financial obligations. As it turned out, there had been a change of command in my absence that did not work in my favor. The new commander was never one of my favorites, and he was not fond of airline part-timers. After he left me cooling my heels in an outer office while he conducted a "meeting," I saw the handwriting on the wall. I would have to look elsewhere for a second job. Later on, another officer, whom I knew and admired, took command of the unit and sent word for me to come and rejoin. But by that time, I had already settled into a part-time real estate career after obtaining my license. Such is life's pathway.

So I settled into a routine of commuting to Atlanta, flying my trips as a B-727 first officer, commuting back home, and working real estate on my days off. I also did a great deal of solo backpacking in the Great Smokey Mountain National Park during this period.

On one of my flight rotations, I flew with a captain by the name of Bob Hedgecock, who was heavily involved with antique airplanes. He lived south of Atlanta, where he had his own grass landing strip and hangar. In this hangar he kept a very special aircraft, the last one of its lot still flying. It was a 1929 Stinson "Detroiter" high-wing monoplane, powered by a Wright Whirlwind J6-5(R540) radial engine. This was the same engine that powered Ryan Aircraft's *Spirit of Saint Louis,* the monoplane used by Charles Lindbergh to make the first solo crossing of the Atlantic Ocean in 1927. The airplane was produced by Stinson Aircraft in several different models, between 1928 and 1933. This one was designated an SM2-AA, 80 series "Junior," because of the smaller five-cylinder engine compared to the seven- and nine-cylinder engines on other models.

As we flew together that month, Bob began to talk about taking the Stinson to the annual Antique Fly-In held in Ottumwa, Iowa. Since my vacation time coincided somewhat with his, he asked if I would be interested in going along with him as copilot. I heartily agreed to what promised to be a great American adventure.

This adventure began on August 31, 1977, at a little municipal airport in Madisonville, Tennessee, just south of Maryville. This location was selected as a pickup point for me, to avoid the "control zone" around the Knoxville Airport, which required two-way radio contact between the tower and all air traffic. Since the Stinson carried no radios, or any electronics for that matter, she had to stay in "uncontrolled" airspace.

As I waited on the tarmac in the heat and humidity of a late summer day, there was very little stirring around the airport except a few songbirds and a hawk circling overhead. Our rendezvous time had passed, and I was getting a little anxious. Suddenly I detected a faint sound off to the south, an unfamiliar sound to me at that time, the distinctive sound of a large air-cooled engine. And it was getting louder and closer. Scanning the southern sky and straining to pick up the source of the sound, I spotted the Stinson for the first time, a high-wing monoplane with red paint, headed straight for the airport. Bob entered the traffic pattern, touched down, and taxied up to the gas pumps near where I was standing. The heat, energy, and sound of the big radial engine immediately caught my attention. This was no ordinary aircraft!

1929 Stinson Junior, Blakesburg, Iowa, 1977

After Bob and I greeted each other, I stashed my "stuff" behind the front seats and began planning our first leg, while Bob attended to the refueling operation. When everything was ready, Bob took his place in the pilot's seat after giving me the engine starting routine. It was then that I better understood why I was now part of the crew. Reaching as high as I could on the topmost blade of the prop, I awaited Bob's commands of "Clear!" and then "Contact!" after which I pulled the prop through as hard as I could. One cylinder fired, and then another, until all five were firing and the engine was running smoothly. I quickly ran around and jumped into the right seat and strapped in, as the fueling attendant pulled the "chocks" and Bob released the brakes for taxi. Waving to the "friend" who had brought me to the airport, and who was to become my wife within a year, we taxied out for takeoff. Lining up on the runway, Bob brought the engine up to full power and released the brakes for takeoff. The noise was deafening as we accelerated down the runway and struggled into the air, with the added weight of a full fuel load and another crew member with gear along with the heat of the day to limit performance. Later, my friend said that seeing this old, antique airplane take off was very special, but she said that she held her breath until we cleared the trees at the airport boundary.

The remainder of this adventure will be related from the diary I kept, commemorating the trip.

August 31, 1977

Madisonville, Tennessee to Madisonville, Kentucky

Flight Time: 2:55 Altitude: 4,500 feet Airspeed: 80 knots

Weather: Hazy with poor visibility into the sun

Landed Madisonville—refueled—set up tent in grass and prepared dinner. Mosquitoes very bad—hot and humid—moved tent to ramp area under wing of the Stinson. Spent a hot, sweaty night—Bob moved out for cooler air and finally gave up battle with mosquitoes and sought refuge in a tiny, screened-in vestibule leading into the base operations office.

September 1, 1977

Madisonville, Kentucky to Jacksonville, Illinois

Flight Time: 2:55 Altitude: 4,500 feet Airspeed: 80 knots

Weather: Still hazy with improved visibility—smooth

Up at 6:30—breakfast—packed up camping gear—pushed the Stinson to the wash rack to give her a final wiping down—propped her at

0810 and airborne at 0820. Went through weak cold front northwest of Jacksonville—cooler temp and less humidity. Made pass over field—wind 10kts from south—avoided crosswind landing on the hard surface runway by discovering a sod strip running north-south. Bob surprised me by saying: "Since its sod, you make the landing." I brought the Stinson around in a tight turn and, with verbal instruction from Bob (increasing only slightly in volume and tone of trepidation), and made my first landing of the trip. Taxied to the fuel pumps—a beautiful airport for such a small city—plenty of ramp space, multiple hangars, and a new operations building—part of a state program to upgrade all Illinois airports. Among the spectators (who always seem to materialize wherever we are) was one Byron Smith, a retired farmer and former county commissioner for Morgan County. Byron volunteered to drive us into town for lunch in keeping with the old barnstormer days when pilots were treated "like kings" (his words) wherever they landed. On the way, he added a bonus by taking us to the opposite side of the field where he hangared his 1949 Piper-Stinson "Voyager" (Piper had bought out Stinson but retained the compound name for the Stinson designs)—a beautiful original, inside and out. Back into his Audi, we drove into town with Byron giving us a running commentary on the history of the town and its progress. The quietness and peacefulness of the downtown area was noticeable after three hours of listening to the Wright Whirlwind engine. After a lunch of fried chicken topped off by cherry pie à la mode, we talked for awhile with the owner, Mary Ralston, who offered to come out to pick us up for Sunday dinner if we'd stop on our way back. On the return to the airport, Byron made a short detour to show us an industry unique to Jacksonville—the only Ferris wheel factory in the world—makers of the "Big Eli" Ferris wheels. Soon we were back at the airport, where we propped the Stinson, said our good-byes to Byron, and took off for the final leg of our journey.

Jacksonville, Illinois to Antique Airport, Blakesburg, Iowa

Flight Time: 2:10

Weather: Scattered stratocumulus, 15 knot headwind, a few scattered showers, visibility: excellent.

Good section lines, highways, and railroads made our "dead reckoning" map navigation easy on this leg—what a sight as we picked up our destination airport! There were *fields* full of antique aircraft, campers, and tents. Several aircraft were in the traffic pattern, and we had to work our way down into the pattern as we circled the airport. Bob made a beautiful approach and received clearance to land by a flagman waving a green flag. Our wash job from the morning went "out the window" as we negotiated several mud puddles into the parking area. With the help of several flagmen and spectators, we taxied into our area and parked next to two other Stinsons of the same vintage and behind two Howard high-wing monoplanes. Again a host of spectators surrounded this new Stinson arrival, examining Bob's new exhaust collector assembly (the old one had rusted out and he found a commercial cookware company that was able to produce a replacement) and arguing about what model the Stinson was and how it was different from the others present and elsewhere.

The Antique airport is well-suited for an event of this type: fields, and rows within those fields, are specified for certain aircraft types and makes. My first inclination was to grab the camera and start shooting. The only problem was which aircraft to shoot first. The oldest aircraft are parked closest to the hangars and operations area, so we are ideally located for watching airplanes coming and going. Antique airplanes were everywhere: parked, taxiing out, taxiing in, landing, taking off, flying overhead in formation, etc. There was a Waco; here came a Stearman; parked was a beautifully restored 1927 Curtiss "Robin," rumored to be in strong running for the Grand Champion Award. Could this be airplane "heaven?"

After a brief walking tour, I pitched the tent under the wing of the Stinson and headed for the Lions Club tent and a barbeque dinner. At 3:00 p.m., movies were shown in the hangar along with a program on UFOs. We turned in at 11:00 with lightning and clouds moving in from the west.

What a rain! Bob punched me about 2:00 a.m., as large raindrops began to fall. I did my usual scramble act to get the rain fly on, and we stayed reasonably dry during the night as two inches of rain fell on the field.

September 2, 1977

What a mess! The airfield was closed for four hours and the morning was spent trying to dry out from the deluge. After breakfast at the "Ladies Bazaar" tent, I toured the antique museum and the concessions area, where there was much memorabilia and souvenirs on display and for sale. I spent the early afternoon watching what limited air activity there was, as many owners refused to tackle the muddy conditions.

I retoured all the fields of aircraft, with particular attention to the Stinson area. I am convinced that the Stinson 180-3 is the "tail-dragger" I would love to own. It is a good-sized, four-place, well-built airplane with leading edge slots for lateral control, even in a full-stalled condition. With the Continental 165 engine, it has adequate power for all conditions, and with a 120 mph cruise speed, it would be adequate for cross-country operation. The big plus, however, is that they are plentiful and reasonable in price. Appreciation in value appears to be a certainty.

After dinner at "Elaine's" tent, I met a gentleman whose hobby is aircraft photography. We discussed cameras and airplanes, and viewed his collection of pictures and slides. A dance soon began in the hangar.

I got homesick, called my "friend" back in Maryville, went back to my tent, and called it a night.

September 3, 1977

More rain during the night. Will it never end? Bought a coffee cup at the Coffee Club stand, put my name on it to distinguish it from the hundreds of others, and had a breakfast of rolls and coffee. Limited flying activity began about 9:30 a.m., and I experienced a "first," a ride in a 1929 "Fleet" biplane, open cockpit, leather helmet, goggles, and all! On the first pass over the field, we were joined by a "Waco" and a "Juggermeister" biplane for a three-ship formation pass. What an experience! The rush of air around your head and an exhilarating feeling not found in closed cockpit aircraft. Traffic was heavy, requiring several passes over the field before we were able to get down into the traffic pattern. Just as we landed, rain began to fall again, shutting down operations for the rest of the day. Later, I went by the Fleet biplane to get more particulars. She was a beautiful orange and white with a five cylinder Kenner engine that makes a distinctive "popping sound" as it fires. I spent the rest of the day retouring the museum, hangars, etc., just trying to stay dry.

About 7:00 p.m., Bob and I decided to join the steak cookout crowd followed by the initial awards ceremony. Surprise!! Bob won the trophy for the best pre–World War II Stinson. It was about now that I realized that Bob was not going to get his airplane off for the trip back tomorrow. The Stinson, with its J65 engine, just didn't have enough power to get us off the soggy sod field. One aircraft had tried it, but crashed at the end of the field, tearing up the airplane, but without serious injury to the unwise occupants.

During the day, two "Staggerwing Beech" airplanes had come in from Tullahoma, Tennessee. One was owned by a Glen McNabb from Jasper, Tennessee. His won the award for the best Staggerwing, and I used the occasion to congratulate him, while at the same time explaining my dilemma of getting back home for my trip on September 5th. Glen obliged me by offering to land me in Chattanooga and instructing me to be ready to go between 7:00 and 8:00 a.m. the following morning. Such a deal! Going back to Tennessee in a Staggerwing Beech, the most beautiful aircraft ever built, by most pilots' opinion, and certainly in my mind.

September 4, 1997

Ottumwa, Iowa to Tullahoma, Tennessee

Staggerwing Beech #N40E

Off: 15:56Z On: 19:20Z   Time: 3:24

Altitude: 9,500 feet

Ground Speed: 150 knots

Pilot: Glen McNabb

Takeoff from Antique Field was no problem for the big Pratt& Whitney radial engine powering the Staggerwing. We were joined on the right wing by another beautiful red Staggerwing and made it a "two-ship" formation along the route. I was able to get pictures of our wingman and was thrilled when Glen unhinged the control wheel and rotated it over to the copilot position asking me to pilot the airplane. Hog heaven! I was surprised to learn upon landing that Tullahoma housed an extensive Beech aircraft museum of which Glen was a partner. After touring the facility and meeting some of Glen's friends, it was back to the airplane for the short flight into Chattanooga.

Tullahoma, Tennessee to Chattanooga, Tennessee

Off: 21:10Z   On: 21:45Z   Time: 00:35

Total Staggerwing Beech Time: 3:59

Total Stinson Junior Time: 7:55

Total Antique Aircraft Time: 11:54

Darkness was falling quickly as we landed in Chattanooga and taxied to the general aviation hangar where the Staggerwing was parked. I said my thanks and good-bye to Glen, hoisted my gear on my shoulder, and found my "friend" waiting for me beyond the border fence for the drive back to Maryville. My adventure into the historical past of aviation was over. But there were other adventures yet to be lived.

I learned later that Bob had gotten off Antique field the next day. While en route, the engine on the Stinson seized, forcing him to make a quick emergency landing on a nearby sod field. Fortunately, the owner had a hangar, and the Stinson was housed there for several months, waiting for repair. I never heard of her final disposition, or whether she ever flew again, but I will never forget my time with her. Later, I had a model constructed to commemorate that trip. It may still be flying from someone's desktop.

✳ ✳ ✳

Returning to the routine of "flying the line" as a B-727 first officer, I was able to grasp the amazing strides that aviation had taken, even in my lifetime. From "wooden airplanes and iron men," the industry had advanced to sleek, jet-powered aircraft, guided by sophisticated onboard avionics and ground-based electronics that could detect and guide myriads of aircraft to a safe landing at their chosen destination. Gone were the goggles, boots, flying scarves, and leather helmets. Now pilots put on double-breasted, tailored uniforms (Delta copied theirs from the US Navy), complete with crisp white shirt, black tie, and polished black leather shoes. Topped off with a "wheel hat" bearing the airline insignia, we looked every bit "military" as we walked down the concourse, inspiring confidence in the traveling public, as we were told. Assistant chief pilots were not immune to "reminding" pilots of the expected standards as they stood in the hallway of Operations, checking shoe-shines and haircuts (no beards, no sideburns, neatly trimmed mustaches only).

There was something of a "hero image," at that time, which went with the job and the uniform. We were not only pilots, but we were the best public relations agents that Delta Airlines could ever have. Marketing managers would ask for pilots in uniform to accompany them on sales calls. Schools asked for pilots in uniform to address their classes on "Career Day" or to explain what makes an airplane fly. Pilots gave out toy wings and airplanes to kids as they boarded, entertained them in the cockpit at appropriate times, and issued signed "First Flight" certificates to young first-time fliers. Kids responded on their own with drawings and notes to the captain, many of which found their way to the bulletin boards in Operations.

Even in our off duty, out of uniform lives, we still represented Delta Airlines, in every sense of the word, in our communities and in our associations. To bring reproach on ourselves was to bring reproach on Delta Airlines. Keep your nose clean, pay your bills, and don't abuse your sick leave benefit; these were words to live by in the Delta "family." Walk carefully or suffer the ire of the chief pilot, who had the power of suspension or termination.

But the advance in pilot's attire was miniscule compared to the atmosphere in which he now plied his trade. Unless you had the added responsibility of outside inspections, you arrived at your cockpit "office," hung your coat on the supplied coat rack, stowed your hat, put your flight kit in place beside your seat, and sat down behind the control wheel with all systems at your disposal for bringing about a safe flight from point A to point B. It was the enormity of change in the environment that made such an impact on me upon my return from the world of old men and antique airplanes. And yet, in spite of my entering the aviation arena in its advanced stage of development, I was pleased to know that as a pilot, I was still a member of that great fraternity of brothers who had gone before.

But there were other aviation "Meccas" to which I had yet to pay homage. That opportunity came the following summer, when another fellow pilot and neighbor, Captain Ernie Hand, invited me to accompany him to the annual Experimental Aviation Association "Fly-In" in Oshkosh, Wisconsin. Ernie had just purchased a seasoned but beautiful Cessna 170B and was interested in building his own airplane from scratch. The clinics and seminars held at Oshkosh would lead him to accomplish that goal a few years later. The air shows and the displays were the big draws for the rest of us.

Although I failed to keep a diary for that trip, the experience still left its indelible mark on my memory. The scenario was similar to the first trip in that we would camp out under the wing and find our food primarily from the concessions at the event. The first thing I recall was our arrival at the fly-in. After a quick trip from Knoxville in the faster Cessna, we entered the arrival pattern with our required radio tuned to the published frequency. Those chosen to be controllers for this event were no ordinary controllers. These were the men of Chicago O'Hare Approach Control, who volunteered their talents each year to keep the hundreds of airplanes from running into each other during this busy three-day event, much as they did on a daily basis with the airline operation at O'Hare. Lining up on final approach with the controller's nonstop directions crackling over the speaker, we listened for our clearance to land behind several aircraft ahead. This was going to be touchy because the spacing between aircraft was very minimal, allowing very little time to clear the runway. Finally we heard the controller say "Cessna 170 cleared to land, clear the runway immediately left into the grass!" Ernie accomplished this maneuver just in time to see an experimental "Vari-Eze" aircraft touch down just off our right wing, as we pulled off into the grass for direction to parking.

I would describe the annual Experimental Aviation Association Oshkosh Air Show as the ultimate experience for anyone even remotely interested in aviation. I never had the opportunity to attend the famed Paris Air Show, but it would have to be something extraordinary to top Oshkosh. Everything was here: "home-builts," war birds, classics, antiques, and even old airliners like the Ford Tri-Motor or "Tin Goose," which began service in the 1920s and was on hand to give rides during the show.

After being assigned to parking, I set up our sleeping tent and spent the rest of the day roaming the displays and watching the action on the airfield, as hundreds of aircraft landed and took their places in the fields adjacent to the airport. Approaching one display tent, I saw a man selling and autographing books for a crowd of people. It turned out that this was Colonel "Pappy" Boyington, commander of the famous "Black Sheep" Squadron in the Pacific theater of World War II. "Pappy" was an early member and "ace" of the famous "Flying Tigers" under General Chennault in Burma and China, where he shot down six Japanese aircraft in his P-40 Curtiss "Warhawk." Afterward, he assumed command of a squadron of "misfits" flying Marine F-4U "Corsairs" off atolls in the Pacific. They went up against the Japanese "Zeros" on a daily basis and took their toll. The Japanese pilots referred to the Corsair as "Whistling Death." Naturally, it was a great honor to meet this hero of World War II and to buy an autographed copy of his book. After digesting the contents of the book, I discovered what a tough, colorful fellow he was, having been shot down and imprisoned by the Japanese until war's end. The long-running television show, *Baa, Baa Black Sheep*, was developed around his experiences, although he claimed the show was fictionalized to some extent. Considering those experiences, his very presence at Oshkosh was a miracle.

The next day, Sunday, the field was closed to arriving traffic, and the crowds assembled in the viewing areas for the commencement of the air shows. It was a beautiful sunny day, with blue skies and a few white puffy clouds. The temperature was pleasant, with light breezes—a perfect day for an air show. The first event included aerobatics featuring many types of aircraft. I particularly remember the demonstrations performed in the biplanes, some featuring "wing walkers" secured to the top wing as the aircraft was put through its paces. Next were performances featuring everything from a "Super Cub" to a Ryan monoplane to a P-38 "Lightning." The "War Birds" came next with a flyby featuring the "Confederate Air Force" based in Harlingen, Texas. This flyby included various bombers and fighters from the World War II era. I particularly remember seeing a T-28, painted up to look like a Japanese Zero, coming across the field trailing smoke, as an F-8U "Corsair" followed behind, simulating a "shoot-down." The climax of the show was a Marine "Harrier" jump jet, which demonstrated its vertical takeoff capability and then transitioned to level flight as it departed the airfield.

As the afternoon began to wane, departure was now the game, as all the assembled aircraft had to depart for home. We cranked the 170B and got into the lineup for takeoff. All went quickly, and we were soon back in the air for a quick trip back to McGhee-Tyson and home. It was time to get back to work and to my role in the modern world of civil aeronautics.

CHAPTER FOURTEEN

"TRANSITIONS"

1978 was a pivotal year in my life as I married the "friend" mentioned previously in these memoirs, Carolyn Dyer, who was to be my faithful and loving wife throughout our remaining years. She continued in her job at a local bank, while I continued selling real estate and flying a full month with Delta, commuting to Atlanta as a First Officer on the B-727. It was a busy time but a happy time.

Once a first officer was established in a cockpit position on a particular aircraft, the training requirements were reduced to an annual ground school, a simulator check, and a line check by a company-designated line-check airman. This training was normally accomplished within a four-day period at Delta's training center in Atlanta, with the line check coming sometime later when the line-check airman could catch you on one of your flights. With my time and years increasing on the B-727, I began to feel that I had "found a home," and I actually began to enjoy these annual reviews.

One of the simulator instructors must have sensed something along that line during one of my annual ground schools. On one occasion, after I completed my simulator check ride, he called me aside and invited me into the office of the Vice President for Training. It seemed that with the explosion of the B-727 onto the scene, there was a great need for simulator instructors, and he wondered if I would be interested in leaving the line and joining the Training Department as a B-727 simulator instructor. They embellished this offer by pointing out the many benefits of the position. These included being home every night, a schedule tailored to my preferences, increased pay, jump seat privileges, and an opportunity to move up the management ladder with the company. I would only have to go back to the line occasionally, to actually fly the aircraft. They heaped compliments about my ground school and simulator performances upon me, for good measure. I was told to think it over and to get back to them if I was interested.

To say that I was flattered by all this attention was to put it mildly. Was this to be a turning point in my career? Over the next few days, I began to digest the offer, considering its advantages and disadvantages for my situation. As I went about this process, something began to become clearer to me about my fellow pilots who had elected to go this route. While several of them were friends and classmates, what was it about their personalities that seemed to stand out to me? I denoted that, for the most part, these were people who did not enjoy being line pilots, preferring instead the coat and tie atmosphere of the Training Department and preferring to rub shoulders with management. Some simply did not want to fly. Others had visions of grandeur, believing that they possessed the qualities necessary for advancement to senior management. In short, this job was all about privilege and politics. Most of all, it involved getting away from real flying and entering the fantasy world of simulated flight. And as mentioned earlier, I recalled how weak these people were when they returned to the line and what an added burden they were to the rest of the crew. Did I really want to follow in the potential footsteps that were laid out before me? After considering all the available options, the answer became crystal clear. It was a resounding "No." I resolved, at that point, to forsake this opportunity and forever be a line pilot.

With the 1970s drawing to a close, I celebrated my tenth anniversary with the company. This precipitated being called into the chief pilot's office to be congratulated and to receive my ten year lapel pin, a small set of Delta wings with a ruby setting. It was a moment of reflection as I looked back over the first ten years with the company and the many changes that had occurred, such as deregulation, a merger, changes in the makeup of the fleet, and the addition of international routes. The one change that stood out to me during this decade was the change in the personnel of Delta itself.

From its inception, Delta Airlines was a "southern" company, employing southern people with southern values, values that were headed for a collision with the Civil Rights movement begun in the 1960s and lasting into the 1980s. With the exception of a few employees such as cabin service personnel, porters, and a couple of pilots, Delta was a "lily-white" airline. Now the federal government was mandating the hiring of "minorities" in all categories for which they were qualified, setting "quotas" for companies to follow. While this transition was accomplished without any serious consequences, there were some instances of trouble when black flight attendants began mixing with our southern crews.

One night I was flying a B-727 trip to Charleston, South Carolina, with a stop in Columbia. On the ground in Columbia, the lead flight attendant came to the cockpit with a complaint. It seemed that the black flight attendant assigned to the trip was not pulling her load and was showing a sullen attitude about being told what to do. The captain left his seat and went back to the galley to talk to her. When he tried to reason with her, she made a comment like, "No 'honky' is going to tell me what to do." The captain turned around and contacted the gate agent, telling him, "This airplane will not leave the gate until this flight attendant is removed from the flight." The gate agent complied, much to the surprise of the offending flight attendant, and we continued on to Charleston with only two flight attendants, our minimum number for flight.

Back inbound to Atlanta, the captain prepared his "write-up," citing the flight attendant for insubordination. But all in all, such instances were rare, and Delta soon became an integrated national airline with minorities filling the entire spectrum of the employee group.

In thinking of this incident, I recall another example where another B-727 captain took matters into his own hands in Columbia, South Carolina. Late one evening during our taxi-in to the gate, the tower advised that our red anti-collision beacon on top of the fuselage was inoperative. Checking the minimum equipment list, we discovered that we could not continue the flight, as it was a required item. Unless we could come up with a replacement bulb for the beacon and some way to get up onto the fuselage to change it, we were stuck until maintenance support could be flown in from Atlanta. What little Delta maintenance there was in Columbia had gone home for the night, and there was no equipment available for reaching the expired bulb. The agent was just about ready to notify Atlanta, when the captain hatched a plan that the two of them agreed would forever be left untold, to avoid possible disciplinary action.

Fortunately, the 727 carried a limited supply of light bulbs, and we were able to find what was thought to be the correct replacement bulb. Taking the bulb and a couple of screwdrivers, the captain stripped down to his pants and T-shirt and asked the gate agent to move the portable stairs as close to the fuselage as possible. Using the vertically extended handrail as a step, he "spread-eagled" his body onto the curvature of the fuselage and began inching his way toward the inoperative beacon. Once in place, he removed the lens and replaced the bulb, yelling down for me to turn on the beacon switch in the cockpit. To the delight of all, the beacon illuminated and began to rotate, casting an eerie aura of white light that must have been blinding to the captain-turned-mechanic. After yelling down to get the switch turned off, he replaced the red lens and began to inch his way back down the fuselage, looking for a foothold on the handrail. We all held our breath as he made it back down successfully, to the applause of a grateful crew and an even more grateful gate agent. As we departed on our way, the thought came to me that sometimes you do what you have to do to "keep the mill running."

That triggers another memory of my time back on the L-100 freighter. We were stranded in the Miami freight terminal one night with a seemingly inoperative oil cooler door on one of the engines. It was supposed to open on landing in order to help cool the engine oil while on the ground, but was stuck in the closed position. Knowing it would take an eternity to get Delta maintenance on the scene, the captain secured a rubber mallet and, standing on the hood of a tug positioned under the engine, gave the recalcitrant oil cooler door a resounding "whack." It immediately opened, and it operated normally for the remainder of our trip. As the captain stated on our departure, "Sometimes you have to 'malletize' things. It's a secret maintenance procedure."

Such actions were largely abandoned with the increased availability of maintenance support at all stations, not to mention the increased fear of incrimination among the pilot group for extending their expertise beyond job-description limits.

To say that the times were changing in the latter years of the 1970s would be putting it mildly. While the nation was struggling with the post-Vietnam era of civil unrest, runaway inflation, exorbitant interest rates, and fuel shortages, the airlines received a "gift" from Democratic President Jimmy Carter and the United States Congress that would change the industry forever. Entitled, "The Airline Deregulation Act of 1978," it basically ended government control of routes and fares, allowing each airline to fly anywhere, at any time, and at any price, all with the idea of producing more airline service at a reduced cost to the flying public, through competition. Critics were predicting that the end result would be the survival of only two or three US airlines. That prediction was played out over the next few years, as nine major carriers that had been profitable under the old system filed for bankruptcy. The great airlines of the past, such as Eastern, TWA, Braniff, and Pan American, were to be no more. Delta, with its conservative management style, was to survive and prosper in this environment, for the time being. Time enough, at least, to complete my airline career.

I cannot leave the era of the Jimmy Carter administration without mentioning the Super Sonic Transport (SST). France and England were pushing ahead with development of a supersonic airliner to reduce the time factor on international routes, all of this with the financial assistance of their governments. US aircraft manufacturers, notably Boeing, submitted plans for an American version, with appeals to the Carter administration for support. In a press conference, Carter stated emphatically, "We are not going to build it," leaving the United States completely out of this pioneering aviation development. France, with its Concorde, and England, with its own version of the SST, did develop the aircraft successfully, and they found a niche in the industry that proved profitable over several years. We used to "drool" when on the ramp at New York's JFK Airport or Washington's Dulles Airport, when we saw these beautiful, sleek supersonic machines take off or land, knowing that we could have been in similar cockpits, were it not for a peanut farmer from South Georgia. The 1970s could not end soon enough.

* * *

This portion of the poem by American poet Robert Frost continued to stick in my mind:

The woods are lovely, dark and deep;

But I have promises to keep,

And miles to go before I sleep.

Those "promises," in my mind, were to all passengers, to get them safely to their destination over the many "miles" that lay ahead, and there were to be many of those.

With the advent of the 1980s, a new wave of optimism and patriotism swept over the country. We had a new Republican president, Ronald Reagan, who would bring the country out of the economic doldrums and restore our respectability on the international stage. He had a taste for "jellybeans" and kept a jar on his desk in the Oval Office. I was quick to emulate this habit by immediately acquiring a jar for my own desk.

President Reagan almost immediately faced a challenge from the nation's air traffic controllers, who had organized and were threatening to strike if their demands for improved pay and working conditions were not met. Ignoring the fact that, as a federal agency, their strike was considered to be illegal, the controllers decided to proceed with a shutdown. This immediately threw the nation's airline schedule into turmoil, with limited operations and only a handful of nonstriking controllers and supervisors to handle the few flights that could operate. President Reagan responded by giving the striking controllers twenty-four hours to return to work or be fired. A few filtered back, but the majority, in their arrogance, refused, thinking that negotiations would continue toward a settlement. How wrong they were! This president was no Jimmy Carter. All striking controllers were fired, new controllers were hired and trained, and after a few weeks of reduced schedules, the industry was back in full operation. As I have mentioned, the greatest outcome of this strike was getting rid of those controllers who were hard to work with, while gaining a complement of new controllers who were a pleasure to work with for the remainder of my career.

Things were also moving rapidly with Delta Airlines. The Lockheed L-1011 was now the "queen of the fleet," the B-747s having been parked and finally eliminated from the inventory due to operating fuel costs.

The three-man cockpit was giving way to two-man crews only, as new aircraft designs began production. The B-757, B-767, and Airbus 300 were a new generation of aircraft destined to replace the nation's aging fleet. These were to employ new fuel-saving technology and avionics that would reduce cost and pilot workload, at least in the minds of the engineers who designed them.

The word was that the DC-8 was destined to be a vanishing breed, but Delta Airlines had a "love affair" with this aircraft that would keep it around beyond its time. Although the company parked the shorter, older DC-8-51s, it kept the newer "stretch" DC-8-61s flying on some of its main routes. Later, Delta pioneered a fuel-saving engine change to these aircraft, producing the DC-8-71. Most of these aircraft ended up eventually in the fleets of UPS and other cargo carriers. But once again, I digress.

At this point, I was moving rapidly up the seniority list, and I began to consider my options for moving up on equipment. Being a commuter, I had to consider being assured of holding a regular line instead of sitting reserve in a motel around the airport, waiting to be called out. Accordingly, I submitted bids with contingencies to ensure that happening.

One day I arrived from Knoxville on my commuter flight and was thrilled, upon checking the bulletin board, to see my name among those slated to become first officers on the DC-8. I was to have one last fling, flying the aircraft that I knew best, in a crew slot that was considered the best on the airline. Again, "Show up with your flight kit" was that position's job description, jokingly coined by the pilot group. In addition, I was to be reunited with many of the captains that I had flown with as a second officer. It was to be an enjoyable, relaxed operation over the next three years, with a nice increase in pay to boot.

Ground school, simulator, and flight training were routinely accomplished, and I was soon scheduled for my first trip. I was amazed anew at the room and visibility I had in the cockpit, compared to the cramped quarters of the B-727 to which I had become accustomed. The DC-8 schedules called for no more than one or two stops in each duty day. I would not miss the multiple stops engineered into the B-727 schedules. Hello, Los Angeles and Miami, good-bye Shreveport and Fort Wayne!

Flying the DC-8, as I have mentioned, was a "handful." That's what you had, a handful of throttles and a handful of a control wheel that moved all the cables leading to the controls—no hydraulically boosted controls here. To say she was responsive to control movements would be much too complimentary. There was a slight time lag that had to be allowed for between the muscle applied to the control wheel and the response from the flight controls on the wings and tail. This was a tough aircraft, and it took a tough person to fly it. Flying it in a crosswind approach and landing was not for the fainthearted. You earned every dollar of that extra pay during those times. On one of my first flights, I asked an old veteran captain for landing tips. He said, "Son, just bring it down about six inches above the ground, wipe the power, and let it settle in from there. Just don't mess with it." And he was right, although determining that "six inches" was always a challenge.

One interesting and unique thing about the DC-8 cockpit was the pet names given to various controls and switches. The manually operated elevator trim switches on the center console, for example, resembled and were appropriately called "suitcase handles." Just to the right were the smaller electric trim switches, which resembled a popular chewing gum shape of that time. Accordingly, we operated "Chiclets switches" when we wanted slower electric elevator trim. The knobbed handle used to manually control the outflow valve was called the "lollipop handle." Then there was the switch used to close off all heat and pressurization to the baggage area, in the event of a rapid depressurization. This was the infamous "dead dog" switch, denoting the condition in which any canine or other animal carried therein would be found in upon landing.

As with most aircraft in the fleet, a small tire-shaped knob was affixed to the landing gear handle, and the flaps handle was shaped like a miniature flap, just to avoid confusion, I suppose. Were the aviation engineers saying something about pilot intelligence?

Although my days on the DC-8 were relatively uneventful, they were not without incident. On one occasion, we were boarding passengers at Houston Intercontinental for a flight to Baltimore, Maryland. I noticed some tall, mostly black fellows in the waiting room, and I was told that we would be transporting the NBA Baltimore Bullets back home after their game the previous evening with the Houston Rockets. The entire first-class cabin was reserved for the squad and their manager. All went well until shortly after the team was boarded. The lead flight attendant was the first to break the news that certain team members were being unruly and uncooperative, even to the point of "pinching her on the butt." This infuriated the diminutive captain I was flying with. Getting out of his seat, he called for the team manager to come forward for a word in the cockpit.

I can still see him looking up and shaking his finger in the face of the tall form in front of him. His words went something like this, (offensive words that matched the offensive behavior of the players. Both uncalled for.) "You get those monkeys under control back there, and if I hear of any more trouble back there, I will have the FBI waiting to meet the aircraft in Baltimore."

The manager said, "Aw, Captain, these boys are okay. I'll take care of it." And he must have done so, because we never heard a word from the first-class cabin the rest of the flight; so much for the ambassadors and role models of the professional sports world.

People have asked me if I ever saw any "flying saucers" during my time in the air. I have always answered in the negative, although I have witnessed initially strange phenomena that turned out to have an explanation. Some of these would include a sudden moonrise over a dark ocean, meteor showers, space "junk" returning to earth in a ball of fire, planets that we could swear were aircraft in the distance, and the northern lights, to name a few.

The one phenomenon that shook me the most, however, was one that has been witnessed by pilots and seamen for hundreds of years. As aircraft and ships move through the electrified air associated with thunderstorms, small licks of amber-colored flames, called "Saint Elmo's fire," begin to build up on certain parts of the ship. This was particularly noticeable on the DC-8 windshield and nose, and the first time you see it, it startles you until you understand that it is normal and no danger to the aircraft.

One night we were flying into Cincinnati, doing our best to navigate around the weather. Finally we had no choice but to enter an area of thundershower activity. The usual "Saint Elmo's" started immediately, but this time it seemed brighter and more extensive than usual. Building very rapidly on the nose, it suddenly discharged with a loud bang, and a ball of static electricity rolled back through the cockpit. Fortunately, we popped out into clear air soon afterward, glad to have the "fireworks" behind us.

When I think of flying into Cincinnati, I recall a sad tale of a sailor flying home on leave to visit the family. He had boarded in Atlanta in a somewhat intoxicated condition, and he was further driven into that state by a few drinks from an indulgent flight attendant. His destination was Columbus, Ohio, our termination point for a short layover. After landing in Cincinnati, and while boarding for Columbus, the lead flight attendant reported that the sailor was "out of it," passed out and unresponsive. Knowing that we could not transport a passenger in this state, the captain had no choice but to have him removed by the local authorities. After we arrived at the gate in Columbus, the passengers deplaned, followed by the crew. Standing in the gate area were an older couple and a young woman holding a baby.

The elderly man asked, "Are all the passengers off? We were expecting our son on this flight. He's coming in from the navy." The captain and I looked at each other and silently agreed that we did not have the heart to tell the true story. We simply said that all passengers were off and that they should check with the agent meeting the flight for additional information. We departed to our layover, decrying the effects of "demon rum."

I could not leave my days on the DC-8 without mentioning the "unpreparedness" of Delta Airlines to handle a weather phenomenon in Atlanta that was confronted routinely in more northern stations. Apparently the powers that be on Delta's "mahogany row" considered Atlanta a "southern" city, somehow insulated from such things as snow and ice. Consequently, there was very little equipment and was even less training on how to keep runways and taxiways clear or on how to deice an aircraft prior to departure. This mindset was to bite Delta Airlines "big-time," several times over the course of my career.

On February 26, 1982, I recorded what I termed the "Great Deicing Caper" in my logbook. A good layer of ice followed by an inch or so of snow had brought this great international airport in Atlanta to its knees. Every Delta gate was occupied with an aircraft, the crews begging for deicing fluid that was in short supply, was late in coming, and had a long application time. My flight was at the gate for five hours during this process. Reports from captains indicating their disgust with the whole operation were submitted up the management chain, but with little impact.

On another occasion, I was stranded in an Atlanta airport motel for three days due to ice, snow, and persistent low temperatures. The airport simply shut down, taking no arrivals and allowing no departures until a runway could be cleared. It took several days to get back to full operation, and the effects were felt throughout the Delta System, at extreme financial loss. Later on, Delta adopted the "car wash" system of deicing, which was first employed, as I recall, at the Denver Airport. Aircraft would simply taxi to the departure end of the runway, pausing along the way at the "car wash" to receive deicing fluid just prior to takeoff. Such were the advancements in dealing with this "northern" weather phenomenon. A major accident at Washington National, involving an ice-laden B-737, resulted in aircraft deicing being given the highest priority later on in my career.

With the airline continuing to expand, I received another notice of "upward mobility," a bid on the Lockheed L-1011. It was September 1983, and all was well with the world. How suddenly that was to change.

* * *

There are certain "turning points" in people's lives that mean that, from that time on, things are never quite the same. Sometimes God needs to get your attention. On the evening of September 28, 1983, such an event took place in my life. Carolyn and I were driving from the Foothills Mall in Maryville, Tennessee, when it happened. As we passed through an intersection, a tractor trailer ran the traffic light and crashed into our right front, knocking our car sideways. It continued on, crushing a car on our left and dragging both vehicles two hundred feet down the highway and into a ditch. Both Carolyn and I were knocked unconscious for a few minutes. I came to with the smell of gasoline in my nostrils, and I realized that we were hurt, but just how much, I did not know. Just one spark would have ignited the fumes, turning the car into a flaming coffin. I was suddenly aware of men opening the doors and verbally assessing our injuries to a waiting ambulance above. The old Buick that we were driving had basic seat belts but no shoulder harness and no airbags. Failing to use the seat belts was a mistake that we both paid for.

My head had contacted the windshield, producing cuts requiring several stitches. In addition, I had broken ribs. However, my wife was not so lucky. She suffered a ruptured spleen, a punctured lung, multiple broken ribs, and a cracked pelvis. Only the hand of the Lord and the skills of the doctors, nurses, and technicians allowed her to emerge from the hospital one month later to begin a long recovery process. During that period, Delta Airlines told me to take whatever time I needed for both of us to recover, and added that by the way, I had been awarded a bid as first officer on the L-1011.

When Carolyn improved to a point where I felt I could leave her in the hands of other family, I contacted Delta Training and advised that I was ready to come back to work. Accordingly, I was scheduled to begin ground school on November 7, 1983. Miraculously, my wife had improved enough to join me in Atlanta for a portion of that time.

The L-1011 was a different kind of aircraft for me, in many ways. I had always flown aircraft with "conventional" avionics and controls. This aircraft, however, was of a new generation, employing the first version of what was to be known as a "glass cockpit." Manually flying the aircraft now gave way to maximum use of the autopilot, flight director, and navigational aids coupled to the autopilot. The pilot gave "inputs" on a panel just below the glare shield, and the autopilot and autothrottles would accomplish the task. Monitoring the changes and "minding the store" actually added to the workload, rather than decreasing it as the designers believed it would. As to aircraft systems, pilots were required only to learn how to operate a system but not necessarily to understand how it worked. Systems by operation became the ground school standard. Only the second officer was given any further in-depth training in system design and engineering. This saved on training costs, but somehow I felt that something was lost in the process. Accordingly, I never had as much confidence in the L-1011 as I had in the other aircraft I had flown. After fiddling in frustration with the "inputs" to produce a desired flight result, most of us clicked the autopilot off and flew the aircraft manually whenever possible. Resistance to change was a common feeling.

Assembled by Lockheed in Palmdale, California, the L-1011 was nicknamed the "Palmdale Pig" or the "Tritanic" by those who flew it. Delta shocked the aviation world when it selected the L-1011 over the Douglas DC-10. Everyone assumed that the DC-10 would be the choice, considering Delta's long history with the "DC" series built by Douglas Aircraft. The difference in operating costs between the two seemed to have been the deciding factor. The "bean counters" in Delta's accounting departments were having their voices heard.

One interesting story related to the very first L-1011 to roll off the assembly line. Each aircraft had what was known as an operating empty weight. Adding fuel, crew, and baggage to this figure produced the take-off weight for a particular flight. It seems that this first L-1011, delivered to Eastern Airlines, weighed several pounds more than subsequent aircraft, and no one could figure out why. The answer came at the first major overhaul, several years later, when the wing bays were opened for inspection. It was then discovered that several sets of tools and various parts were left in the wings by work crews rushing to meet the rollout deadline. When these much-traveled items were removed, the operating empty weight fell back into line with that of the other aircraft in the fleet.

The L-1011 was the first aircraft I flew that required "call-outs" during landing. This was due to the nose-high attitude and due to the fact that the cockpit was still several feet in the air when the main wheels touched down. The second officer would look over the pilot's shoulder and call out the readings on the radio altimeter, as the aircraft neared the runway surface. The readings would usually begin at fifty feet, going to forty, thirty, twenty, ten, five, and finally to touchdown. The only advantage to this system was that hard landings could now be blamed on the second officer. That excuse ran out, however, with the advent of later aircraft that computerized the call-out system and eliminated the second officer position.

The L-1011 was flown as a "nose-high" aircraft throughout all phases of flight. When flight planners slowed the airspeed during cruise in order to save fuel, this action aggravated the situation, producing a steep deck angle in the passenger cabin. We had to hear continual complaints from the flight attendants about having to "walk uphill" during their meal service on longer flights. In addition, the air circulation was poor in the rear of the aircraft, where the smoking section was located. Having to work or ride in that area, designated "D" zone, was a lung-challenging experience. Fortunately, Delta Airlines declared a "no smoking" policy on all domestic flights shortly thereafter, eliminating both the exposure to secondhand smoke and the need to clean the outflow valve area, which was usually stained or dripping with tar.

Trips on the L-1011, during the time I flew it, were decidedly different from those of other aircraft. Delta began serving the "island trade" with heavy turnaround schedules to Bermuda, Puerto Rico, and the Bahamas. This service was tied in with the cruise ship schedules serving those areas, so there was always a festive air among the passengers onboard. Putting all dress codes aside, passengers came and went as their vacation experience dictated. Gone was any semblance of good taste as male passengers deplaned in "tank tops," cutoff shorts, and "flip-flops," carrying the obligatory five bottles of rum in a box especially designed for the purpose. Their sunburned spouses followed behind with shopping bags full of whatever the islands had to offer.

All in all it, was great fun, with the exception of dealing with the island ground personnel charged with getting the flight in and out. To say that things moved a little slower in the islands would be an understatement. "It's the islands, 'mon,' relax!" was the advice given as each arrival was slowly and laboriously unloaded, refueled, and reloaded for departure—no hurry here, as we saw the time tick up ever closer to scheduled departure time. On occasion, we would have a few hours to kill, which we would spend rattling over the island roads in a rented taxi, perhaps to a suggested oceanside restaurant for lunch or to comb the duty-free shops for bargains too good to pass up. The only layover in the islands was in San Juan, Puerto Rico, where I spent many hours exploring Old San Juan and its history. As I sat on the promontory of El Morro, the ancient Spanish fort, it was difficult to imagine Christopher Columbus sailing into the same harbor below in 1493, or to imagine the fact that one shell from an American warship in 1898 destroyed the flagpole atop the fort, resulting in surrender of the island to US forces during the Spanish-American War. All this, plus the weather and the excellent food, made San Juan a favorite layover spot for me, both then and in future years on other aircraft.

There are three significant events, relative to the L-1011, that I deem worthy to include in these memoirs. The first of these occurred on August 2, 1985. I was on vacation at the time, spending the night at a Holiday Inn in Roanoke, Virginia, en route to Colonial Williamsburg. Turning on the television, I received a shock. A major air disaster had occurred in Dallas, involving a Delta L-1011 with a flight number that was familiar to me; it was a flight on my line of time for the month, although not on the same day. The facts of this accident are best told in a special report by correspondent Chris Kilroy, reporting for AirDisaster.com:

"August 2, 1985 is a day Dallas, Texas will never forget. Throughout the afternoon, the weather was typical Texas; Hot temperatures, low humidity, and sunny skies. At 4:03 PM eastern daylight time, Delta Airlines flight 191, a Lockheed L-1011-385-1 lifted off from runway 9L at the Fort Lauderdale/ Hollywood International Airport. Aboard the aircraft today were 167 passengers and crew traveling to Los Angeles with a stop at Dallas/Ft. Worth. As the flight cruised over the vast farmlands of Louisiana, something strange began to happen at Dallas.

In command of Delta 191 was Captain Edward Conners, a 14,000 hour pilot who was highly respected at Delta. Assisting him on the flight deck was First Officer Rudolph Price, hardly a novice, and Second Officer Nick Nassick. Nassick actually re-wrote the technical manual for Delta L-1011's some two years earlier and he probably knew the inner workings of the airplane more than anyone.

As the plane approached the beginning of the standard terminal arrival route, air traffic control gave the crew a vector to "turn heading 290 to join the Blue Ridge 010 radial and track inbound." Seeing a thunderstorm cell at that heading, and not being one to trifle with heavy weather, Captain Conners decided to turn to a heading of 255 and turn back to 290 before he got to Blue Ridge…this would give the passengers a much smoother ride.

Meanwhile, off the end of runway 17L at Dallas-Fort Worth (DFW), a huge updraft had begun to form and a thunderstorm was forming with more energy than 100 nuclear reactors. All of this, however, was disguised in the form of puffy, white clouds. At the National Weather Office in Dallas, the aviation meteorologist, George Encinas, decided to break for an early dinner since nothing was on his scope. When he returned he learned that an airliner had crashed at DFW.

Turning onto final approach, flight 191 was at 2,000 feet AGL (above ground level) with the landing gear in motion. The landing checklist was performed without incident. 191 was four miles in trail of a Learjet (N715JF) for the runway, and throughout the entire ordeal, 15JF never reported any abnormal weather phenomenon. Approaching 1500 feet, F.O. Price commented "there's lightning coming out of that one." Captain Conners, surprised, replied "what?" "There's lightning coming out of that one." "Where?" "Right ahead of us." That was the first sign of trouble in the cockpit of Flight 191.

Descending through 800 feet, something very odd began to happen. The plane was speeding up, but no one was touching the throttles. The Vref (landing reference speed) for the airplane's weight was 149 knots, and the plane had accelerated to 173 knots before Price (who was the pilot flying), closed the throttles to slow her down. Captain Conners recognized this as the first signs of wind shear, and warned Price: "Watch your speed. You're gonna lose it all of a sudden, there it is." Price advanced the throttles. "Push it up, push it way up. Way up, way up, way up," exclaimed Connors. From the beginning to the end of this sentence, the aircraft's speed dropped from 173 to 133 knots. As Price gave it full power, Conners said "that's it" as the speed began to rise. His voice filled with terror, the Captain then exclaimed "Hang onto the son of a bitch," as the speed dropped to 119.

To avoid a stall, the pilots pushed the nose over…their vertical speed increased to 1,700 feet per minute and the ground proximity warning system began to sound an alarm. The last words heard in the cockpit were various expletives.

The aircraft landed in a field, bounced in the air, and came down again on Hwy 114, a very busy 6-lane thoroughfare adjacent to the airport. A small Honda was crushed by the no. 1 engine, killing the driver, and shutting that engine down. The differential thrust with the failed engine caused the plane to veer left, and it struck two 4 million gallon water tanks at a ground speed of 220 knots.

On that dark day in Dallas, 167 passengers were driven literally into the ground by Mother Nature. Unfortunately, 136 of them did not live to tell their story."

AirDisaster.com: Special Report: Delta Airlines Flight191,

January 15, 2012

A pall of sadness settled over the remainder of my vacation trip as the television images of the blackened L-1011 tail section kept center stage in my mind. And the questions went on. What had happened? Who were the crew members? Were they classmates known to me? Would it have been the same for me if I had been at the controls? All of these questions, with the exception of the last, were to be answered in the days and weeks following. The crew list was released shortly thereafter, and although it was of little solace, it did not list anyone I knew personally. The thing that did jump out at me was that this captain was out of the Training Department. The other thing was that the first officer was flying the aircraft. I have related my experiences of what it was like to fly with Training Department captains elsewhere in these memoirs, and I will not belabor that point here or imply that there was any culpability on his part. However, it occurred to me that the first officer was being "instructed" throughout the approach and that there was some confusion as to who was controlling the aircraft.

Did the crew get into a situation from which recovery was impossible? That question was to be addressed in every L-1011 simulator training session over the next several months. Recovery from a wind shear microburst on final approach was a scenario that every L-1011 pilot would face, as programmers attempted to duplicate the flight conditions of Flight 191 in the simulator. As time went on, technology went to work supplying wind shear detecting Doppler radar at major airports as well as wind shear warning devices aboard most commercial aircraft.

The gruesome aspects of this accident were to come home to me upon return to work. I thought that surely, with all the bad press precipitated by Delta Flight 191, the company would exchange that particular flight number for another. But no, there it was on my rotation sheet: Flight 191, FLL to DFW to LAX, and it was my leg to fly. Flying that flight, taking off and landing on the same runways, hearing that call sign throughout, and seeing the smashed, blackened water towers where another 191 came to rest was a " ghoulish" experience. Even the tone of the air traffic controllers' voices seemed to be more serious and sympathetic when responding to our calls.

Reality really came to roost when we arrived at the gate in Dallas. It seemed that we were scheduled for a delay, one long enough to allow us to hitch a ride to a maintenance hangar across the field, there to view the remains of Flight 191 that had been recovered from the crash scene. Entering the dimly lit hangar from the bright sunshine outside was one of the most eerie experiences of my life. After getting adjusted to the lighting, I could make out the blackened tail section lying on its side, with passenger seats hanging out. Here was a landing gear, and over there an engine cowling. Otherwise, there was nothing recognizable in the mounds of debris that made up the remainder of the aircraft. It was the equivalent of looking at a smashed eggshell, and that was the revelation that came to me at that point. The large, heavy-looking aircraft that we flew were nothing more than aluminum eggshells with engines attached. I resolved to handle them accordingly.

The second event was an air disaster of a different sort, one to which I was an eyewitness. January 28, 1986, dawned cloudy and cold in New York as we reported for sign-in at LaGuardia Airport to fly Delta Flight 93, with our destination, Nassau in the Bahamas. I had flown this flight three other times earlier in the month, and I had the route down pat. The weather was forecast to be good, and the whole crew was looking forward to the warmth and sunshine of the islands, even though we would have very little ground time before heading back to Boston. As I programmed the onboard navigational computer, I noticed that the last portion of our flight involved a route change; instead of flying the usual Atlantic route, located some distance off the east coast, we would take an inland route down over the Florida peninsula and would turn due east for Nassau. In the Notices to Airmen attached to the flight plan was this message: Reroute due Space Shuttle launch Cape Kennedy.

At 8:53a.m. (EST), we departed the gate to join the lineup for takeoff on LaGuardia's runway 31.Originally designed for aircraft of the1930s, this runway had been lengthened with a concrete pier extending into the East River in order to accommodate aircraft like the L-1011. Takeoff and landing at LaGuardia was always a challenge and would best be described as landing or taking off from an aircraft carrier. Any miscue, and you were sure to get wet. There was no room for error and no place to go if you made one.

On takeoff, we watched the edge of the pier disappear under the nose as we raised the gear and climbed out over the city, our heart rates settling back to normal. Turning left over upper Manhattan, we crossed the Hudson River and headed south to join our departure route. At approximately 11:30 a.m., we were positioned just north of Jacksonville, Florida, cruising at thirty-five thousand feet, when an unidentified voice came over the radio saying that the space shuttle Challenger had just lifted off from her launch pad at the Kennedy Space Center. Sure enough, there ahead and slightly off to the left, we saw a white, vertical column of water vapor and exhaust rising from the ground and rapidly passing through our altitude. Shortly thereafter, the vertical column underwent a change, with one small portion continuing erratically upward and the larger portion arcing over and back down toward the earth in a weird looking smoke trail. I assumed that this was a normal separation of a booster rocket attached to the shuttle, but I was shockingly corrected a minute or so later by that same voice over the radio: "She didn't make it." What we had seen was the explosion of the Challenger a few seconds after launch, although we did not know what was happening at the time. The Wikipedia online encyclopedia gave this account:

"The **Space Shuttle *Challenger* disaster** occurred on January 28, 1986, when Space Shuttle Challenger broke apart 73 seconds into its flight, leading to the deaths of its seven crew members. The spacecraft disintegrated over the Atlantic Ocean, off the coast of central Florida, United States at 11:39 a.m. EST (16:39 UTC).

Disintegration of the entire vehicle began after an O-ring seal in its right solid rocket booster (SRB) failed at liftoff. The O-ring failure caused a breach in the SRB joint it sealed, allowing pressurized hot gas from within the solid rocket motor to reach the outside and impinge upon the adjacent SRB attachment hardware and external fuel tank. This led to the separation of the right-hand SRB's aft attachment and the structural failure of the external tank. Aerodynamic forces promptly broke up the orbiter.

The crew compartment and many other vehicle fragments were eventually recovered from the ocean floor after a lengthy search and recovery operation. Although the exact timing of the death of the crew is unknown, several crew members are known to have survived the initial breakup of the spacecraft. However the shuttle had no escape system and the astronauts did not survive the impact of the crew compartment with the ocean surface."

Wikipedia Encyclopedia

Space Shuttle Challenger disaster

January 30, 2012

An atmosphere of gloom settled over the crew that even the warmth of the tropical sun could not dispel upon our arrival in Nassau. So many lives lost, including a female school teacher selected for the mission. Had the shuttle's past successes produced such an air of overconfidence, or had its launch become so routine, that we felt we could now send anyone into space? This tragic setback in the nation's space program was to haunt NASA for many months to come, as President Reagan suspended the program. That weird-looking smoke trail, shooting out and over like a roman candle, became etched in my mind for all time.

The third event that comes to mind relative to the L-1011 was more personal and involved one of my favorite holidays, Saint Patrick's Day. And what better place to celebrate the "wearing of the green" than America's most Irish city, Boston, Massachusetts? I was developing a measure of seniority on the L-1011 and was scanning over the bid sheet for the month of March, 1986, when I spied a trip that included a choice layover in Boston on the big day. I bid and won the trip, and my plan was set in motion. My wife would join me in Atlanta, replete with our celebratory green gear, and would accompany me to Boston to help the citizens celebrate on March 17th.

All went exactly as planned until I entered the cockpit and prepared to get into the copilot's seat. These L-1011 seats were the first to be electrically powered, replacing the manually operated spring handles used on older aircraft. The controls were located on the left side of the seat, opposite the center console (for the first officer), with the switches guarded by a small bracket attached to the seat. Getting into the seat required stepping over with your right leg and then squeezing your left leg between the seat and the console. I had performed this maneuver on many occasions, but this time something went terribly wrong.

Somehow, my left leg, in passing through this narrow slot, actuated the "Forward" switch of the seat control driving the seat left and forward, pinning my leg against the center console. Fortunately, a Delta mechanic was in the cockpit, saw what was happening, and quickly pulled the appropriate circuit breakers, shutting off the seat motor. Otherwise, the seat would have continued forward, completely crushing my leg. But now I was trapped like a rat! Sweat began to pour from my face as I struggled to find some relief from the pain and the awkward stance I was in. With power shut off to the seat and with my leg blocking the controls, my extrication from this predicament was in doubt, and my fear factor began to rise.

Again, however, the mechanic onboard came to the rescue. Analyzing the situation, he saw that the only solution to freeing this trapped pilot "rat" was to remove the seat, which was attached to the cockpit floor with a series of bolts. After obtaining authorization from maintenance control and then rounding up some assistance, he went to the task, and several minutes later removed the last of the bolts. With assistance, he slid the heavy seat backward and to the right, and my leg came free. Oh, blessed relief!

But now I was unable to walk, and the extent of my injury was unknown. I hobbled off the aircraft and into a wheelchair that had just been used to board disabled passengers. Someone placed my coat and flight kit in my lap, and an agent pushed me down the Jet way and into the gate area, where a surprised Carolyn was waiting to board. We both knew at this point that Boston was not to be. Seeing one of the pilots in a wheel chair was not good "PR" for the waiting passengers, so I was quickly wheeled away from the gate as my replacement hurried down the Jet way to avoid a delay.

Fortunately, there was a flight leaving for Knoxville at a gate nearby. After obtaining "emergency" pass priority for the two of us, I was wheeled onto the aircraft, and we were soon winging our way back home. First stop was Blount Memorial Hospital Emergency Room in Maryville, where x-rays proved negative and the diagnosis was a severe contusion of my left calf. I celebrated Saint Patrick's Day for the next few days propped up on the sofa with my leg elevated. Such are the happenings when the plans of man go awry. I always wondered if the copilot who replaced me had as much enjoyment on that Boston layover as we intended to have.

Once again, the winds of change were blowing relative to my career. My days on the L-1011 and my days as a first officer were rapidly drawing to a close. On December 12, 1985, I had received an "Advance Entitlement" for a captain's position on the Boeing 737 in the Atlanta base. You will recall that this award was something like a "promise" of a position, when and if the needs of the company were such as to make it a reality. Now, in the spring of 1986, that reality came to pass. My "entitlement" was converted, and I was scheduled to begin ground training in April. On the evening of March 28, 1986, the captain steered the aircraft into the gate in Atlanta on my last L-1011 flight. I ran the electric seat back, picked up my flight kit, and walked off the aircraft, never to occupy a copilot seat again. Now it was my time to be a captain.

CHAPTER FIFTEEN

"JUNIOR CAPTAIN"

Seeing my captain's bid posted on the bulletin board in Operations produced a myriad of emotions. The first was joy that I had, at last, attained the opportunity to occupy the highest position possible on a commercial flight crew—the left seat. This was quickly followed by questioning fear and trepidation. Could I hack the course? What kind of captain would I be? How would I handle the responsibilities of command? Suddenly, the comfort of being a copilot first officer-type with someone else calling the shots was very appealing. It was some consolation, however, to recall a statement made to me during the hiring process over sixteen years earlier: "You are here to become a captain." And so it was now time to fulfill my reason for being.

Since this captain's bid was an "Advance Entitlement," it did not mean that I would launch into training immediately. Rather, it meant that I would begin the checkout phase in keeping with my seniority, as class slots became available at some future date. Finally, after nearly four months of continuing to fly first officer on the L-1011, I was "converted" to B-737 captain on April 1, 1986, and was scheduled to begin training immediately.

As with every aircraft I ever flew, the training regimen began with "ground school." Accordingly, in that first week of April, I reported to the familiar surroundings of the Center for Disease Control (CDC) training building in Hapeville, Georgia, near the Delta general offices, where I had spent so many hours in times past. Walking into the classroom, I found myself in a rather small class that included other B-737 captain candidates, with a corresponding number of first officer candidates. For the next two weeks, we would take the B-737 apart and put it back together, system by system, prior to moving on to the simulator. The instructor was an animated type who kept us entertained while teaching the rather dry intricacies of each aircraft system. I remember that he would award "attaboy" stickers to those who excelled in class and on exams. He was also a confidence builder who said such things as, "If they can teach camel drivers to fly this airplane, I know you guys can do it too." This was a somewhat racial reference to the fact that Boeing had sold a number of B-737s to Middle Eastern countries. It seems that every academic class develops a personality of its own, and ours was no exception.

They say that there is one person in every class, however, who makes it hard on everyone else, and we had ours—a fair-haired first officer candidate who seemed to delight in knowing the answer to every question and, in the process, embarrassing us older captain types who were a little slow in responding. The instructor tried to rein this guy in when he wanted to delve deeply into the "theory" behind certain aspects of B-737 engineering, and discreetly failed to recognize him when his hand shot up with a question at "quitting time." Most of us knew that "being smart in things that don't matter" would be of little use in flying the B-737, but apparently this was lost on our classroom nemesis. Somehow we sensed that there would come a day of retribution.

As to the B-737 itself, it was a tough little aircraft, often referred to as the "Fluff" or the "Flying Football" because of its symmetrical shape.

It had an older design incorporating much of the technology found on the B-727, and it was designed to carry smaller loads and get into places where other aircraft could not go. Delta found a fit for the aircraft in its route structure, and the company ordered newer models, incorporating advanced control and navigation systems, to augment the fleet picked up in a merger with Western Airlines. As fate would have it, the new models went to the old Western bases, and the old models were brought in to Atlanta for us to fly—more on that later. I was just happy to be in the B-737 program instead of the alternative. That alternative involved the evolution of the old DC-9 to a design ushering in the MD-80 series, which was nicknamed the "mad dog" by those forced to fly it. (As one "mad dog" captain said, "I don't care what they do to it, it's still a DC-9.") I didn't know it at the time, but I would never fly anything other than Boeing equipment for the remainder of my career, and for that, I am thankful.

With ground school behind me, the simulator phase was set to begin. This phase all went smoothly, and I was put up on the schedule for my FAA oral exam. I assumed that the exam would be conducted by an FAA flight examiner. But what I didn't know was that, due to a shortage of personnel, the FAA had just completed a program with Delta, naming a number of the Delta flight training instructors as "designated FAA examiners" to conduct these "airplane orals." Not knowing this, I walked into the examination room, attempting to hide my nervousness. And although I felt fully prepared in my knowledge of the B-737, I still felt what I would call the "suspicious tension" that always existed on the part of the pilot group when the FAA was around. I mean, here was a fellow (in my mind at least) who envied the position I was about to attain and who had the power to delay or to end that process, based on my performance. Accordingly, I was rather formal and tight-lipped, answering, "Yes, Sir" and "No, Sir," avoiding any needless chitchat. The examiner proceeded to check my license, my air transport rating written exam certificate, my current physical, and my training records, after which we launched into an hour-long question and answer session on B-737 aircraft systems.

All this went well, and shortly afterward, he called for a short break. Sitting in the break area over a cup of coffee, the "examiner" made some comment about wanting to get out of the Training Department and back to flying the line. I said something like, "You mean you're not with the FAA?"

He laughed, replying in the negative and explaining the aforementioned "designee" program. "But you will see the real guy on the last two legs of your line check," he said. "He'll be the one to write your ticket." Relaxed and somewhat relieved for the present, I successfully passed the remainder of the oral exam—one more step completed on my journey to captaincy.

With ground school and simulator behind me, it was on to flight training, the goal of which was to show that we could take off and land the aircraft, in preparation for our upcoming line checks. One morning, a few days later, I reported to Operations to meet my flight instructor. We were joined by one other captain-candidate, plus the "know-it all" first officer candidate from our ground school class. It was decided during a short briefing that we would fly to Augusta and remain in the traffic pattern, each man getting his "three bounces" (landings), before we returned to Atlanta. Since the other captain-candidate was senior to me, he took the first turn in the left seat, while the rest of us did the preflight inspection. The flight to Augusta was quick, smooth, and uneventful, and we were soon into the traffic pattern. I observed from the jump seat as the other captain-candidate satisfactorily completed his required three landings, after which the instructor asked us to change seats. Having been able to observe, I quickly "got the picture" and accomplished three landings, the last being a perfect "grease job," upon which the instructor said, "I've seen enough."

Now it was time for "Mister Smart Guy" first officer to get into the right seat and to show us up with his aviation skills. His first landing attempt was a bone-jarring assault on the earth that made us grimace. The next was even worse. Round and round the traffic pattern we went, each landing an unnerving event. After ten or so attempts (we quit counting), the instructor decided that we had wasted enough jet fuel, so he set course for Atlanta. During the debriefing, we captain-types were signed off, with compliments for our efforts, and were dismissed to go on our way. We lingered long enough, however, to observe the dazed and embarrassed first officer shaking his head and muttering to himself as he was being debriefed and rescheduled for additional flight training. "I just couldn't get the picture," he kept saying. Leaving the room, the other captain-candidate and I could not resist a mutual grin as our revenge and retribution was now complete. In the end, landing the B-737 that day was one answer the first officer did not have.

With ground school, simulator, and line oriented flight training behind me, I now had my air transport pilot rating on the B-737 in hand. The only remaining items were the initial captain's line check, and most importantly, meeting up with an FAA flight examiner who would "write my ticket," the license authorizing me to fly the B-737 as captain in airline operations.

The line check was a series of flights where the aspiring captain sat in the left seat (the captain's seat), and a company-designated "line check airman," who was a line captain himself, sat in the right, or copilot's seat. The regular copilot either sat on the cockpit jump seat or took a seat in the cabin. On April 26, 1986, I departed on a four-day trip, acting as captain, with layovers in Amarillo, Texas, Pittsburgh, Pennsylvania, and Norfolk, Virginia. Coming out of Norfolk on the fourth day, we would fly direct to Dallas-Fort Worth, Texas, and then back home to Atlanta with a stop in Baton Rouge, Louisiana. The FAA flight examiner was scheduled to board in Dallas, take his position on the cockpit jump seat, and observe my performance for the last two legs inbound to Atlanta. Based on that performance, he would be the final authority in granting my license.

All went well throughout the first three days of the trip, with the line check airman basically giving me tips about flying the airplane on the line and helping me transition from the training environment to the "real world." On April 30, I landed the B-737 at DFW and taxied to the gate. While the aircraft was being serviced for the outbound trip, I was met by the FAA examiner, who entered the cockpit, introduced himself, and began to check my qualifying paperwork, my current first-class physical, and so on. I was a little nervous, but by this time, I was so immersed in the B-737 that I was confidently ready to "get it on." I was a little surprised when the examiner said that he would only ride with us on the first leg to Baton Rouge, as he had to get back to Dallas to give another rating ride. One shot would be all I would get.

After I briefed the senior flight attendant on the pertinent data relative to our short flight to Baton Rouge, the passengers were boarded, the boarding door was closed, and we called for "pushback." Taxi and takeoff were routine, and we were soon leveling at cruise altitude. I had turned the seat belt sign off on climb-out, to allow the flight attendants to move around the cabin, but as soon as we leveled off, we began to experience light clear-air turbulence. Should I turn the seat belt sign back on, or should I ride it out for a little bit, hoping that the ride would improve? The examiner made the choice for me by saying something like, "It's probably a little rough back in the cabin." Somewhat chagrined, I quickly reactivated the seat belt sign to the "on" position and began preparation for the descent and approach into Baton Rouge. Had I made a grave, disqualifying error of judgment with the seat belt sign? I put it into the back of my mind as I initiated the descent. As weather conditions would have it, the Baton Rouge Airport was "in sight" a good distance out, and the tower controller cleared us for a visual approach and landing on the north-south runway. As I rolled the airplane to line up with the center-line of the runway, it suddenly dawned on me, "After all the study and training, all I have to do is land this B-737 on that runway and I am a Delta captain!" The excitement began to grow in me as I "greased it on" and taxied to the gate.

When the engines were shut down, the examiner leaned over my shoulder and said, "Congratulations, Captain Butcher," and handed me my license. It was all over in one respect, but it was the beginning of something new in another. As the examiner left the cockpit, there was celebration all around, as I thanked the crew for their support and received their congratulations in turn. The final leg of the trip back to Atlanta was flown by a giddy and happy crew, especially the captain.

Junior Captain 1986

On May 1, 1986, I was "converted" to a permanent position as captain on the B-737 in the Atlanta base. I received the standard congratulatory letter from the director of Flight Operations, along with an invitation to meet him in his office to receive my captain's wings. After wandering the halls of "mahogany row," I finally located his office and was ushered in for the presentation and a short chat, much of which centered on the level of responsibility inherent in my new position. I distinctly remember him saying something like, "When you taxi the 'Widget' [the triangular-shaped Delta logo painted on the tail of every company aircraft] away from the gate for the first time, it will be the loneliest moment of your life." And he was right. Now I would only be able to look to myself.

As a member of ALPA, the union organization that represented the pilot group, I was reminded of the "Code of Ethics" to which every professional airline pilot was bound:

CODE of ETHICS

An Air Line Pilot will keep uppermost in his mind that the safety, comfort, and well-being of the passengers who entrust their lives to him are his first and greatest responsibility.

An Air Line Pilot will faithfully discharge the duty he owes the airline that employs him and whose salary makes possible his way of life.

An Air Line Pilot will accept the responsibilities as well as the rewards of command and will at all times so conduct himself both on duty and off as to instill and merit the confidence and respect of his crew, his fellow employees, and his associates within the profession.

An Air Line Pilot will conduct his affairs with other members of the profession and with ALPA in such a manner as to bring credit to the profession and ALPA as well as to himself.

To an Air Line Pilot the honor of his profession is dear, and he will remember that his own character and conduct reflect honor or dishonor upon the profession.

Having Endeavored to his utmost to faithfully fulfill the obligations of the ALPA Code of Ethics and Canons for the Guidance of Air Line Pilots, a pilot may consider himself worthy to be called…an **Air Line Pilot.**

With my new wings attached to the uniform as a reminder of my newly acquired responsibility, I set out on my captain's journey to become a true Airline Pilot.

* * *

Since I was not senior enough to hold a regular line, my first order of business was to find housing for the periods that I would "sit reserve," waiting to be called out when needed. Luckily I had made some contacts in the rental office of the CDC building where I had undergone training. This office managed a few apartments on the upper levels of the building, and by chance, one of the small one-bedroom apartments became available, so I jumped on it with a month-to-month lease. With a few linens from home and a trip to the grocery store, I was soon set up. I turned on my rented "beeper" and sat back, waiting for crew scheduling to "call me out" for a trip.

And then, for two weeks, absolutely nothing happened—no beeper alerts, no phone calls, nothing. It even got to the point that instead of crew scheduling calling me, I would call them, just to check on the current situation. I was "antsy" to fly, to get out of that apartment, and to get out into the system again.

Finally I was delivered. On May 15, 1986, crew scheduling called, assigning me to a trip the next day. I alerted my wife, who came down that evening to join me. The trip was a two-day trip that started out with a leg to Columbia, South Carolina, then on to Charleston, and back to Atlanta. Since seating was tight for pass riders out of Charleston, my wife would fly with me to Columbia and then board a westbound flight back to Atlanta. As it turned out, she would be onboard for my first flight as a captain and my last flight as a captain. Little did I know what lay between. But all went well on this day, and despite a little nervousness, I survived to grease it on the runway in Columbia, where I said good-bye to my wife and pressed on to Charleston and the remainder of the trip. As I settled in to my new position, I began to understand that being captain was not all that bad.

The following few months were spent settling in as a new captain on the B-737 and building enough flight time to be removed from the "high minimums" restriction. This was a weather restriction placed on new captains, which added ceiling and visibility values to the "published minimums" already in place, until the captains acquired one hundred hours in the airplane. Although it was protection for new captains and never came into play for my part, it was nice to reach that one-hundred-hour plateau and have my name removed from the list. This goal was reached rapidly, facilitated by my living close to the airport and being available to crew scheduling on short notice. By letting them know that I was standing by in my apartment and was ready to take a trip on a moment's notice, I developed a win-win situation that allowed me to build time and allowed the crew scheduler to cover a trip quickly, without having to call out a captain who lived miles from the airport. In addition, when I neared the end of my on-call days, they would often release me early to go home, if there was no immediate need in sight.

Another restriction placed on captains was "airport familiarization." This basically began as a requirement to be qualified to fly into your destination airport, either by having been there previously or by flying with someone else who had. With the rapidly expanding route structure and upward mobility of the pilot group, this became a real headache for Operations in determining who could or could not fly a particular rotation of trips. The company quickly solved this problem by producing a set of slides for each airport in the system and by getting them approved by the FAA as meeting the requirement. These slides showed visual approaches to all useable runways at each airport, with warnings about any local terrain or obstacles. The captain was then responsible for viewing the slides for each airport and initialing a roster indicating that he was qualified into each airport on his rotation. There were a few airports, like Jackson Hole, Wyoming, that required an initial familiarization by an airport-qualified check airman. Luckily, I never had to fly into any of those "hard to get into and out of" airports.

By coming to the B-737, I was introduced to a whole new set of cities into which I had never flown. Now I would see smaller cities like Pensacola, Norfolk, and Greenville in the southeast and nearly all cities in Texas and Oklahoma further west. The need for the B-737 was particularly acute out of the Dallas-Fort Worth base. I recall being sent there for several rotations involving four days of nothing more than shuttling in and out to places like Austin, El Paso, Lubbock, Amarillo, and San Antonio, as well as to other outlying cities such as Tulsa, Albuquerque, and Oklahoma City.

As crew members, we dubbed those rotations as "the search for the ultimate Mexican restaurant." Every layover was spent in diligently carrying out this search, based on local recommendations. Hotel employees would transport the crew, or even offer the loan of a car, to the location of the best-rated Mexican food in the area. It might be a fancy place, but more than likely would be a "hole-in-the-wall" or even, on one occasion, someone's home. After taking our fill, we would continue the search the next night in another city. While it was a close race between El Paso and Albuquerque, the ultimate result of this search was a net weight gain of twenty pounds during my first six months on the B-737. Ultimately, I was delivered from the DFW shuttle and my Mexican feasts, only to be further tempted in places like Mobile, Alabama, where obtaining a fried shrimp and oyster "Po'Boy" sandwich at the airport café was mandatory when transiting that station.

Was I destined to be a fat captain? I certainly was getting a good start. I recalled the old captain who always said, "I know our flight schedule, but what is our eating schedule?" Somehow, as I mentioned earlier, flying and eating just seemed to go hand in hand.

The most memorable flight I ever had in the B-737 could be entitled, "The most scared I ever was in an airplane," or "A junior captain learns his first big lesson." As the saying goes, "There are old pilots and there are bold pilots, but there are no old, bold pilots." After a few months in the captain's seat, I was beginning to "settle in" and think that there wasn't too much out there that I couldn't handle. Mother Nature was to prove me wrong.

It all started late on the afternoon of July 20, 1986. Lifting off from Atlanta en route to Pittsburgh, Pennsylvania, I climbed the B-737 to cruise altitude in clear and smooth weather conditions. It looked as though it was going to be another routine flight. To say I was wrong would be an understatement. As we continued northeast, I began to see a line of high, towering clouds off to my left front. I recalled that a weather advisory had been issued for a fast-moving cold front coming out of the Ohio Valley, but I had dismissed it as not affecting my route of flight. The south end of the front consisted of a broken line of thunderstorms, and I could easily have deviated early on to the northwest and gotten on the "backside" of the front. But being the young, bold captain that I was, I elected to proceed on course and to ignore that option for the time being, thinking it would be available when I was nearer my destination. As we continued on to the northeast, the thunderstorms became a solid line, moving very quickly and beginning to affect our course. I began to realize that this line of thunderstorms was now between me and my destination. As I neared a point where Pittsburgh was straight off my left wing, I had reached a decision point.

An "older" captain would have landed at nearby Washington Dulles Airport and waited for the thunderstorm line to pass over before continuing on to Pittsburgh. But the "bold" young captain would have none of that. I had to get my aircraft and passengers "home" to Pittsburgh, thunderstorms or no thunderstorms. Using the airborne radar picture, I began to search for a "hole" to get through the line. Perhaps it was only my imagination, coupled with overconfidence, but I thought I saw a lighter area on the scope and asked for a heading to penetrate this line of storms that were as black as ink and boiling like an atomic cloud.

As the aircraft entered the clouds, it was as though a giant hand had grabbed the aircraft and begun shaking it like a baby's rattle. The shaking was so bad that my eyes could not focus on the instruments. This was accompanied by alternating downdrafts and updrafts, producing wild changes in the altitude and attitude of the aircraft. How much could the B-737 take? She was at the mercy of the storm cell, as I had basically lost control of the airplane. We were just along for the ride. Then, just as it seemed that all was lost, the thunderstorm spit us out like a watermelon seed into the clear, smooth air on the west side of the line.

Shaken, but apparently still in one piece, I quickly regained control, asked air traffic control for descent, and landed at Pittsburgh. The deplaning passengers just shook their heads as I stood in the doorway to offer a lame excuse for the "amusement park" ride to which they had been subjected. I apologized to the flight attendants and deplaned into the terminal, weak-kneed and still shaken. A call home to my wife brought some comfort and encouragement (I needed a hug), and the tension lifted enough to help me concentrate on the details of the flight back to Atlanta, which did not come *near* any lingering thunderstorm.

That flight was a nightmare, not soon forgotten. For years I would wake up in the middle of the night, relieved that it was only a dream. As an experience, it shaped my future as a captain. Never again would I knowingly penetrate an area of severe weather in an attempt to stay on course and arrive at my planned destination. "Weather avoidance" and "course deviation" became my watchwords until the end of my career. I had learned a valuable lesson: "It's not nice to mess with Mother Nature." I was determined to become an "old" pilot.

* * *

Having arrived at this point in these memoirs, it seems appropriate to pause for a time and move into another area closely associated with aviation, which would be humor. It was not unusual on the flight line for a joke to be told in Atlanta on the early morning "push" and to have that same joke told throughout the Delta route system and beyond by noon that same day. Humor, according to medical research, relieves stress, so perhaps that was the reason it was so regularly used by all those working in an airline environment.

I have tried to divide this subject into several categories in an effort to provide some sense of organization: pilot to pilot, traffic controller to pilot, rules for flying, and dealing with passengers. There were so many of these that the scope of these memoirs will only allow a sampling at best. Some of these witticisms may overlap, so I apologize to the reader in advance as you wade through this plethora of mirth.

In the pilot to pilot category, there are two examples that come to mind. The first of these I will call "bulletin board" humor. Woe to any pilot who would post *anything* on the company bulletin board in any crew base. His posting immediately became fair game for "additional comments" by any other pilot. Since reading the company postings was mandatory, all pilots sooner or later gathered at the bulletin board to check the latest company advisories, union news, items for sale, gripes, and complaints.

I particularly remember one notice posted by a new second officer at the beginning of the winter flying season. It read something like this:

"Whoever took my topcoat from the rack in the crew lounge, please return it. I am a poor Second Officer, and cannot afford another. In addition, my car keys are in the left pocket. Thanks." John Smith, S/O, ATL.

Added to the bottom of the notice was this additional comment by the "guilty" fellow pilot:

"John, I will try to get that topcoat back to you as soon as the weather warms up in the spring. By the way, where did you park your car?"

As I said, pilots could be merciless in these situations.

The second example includes the myriad of practical jokes that one pilot would pull on another. I distinctly remember one captain who acquired all the necessary official forms and who scheduled one of his fellow captains for an "audit" with the local IRS office in Atlanta, requiring him to report at a specific time with all his tax records. While the victim pilot "sweated out" having to undergo the dreaded audit, his "buddy" rounded up a few other captains, let them in on the joke, and arranged to meet the "auditee" in the lobby of the IRS building. After the surprise was pulled, a good laugh was had by all, and the relieved captain was taken out for a free lunch. I don't recall any murders or other physical retaliation connected with these capers, but those responses must have crossed the minds of those so targeted.

One last story in this area involves the "unknown pilot" who keys his mike to add the "punch line" to a fellow pilot's lament, and there were many of those, as this example shows:

Lufthansa flight on the ground in Munich, Germany, requesting clearance (in German):

"Ground, what is our start clearance time?"

Ground Control (in English):

"If you want an answer you must speak in English."

Lufthansa (in English):

"I am a German, flying a German airplane, in Germany. Why must I speak English?"

Unknown voice from another plane (in a beautiful British accent):

"Because you lost the bloody war!"

The second area of airline humor revolved around the continuing, sometimes testy, relationship between airline pilots and the air traffic controllers who guided them. Each party was continually trying to make his or her own work easier, and for the most part, when it was a win-win situation, the pilot was granted the request to do what he or she wanted with the aircraft. The following are supposedly some actual radio exchanges between pilots and controllers:

ARTC: "Delta 351, you have traffic at ten o'clock, six miles!"

Delta 351: "Give us another hint! We all have digital watches!"

ARTC: "TWA 2341, for noise abatement, turn right forty-five degrees."

TWA 2341: "Center, we are at thirty-five thousand feet. How much noise can we make up here?"

ARTC: "Sir, have you ever heard the noise a 747 makes when it hits a 727?"

"Rules for Flying" are as old as the airplane itself. Actual regulations written by the Army Signal Corps in 1920 included some of the following:

- Don't take the machine into the air unless you are satisfied it will fly.

- In taking off, look at the ground and the air.

- Learn to gauge altitude, especially on landing.

- If you see another machine near you, get out of the way

- Don't attempt to force the machine onto the ground with more than flying speed. The result is bouncing and ricocheting.

- Pilots will not wear spurs while flying.

- Pilots should carry hankies in a handy position to wipe off goggles.

While the latter two rules faded with history, the first five are as valid today as they were in 1920.

Another list containing "Rules of the Air" was a bit more whimsical:

- Every takeoff is optional. Every landing is mandatory.

- If you push the stick forward, the houses get bigger. If you pull the stick back, they get smaller. That is, unless you keep pulling the stick all the way back; then they get bigger again.

- Flying isn't dangerous. Crashing is what's dangerous.

- It's always better to be down here wishing you were up there than up there wishing you were down here.

- The *only* time you have too much fuel is when you're on fire.

- The propeller is just a big fan in front of the plane used to keep the pilot cool. If it stops in flight, you can actually watch the pilot start sweating.

- When in doubt, hold on to your altitude. No one has ever collided with the sky.

- A 'good landing' is one from which you can walk away. A 'great landing' is one after which they can use the plane again.

- Learn from the mistakes of others. You won't live long enough to make all of them yourself.

- You know you've landed with the wheels up if it takes full power to taxi to the ramp.

- There are three simple rules for making a smooth landing. Unfortunately, no one knows what they are.

- Always try to keep the number of landings you make equal to the number of take offs you've made.

- You start with a bag full of luck and an empty bag of experience. The trick is to fill the bag of experience before you empty the bag of luck.

Back in my air force days, a fellow instructor pilot and I came up with our very own version of "Rules for Flying:"

"Never fly at night, or in the weather, or when the wind is blowing. The rest of the time, do it very carefully."

Unfortunately, I had to violate my own rule on most occasions.

There are other rules that I would characterize more as "observations" than actual rules. Here are some from a list published by a Captain Len Morgan:

- An airline pilot is a confused soul who talks about women when he's flying and about airplanes when he's with a woman.

- A comment about how well things are going is a sure guarantee of trouble.

- A "greaser" landing is 50 percent luck; two in a row is all luck; three in a row and someone's lying.

- There are four ways to fly: the right way, the wrong way, the company way, and the captain's way. Only one counts.

- The owner's manual that comes with a five hundred dollar refrigerator is better than the one you get with a five hundred million dollar airplane.

- "Please see me at once" memos from the chief pilot are distributed only on Friday after office hours.

- Everything in the company manual—charts, graphs, policies, federal regulations, warnings, the works—can be summed up to read, "Captain, it's your baby."

- Most airline food tastes like chicken because most airline food *is* chicken.

- A thunderstorm is rarely as bad as it looks from the outside; it's always worse. (See personal experience above)

- A jet engine operates on a simple principle: suck and squeeze, blow and go. (Obviously stolen from my old UPT instructor)

While pilots had little contact with those employees who had to deal directly with the flying public, our hats were always off to them. Here are a few examples from a list of exchanges compiled by a Washington, DC, airport ticket agent. The list is entitled, "Why our country is in trouble."

I had a congresswoman ask for an aisle seat on the airplane so that her hair would not get messed up by being near the window.

I got a call from a candidate's staffer, who wanted to go to Cape Town. I started to explain the length of the flight and the passport information. Then she interrupted me with, "I'm not trying to make you look stupid, but Cape Town is in Massachusetts." Without trying to make her look stupid, I calmly explained, "Cape Cod is in Massachusetts; Cape Town is in Africa." Her response: Click.

A senior Vermont congressman called, furious about a Florida package we did. I asked what was wrong with the vacation in Orlando. He said he was expecting an ocean-view room. I tried to explain that's not possible, since Orlando is in the middle of the state. He replied, "Don't lie to me. I looked on the map, and Florida is a very thin state.

I got a call from a lawmaker's wife, who asked, "Is it possible to see England from Canada?" I said, "No." She said, "But they look so close on the map."

An Illinois congresswoman called last week. She needed to know how it was possible that her flight from Detroit left at 8:30 a.m. and got to Chicago at 8:33 a.m. I explained that Michigan was an hour ahead of Illinois, but she couldn't understand the concept of time zones. Finally I told her the plane went really fast, and she bought that.

A New York lawmaker called and asked, "Do airlines put your physical description on your bag so they know whose luggage belongs to whom?" I said, "No, why do you ask?" She replied, "Well, when I checked in with the airline, they put a tag on my luggage that said 'FAT,' and I'm overweight. I think that's very rude." After putting her on hold for a minute while I looked into it (I was laughing), I came back and explained that the city code for Fresno, California, is "FAT" (Fresno Air Terminal), and the airline was just putting a destination tag on her luggage.

A senator's aide called to inquire about a trip package to Hawaii. After going over all the cost info, she asked, "Would it be cheaper to fly to California, and then take the train to Hawaii?"

I just got off the phone with a freshman congressman who asked, "How do I know which plane to get on?" I asked him what exactly he meant, to which he replied, "I was told my flight number is 823, but none of these planes have numbers on them."

A senior senator called and had a question about the documents he needed in order to fly to China. After a lengthy discussion about passports, I reminded him that he needed a visa. "Oh, no I don't. I've been to China many times and never had to have one of those." I double-checked, and sure enough, his stay required a visa. When I told him this, he said, "Look, I've been to China four times, and every time they have accepted my American Express."

The maker of the list concluded by saying, "Now you know why the government is in the shape it's in."

I'll add the tenth example I heard from a gate agent in Atlanta:

A prospective passenger calls up reservations and says, "I want to go to Maconga." The agent politely replied that Delta did not serve a destination by that name, to which the person replied, "It shor do! Right here on this Delta timetable it say 'Maconga,' M-A-C-O-N, G-A.

One last example in the more serious side of this area involves the impact that Hollywood has had on the aviator persona. In the mid-eighties, the flight sequences of the movie, *Top Gun,* had a tremendous motivational impact on military fighter pilots. To head off the inevitable disaster should these staged maneuvers be "tried at home," the commander of one navy fighter squadron published the following:

Subj: Airborne Professionalism

"It has come to my attention that since the premiere of *"Top Gun"* there has been an increase in aircraft speed approaching the break (450 + Knots), low transitions on departures, pylon turns around the TACAN, and in general "hot dogging" around the field. Reducing the margin of safety in an attempt to impress someone on the ground is totally unprofessional. I am not impressed and you shouldn't be either."

While "professionalism" was the watchword for every airline pilot, there was still something buried deep within the psyche of each pilot urging him or her to climb into the airplane and fly under the local bridge.

In summary, a sense of humor was an invaluable trait for those destined to earn their living in the field of aviation.

CHAPTER SIXTEEN

"INCIDENTS AND WAR STORIES"

On September 29, 1986, I was in command of Flight 1049, scheduled to depart Dallas-Fort Worth, Texas, to Baton Rouge, Louisiana, in the early afternoon. Start and pushback was normal and on schedule. On our taxi-out, we joined a long line of aircraft waiting to takeoff on runway 17R. This was not unusual, as American Airlines launched their afternoon "push" at the same time as we did. This was a business technique that all airlines used in competition with each other. Unfortunately, it usually resulted in long takeoff delays.

It was a very hot day, and as we inched along in the queue, I was making every effort to stay off the aircraft brakes, as they were prone to heat up rather rapidly, particularly on a hot day in Dallas. Suddenly a voice crackled over the ground control frequency from the aircraft immediately behind us: "Delta 737 passing taxiway ____, you have smoke coming from your left main gear." Hey! That was us! At about that time, the tower confirmed what I feared, that smoke was beginning to boil out from under the left wing.

Remembering that where there is smoke, there is fire, or at least the potential for fire (the thing a pilot dreads most), I declared an emergency and summoned fire and rescue to the scene. While that was in progress, the tower was in the process of clearing all other aircraft from our immediate area. In the meantime, I called the flight attendant in charge (FAIC) to the cockpit for a face-to-face briefing in the event that we had to evacuate the aircraft by means of the slides and the over-wing doors located on the right side of the fuselage. As I was advising the passengers of our situation, fire trucks, along with Delta maintenance, arrived on the scene.

A maintenance man ran under the wing and quickly assessed the situation. Apparently he had seen this situation before. He established radio contact with me and advised that we had lost fluid from one of the aircraft hydraulic system reservoirs located in the left wheel well. That leaking hydraulic fluid was dripping on the left main wheel brake, producing the smoke, but with no danger of fire, as the fluid itself was not inflammable. This was "music to our ears!" However, he advised, we would not be able to taxi. The hydraulic leak would have to be repaired, the wheel changed, and the aircraft towed back to the gate.

I passed all this information to the passengers and to the station personnel, who elected to send out a set of mobile stairs and a "people mover" to deplane the passengers and return them to the terminal.

Maintenance quickly completed their work, and we were soon back at the gate for another "go at it." This time, all went well, and we arrived in Baton Rouge only two hours and fifteen minutes late. Surprisingly, we did not lose a single passenger from our first attempt, as was usually the case when there was an event of this nature. After apologizing for being late and thanking the passengers for sticking with us, I received several compliments on our handling of the situation during the deplaning in Baton Rouge. Later, after writing letters of commendation for Dallas maintenance and all of the flight crew onboard, I was pleased to receive a personal letter from the vice president for Flight Operations, praising our professionalism in this matter.

One day, after a few more months on the B-737, I was struck by the thought of how routine airline flying had become. With improvement in airframe technology and engine reliability, and with continual maintenance, the flying public was beginning to accept air travel as a preferred alternative. For my part, I had developed great confidence in the Boeing Company for the airframes they built and in the Pratt & Whitney jet engines that powered them. If it had not been for the challenges of weather, flying these modern-day jet airliners would have been a complete and total pleasure. As one fellow captain expressed it, "I'd fly for nothing on beautiful days, if they would pay me double the rest of the time."

Most of the day-to-day aircraft problems now dealt with warning lights, instrument failures, and other "nuisance" items. Read on!

On the afternoon of November 29, 1986, I departed Atlanta in the late afternoon with Flight 621 en route to Mobile, Alabama. The weather at the destination was forecast to be good, with some smoke and haze reducing visibility. After contact with approach control in Mobile, we were guided by radar vector and established on a straight-in final approach to the landing runway.

Since it was my leg to fly (captains normally alternated flight legs with the first officer), I set up the flight instruments and coupled them to the autopilot for a "coupled" approach utilizing the ground-based instrument landing system. It was required that each aircraft accomplish one of these approaches periodically in order to confirm that all systems were operating normally.

At approximately six miles out on our final approach, we configured the 737 for landing by lowering the landing gear and extending the wing flaps. The tower cleared us to land as I sat back, watching the autopilot fly the airplane and waiting to catch sight of the runway ahead.

Suddenly, the autopilot disconnected with an accompanying warning siren and with flashing lights. In addition, my attitude director indicator froze, showing only red flags. I was now hand flying the airplane with no primary flight instruments and no contact with the ground or the runway—not a condition in which any pilot wants to find himself. I quickly glanced at the first officer's instrument panel and saw, with relief, that his attitude director indicator was working. I immediately transferred control of the airplane to the first officer for continuing the approach while I monitored with my "standby" flight instruments, which comprised a small attitude indicator (a throwback to the early days of aviation that did not rely on electrical power) and the standby or "whiskey compass" (another throwback utilizing a compass rose floating in a sealed case filled with alcohol).

Soon thereafter, we broke through the haze and smoke and picked up the runway, and the first officer continued with a normal visual approach and landing. Taxiing in, I knew that we had a major problem with the flight instruments and that we would very likely incur a delay. I was not to be disappointed, as it took three hours for a new attitude director indicator to be delivered from Atlanta via the next inbound flight, along with a mechanic to install it and run an extensive check of the system. On the night flight back to Atlanta, I wondered what the results would have been had we been in worse weather conditions. It came to me that although I had to have complete confidence in my flight instruments, they were not infallible.

A couple of stories that come to my mind at this point also concerned warning lights and switches.

People who worked the baggage underneath the airplane were a little different "breed of cat." They tended to be a fun-loving group of people who threw their backs into the boring, laborious job of loading and unloading baggage. At times, the flight crew would join them in this task when we were running late or when a quick turnaround was in our best interest. These fellows were not beyond going to extremes with those "baggage brothers" who, for whatever reason, got on their bad side. One night, a DC-9 pulled into the gate in Knoxville. When the front baggage bin was opened, there sat a baggage handler who had made a non-volunteer flight from Atlanta. Fortunately the front bin was heated and pressurized, or else this flight would have had deadly consequences. Apparently, his buddies back in Atlanta knew what they were doing. This same scenario was played out a short time later, when a DC-8 pulled into the gate in Kansas City with the same result (I never found out if it was the same guy).

Naturally the company could not condone these actions, so an engineering order was sent out to install a switch in the cargo compartment that could be activated by anyone accidently or intentionally left in the compartment after the door was closed. This activated a light in the cockpit, alerting the crew that that there was a non-volunteer passenger trapped in the cargo bin. This apparently put an end to these high jinks, as I don't recall a similar incident. However, the airline industry continued to have trouble with people trying to hitch free rides by climbing up into the wheel wells, always with fatal results.

The second story that relates to warning lights and switches involved the constant, often frustrating efforts of pilots to keep the cabin at a temperature agreeable to the flight attendants. A call to the cockpit that it was "too cold in the back" was usually followed by another call a short time later that "it's too hot back here." Mix that with the varied "comfort indexes" of the cabin crew, and you can understand the problem. One solution that seemed to work on the DC-8 was to put a rheostat switch at the rear flight attendant jump seat location. This switch was designed to give the flight attendants the privilege of controlling the temperature themselves, within a range of plus or minus two degrees. After installation of this switch, calls to the cockpit dropped dramatically. The odd thing about this whole situation was that, according to unnamed maintenance sources, the switch was never hooked up.

Thus I finished the year of my captaincy. While 1986 was a major turning point in my career, I was looking forward to building on that with the dawning of 1987. I had been a flight engineer and first officer for over sixteen years. With the economy growing and Delta expanding, it seemed that the sky was the limit.

With the acquisition of Western Airlines finalized, Delta began the process of combining the two airlines into one during the early months of 1987. The crew bases now available in Salt Lake City and Los Angeles were new to "old Delta" pilots. New routes now included trips to Mexico and Alaska.

As in the merger with Northeast Airlines in 1972, the most important thing on every pilot's mind was where he or she would end up on the combined seniority list. There were two methods that were traditionally used to accomplish the most challenging task of combining the lists: date of hire and years of service. The "date of hire" option simply took the date each pilot was hired by each respective airline and used that solely to determine the integrated list. The "years of service" option, however, considered date of hire, but subtracted all the time that a pilot had been furloughed or had been otherwise inactive during his or her career. Since the Western pilot group was somewhat older than the Delta group, they naturally preferred the date of hire method. But since Western had had several furlough events during its recent history, the Delta pilot group held out for the years of service option, which was the one adopted. After much grumbling, complaints, and tweaking the list to protect Delta's most senior pilots flying the larger equipment, the list was finally integrated. Due to the expanding airline, there was little, if any, loss of pay or position. I do remember one pilot who had been furloughed by Western and who was hired into my class with Delta. When the list was combined, he was substantially ahead of his classmates at Western who had not been furloughed. Such are the vagaries of an airline career.

For the airlines, the year 1987 could best be characterized as the beginning year of the "gate hold." Due to mergers and new entrants into the system, air traffic control could not possibly handle the increase in air traffic and continue to meet required federal safety and separation criteria. The consequence was that many flights, particularly at smaller outlying stations, had to hold at their departure gates, awaiting a slot in the skies. Sometimes the flight would depart the gate, only to be held on the ramp before receiving a "release" from air traffic control to take off. A few times, the delays that I experienced would be so long that I would have to taxi the aircraft back to the gate, shut down engines, and allow the passengers to deplane. As you might suspect, this was all very frustrating for passengers, crew, station personnel, and air traffic control. I found that communicating with my passengers and telling them the truth about the situation was always the best course. Seasoned passengers were quick to pick up on any overly optimistic offerings over the cabin PA system, and an outright lie could have all manner of repercussions. One captain who had to divert to another airport due to weather "promised" his passengers that buses would be "standing by" to whisk them to their destination. Unfortunately, he failed to confirm that with the company. When nothing of the sort was awaiting these expectant travelers, the term "irate passenger" was barely enough to define the backlash. For weeks, the pilot group received all manner of letters and memos reminding us not to promise passengers anything we could not confirm.

Another advisory that came down was to watch what was said over the PA system. While it was good to give the passengers flight information and to keep them updated on the weather at their destination, anything else, such as attempts at humor or offhand comments, could be offensive. One captain learned this the hard way. Before a new runway was built in Jackson, Mississippi, flights were forced to land on one that was in such bad shape that the landing roll was like riding a bucking bronco. One morning, a DC-9 captain, who was apparently a veteran of this experience, picked up the PA phone on taxi-in and said, "Ladies and gentlemen, that landing roll was brought to you by the mayor of Jackson, Mississippi. You all have a good day now, you hear." What he didn't know was that the distinguished mayor himself was onboard the flight. Not only that, but he was a major stockholder of Delta Airlines. After a conference with the chief pilot back in Atlanta and some time off to "think about it," the offending captain was returned to the line, older and wiser. Personally, I was never really comfortable speaking over the PA, but regarded it as a necessary duty and was certain to stick with the facts only.

Other than the increase in ground delays there is little reflected in my logbooks that would make 1987 anything other than a routine year. One thing that was noted, however, was the increase of FAA examiners riding with me on the cockpit jump seat. Whenever they were onboard any flight, they were required to give the crew a flight check. Whether this was just due to coincidence, to an increase in examiners, or to the fact that I was a new captain needing additional observation, I never knew. While I was confident in the B-737 and in my abilities to perform the duties of captain, it was still somewhat of a nuisance to have someone "looking over your shoulder" while you were performing those duties. My approach to this was to perform exactly as I had been trained by Delta. Then, if the examiner found any discrepancy, he could take it up with the company.

It sounds strange, but I also welcomed the opportunity to "show this guy" what real professionals we were. Was I becoming a cocky captain? One night in Atlanta, an FAA examiner boarded the flight for our last leg of the day to Greensboro, North Carolina. I had only been into Greensboro a few times, and the weather was right at minimums for landing, with thunderstorms and heavy rain. Couple that with the onset of fatigue and now with the "FAA factor," and it did not look like a good way to end the evening. Arriving in the Greensboro area, we were using radar to navigate around the storm cells, while lightning was all around us. Turning onto final, the aircraft was buffeted by wind and rain as we configured the B-737 for landing. With the aircraft coupled to the autopilot for the approach, I kept my eyes glued to the instruments as the first officer made his altitude "call outs" and looked outside, trying to pick up the runway. Just as I was ready to call for a missed approach, the first officer yelled, "Runway in sight!" I disconnected the autopilot at that point and made a perfect grease-job landing on the rain-swept runway. That produced an unusual, "Nice going, Captain," comment from the examiner as we rolled out on the runway. Pilots live for such words. Professionals we were, particularly on that night with the FAA watching.

What seemed to begin at about this time in my career was an increase in problems dealing with passengers in the cabin, coupled with their complaints about the service. With the increase in routes, multiple changes in crews and equipment, and communication failures, such incidents were bound to happen.

Most complaints, heretofore, were confined to the New York-Florida routes, where pleasing New Yorkers was never easy. I always felt that the flight attendants working those flights should have received "combat pay" for what they had to put up with. I recall one flight that departed LaGuardia for West Palm Beach. As the flight crew, we worked very hard to find the smoothest altitudes, to dodge all thunderstorms along our route, and to fly a slow, easy approach to the runway. On one occasion, I accomplished all these things, greased the airplane onto the runway, and arrived at the gate ten minutes ahead of schedule—the perfect flight. Right? Wrong! As I stood in the doorway to say good-bye to the folks, expecting at least one compliment, the only comment I got was from one "grand dame" New Yorker. Shouldering her fur and finery as she passed by, she glanced up at me and said, "Dinky little lunch." These were the standards on which flights were judged, at least for that segment of the air travelling public.

With the uptick in cabin complaints, Delta devised a "Flight Attendant Report Form" listing forty different codes for logging complaints and/or problems, along with a "comments" section that could run several pages, depending on the issue involved. The FAIC was required to send a copy of any such report to me as captain, in the event that I was called on for any additional input. Normally the flight deck crew was unaware of these incidents until the report showed up in the captain's mailbox. Succinctness was not a flight attendant literary characteristic, and reading one of these meandering epistles was a chore. I offer the following from one FAIC to prove my point:

May 28, 1987 Flight 786 Atlanta to Houston Code 38

"Had an incident upon arriving in HOU involving passenger _____ and his wife. Mr._____ was already onboard the flight to HOU when we picked the flight up in ATL (It was a thru flight). He was a carry-on passenger (a cancer patient) and the FAIC that was deplaning in ATL advised me that Mr.____ would need to be carried off in HOU. During the flight, he seemed to be O.K. He walked to and from the rest room, slept during a large portion of the flight. Shortly before our initial approach into HOU, Mrs. _____ spoke to F/A _____ and requested for her and her husband to deplane first when we landed. Mrs. ____ seemed concerned that her party meeting her was concerned about them as we were running quite late. However, she did not mention any urgency regarding her husband's immediate physical condition, nor did her husband show any obvious signs of an emergency medical condition. F/A ____ politely advised Mrs._____ that our normal procedure (and we assumed this was a normal carry-off situation) was for them to wait until all other passengers deplane first before her husband could be deplaned. According to F/A_____, Mrs._____ was agreeable and did not mention any need for emergency assistance at that time. F/A_____ then came to F/C where I was working and told me of this conversation between her and Mrs.____. I then immediately went to the back cabin to speak with Mrs.____ myself and I explained our normal carry-off proce- dure to her again as F/A____ did. She again seemed agreeable and under- standing and, again did not mention that her husband needed any emer- gency medical provisions. She did however mention to F/A_____ earlier that she was concerned that we were so late arriving in HOU (1 hour late) as apparently she had people meeting her in HOU and were going to go straight to the hospital. F/A _____ said that Mrs.____ was quite ambiguous about this and Mrs._____ just seemed generally uptight and stressed. Upon landing in HOU, during taxi-in, Mrs.____ came running up to First Class in a panic and said her husband was very ill and needed an ambulance. I immediately asked the Captain to radio for EMTs. We remained on the taxi way for several minutes while waiting for another aircraft to vacate our gate, which caused us to be delayed even more and, of course, made Mrs.____even more anxious. She said she was worried that her husband might be going into a coma from a high level of calcium (he has leukemia). He was very listless at this point and didn't appear to even be able to walk. Once we reached the gate our Load factor (sit- ting on forward jump seat) immediately jumped off the plane to phone Mrs.____'s doctor at Mrs._____'s request. I made an announcement for all passengers to remain onboard (as the _____s were sitting toward the rear) and within no more than 4 or 5 minutes the EMTs were at the gate. After all other passengers deplaned the EMTs tended to Mr._____ until the ambulance arrived just a few minutes later. While on the ground in HOU Mrs._____expressed her disenchantment with Delta because: #1 we were an hour late which she said contributed to her husband's condi- tion upon arrival, #2 because we were not prepared to offer her husband immediate emergency care when we arrived. However, I must reiterate that we were not aware of her needs and her husband's condition until we landed. Mrs._____ did not communicate with us enough in order to be prepared with an ambulance in HOU on arrival. From talking to her during the flight she did not convey to us any emergency, urgent needs.

The EMTs and ambulance did arrive very quickly and we were grateful for that. We felt that we did everything we possibly could considering the circumstances and the lack of communication."

If the reader is still awake after following this meandering maze of flight attendant/passenger interaction, he or she can see that the main focus of these detailed write-ups was to give the company side of an incident that could possibly end up in a lawsuit, and there were many of those. If Delta's PR department couldn't smooth things over with free passes for another flight, there was an entire legal department in place to deal with such issues. These lawyers must have earned their money, as it was my understanding that very few lawsuits against the company were successful.

As the New Year, 1988, was ushered in, air travel would take a darker, more tragic turn in terms of incidents. It sounds trite but true: things would never be the same again.

The year began in a very routine fashion. After settling into the left seat of the B-737, I was beginning to hold a regular line of time, and was moving up on the seniority list. It seemed like nothing but blue skies ahead. I was able to give up the "commuter" apartment at the airport along with the beeper and to devote myself to the rigors of commuting to the Atlanta Airport from home in Maryville, Tennessee.

Commuting on Delta Airlines during this particular period was not for the faint of heart. Since Delta used the cockpit jump seat as an item in contract negotiations with the pilot group, the company would not grant its use to commuting pilots for several years to come. Since the majority of the pilot group did not commute, it was always one of the first items dropped at the negotiating table. This worked a tremendous burden on pilots trying to get to work. We were now thrown in with all other revenue and non-revenue passengers attempting to board any given flight. Naturally, all revenue passengers were boarded first, followed by non-revenue passengers based on date of seniority. This made acquiring a seat on any given flight a real adventure.

Delta did award an annual pass to employees after ten years of service. This gave me seating priority over other employees with less service time. As a backup, though, I purchased a half-fare ticket, which would put me ahead of any non-revenue passengers if the flight looked close. My system was not to plan on standing by for any flight within four hours of my report time in Atlanta. This would allow enough time, as a last resort, to make the four-hour drive to the employee parking lot at the Atlanta Airport. I had to do this on more than one occasion. To take some of the pressure off, I would often catch a late flight to Atlanta the night before, obtain a motel room, and then fly an "early bird" trip the following morning. Even this was risky, and in addition, it involved additional expenses. Although most airport motels gave airline employees a price break, the Howard Johnson Motel on Virginia Avenue in Hapeville, Georgia, gave us the best deal, and it became a home away from home for many commuters.

The flip side of commuting to work on Delta was standing by for a flight to get back home. Although the pressure to meet a sign-in deadline was absent, it was still a nerve-racking experience, and it added on to the fatigue from a full day of flying. Missing the last flight of the day meant another night in the motel and being back at the airport the next morning to stand by for the first flight of the day. A few times, I would catch a flight to Chattanooga and "deadhead" a rental car to Knoxville, just to get home. Another plan to get to Knoxville was to catch a flight to Nashville, then connect to another Delta flight coming from Dallas-Fort Worth. Getting home was the key, and no method was ignored. Once, after all flights out of Atlanta were cancelled due to snow and ice, I took a big chance. I rented a car at the Atlanta Airport and drove home, over ice covered roads, in a continual snowstorm. Vehicles were abandoned in ditches off the side of the road, and I vividly remember a large overturned truck off to the side, with its wheels eerily pointing to the sky.

The reader might ask why, with all this trouble, a pilot chose to commute long distances to the crew base. While there were perhaps many reasons, it really boiled down to a pilot living where he or she wanted to live and also avoiding the exorbitant income taxes levied by many states, including the state of Georgia. Delta did not like it one bit, but they could do little about it. But woe to the commuting pilot who failed to make sign-in time or who tried to use sick leave when that last flight to Atlanta was missed. The pressure to get to work and to be ready to fly never let up. Even after my retirement, I continued dreaming about flying for many years thereafter, including nightmares about missing my sign-in time or losing my flight kit.

In July of 1988, the "blue skies" that seemed to lie ahead suddenly turned gray. As previously mentioned, I had developed the habit of scheduling an appointment with my personal physician a month or so prior to my FAA physical. This was a "backup," just in case there was an issue that might prevent me from retaining my "Class A" physical certificate. Up to this point, everything had always checked out normally, and I would relax a little, knowing that when I reported to the FAA medical examiner, I should have similar results. This time I was in for a real shock. Although my blood pressure had been hovering around the upper limits for some time, it was now well above the limits and would require medication to keep it well-controlled. I did not immediately understand the time factor involved in finding and "tweaking" the right combination and dosage of drugs to address my problem. What I did know was that this was a "grounding" issue until the problem was solved. Flying while using prescription drugs was strictly prohibited, unless they were specifically approved by the FAA. My doctor immediately started me on a low dose of one class of drugs, with orders to check back with him weekly. I left his office somewhat shattered. Was this to be the end of my flying career?

My first call was to my chief pilot, to advise him of the situation. He was very understanding and encouraging, advising me to work closely with the FAA doctors, located in Denver, Colorado, who had been retained by the Air Line Pilots Association to handle such situations. While his words were consoling, the hard, cold fact was that I was now on medical leave until my blood pressure could be brought under control.

After contacting the ALPA aero medical office in Denver and establishing a case number, my doctor and I began the tedious process of finding a drug or combination of drugs that would treat my condition without side effects. Each week, I would report for a blood pressure check and a continual upward dosing of the first class of drugs. When I reached the maximum dosage of that drug, another drug from another class was added. Finally, after two months, my blood pressure began to drop into the "high normal" zone with no side effects. After determining that it could be well-controlled on that dosage, my doctor wrote a letter to the FAA doctors in Denver, so stating. My drugs were approved for use, and I was released to return to flight status, pending an FAA physical.

With this accomplished, I contacted my chief pilot, who advised crew scheduling that I was ready to return to the cockpit. I had been away for over two months. Thanks to my union and to close coordination between the doctors involved, it appeared that my airline career would continue. The curse of high blood pressure would also continue, all the way to retirement and beyond, even necessitating the addition of a third class of drugs later on.

I was allowed to bid a line of time for October 1988, but because the extended medical leave had caused me to go "noncurrent" in landings and other requirements, I would have to undergo three days of training before I could return to the line. The only B-737 training going on at the time was being conducted in Salt Lake City, Utah, so to Salt Lake

I would go. With this completed, I returned to Atlanta, a full-fledged, qualified captain on the B-737once again.

At last, on October 21, 1988, after nearly three months away, I returned to the line, ready to press on to whatever lay ahead. It had been a long day's journey into night.

The remainder of 1988 was relatively uneventful. For the aviation industry and the rest of the world, however, an incident occurred on December 21, 1988, that would also change things forever.

Heretofore, the major man-made threat to aviation was the occasional hijacking of an aircraft for political purposes. Few people were killed, the aircraft involved usually survived, and air travelers suffered through these ordeals of inconvenience with resignation to the situation. The emphasis in aircrew training was centered on acquiescing to the hijacker's demands while protecting the rest of the crew, the passengers, and the aircraft. On that date in late December of 1988, the stakes would go up dramatically.

In 1985, an Air India aircraft had disappeared over the Atlantic Ocean without a trace and with no radio transmission to indicate any difficulties. While an onboard bomb was suspected, it was never proven, and the event soon faded from news coverage and was soon forgotten. This time, however, the evidence was all too apparent.

Climbing out of London en route to New York, Pan American Flight 103, fully loaded with fuel, freight, and passengers, was nearing cruise altitude. Suddenly, over the small Scottish village of Lockerbie, the unimaginable happened. In a tremendous explosion, the Boeing 747 was blown to pieces, scattering the debris of bodies, baggage, and bits of the aircraft over the countryside below. The largest piece of the aircraft found on the ground was the front section of the nose. This piece, displayed with the blue and white paint scheme of Pan Am, was shown over and over again by every news agency for weeks to come. While the world was trying to cope with the enormity of this disaster, it was quickly traced to a Libyan terrorist group, who claimed responsibility. For those who might be interested in more of the details surrounding this tragedy, I would direct them to the many sources available on this particular incident. The sobering realization for all of us, at the time, was that the world and the airline industry in particular, had entered a new age: the age of terrorism.

Borrowing from some obscure passage from their Koran, Muslim fanatics were now declaring Jihad, or holy war, on the "infidels" of non-Muslim countries, particularly the United States, the ultimate supporter of Israel, the fanatics' blood enemy. The fact that this war was being taken to the skies and to the nations' airlines was one that was not lost on those of us who did the flying. Ramped up security and increased ground training on how to handle a terrorist threat aside, we knew that we were "sitting ducks" for a well-planned and determined attack by these fanatics, who were willing to die for Allah and for the rewards that were promised beyond this life. While the threat seemed rather small for those of us flying the B-737 into the Fort Waynes and the Charlottes of this country, it could not be dismissed. In this new age, anything could happen. The year 1988 was drawing to a close. What would the future hold?

* * *

The year 1989 began with the welcome news that I had won an Advance Entitlement to upgrade to captain on the Boeing 727, my old "friend" on which I had spent seven years as first officer. On January 30, 1989, I flew my last flight as captain on the Boeing 737. It had been a great three years. I had enjoyed getting into the smaller cities, and I had logged much in the way of flight hours and experience. But now it was on to the next step in my journey up the ladder to increased responsibility (and pay) on larger equipment.

Vacation was next on the list, and I must interject at this point that Hawaii was always the destination of choice when it came to vacation, particularly during the winter months. While I enjoyed vacation time in other areas of the United States, notably in Arizona, Maine, South Dakota, and Florida, Hawaii was always the best. And while others longed to ski the slopes of the Colorado Mountains at such times, I was looking for palm trees and balmy breezes. While other foreign locales were perhaps more pristine, I always considered the islands of Hawaii to be the closest thing to paradise within our United States. Fortunately, I was able to spend seven vacations there over the years, visiting and enjoying all that the accessible islands had to offer.

In summer months, the locale of choice was Alaska, and again, I was fortunate to make three excursions into that state, fishing for king salmon and halibut. I always joked that the smartest mammals on the planet were the humpback whales; they spent their summers frolicking in the cool waters of Alaska and then migrated to the warm waters of Hawaii in winter in order to rest and have their young—all of this broken by two leisurely ocean cruises. You can't convince me that animals are "dumb."

In any event, my time in paradise had to come to an end, and on February 19, 1989, I reported to the Atlanta Training Center for ground school on the Boeing 727. Since I had flown the aircraft previously and had not strayed too far from Boeing engineering during my time on the Boeing 737, the ground school, simulator, and checkout were a breeze. I did have to adjust to going back to a three-man operation in the cockpit, but with the workload distributed three ways, it made for an even more relaxed atmosphere. On March 24, 1989, I flew out on the series of flights making up the initial operating experience portion of training, which visited new airports like Ontario, California, as well as old acquaintances like Los Angeles and Portland, Oregon. It was good to be back on the west coast once again.

One thing that I had given up on upgrading to the Boeing 727 was "seniority on equipment." While I was able to hold a regular line and some reasonably good trips, I could not often choose my days to fly. Thus, weekends and holidays went to those of greater seniority. When it came to Christmas in particular, many of my fellow pilots adopted the idea of "Christmas off at any cost," even if it meant suffering through a bad schedule the remainder of the month. I did not object to this line of thinking, but when the Boeing 727 bid schedules came out for December 1989, I was presented with a viable alternative. On one of the lines of time was a trip that departed Atlanta on December 23rd and returned on December 26th. Interestingly, the layover on Christmas Eve was in Knoxville, Tennessee, with a late departure the next day, Christmas day. I figured that no one but me would want to be stuck at the Knoxville Airport on Christmas, so I bid this line of time as my number one choice. Since it was one of the better trips in the month, I held my breath until the bid awards were posted. Sure enough, there was my name along-side my first choice. All went well, and I was able to spend an enjoyable Christmas at home. Sometimes you can have your cake and eat it too.

All in all, 1989 was a good year. I had moved up on equipment, passed my twentieth anniversary as a Delta pilot, and was looking forward to the final decade of my flying career. On December 31st, I walked off the airplane on my last flight of 1989 and said "good-bye" to the 1980s.

January 1990 did not get off to a very auspicious start. Since the Boeing 727 was not equipped with the most up-to-date avionics, getting into airports with very low visibility was difficult at times. While this situation rarely occurred, it did on my very first flight in 1990. On January 7th, I departed Atlanta at 11:45 p.m., bound for Savannah. Heavy fog was developing around the airport, but it was forecast to be at or above our minimums for visibility upon our arrival. Operations believed that we could make it in, so after adding extra fuel, we proceeded accordingly.

After lining up on runway 09 at Savannah, we coupled the autopilot for an approach. I was flying and monitoring the approach, while the first officer was straining his eyeballs for any evidence of the runway environment. As we neared our minimum altitude, all configured to land, I listened for him to say, "Runway in sight." Instead, as we reached a point one hundred feet above the supposed runway surface, in the blackest black I can ever remember, he said, "No contact." I announced, "*Go around!*" and ran the throttles forward to initiate a "missed approach." I had done this in the simulator several times and relied on that training to get us out of the black hole into which we had descended. After notifying the tower of the missed approach, we received a call from our ramp control saying that they heard us but never saw us, and would we want to take another shot at it? I keyed the mike and said that the only place this airplane was going was back to Atlanta, Georgia. Ramp control laughed and bid us a good evening, as we requested clearance back to Atlanta. While the few passengers we had onboard were disappointed not to get into Savannah, they all seemed grateful that we were out of the foggy skies and back on terra firma, even though it was not at their preferred destination. I recount this event because, for the first time as a captain, I was not able to bring a scheduled flight to completion at the scheduled destination. I learned that sometimes, there are places you simply can't go with an aircraft. I hoped that this was not an omen of things to come in the year 1990. Happily, this was not the case, and the following months were flown with only minor problems disrupting the schedule.

One major development that benefitted the entire airline industry did finally come to fruition in the year 1990. Delta Airlines was one of the first to announce that it would now be a nonsmoking airline on all its domestic flights. This was "music to the ears" for those passengers and crew alike who had had to breathe the secondary cigarette smoke from passengers or crew members who had the habit. Even with the division of the cabin into "smoking" and "nonsmoking" sections, the problem of air quality had continued, and the entire cabin often reeked of tobacco smoke. It was even worse in the confined area of the cockpit.

I recalled my days as flight engineer and copilot, when I was forced to breathe the smoke of the captains I flew with, most of whom smoked. I recall one miserable month on the DC-8, when I was paired with a pipe smoking captain and a copilot who smoked rum-soaked "Crooks" cigars. The captain would light his pipe, and the whole cockpit would fill with smoke. Then he would start talking, and the pipe would go out, requiring lighting all over again. This went on innumerable times during the four-hour flight from Atlanta to San Francisco, with the copilot adding his less-than-fragrant smoke to the mix. I had an "eyeball" outlet at my engineer's panel that delivered fresh, air-conditioned air. Using it, however, only served to collect the smoke and blow it into my face. The dry cleaners loved it, though, when I brought my uniform in each week for cleaning.

Banning smoking onboard did not mean that passengers would all abide by the rule, however. Smoking in the onboard lavatories became a problem, requiring maintenance to install smoke detectors in an effort to deter this practice. After an incident where a cigarette butt deposited in the lavatory waste can caused an in-flight fire, it became a federal offense to smoke on any domestic flight. International flights continued to allow smoking for a few years but soon discontinued the practice. This was soon followed by nonsmoking rules in the airport terminals as well. Not many were sad to see the "wicked weed" depart from the scene.

With retirements increasing and Delta beginning to offer incentives for early retirement, I began to advance up the seniority list rather rapidly. Accordingly, I put in a bid to move up to the next level, either a captain's position on the Boeing 767 or a captain's position on the Lockheed L-1011 still being flown internationally(more on that later). Since the Boeing cockpit avionics were virtually identical, the B-767 bid would also include flying the Boeing 757. I was surprised but not shocked to see my name listed for an Advance Entitlement with training to begin on the B-767in December of 1990.

On December 1st, I landed in Atlanta on my last flight as a Boeing 727 captain, and on December 5th, began ground school on the B-767. With the classroom schedule allowing for weekends and holidays, one thing I was certain about was that I would definitely be home for Christmas in 1990.

CHAPTER SEVENTEEN

"MOVING ON UP"

January 1991 found me, once again, undergoing training on another aircraft. What I did not know at the time was that this would be the last one I would fly in my airline career. But what an aircraft to end a career on! The Boeing 757 and Boeing 767 were the culmination of all the Boeing aeronautical engineering that had gone before. Powerful, fuel-efficient, the latest avionic technology, easy to fly, comfortable cockpits, able to climb above the weather—these were just a few of the superlative characteristics of these wonderful flying machines. The pilot group immediately fell in love with these airplanes as they supplanted the Lockheed L-1011 as "queens of the fleet." With economic times being so good, Delta employees, who bought into the concept of the "Delta family," even took a pay cut to buy a B-767 as a gift to the company. Later, under failing economic conditions, Delta management sold out the employee group, bringing an end to the concept of family, and making me glad that I had not participated in this scheme.

Notwithstanding, all was "clear skies ahead" in 1991 as I settled down into the routine of ground school and simulator training in Atlanta. I have never added it up, but I do believe that I spent more time training than actually flying. This time, however, there was a new twist to receiving the captain's type rating. It would now be accomplished in the simulator. Thus it came to pass that after successfully completing my check ride, administered by an FAA company designee, I departed the simulator fully qualified to fly the airplane, *having never set foot on the actual airplane itself!* This was how far flight simulators had come. Any and every conceivable flight condition and situation could be completely duplicated. And I was not to be disappointed when I reported for my initial operating experience with the line-check airman; the airplane did fly just like the simulator!

As with all move-ups on equipment, I gave up seniority and found myself a very junior B-767 captain. But I wasn't thinking about that when I "deadheaded" from Atlanta to Cincinnati on February 3, 1991, to fly my first trip on the airplane. To uphold tradition, my wife joined me there to be onboard for my first flight as a "new" captain. After a smooth, uneventful flight to Salt Lake City, we enjoyed a nice layover together in that city, and deadheaded together back to Atlanta and home again.

One of the flights on my initial operating experience was from Los Angeles to Mexico City, and Delta soon thereafter inaugurated service from Atlanta to Mexico City as well. This introduction to true international flying presented additional problems for those who flew the route. No water was to be boarded in Mexico on any Delta aircraft, due to the level of pollutants. Consequently, we had to ensure that we had full water tanks before departing Atlanta. In addition, all garbage on the return flight had to be placed in red, sealed bags for incineration upon arrival back in Atlanta. Food boarded in Mexico was prepared under strict sanitary conditions, to alleviate the dangers of food poisoning. Some crew members who had experienced their own version of "Montezuma's Revenge" refused to eat it, and carried their own "lunch" and bottled water for the return flight. There were other requirements to be met as well, involving customs declarations and immigration.

All of this could have been tolerated had it not been for the problems flying into Mexico City itself. As the city lay down in a "bowl" and was ringed with high mountains, strict adherence to navigational procedures was an absolute necessity. This could be easily compromised when dealing with the Mexican air controllers. Most spoke rapid, broken English, requiring you to "listen up" and verify all flight instructions along the arrival corridor. Sometimes, in the midst of all this, they would jabber in rapid-fire Spanish to other aircraft flown by their countrymen. Add to this the fact that thunderstorms were a common occurrence in the vicinity of the airport, and the reader can see that the pilot flying into Mexico City really earned his or her money.

One of my trips involved a layover, which presented even more dangers. The cab ride to the layover hotel was akin to an amusement park ride, as we dodged dangerously in and out of traffic over bridges that had been damaged by the latest earthquake. To leave the hotel for sightseeing or for food involved the possibility of being robbed or receiving a good dose of dysentery. Luckily, bottled water was provided in the room for drinking and tooth brushing, so there I stayed until pickup the next morning. I had been told that the breakfast buffet at the hotel was safe, so I hesitatingly partook of what was offered. Perhaps it was the milk I drank or the fruit that was placed on a bed of lettuce washed with the local water; either way, the food began to act on this "Gringo's" digestive system in unkind ways during the return trip to Atlanta. Just when I thought I had beaten "Montezuma," he got me "in the end."

I failed to mention the dangers of simply breathing the local air in Mexico City. That could best be demonstrated by an incident that occurred at the airport one evening. We were seated in the 757 cockpit, awaiting final paperwork, when a rain shower passed over the field. Instead of rain drops, the shower became "mud drops" as the rain precipitated the pollutants in the air and deposited them on our windshield, obscuring our view. After the "mud" ended, we had to take a short delay in order to have the windshields cleared of Mexico City "air."

I often reiterated the facts of flying into Mexico City with my fellow pilots, with this rhetorical question: Why would anyone want to fly into a place where you can't eat the food, drink the water, or breathe the air? As one might guess, I attempted to avoid Mexico as often as possible. When I was senior enough, I avoided lines of time with Mexico City as a destination. In addition, when trying to pick up trips to fill out the month, I was always careful to write "NO MEX" on my bid slip.

The only other incident that I can recall requiring me to remain in the hotel during a layover did occur in 1991. A mosquito alert was posted for stations along the Florida east coast, as several people had contracted encephalitis. A few had died as a result. I had a layover that month in Melbourne, Florida, which was the center of this warning area. The crew was briefed accordingly, and we took every precaution, including wearing long-sleeve shirts and perfuming ourselves with mosquito repellent while in the area. Such are some of the dangers inherent in an airline career.

All in all, however, obtaining good food and taking in the local sights on a layover was rarely a problem. The following are some of my favorite cities, with the best of both:

San Francisco: Fisherman's Wharf, Chinatown, Golden Gate Bridge, Cable Cars

New York: Carnegie Deli, Rockefeller Center, Central Park, Statue of Liberty

Chicago: Deep dish pizza, Lake Michigan waterfront, Wrigley Field, Rush Street

Philadelphia: Cheese steaks, Franklin Mint, Independence Hall, Liberty Bell

San Antonio: Mexican food along the River Walk, boat rides, the Alamo

Seattle: McCormick & Schmick's Seafood Restaurant, Pike Street Market, and the Space Needle

Santa Monica: Restaurant atop the Huntley House, Palisades Park, the Pier

Bangor: Cap Morrill's lobster, Bass shoe factory, side trips to Bar Harbor

Boston: Legal Sea Foods, Boston Common, Old Ironsides, Boston Market

Charleston: Shrimp and grits, The Battery, the historical district, The Mills House

Savannah: Riverwalk down under, the parks, Paula Deen's headquarters

Cincinnati: Five-way chili, the train depot, businessmen's baseball matinees

New Orleans: Felix's Restaurant & Oyster Bar, Bourbon Street, Café Du Monde, Jackson Square

Fort Lauderdale: Sunshine, beach, the mall, cruise ships, the Jungle Queen Riverboat

San Juan: Cuban Food, the Old City, El Morro Fort, the Caribe Hilton

Washington, DC: Smithsonian Museums, Georgetown, the Capitol, monuments

While almost every layover city had something to offer, these cities were the best of the best, to my recollection, and I felt very privileged to have experienced each one.

This next subject I would entitle "airports of aggravation," meaning airports that required using all your skills and judgment to put your airliner in a position to make a safe landing without the need for violent maneuvering and without stress to the passengers. I have already mentioned Mexico City and the "Rudy Patrick" approach to the downtown Kansas City Airport, but I will mention three more that no pilot particularly looked forward to flying into.

For some reason (most likely convenience), "close-in" airports continued to be used into the jet age, even though those airports were designed for a past age of slower, propeller-driven aircraft. As aircraft were engineered to be larger and faster, getting into these shorter runways and getting the aircraft stopped became a tight proposition.

The first of these airports was (and probably still is) Washington National Airport (later renamed Washington Reagan), close-in to our nation's capital. While Washington Dulles was just a few miles away, with runways long enough to handle the space shuttle, those who worked or planned a visit in our nation's capital overwhelmingly chose to go into National, which was just a short cab ride away. What was convenient for the passengers, however, was a challenge for the airline crews when landing to the south on runway 18.

Beginning about ten miles northwest of the airport and situated over the Potomac River, the pilot had to arrive at a preset altitude and airspeed. Following the course of the river for noise abatement in the surrounding neighborhoods, the pilot had to configure the airplane for landing and then had to descend to other preset altitudes at certain distances from the airport until he or she picked up the runway visually. Being careful to avoid the prohibited area around the White House, the pilot then had to execute a rapid, sharp, descending right-hand turn, short of the Jefferson Memorial, in order to bring the aircraft in line with the runway. The rapid descent continued until approximately fifty feet above the runway, at which point the pilot would break the descent, close the throttles, and "plant" the aircraft on the runway. With maximum engine reversal and braking, the pilot would bring the aircraft to taxi speed in the remaining runway, only to be advised by the tower to "expedite off the runway," as another aircraft was close behind for landing. To say that all this was an adrenalin "rush" would be putting it mildly. Thankfully our hearts were beating normally as we stood in the cockpit door and bade our Washington, DC visitors a "good-day."

The second airport worthy of mention in this area was New York's LaGuardia Airport, another of those built for a previous age of aviation, with no room to expand. As previously mentioned, a portion of runway 13/31 was built on piers extending into the East River. In addition, just a few miles away was New York's Kennedy Airport with multiple long runways, enough to land even the supersonic airliners of that day. But once again, remaining close-in to the city was everything. This put tremendous stress on the aircrews that flew into and out of LaGuardia. The approach to runway 31, while not quite as harrowing as that of Washington National, still required a coordinated crew effort to meet the altitude, airspeed, and airspace requirements that ended with a "hair-raising" turn around Shea stadium, home of the New York Mets. Once lined up, the approach followed the previous scenario to a firm touchdown, followed by maximum braking to avoid going beyond the pier and into the river. I remember noting that the New York police and rescue personnel always kept a number of boats near the end of the pier, just in case. Getting into and out of LaGuardia Airport was always a "hassle," with many departure delays due to the volume of traffic and the proximity to other major airports in the area. Bird strikes were also a problem. In later years, a US Air captain became a hero when he lost both engines due to bird strikes, on takeoff out of LaGuardia. With superior airmanship, he was able to land the airliner safely in the nearby Hudson River, without loss of life.

The third airport worthy of mention was San Diego, California. The approach to Runway 25 at this airport was deceptive in that it also sat down in a "hole," requiring a steep approach over tall buildings that seemed to reach up and touch the airplane. I can remember seeing people on the upper floors of these buildings enjoying drinks and dinner, as we descended, trying to meet the noise abatement and altitude requirements. Airspeed control was mandatory because touchdowns tended to be far down the runway, again requiring maximum braking to bring the aircraft to a stop. Before my retirement, one Delta captain landed "long and hot," using up all of the available runway and ending up on the "overrun" with damage to the airplane.

While there were other airports requiring extra caution and increased blood pressure, the majority were handled in a routine manner, with only minor aggravations. Some, with extra long runways, light traffic, and long, shallow approaches over unpopulated areas, were a pleasure to fly into at times. Other aggravations, beyond the airports themselves, were short flights between co-terminals. A good example was the route from Fort Lauderdale to Miami. This five-minute flight required rapid accomplishment of checklists as well as timely communications with air traffic control in order to bring about a safe flight. As one captain put it, "Like flying copilot on the DC-9, you are busier than a one-armed paperhanger, getting it all done."

Another aggravation worthy of mention was the "test hop." After an aircraft came out of overhaul or some type of major maintenance at the

Atlanta "jet base," it had to be flown by a crew and certified for reentry into passenger service. If you were on reserve and were near the airport, as I was on many occasions, you got the nod. With maintenance personnel onboard, and often after a lengthy delay, we would take off and remain in the local area, trying to stay clear of the arrival and departure routes. After maneuvers and flight checks of various components, the onboard maintenance supervisor would determine that all requirements had been met. After landing, the appropriate paperwork would be completed, the crew released, and the aircraft, in most cases, returned to the line. While the "test hop" was somewhat interesting and was a change of pace, I was always interested in being assigned a trip that was *going somewhere*!

In addition to the normal hazards to flight, such as clear-air turbulence, icing, thunderstorms, or wind shear, there was one last "aggravation" that put additional pressure on pilots operating in and out of some of the nation's airports. It was always a mystery to me why a city would build an "international" airport, allow all manner of housing to be built around it, and then entertain noise complaints from the residents who chose to live there. Aviation law is rife with lawsuits over aircraft noise. Farmers have sued because their chickens quit laying eggs or their cows quit giving milk—all due to jet traffic passing overhead.

These complaints precipitated every type of "noise abatement" procedure, depending on the geography around the airport. Some procedures required sharp turns to a published heading immediately after liftoff. Others required unusually steep climbs and/or reduction of power during the critical phase of takeoff. Still others would not allow takeoffs during certain hours of the day. Noise monitors were set up in the departure corridors to identify offending captains, who usually received a notice from their chief pilot, requesting an explanation. I caught on to the best response to such requests while flying with some of the older captains, years earlier: "Safety issues of this particular flight precluded adherence to the published noise abatement procedures." Mentioning "safety" nearly always ended the matter. Installation of "hush kits" on the jet engines of older aircraft and the development of quieter engines for newer aircraft helped reduce some of the noise. However, jet noise was always a problem during my career, both for the aircrews as well as for the residents who chose a convenient place near the airport to live.

My best story about noise abatement occurred one morning while waiting in line for takeoff at New York's JFK Airport. A British Airways jumbo Boeing747 had just taken off on runway 31and was turning east, bound for the motherland, when the tower controller said, "Speedbird 747, be advised that you have set off the noise monitor on runway 31." With very little pause, the heavy British accent replied, "Tell it to the bloody queen!" Obviously, this chap was not a "royalist."

* * *

With the end of 1991, I was moving up on the seniority list rather rapidly, in fact, rapidly enough to hold a regular line of time and to give up sitting reserve near the airport. Most of the trips now involved longer flight legs to places like Anchorage, Bermuda, San Juan, Nassau, Las Vegas, San Diego, and the aforementioned Mexico City. While my career was changing in a good way, the airline industry was changing in a not so good way. Because of fuel costs and rising, deregulated competition, many airlines were struggling to make a profit. Some folded completely and went out of business. Others sought the avenue of "merger" with another more profitable airline. Delta had already absorbed Chicago and Southern Airlines, Northeast Airlines, and Western Airlines, so it was no surprise when Delta announced that it was purchasing Pan American Airlines, the airline that I had yearned to fly for so many years previously. With this purchase, Delta spent a lot of money and received little in return. I have always equated the temporary demise of Delta Airlines with this purchase, although I'm certain there were other factors.

One thing that the company introduced during this period was a "B" scale (lower) rate of pay for newly hired pilots. This was repugnant to the pilot group, who fought it in contract negotiations with the company, without success. These drawn-out negotiations also resulted in loss of many of the benefits we had attained over the years. They were given up supposedly to help the company's "bottom line" and to protect the existing pay rates. It seemed that the entire airline industry was descending into chaos, and there was much polarization of the relationship between the pilot group and Delta management. The days of the "Delta family" were seemingly numbered.

In April of 1992, an event occurred on the nation's west coast that bears inclusion in these memoirs. In Los Angeles, a black man who was a habitual criminal was severely beaten by four white policemen during an effort to take him into custody. This effort was videotaped and shown repeatedly to the nation by the media. When charges were brought against the policemen for brutality and were then dropped, it produced a spark in the black community that began six days of rioting, looting, assaults, arson, and murder. Fifty-three people were killed and hundreds injured, and property damage was estimated at one billion dollars.

During this time, people began shooting at airplanes as they descended over the riot-torn neighborhoods when landing to the west. Thereafter, all landing aircraft had to fly west, out over the Pacific Ocean, execute a change of direction, and land to the east, regardless of wind or weather. The army and National Guard were called in to "put out the fire," even posting details of soldiers on the beaches underlying the approach paths when aircraft were landing.

On April 30, 1992, I was piloting flight 6600, a Boeing 767 from Atlanta direct to Los Angeles. The flight involved our arriving there in late evening, and as we approached, we could see the fires burning from miles away, with flames reaching high into the sky. It seemed that a good part of the city was on fire. I deviated well south of the city, descended over the ocean, and turned back toward the airport. Luckily there was only a slight tailwind as we lined up on Runway 07 Right. We held our breath as we hit the coast and descended the few remaining feet to the runway, hoping that the soldiers were on alert. It had been twenty-seven years since I had had to worry about ground fire while landing an airplane. How sad that it had to occur in America.

On arrival at the terminal, we were informed that we would not be transported to our normal layover hotel, due to the security status of the city. All of Los Angeles was on a curfew lockdown until the riots could be quelled. As a result, our crew, along with others, was housed at a hotel within the terminal rather than risk the potential dangers of the long drive to a downtown location. Now, in addition to the many hazards to aviation, "riots" had to be added to the list. Fortunately the rioting lost steam after the six days, and the city was brought back under control. Still, there was some apprehension on subsequent flights, while descending over the riot neighborhoods and hoping that the shooters had been permanently silenced. As to the remainder of 1992, all went well as I settled into the captain's seat on the Boeing 767 and into the routine of airline operations.

* * *

I will pause at this point to address two topics that always seem to arise when people discover that flying was my profession. As I said earlier, the first of these is always the question, "Have you ever seen any UFOs (Unidentified Flying Objects) or 'flying saucers' up there?" My response always seems disappointing to the questioner when I say, "No," but I always go on to add that it doesn't mean they aren't there, perhaps in another dimension. I also recount the times when I thought a star to be an aircraft, or an aircraft a star, while flying at night. There were also encounters with weather balloons, meteorite showers, the northern lights, and various optical illusions that proved false.

I do recall a flight during my air force days that gave me a "start" for a few moments. I was piloting a C-130 eastbound over the Pacific one night, when a giant light appeared ahead on the horizon. It rose so quickly and was so large that it startled me for a moment. It was then that I realized that it was a "harvest moonrise," brought on rapidly by my speed toward the eastern horizon. I had never seen that before, so I guess it could be classified as a UFO, if for only a few moments.

Another question I get, at times, revolves around the celebrities that I had a chance to meet during my career. While most well-known people moved around the country in their own private or chartered airplanes, there were a few who chose to use the airlines from time to time or in special situations. I have already mentioned sports teams and the White House press corps, but there were many individual encounters as well.

One evening at New York's JFK Airport, I reported to the DC-8 making up our night flight to Houston. The first-class section had been completely reconfigured to accommodate a stretcher case and medical attendants. After the "coach" or "tourist" cabin was boarded, the patient was boarded with his retinue, and we made ready for departure. The patient, in this case, was the famous bandleader Guy Lombardo, who was going to the Houston heart center for treatment. During the flight, after being assured that it was no trouble, I asked for and received his autograph on a Delta postcard, a process that I followed on other occasions with other celebrities.

On another day, I was flying as first officer on a Boeing 727 inbound to Cincinnati, when it was discovered that the astronaut Neil Armstrong, the first man on the moon, was onboard. The captain, with full support of the crew, put company policy aside and invited him to join us in the cockpit for the approach and landing. We put him on the jump seat and equipped him with a headset so he could listen to all communications. I remember that he was not too impressed with the way air traffic control handled us, and he said so in a "colorful" way. At the gate, he chatted with us for a few minutes and signed autographs all around. I wondered if landing on the moon was as difficult as getting into some of our nation's airports.

One morning in Atlanta, I was headed down the Jetway before passenger boarding, when an agent told me that he had just preboarded a "special" passenger. I stashed my stuff in the cockpit and peered around the first-class bulkhead. There sat award-winning actress Jessica Tandy. I told her how much I appreciated her talent, and she responded graciously with a thank-you and another autograph to add to my collection.

I could recount the particular instances of other encounters, but will only conclude with a few of the personages I remember. These include famous athletes Pete Rose, Pee Wee Reese, Wilt Chamberlain, Andre the Giant, Caesar Cedeno, and longtime Boston Celtic's coach, "Red" Auerbach, comedians Robert Klein, Jerry Lewis, and Jerry Clower, songstress Brenda Lee, newsman Frank Blair, Dan Blocker (TV's "Hoss" Cartwright of *Bonanza*), and everybody's favorite cowgirl, Dale Evans. If the young minds of future readers are not familiar with these names, I would refer them to a *Who's Who in American History* publication. While most passengers were just common, everyday people who were appreciated for their business, having a celebrity onboard added just a bit of "spice" to the routine.

One other question that always comes came up, particularly from the younger set, is, "How fast do you go up there?" I begin by saying that the speed across the ground depends on several factors such as altitude or winds, with the short answer being around 600 mph. I then proceed to explain that all the jet aircraft I flew were operated at subsonic (below the speed of sound) speeds, with the exception of the T-38 trainer, which could fly at supersonic speeds. Then I move on to the fact that all subsonic jets are flown at a percentage of the speed of sound. The term

"Mach 1" has been used to identify the speed of sound; therefore, anything slower would be expressed as a percentage of Mach1, for example, .78 Mach, .80 Mach, and so on. After receiving blank stares after this technical explanation, I usually say, "Just forget all that, and just know that we go very fast."

* * *

As fuel prices continued to climb, the industry began to develop more fuel-efficient jet engines and to assign specific Mach speeds for best fuel economy. I do remember that some of the control surfaces on the early DC-8s I flew as a flight engineer could reach the speed of sound. This level was discernible as a slight shaking of the airplane. One night, on a flight from San Francisco, the captain "let the big dog (DC-8) eat" all the way to Atlanta, right up to the maximum airspeed warning needle. We landed twenty minutes under schedule, which pleased all the passengers, one of whom said upon deplaning, "That was a great flight captain, but what was all that light turbulence about during the flight?" The captain mumbled something about being on the edge of the jet stream, as the first officer and I looked at each other with a sly grin. Those old captains back then had a habit of going "full speed ahead" at all times, regardless of what the company flight plan called for. Fuel was cheap, and even some experts within the company thought this was the best speed to fly for scheduling purposes. Sometimes the old captains would level at cruise altitude and forget to pull the throttles back. On one flight, I watched a first officer begin to squirm as the airspeed began to approach the over-speed warning siren. Finally he turned to the captain and said, "John, reckon you oughta trot 'em for awhile?"

The year 1993 began with the inauguration of a new president, Democrat William Jefferson Clinton, better known as "Slick Willie" to those of opposite political leanings. This "new liberal era" produced great gains for those seeking equal rights, such as gays and lesbians and women in general. Same-sex "civil union" couples were clamoring for the right to marry. Gays and lesbians, who heretofore had been banned from service in the armed forces, were now granted entry under the "Don't ask, don't tell" policy outlined for military recruiters and enlistees. Later on, they were allowed to serve openly. Women were ordained as priests, integrated into the military services, and appointed to high offices in government that had formerly been held only by men.

On the international scene, tensions between the United States, Russia, and other members of the Soviet bloc were easing as new sets of treaties were signed with Russia and with other newly liberated nations. Other tensions, however, were increasing, as Moslem "Jihadists" raised the level of terrorist activity around the world against the "great American Satan" and against all Jews and Christians. This was first brought home on American soil in the most violent way possible. As all America was sleeping, thinking the country immune from terrorist attack, the alarm clock went off on February 26th. A vehicle loaded with explosives was driven into the parking garage of the World Trade Center in New York City. The detonation and resulting explosion killed six people and injured scores of others. Acts of terror had reached the American continent at last, an omen of more terrible acts to follow.

On the airline scene, this escalation brought on many changes. In training classes, emphasis was placed on acting out scenarios involving the activities of terrorists, hijackings, and bomb threats. Airport security was increased, and later, a color-coded terrorist alert level was instituted nationwide. As the airline industry continued its economic freefall, Boeing Aircraft laid off fifteen thousand industry workers. The year 1993 was not off to a good start, and the future did not look much better. How far the experience of flying on the nation's airlines had fallen. With deteriorating onboard service, deregulated competition, and increased predeparture security screening, flying for the American public had developed into a "hassle."

With the increase in tension and stress, incidents of confrontation between passengers and airline personnel began to escalate. While I was fairly insulated from most altercations behind the safety of the cockpit door, I was sometimes brought into the problem when a decision had to be made relative to a passenger boarding or continuing on one of my flights. An increase in passengers' predeparture alcohol consumption often added to the problem. A few travelers would arrive at the gate having "had too much," as the saying goes. Gate agents would often try to board these individuals, just to get rid of them. One afternoon, back when I was on the B-727, this idea did not work out too well for one Kansas City gate agent.

I was in the cockpit, readying the jet for departure to Atlanta ,when the "A-line" flight attendant came up to complain of a drunk who had been boarded in first class, over her objections, and who was now being an obnoxious nuisance in the entire cabin. I had learned over the years always to defer to the judgment of the flight attendants as to who goes and who stays in these situations. Accordingly, I sent word to the gate agent that this aircraft "would not turn a wheel" until the offending passenger was removed. Realizing that he had been "outflanked," the gate agent quickly responded by having the offending passenger removed. After a quick rework of the passenger manifest, the boarding door was closed, and we pushed back on time for a pleasant flight to Atlanta for both passengers and crew.

Another incident along these lines occurred on a B-757 flight originating in Portland, Oregon, with a short flight scheduled to Seattle and then on to Atlanta. Boarding in Portland was a group of boisterous young men bound for Atlanta, who had spent a little too much time in the airport bar. One member of this particular group carried the party spirit too far by putting his hands on one of the flight attendants, showing off for his buddies, and making a general nuisance of himself during the flight to Seattle. After complaints by the flight attendants, I called ahead to have the young man removed from the flight and to have him denied boarding for the continuation of the flight to Atlanta. This was accomplished, much to the offender's surprise, as the passengers waiting in Seattle were being quickly boarded. From the cockpit, I could see the gate waiting area as it quickly emptied, leaving only our offender sitting alone, contemplating his situation.

The gate agent arrived at the cockpit with the final paperwork, all prepared to close the door, when he said, "Captain, what do you want to do with that guy out there?" The A-line flight attendant was standing there as well, so I told the agent, "It's up to her." She thought for a second and said, "If he can behave himself, I'll take him." I told the agent to go get him and to have him stop off at the cockpit on the way in. When he showed up, looking sheepish and stone cold sober, I told him to go back and sit down, adding that if there was any more trouble out of him, I would land at the nearest suitable airport and have him arrested by the FBI. He seemed so happy to be back onboard that I believe he would have agreed to any terms. Sometime during the flight to Atlanta, I called back to the cabin to see how our boy was doing. "Oh, Captain," came the answer, "he has been a perfect angel; haven't heard a peep out of him, and he is now sleeping like a baby." Sometimes the exuberance of youth has to be reined in.

Since I am dealing with this area of problem passengers, I will relate one last incident that occurred a few months prior to my retirement. The flight in question originated in Fort Meyers, Florida, bound for Atlanta. Two seemingly nice older ladies were boarded in the first-class cabin and were served drinks while the other passengers were boarding. All seemed to go well during the first portion of the flight, but things changed radically as we neared Atlanta. I will never know the exact details of what happened between one of the women and the flight attendants, but this one lady suddenly became belligerent. Verbally and physically abusing the flight attendants, she rose from her seat, marched to the cockpit door, and began banging on it, demanding to see the captain. The flight attendant used the call system to give us a "heads up" on the situation, and since we were near the descent point into Atlanta, I picked up the PA microphone and advised all passengers to return to their seats, to fasten their seatbelts, and to prepare for landing in Atlanta. This seemed to get through to the woman, who complied, while still giving the flight attendants fits. During the descent, I called ahead, advising that we had a belligerent passenger onboard and requesting assistance upon arriving at the gate. When the cabin door was opened at the gate, the agent asked all passengers to remain seated while law enforcement personnel and Delta passenger service agents dealt with the lady passenger. I did not witness her removal from the airplane, but I was told later that she had to be put in a strait jacket and placed in a padded cell at the airport. It seems that demons of all description hitch a ride on the nations' airlines from time to time. This lady must have filed an enormous lawsuit against Delta, for even after my retirement, I continued to get correspondence relative to this incident, asking for my role and for my recollection of the facts.

It seemed that the airline environment was increasingly bringing out the worst in the traveling public. I now understood more clearly the statement made by that old-time captain who had remained on the all-cargo operation for many years: "freight don't talk back"

* * *

With the beginning of 1994, I was continuing to move up on the pilot seniority list. This allowed me to bid and hold better days off, fly better trips, and better coordinate both of these with my commute from Knoxville. On the aviation front, things were relatively static, the only new thing being the formation of so-called "alter ego" airlines. These were offshoots of the major airlines, formed for specific markets and designed to get around the union contracts that the "majors" had to contend with. United had its "shuttle," American its "express," and Delta its "connection." Most of these operated into smaller stations with smaller equipment and at a substantial savings in cost. Pay and benefits for those employees was far below the levels enjoyed by those who worked for the major airlines. A good portion of those pilots were new to airline flying, and they looked at the job more as a stepping stone to getting on with the parent company. The danger for the major airline pilots was the loss of flying time in some markets. These arrangements were monitored closely, and contract language was adjusted to forestall any abuse. Later on, the majors would form "wholly owned subsidiary" airlines that could operate totally free of contractual restraints.

The big event of 1994, for me, began on April 1, when my wife and I boarded an L-1011-500 in Atlanta for a tour of the Holy Land. Having undergone a recent spiritual transformation in our lives, we were looking forward to "walking where Jesus walked" and enjoying the fellowship of other believers who were on the same tour. After an aircraft change in Paris (a B-767ER, meaning "Extended Range"), we continued on to Israel, landing at the Ben Gurion International Airport near Tel Aviv the following day.

Since we were two days early for the beginning of the tour, we elected to remain in the Tel Aviv area until all the other tour members arrived. After settling into a nearby hotel, we soon found ourselves in the crowded marketplace of Joppa (Jaffa), a historic seaside town where the biblical Jonah began his ill-fated voyage to Tarshish. A highlight was wading in the surf of the Mediterranean Sea. The next day, we visited the Museum of the Diaspora, which showcases the Jewish experience over twenty-six hundred years since the destruction of the temple in Jerusalem. That history was profiled in displays from the various countries to which the Jews were exiled. Finally, all the fellow Christian believers arrived, and we departed next day for Jerusalem and the start of our tour.

Touring the Holy Land is to walk down the timeline of Judaism and of early Christianity. Being there made the Holy Bible come to life, with stops at so many of the locations mentioned therein. The highlight for me was a boat trip on the Sea of Galilee, during which the captain cut the engines and allowed us to drift while we had a short church service. Afterward, we had a sumptuous dinner of St. Peter's fish at a lakeshore restaurant. Taking communion at the Garden Tomb was another highlight I must mention. While the details of this experience would go beyond the scope of these memoirs, let me say that Israel is a beautiful, vibrant country, the crossroads for so many of the world's religions. While we were there, the weather, the food, our tour guide, and our accommodations were perfect in every way, and I would recommend this experience to anyone who calls himself or herself a Christian. On April 24th, we retraced our route with flights back to Atlanta, and we arrived home spiritually refreshed and ready to get on with life.

One of my first flights back on the line was a trip involving a flight from San Francisco to New York's Kennedy Airport. I mention this flight because it brought home to me the beauty of this country as well. Taking off from San Francisco, we climbed out over the sunlit bay. As I looked back off the left wing, I saw the Golden Gate Bridge, almost enshrouded with fog, its piers rising above, reflecting that familiar deep red in the sunlight of morning. Ahead were the Sierra Nevada Mountains, capped with snow and cradling beautiful Lake Tahoe. Continuing eastbound, we crossed the Great Basin of Nevada with the rugged, snowcapped Rocky Mountains looming in the distance. With a good tailwind, we were soon over the Great Plains, the "breadbasket" of the nation, with its large tracts of agricultural land just beginning to bloom with the food to feed our country as well as others around the world. Crossing the Mississippi River, we surveyed the neat farms of the Midwest, continued on over the shorter peaks of the Alleghenies, and began our descent into the New York area. Since JFK airport was landing traffic to the west, we passed over the city, continuing east out over the Atlantic, with a turn back to the west for landing. During this maneuver, we could see Manhattan Island, all the connecting bridges, and the Statue of Liberty holding her torch high. What really came home to me was that, in one short flight, we were able to see all the beauty of America at its best and none of its ugliness. Cruising at forty-three thousand feet covers over a "multitude of sins."

On August 3rd, I was scheduled to captain Flight 166, a B-757 out of Cincinnati, bound for Philadelphia. It was a night flight, and as we were climbing over Dayton, Ohio, one of the flight attendants called the cockpit to report a medical problem in the cabin. It seemed that a male passenger was suffering from what appeared to be a heart attack, and he was receiving CPR on the aisle floor. I told her to see if there was a doctor onboard, which fortunately there was. I immediately declared an emergency, and requested an emergency descent into Columbus, Ohio, which was just below. Seven minutes later, I had our patient at the gate and in the care of emergency medical personnel.

While we were topping off our fuel and getting a new flight release for continuing our journey, the gate agent came into the cockpit with a message from our passenger patient. It seemed that after receiving treatment from the EMTs, he was feeling better and was asking if he could get back on board. Trying not to be too shocked at this message, I replied, "The only place that man needs to go is to a hospital; request denied." I could see myself landing every few miles along my route to seek medical treatment for an individual who should not have been flying in the first place. I never found out what happened to the man, but I always hoped that he made it to Philadelphia and lived a long, healthy life.

At about this time, the spiritual awakening that my wife and I had experienced precipitated a move to Johnson City, Tennessee, to be near the church we believed to be preaching the Truth. Now I would be commuting to Atlanta out of the Tri-Cities Airport, which served Johnson City, Kingsport, and Bristol, Tennessee. This worked out very nicely as long as Delta was serving the airport with jet traffic. Later, Delta pulled this service out and left it to the company's connection carrier, Atlantic Southeast Airlines. Smaller, older, propeller-driven aircraft resulted in a decrease in seating. Increased maintenance problems and unreliable scheduling also made commuting on Atlantic Southeast a real venture. Later, after the Delta pilot group negotiated and received authorization for us to occupy the cockpit jump seat on connection carriers, some of the stress was alleviated, although not all.

One event that I will always remember occurred one night on the ramp at Los Angeles Airport. I was sitting in the cockpit preparing the B-757 for a nonstop flight to Atlanta. Suddenly, and with no warning, the aircraft began to rock violently from side to side. Then everything went dark. As I was trying to analyze the situation and determine what course of action to take, a mechanic entering the cockpit announced that we had just had an earthquake and that the rocking of the aircraft had pulled the external power cord out of its socket. With power restored and hearts beating at a slower rate, we reinspected the aircraft for any possible damage. Finding none, we boarded our passengers and departed, very glad to be leaving the country's earthquake zone, an area that scientists and prophets alike have predicted will slide into the Pacific Ocean one day. My thought then was to let it happen after my retirement.

Other than experiencing increased air traffic delays, and with no other major incident on the airline to report, 1994 ended on a very good note. Things were going well.

CHAPTER EIGHTEEN

"POWERING DOWN"

The year 1995 was relatively uneventful, as far as flying the line was concerned. My trips early in the year involved long layovers in Hartford, Connecticut, so my wife and I took those opportunities to explore the New England countryside. On one such occasion, we rented a car and explored the small picturesque towns and villages of western Connecticut and Massachusetts, stopping at antique shops and other sites along the way. People were apparently very trusting in these remote areas. We stopped at one rather large antique barn and entered to find no one minding the store; we saw only a sign saying that if we saw something we were interested in, to go to the big house nearby and ring the bell. While we found nothing to pique our interest, thereby not having to follow those instructions, I had an eerie feeling that we were still under surveillance. On another trip, we again rented a car and headed east, stopping at New London, Connecticut, to visit the USS Nautilus, the nation's first atomic submarine, and also to see the museum outlining the nation's history of the construction and use of the submarine in wartime. Continuing on in to Rhode Island, we ended up in Newport, summer residence to the rich and famous, where we viewed the seaside mansions of Lady Astor and others, followed by a candlelight dinner at one of the small restaurants in the village. After a nighttime drive back through the countryside, we arrived back at our motel, very tired, but satisfied that we had done justice to our allotted time. Later on, after retirement, we returned to New England, spending an entire vacation touring the Maine coast, then turning westward, crossing the White Mountains into New Hampshire and Vermont. All of this area is full of history and beauty, and I enjoyed all of the time I was able to spend there.

As the year wore on, I began to have foot trouble. I had developed large bunions on both feet and had begun to hobble a bit as I walked down the airport concourses, trying to carry my gear and keep up with the rest of the crew. In July, I realized that I had to do something about it. After consulting with a foot surgeon and explaining the situation to my chief pilot at Delta, I reported to the hospital for surgery to correct the problem. While the surgery went well, and I was released to go home, the healing and recuperation period was to take me through September, before I was able to give up both the crutches and my trademark limp and go back to work. As always, after being off for any significant time, Delta put me through four days of recurrent training in early October before allowing me back in the captain's seat on the B-767. Although my recuperative period was enjoyable, to a certain extent (I had the best nurse ever), it was good to get back to my life's work and to see San Francisco and Seattle again.

This was short-lived, however, as I had one more vacation scheduled for the last two weeks of October. I had always wanted to do some international travel, and although we had done a short trip to London to see the queen, I was anxious to see some of the European continent. As it turned out, one of the male flight attendants that I flew with was the son of a couple associated with our church. They were German by birth, having immigrated to this country in the aftermath of World War II. After we visited in their home in Mobile, Alabama, and saw that they had a desire to revisit their fatherland, we all decided to travel together, and we set our departure date to coincide with my vacation. Since they spoke fluent German, it made everything so much easier for us. By allowing them to map our itinerary, we were able to see the "touristy" sites while visiting in the homes of their friends, as well as attending church services along the way. After visiting the German National Tourist Office in New York for updated travel and passport information, then packing and picking up an English-to-German phrase book, we soon met our hosts in Atlanta for departure to Frankfurt, Germany, aboard an L-1011-500.

After landing, we piled the luggage in the back of our rented Volkswagen Passat station wagon and headed south toward the Black Forest. Siegfried, our male host, knew every square foot of southern Germany, according to his son, but with the complexity of highways and the autobahn, we were forced to stop from time to time to get directions. The German language is not pleasant to the ear, and the requests for directions sounded as though the two participants were on the verge of a fistfight, with all the gesturing and raised voices. But satisfied that he was on the right track, Siegfried returned to the driver's seat and soon had us on our way to our first stop.

Over the next few days, we traveled around southern Germany, ending up in Bavaria, staying in the bed-and-breakfast inns along the way. A side tour through Austria to the ski resort peaks of the Italian Alps was a highlight, as well as a visit to the royal castle of Neuschwanstein, home to the mad "fairy-tale king" Ludwig and the inspiration for Disney's Sleeping Beauty Castle at Disneyland. Another highlight was a visit to the Mercedes factory at Stuttgart, where we watched a new Mercedes roll off the assembly line every sixty seconds, after being put together largely by mechanized robots.

One day, while staying in the small village of Klais, we decided to board a train to Munich for some shopping. To say that the trains run on time in Germany would be an ultimate truth. Our train was scheduled to arrive at 9:37 and depart at 9:39, and that was precisely what it did; precision is a very German characteristic.

The quality of manufacturing is another German trait that I can attest to, in that everything I purchased on that shopping trip, I still have as of this writing. One other item worthy of mention here concerns the walled-off areas of Munich, which still contained bombed-out sections of the city. These were a remnant of World War II and had not yet been reclaimed, and this was a very eerie sight indeed. To say that Germany was the cleanest, neatest country I was ever in would be an understatement. Even the barns were tile-roofed, the roads were free of litter, and there was very little, if any, visual pollution.

I noticed a monument in the circle square of one village, which displayed thirty or so pictures of young men in military uniform—all killed in World War II—all the flower of that generation for this particular village. It reminded me that there were similar monuments on the courthouse lawns of America, memorializing that same type of loss.

The aforementioned church services were interesting. My wife and I were fitted with headsets, and while the pastor preached in German, we listened to the interpretation in English. While the words and music were strange to our ears, the spirit of kinship was the same, and we enjoyed sweet fellowship with these gracious brothers and sisters of like faith.

The food was good overall—no fast food restaurants—and the water was bottled. In fact, the Germans made much ado about their bottled water, almost treating it like wine. One thing I do remember in the food line was a "brotchen," sort of a cross between a biscuit and a bagel, which I gobbled up at every opportunity. Fancy desserts were the order of the day, and everyone, us included, paused around 4:00 p.m. to have one of these delicious pastries and a cup of coffee.

Soon we ran out of days, as our time in Germany drew to a close. After a short trip to the airport at Munich, we boarded a Delta B-767ER for the long flight back to our own homeland and the continuation of our lives as Americans. All in all, I enjoyed the trip. Now it was back to the standard American diet, my part in its aviation transportation industry, and the balance of 1995.

With a full month of flying in November and an even fuller schedule the first twenty-four days of December, I was able to build a "bow wave" of flight time. This prevented me from flying the last week of December, due to overtime restrictions. As a result, I was able to be home on Christmas and for the rest of the year. Seniority was beginning to show.

As the year 1996 came in, I began to realize that I had only a little over three years left before retirement. I would be sixty years old in September of 1999, and I could not fly for Delta beyond the end of that month. October 1, 1999, would be my mandatory retirement date. I was very happy with where I was on the B-767, and I was determined to remain there for the balance of my career, thereby avoiding an upgrade to any other equipment. That determination was to receive a shock, however, when I discovered my name on a Lockheed L-1011-500 Advance Entitlement bid. How could this have happened, since I had not submitted a bid? Or at least, I thought I had not. As it turned out, I had, back when I had submitted my bid for the B-767. In my zeal to upgrade from captain on the B-727, I had listed the L-1011-500 as first choice, and I had failed to remove it after I was awarded the B-767 bid. It had remained on file all this time and had come back to bite me in the twilight of my career.

What to do? My distaste for this aircraft, the low seniority position I would have, and the stressful international schedules I would fly were not the way I wanted to end a career. I immediately got on the phone with the individual responsible for the bid awards and began to plead my case to be removed from the list, even to the point of threatening to take early retirement as a last resort. Apparently he sensed my determination, and he stated that he would see what he could do. These bids were virtually "set in stone," and getting one changed was almost unprecedented. After being on "pins and needles" for a few days, I was relieved to see a bulletin board posting relieving me of the bid and giving it to the next applicant junior to me. I hope that whoever he was, he was as happy receiving the bid as I was in having it taken away. By means of a narrow escape, I was to remain a "Boeing only" captain for the remainder of my career.

In its various models, the Boeing 767 category offered a great deal of variety, calling on slightly different piloting skills. First there was the B-757, the narrow-bodied, overpowered machine that was easy to fly and land and was quick to climb above the weather. It was the pilots' favorite, and I was always glad to see it sitting at the gate when I arrived. Then there was the Boeing 767-100, the model that first came into the Delta inventory. It was shorter, slower to climb, and something of a "lumbering beast" to fly. Landing this model was completely different from all the others. With its shorter wheelbase, the nose had to be pulled up to an extreme angle to get a good touchdown. This called for skill in managing airspeed, sink rate, and height above the runway. Once that skill was mastered, though, a "grease job" was the outcome more often than not. The third model to come into the Delta inventory was the Boeing-767-200. This was a "stretch" model of the "100" series. With its longer wheel base, it was more "flat," landing like the old DC-8s. As that old captain had put it so many years before: "Just bring it down about six inches off the ground, retard the throttles, and let it settle in from there." Again, finding that six inches was the key. After Delta absorbed Pan American Airlines, they acquired all of that failed airline's international routes and became a major player on the transatlantic scene to Europe, and then to South America sometime later.

With the success of the B-767 on the domestic scene and with the aging of the L-1011-500 fleet, Delta once again turned to Boeing and began taking delivery on the Boeing 767ER. With more fuel capacity and more powerful and fuel-efficient engines, this aircraft was tailor-made for Delta's route structure. At first this model was restricted solely to the international routes, but as time went on, these planes began to fill in on some domestic routes as well. This was one "going machine," and with the reduced fuel and weight loads common on the domestic routes, it climbed like a homesick angel and was easy to fly and land. With all these models, it was impossible to fall into the boredom that was common on single model categories. I always counted it a blessing to serve out the last years of my career flying these wonderful machines.

In addition to the weather hazards to aviation, there were other hazards stemming from contact with passengers. While I'm certain that I picked up my share of cold viruses from mingling with all those people over the years, sometimes the threat was more serious. It was rare, but on a few occasions, I would get a note in my mailbox advising me that after such and such a flight, passenger John (or Jane) Doe had since discovered that they had chicken pox, measles, mumps, AIDS, etc., and telling me to take whatever precaution I saw fit. Luckily, my immune system was up to speed, and I failed to acquire any of these communicable maladies.

I do remember one story that apparently got one passenger, as well as Delta, into a lot of hot water. It seems that a radioactive shipment had somehow leaked into one of the baggage bins on one particular Delta flight. This aircraft went on to fly several flights before the leak was reported. Not knowing the consequences to the passengers on these flights, there was nothing to do but contact all of them and alert them to the possible exposure to radioactivity. All went well until Delta attempted to contact one male passenger and companion who had made a quick trip to New York from Houston, Texas, over a weekend. When the phone call was made to the man's home, his wife answered the phone. When the purpose of the call was explained and the flight to New York mentioned, she replied, "What trip to New York?" I always wondered how her husband explained that one, and whether or not the radioactivity exposure might have been less hazardous to his health.

One "hazard to flight" that *was* related to weather was the braking capability of aircraft on ice and snow covered runways. While the ground crews normally did an outstanding job of clearing those runways, particularly at the larger airports, there were times when equipment was lacking or when they simply could not keep up with the freezing weather phenomenon at hand. Enter the James Brake Accelerometer. This was an instrument attached to a wheel and towed behind a vehicle to measure the "braking coefficient" of the landing runway. The users having obtained a measurement, this information would be passed to the tower to be disseminated to aircraft landing on that runway, with braking action being reported as "good," "fair," "poor," or "nil." Naturally, no captain would consider landing with a report of braking being "nil." It was the "poor-to-nil" report that put the burden on the captain, and a few of them, trying to land in those conditions, found themselves slip-sliding away , trying to stop the runaway locomotives they were piloting.

My decisions in these situations had been set long ago when copiloting a B-727 into the short runway at Lexington, Kentucky. Arriving in the area one Thursday morning, we discovered that no aircraft had landed there for two days, due to an ice storm followed by several inches of snow. A few miles out, we contacted the tower and requested a braking report. The tower replied, "Stand by; we are working on that." With the aircraft configured for landing and getting closer, I queried the tower again for a braking report. "Yes, Delta, I have that report for you. Braking action reported 'poor-to-nil' by a dump truck." The captain immediately advanced the throttles, gave me the signal to raise the landing gear, and keying the mike, said, "Lexington Tower, thanks for that report; we'll see you next Thursday." After completing the missed approach, we continued on to Chicago O'Hare and to a runway with a better braking coefficient. Fortunately, the memory of that experience kept me out of some "slick" situations during my career.

On July 10, 1996, an event occurred that comes to all who have aging parents. My father, Jesse Lee Butcher, had been sick for some time with stomach cancer. He had been fitted with a feeding tube and had been sent home to the condominium he and my mother occupied in Knoxville. I had left on a trip back on July 8th, with layovers in San Francisco and New York. On the morning of the 10th, I departed New York's LaGuardia Airport, bound for Atlanta. As I taxied into the gate, I noticed the chief pilot standing in the Jetway. His presence immediately let me know that something was wrong, and my mind turned to my father. After the passengers deplaned, I packed up my gear and walked off the airplane. Sure enough, my suspicions were correct, as he informed me that my father had passed away. I was relieved from the balance of the trip and told to take all the time I needed to attend to family affairs in this situation. I immediately got an emergency pass and was on the first available flight back home. On that flight, as I was pondering the events of the next few days, I recalled what someone once said: "A man does not begin to live until his father dies." That thought brought the realization that the paternal generation ahead of me was gone, and that I would now step to the front line to take his place—the last place before my own departure. I wish I could say that my father and I were close, but generational differences, education, and an early departure from under his headship prevented that from happening. But I did try to maintain contact with him and show the respect due his position in the family. After helping my mother with all the arrangements and receiving the condolences of friends and family, I returned to my job on July 24th, with a slightly different perspective on life.

* * *

Later that year, the Atlanta base began flying into several new stations, two of which were Tucson, Arizona, and Vancouver, British Columbia, Canada. My wife and I had a special place in our hearts for Tucson, as it was home to many believers connected with our church. We had made three winter vacation trips there in the past, exploring the area, enjoying the sunshine and the food, visiting Mexico, and attending local church services. So it was good to be back in that area, although I had little time on the short layovers built into the flight schedule.

In August of 1996, I began flying into Vancouver. It was on one of those flights that I experienced a weather phenomenon that I had seen before, but not in such a special way. It was late afternoon when we arrived in the vicinity of the airport. A small rain shower had just moved over the field, with clearing and bright sunshine out to the west. We continued in that direction behind several other aircraft, before turning back to the east for our final approach and landing. As we completed the turn to final, we observed the most brilliant and vivid rainbow just ahead, forming a perfect bow over the final approach course. I was totally awed as we passed under the rainbow, our shadow mixing with all the colors. After landing, the first officer and I agreed that it was one of the most memorable things we had ever witnessed in our flying careers. We had seen many rainbows, but had never flown under and through one. I keyed the mike after landing and asked the tower if this was the way all arrivals were welcomed to Vancouver.

Two major air disasters occurred in 1996 that brought about changes in the industry. The first of these occurred on the afternoon of May 11, when a DC-9 formerly owned by Delta but now owned and operated by ValuJet, one of the new low-cost airlines departed the gate in Miami. In the cargo hold were five boxes of oxygen generators that had reached their expiration date. These generators were used to supply supplemental oxygen to the passengers in the event of a rapid decompression. Sometime during taxi-out, one of the generators fell out of its packaging, produced a spark, and started a fire in that compartment, which was so constructed as to suppress any such event. But with these oxygen generators feeding the fire, it continued to burn as the aircraft took off. Shortly after takeoff, the flight attendants reported intense fire and smoke in the cabin. With no way to fight the fire, the pilots declared an emergency and sought the nearest airport to get the airplane on the ground. But it was too late. The

DC-9 crashed into a remote area, hitting the ground at over five hundred miles per hour, killing all passengers and crew instantly. The investigation revealed that improper packaging and placement of such a hazardous material in the cargo hold were the causes. After this accident, there was a tightening of restrictions for carrying hazardous materials on all flights. One provision was that any hazardous material would be reported to the captain before being loaded, stating what it was and that it was properly packaged. He would then consult a checklist of various classes of hazardous materials in order to confirm whether or not it could be carried. Since the captain was the final authority, it was my policy to deny boarding to nearly all of these materials, as it was most of my fellow captains.

One thing I was always glad to carry, however, were human organs for transplant. These were carried safely in the cockpit and delivered immediately to the agent meeting the flight. Most of these were human eyes. As one of these packages was being strapped into the jump seat one morning, my first officer said, "It's always good to have another set of eyeballs in the cockpit."

The second major air disaster of 1996 resulted in the "most extensive, complex, and costly air disaster investigation in US history," according to Wikipedia, the online encyclopedia. It was the second deadliest US air disaster up to that time, and its cause was subject to much speculation for a long time afterward. On July 17th, TWA Flight 800 departed New York's JFK Airport, bound for Rome. Twelve minutes after takeoff, the Boeing 747 suddenly exploded, scattering aircraft parts and the bodies of all two hundred and thirty souls aboard into the Atlantic, just off the shore of Long Island. Immediately, the cause was thought to be a terrorist attack. When this could not be confirmed, other theories began to abound, including the idea of a missile attack and even mentioning the US Navy as a possible source. After over four years of investigation and trying to piece the aircraft back together in a hangar, the final National Transportation Safety Board report listed the cause as fuel vapors that were ignited by a faulty pump in one of the aircraft fuel tanks. Changes to the nation's commercial fleet were initiated within a short period thereafter. I point out these events not only because they occurred during my career, but to show that for nearly every safety improvement made in the aviation industry, somebody, or several somebodies, had to die.

As the year 1997 began, I had again moved up significantly on the Delta Airlines seniority list. I began the year as pilot number 540. Since many of those ahead of me were scattered among the other bases, were on extended sick leave, or were nearing their retirement date, my *effective* seniority number was somewhat higher. As such, I was able to pick my trips, centering my monthly bid on Atlanta departure and arrival times in order to produce a timely commute to and from work. With this factor being the point of emphasis, it was unusual not to get my first choice.

Since layover destinations and times were less important in bidding, I managed to see most of the older Delta stations during the year, plus a few new ones such as Santa Ana, California, Saint Thomas, the Virgin Islands, and Bermuda, where we were forced to use the ancient high frequency radio system to communicate with air traffic control. Hearing the pops, crackles, and static in my headset reminded me of my air force days, back in the C-130 over the Pacific Ocean. At least all this kept things new and interesting.

With air traffic becoming congested all around the nation, fuel planning became paramount. This again produced some "conversations" between Delta Flight Control, who normally wanted to carry the minimum required fuel load, and the captains, who "had been there before" and who wanted extra fuel. Various combinations of traffic and weather could produce some horrendous delays in holding patterns near the destination airport. The last thing any pilot wanted to do was to bore racetrack patterns in the sky, in all kinds of weather, with several other aircraft nearby, then have to divert to another airport for more fuel, then take off and climb back up into the holding pattern while hoping he or she had not lost the previous place in the stack. Luckily, this only happened to me three times, as I recall, and all involved either New York or Atlanta. The New York incident meant having to descend into Philadelphia after an extended hold over that city while trying to get into New York's La Guardia Airport during bad weather. It was not unusual to be something like number thirty-five to land or take off at that airport, even during the best of conditions. Again, it seemed that everyone wanted to land at "close-in" LaGuardia. The other two events were due to a combination of bad weather and poor fuel planning by both Flight Control and me, the captain. Both involved diversions into Birmingham, which along with Knoxville, were the favored alternate airports in the event of bad weather in Atlanta.

I distinctly remember the one incident involving a Seattle to Atlanta flight. I had checked with Flight Control concerning the fuel load, as it was right at the minimum load necessary to meet the flight requirements. The dispatcher said that there was a very slight chance of a thunderstorm in the Atlanta area, but that it should not develop until after our arrival time. I accepted that report, and we launched off for Atlanta, climbing into the cool air of a Seattle morning, with Mount Rainer and its snowy summit off to our left. As we crossed the Mississippi River at Memphis, the weather in Atlanta began to change rapidly. With all the traffic converging on the airport, we were instructed to anticipate holding delays. I could see "the handwriting on the wall" and immediately requested clearance to Birmingham. Having received that, I instructed the first officer to advise Delta Flight Control of our plan. I was prepared to get some "static" in return, but none came.

After landing in Birmingham, we were fortunate to get an open gate, and we began the refueling process for continuing our flight to Atlanta. As we watched from the waiting area in the terminal, the sky suddenly became filled with Delta jets, landing one after the other and trying to find a parking place on the ramp. With no access to a gate, the passengers and crews were forced to remain on board, and with limited refueling capability, there was obviously going to be a long ground delay for all. At about the time the last Delta jet landed (there must have been twenty or so by now), we received word that the weather was clearing in Atlanta, so we pushed back from the gate, made our way through the conglomeration of Delta jets, and took off for home base. Understandably, there was no other traffic to contend with, and we made it to our gate in minimum time. I often wondered, thereafter, how long it took Delta to recover all those aircraft and how the daily operational briefing went the next morning for those dispatchers who had dropped the ball on fuel loads the previous day. The major problem for the crews was that it made for some very long crew duty days.

In my airline career, I was fortunate to fly with some of the most skilled, intelligent, and motivated fellow pilots, with only a few exceptions. Each one knew his place on the crew, and we normally operated as a well-oiled machine from start to finish. One thing I was not fully prepared for was to have a woman as a copilot. To avoid discrimination lawsuits, Delta had begun hiring a few qualified women in previous years. By the time I became a senior captain, some of these had worked their way up the seniority list to hold first officer positions. In fact, that year, 1997, saw the appearance of the first black female captain on one of United Airlines' small shuttle airlines. While I did not consider myself chauvinistic to a fault, I did hold some prejudice toward these women in that Delta was forced to hire them, to the exclusion of male pilots who needed the jobs as "breadwinners," and also due to the generally held idea that they were "weak" in critical situations. After one female flight engineer caused a DC-8 engine to flame out due to fuel mismanagement, that idea gained support within the pilot group. In addition, letters were sent out, cautioning all pilots working with these women to mind what they said in order to avoid any complaints of sexual harassment. Now it was my turn to be challenged by the presence of a crew member who was not really welcome in my cockpit. By being totally professional, exercising enhanced supervision, and remembering that they were there to assist and learn, I got along fine. I must admit, however, that it was always nice to get back to flying with my own gender.

With the proliferation of drugs into our society, testing for drugs was mandated for all airline pilots at about this time. Delta had been drug testing pilot applicants for some time, but now the requirement was raised to include all active pilots as well. This included scheduled testing as well as random tests, normally upon return from a trip. I always thought this strange in that a positive test would mean that the pilot had been flying around for three or four days with drugs in his or her system. The pilot group insisted on "dual urine samples," to be sent to different laboratories, to help insure against "false positives." Not being a user of any unapproved drugs, I was not particularly concerned about these tests, although I was always relieved to receive a copy of the results in my mailbox with a "negative" score. The greatest hassle I had was when trying to make a quick connection to a flight home, but having to be delayed for random testing. During my lifetime, drugs came to be the greatest enemy of all, far beyond the threat of any foreign foe and with a multitude of tragic consequences.

With the exception of a few troublesome cockpit warning lights and a few problems with Delta's ground support equipment at New York's JFK Airport, my flight schedule for 1997 ended on a good note. And to do it up right, we took some of the family for a "Christmas in Hawaii," returning as the New Year 1998 began; only one year and nine months until my mandatory retirement date.

And then, suddenly, I received news relieving me of a financial burden that I had carried for many years. With everything falling into place financially, it became clear to me that I could retire at the end of September, this year—1998. There was a small penalty assessed for retiring early, something like 3 percent per year to my pension benefit, but I considered it insignificant, considering the hardships of commuting. Accordingly, I notified Delta Personnel that I wished to retire on October 1st—the first day of the month following my 59th birthday—and the request was approved.

The thing that always seemed so far out there in the future was now only a few months away. It was hard to imagine just what it would be like with no more worries about commuting, battling severe weather, training, check rides, physicals, and the pressure of dealing with passengers and flight schedules. I had seen some pilots who did not know what to do with themselves after mandatory retirement. Some died soon after. Others continued to fly with non-scheduled freight airlines that were under less restrictive age and physical requirements. Still others continued to show up in the crew lounges, not knowing what else to do except go to the airport. The word was that the golf course would work for about a year. After that, you had to find something to "do." It was a little scary, but one thing I knew: I would be able to sleep in my own bed at night from that point on.

With retirement looming, my cockpit demeanor began to change somewhat. I wanted nothing to happen on the remainder of my watch that would mar my record of never "bending the tin" or injuring a passenger. I had always desired that, of course, but I wanted it even more so now. I even leaned on my first officer crew members, telling them that it was their job to "nurse" this old captain through to the end before I was "turned out to pasture." Some even bought into that concept, and I enjoyed these last few months of flying like I had enjoyed no other.

Those few months involved my flying a large number of trans-continental flights that had been added to the Delta schedule, primarily out of Boston and New York to San Francisco, Seattle, and Los Angeles. Passenger loads on these flights were usually lighter than normal. With the distance and headwinds to consider, each aircraft took off with near maximum fuel loads. I flew several of these flights during those last few months of my career. Little did I know that, even then, there were those who were studying these flights with evil intent for the future. Three years later, on September 11, 2001, fanatical Muslim terrorists hijacked four of these flights to carry out the greatest attack ever made on American soil. While the nation mourned its dead, we all knew that nothing would ever be the same again. While there were no Delta flights involved in this dastardly act, I always wondered, had the terrorists gotten their agenda together earlier, if one of our flights would have been chosen, and if so, whether I might have been in the captain's seat. Oh the mystery of God's grace!

With the passage of time, the career plan of a man's life must reach its point of fruition. That began for me on September 22, 1998, when I began a four-day trip with layovers in San Diego, New York, and Denver. I had purchased a video camera to record the event, and my first officer agreed to be the camera man. While copies of that recording might still be in the hands of my progeny, I can still vividly remember the details of that last series of flights. One thing that stood out to me was on the third day. As we taxied out at JFK Airport for departure on runway 13, the first officer panned the camera across the skyline of Manhattan. There, in beautiful detail, were the twin towers of the World Trade Center, soon to be no more.

I had mentioned something about the 24th being my birthday. The first officer had purchased a small birthday cake at one of the downtown bakeries and had somehow kept it hidden from me during the long limo ride to the airport. At about the midpoint of our flight to Denver, the flight attendants mobbed the cockpit, singing "Happy Birthday," presenting me with a card signed by the entire crew, and passing slices of the cake all around. This was only the beginning of the thoughtfulness shown me by the people I worked with, on this career-ending series of flights.

Finally the day came: my last day as a Delta pilot. It dawned clear and sunny on the ramp in Denver for our flight to Atlanta. While it was a first officer responsibility, I elected to do the preflight "walk-around" inspection of the Boeing 767, with the first officer videoing and making certain that I didn't omit something. With that duty completed, we readied the aircraft for departure and took off into the rising sun—a sun that would set on my career.

With good weather and an even better tailwind, we blocked in at the gate in Atlanta, twenty-one minutes under schedule. Thankfully there were no delays, as I was anxious to rendezvous with Carolyn, who was to fly in from Knoxville on a flight scheduled to coincide with my arrival time. She would accompany me on my last two flight segments, a turnaround to Savannah and back. I found her flight's inbound gate and was relieved when her aircraft pulled into the gate—a few minutes late, but still with plenty of time for us to board the Savannah flight together. As a favor extended to retiring pilots, Delta had granted the spouses and immediate family confirmed seats on their final flight segments. This relieved all the pressures and worry about getting in place and onboard for that last flight.

With Carolyn at my side, I arrived at the gate. Sitting there was a brand new Boeing 757, just fresh from the factory, all shiny and bright with its Delta paint scheme. What a way to end a career—my favorite airplane, and a brand new one at that. I picked up the paperwork, explained the situation to the agent, and accompanied Carolyn to the cockpit, where I parked her in the first officer's lush sheepskin-covered seat. After giving the flight attendants the usual safety briefing, I added the details of my retirement and requested that they keep a close watch on this lady, who would be riding in the cabin. They entered into the spirit of the occasion, and after the first officer took pictures and video, everyone took their positions as we pushed back from the gate.

The flight to Savannah was short and sweet, and the aircraft flew and landed beautifully. After I parked the 757 at the gate, Carolyn and I walked into the airport terminal for a dish of ice cream during our short ground time. Returning to the gate, I explained to the agent that this was to be my final flight and that we would be going out onto the ramp for some picture taking. It was a pleasant day, with all the familiar smells of the ramp—jet fuel, heated rubber, hydraulic fluid, etc. As we passed the number two engine, I lifted Carolyn into the nacelle of the big Pratt & Whitney engine, for a special picture. Another was taken with both of our heads extended out the captain's sliding side window.

Last Flight, September 25, 1998

Finally, time caught up with us, and it was time to go. Flight 1273 of September 25th, 1998, ship number 687, was ready for departure to Atlanta. As we began our pushback on time (5:28 p.m.), all the gate agents were assembled in the Jetway, giving me a final salute and well-wishes for a happy retirement. Taxiing out was rather weird. Was it possible that this really was the end, the career-ending day that had been reckoned for me since the day I flew that old Super Cub, many years previously? But I couldn't be emotional at this point. I had to be a dedicated professional and consider the safety of all aboard, one last time.

By regulation, spouses were not allowed to ride in the cockpit jump seat. Some retiring captains ignored this rule, allowing their wives to witness that last landing up front. But I wanted to keep my record clean to the end. Besides, in the event of an emergency, I felt that the cabin was the safest place that Carolyn could be. That did not stop me, however, from having her join me in the cockpit once we arrived on the ground.

After my career-ending landing, I asked for an unused, alternate taxiway to the terminal and brought the 757 to a stop. Setting the parking brake, I picked up the interphone and explained to the passengers that this was my final flight and that I would like for my wife to join me in the cockpit for the taxi to the gate. I could hear the applause from the cabin as the cockpit door was opened and she came in, to occupy the jump seat. I then proceeded to offer my thanks for so many things. First, to my Lord and Savior Jesus Christ for watching over me all through the years, then to Boeing Aircraft Corporation and the engine division of Pratt & Whitney for building such wonderful airplanes, and to Delta Airlines for giving me the opportunity to fly them. Finally, I expressed my appreciation to all the passengers who had elected to fly with Delta over the years and to all my fellow crew members who had shared in all my experiences.

With this done, I contacted Atlanta ground control and asked if they had their speaker on in the tower. After receiving a reply in the affirmative, I went on to announce my retirement and to thank all the controllers for the fine job they had done over the years in keeping all of us pilots safe from one another. The controller thanked me and wished me well in all my future endeavors.

With this, I requested clearance to the gate and began a slow taxi. Word of my retirement flight had apparently reached the airport fire house because, as we turned into the ramp area, there were two large fire engines standing by, right and left of the taxiway centerline. As we approached their position, they raised their water cannons and created an arched "rainbow" of water as we passed under and through. The first officer was quick to advise the passengers that this was a tradition started by Atlanta Fire and Rescue to honor retiring captains and that they should not to be alarmed.

Retirement Salute, September 25, 1998

Finally I turned into the assigned gate, following the parking light signals that had long replaced human hands, and brought the 757 to a stop at the gate at 6:47 p.m. After the parking lights extinguished, indicating that the wheel chocks were in place, I released the parking brake, turned to the first officer, and said, "It is finished." I was greeted by more applause and well-wishes, as I stood in the doorway one last time to say good-bye to the "folks." After the last passenger was off, the cabin crew presented me with a "Happy Retirement" gift of a bottle of champagne (which I still have as of this writing), wrapped with a white cloth dinner napkin on which they had added their signatures, and gave me their well-wishes as well. Packing up my flight kit one last time, I stepped off the airplane and into retirement.

As Carolyn and I walked up the Jetway, I could not help but recall, once again, the last stanza of the Robert Frost poem, "Stopping by Woods on a Snowy Evening:"

The woods are lovely, dark and deep.

But I have promises to keep,

And miles to go before I sleep,

And miles to go before I sleep.

Now I could sleep. I had kept all my promises.

EPILOGUE

In these memoirs, I have attempted to present a "slice of life" showing what it was like growing up in the latter years of the twentieth century and becoming a part of this country's aviation industry.

My story did not end when I walked off the aircraft for the last time. In fact, in a sense, it had only begun. Retiring at such a young age was discomforting to some people. "You are too young to retire." "What will you do now?" "You really need a job." These were some of the comments I received from well-meaning friends. While I did consider the possibilities of a second career, I had spent too many days and nights away from home to give myself fully to another occupation. Due to the financial security given me by my retirement benefits, I never needed to work for money again. One retired captain put it this way, "A bad retirement day is better than a good day working."

While I was able to sleep in my own bed from that point on, I could not escape the sense of responsibility that had been drilled into my psyche over the years. I continued to "fly" and "travel" in my dreams. Sometimes these took the form of nightmares, dealing with emergencies, thunderstorms, or the aforementioned fear of losing my flight kit or being late for sign-in. I would awaken, relieved to know that it was only a dream.

Activities and travels consumed the greater part of my time now. I did take up the predictable golf game, but I embellished that with skeet shooting, deer hunting, fishing, kayaking, and teaching myself to play the bass guitar. When none of these were on the schedule, I contented myself with computing, writing on these memoirs, and engaging in church activities that included everything from singing and reading from scripture during services to producing sermon segments for broadcast on the local radio station.

My church travels included missionary trips to Panama and Venezuela, plus convention meetings in Vancouver, British Columbia, Canada and Phoenix, Arizona. Family travels included father-son trips, floating the Colorado River, fishing in Alaska, and attending "school" at the Arnold Palmer Golf Academy in Florida.

After vacations in Hawaii, Maine, and the Black Hills of South Dakota, Carolyn and I settled down to car travel only, spending our winter months in Florida and enjoying our condominium on Norris Lake near Knoxville, Tennessee. I did not miss flying, and with all this, I often wondered how I had ever had time to work.

There are two great revelations that came to me late in life. The first of these can be expressed in the statement that "your health is your greatest wealth." The death that is dealt to us, little by little, by the "standard American diet" and by a sedentary lifestyle is well-documented and is responsible for the sick, obese nation that we have become physically. I never believed myself to be immortal. However, I was finally fortunate enough to understand God's nutritional and physiological laws to the extent that I did not have to be sick and that quality of life was equally as important as quantity.

The second, and greatest of the two, was the revelation of Jesus Christ and his power to guide me into all truth; to overpower my life, and to grant me the unspeakable joy of knowing him in the fullness of his Word. The reader will never understand this until the power of his Spirit has swept over your soul and you know, beyond a shadow of a doubt, that you are one of his, the guilt and shame of the past notwithstanding.

With these revelations, I ventured into the unknown of my retirement years being able to say, truly I have lived.